HOW TO
SOLVE
ANY
PROBLEM
IN LIFE.

HOW TO SOLVE ANY PROBLEM IN LIFE.

THE ROOT CAUSES OF EVERYTHING

How to Solve Any Problem in Life

ISBN: 978-1-5272-9305-2

First published 2021

CONTENTS

INTRODUCTION

Do you ever feel as though your life isn't what it was meant to be? Do you ever feel as though no matter what you've achieved it's never enough? As though there's something missing? A hole deep inside you can't fill no matter what you do, gently nagging away at you every day?

Do you feel unfulfilled, alone or stuck? Do you feel as though no-one really understands you or knows who you really are? Do you ever worry about what other people think of you or spend your time thinking too much about what those other people are doing?

Do you drink too much alcohol to get you through the week? Do you take drugs or watch too much porn? Do you find yourself compulsively picking up your phone to check for messages or to scroll mindlessly through social media accounts? Do you gamble or work too many hours? Do you struggle to sleep or have stomach problems?

Do you ever explode with anger at what later feels like the smallest thing? Do you lie? Do you cheat? Do you manipulate? Do you need to be in control of everything around you? Do you bite your tongue and not say what you really want to say?

Do you suffer from depression or any other mental-health issues, or do you have any physical health issues the doctors can't cure?

If you could start your life all over again, would you make different decisions? Would you change the life you have if you could do it without anyone ever knowing how you really feel?

If you answered yes to any one or more of the above questions, I know how you feel.

For my first 38 years on this planet I did what everyone told me I should do. I worked hard, built a career, earned lots of money, bought houses and a flash car. I built businesses and married a beautiful woman.

Yet by my mid-thirties I was depressed. I fantasised about ending my life. I felt empty and alone, unfulfilled and haunted. I couldn't sleep at night, had many addictions and suffered from chronic illnesses. My body ached with the struggles of the world.

So, I decided to tear it all apart and discover the root causes of everything I was experiencing. To question every aspect of life. To challenge all the stories we are told about how to be happy.

I invested all the money, time and energy I had into this one quest. The only adventure left worth fighting for. I worked with a therapist and coaches, I read countless books and consumed as much information as I could from all corners of the globe.

And I found what I was looking for. The Holy Grail. I found the causes of all the suffering in the world. Of all the hurt and pain we endure every day. The simple explanation for it all.

It transformed my life. From what had been the darkest years I found something I never thought possible. Peace. Contentment. The addictions faded away, as if by magic. Chronic illnesses that I'd been told were incurable largely disappeared, like dust drifting in the wind.

I appreciate that it sounds insane. The old me would have read this and thought I'm crazy. But it's not only me that these secrets have worked for. I discovered a whole world of people that already believe in them and who live in a place that exists alongside the societies we consider normal.

I began to share the lessons I'd learnt with others and have watched in amazement as people all around the world have transformed their lives. People just like you. Of all races, genders, nationalities, religions and sexualities. People from all walks of life. Each of them as amazed as I was at how simple the solutions are that no-one tells us about. Hiding in plain sight all this time.

I wondered why the work I was doing with people was so effective when many of the people I was coaching had already worked with therapists and coaches without any success. Then I read a popular coaching book a few months ago that contained a great line. It said you can only coach someone as deeply as you've been coached, which is why so many coaches struggle to make a real impact on people – they haven't done enough work on themselves.

It made me realise that one of the main reasons my methods have been so profoundly effective with so many different people all around the world is because I've been to the Gates of Hell and back on my own adventure.

I've gone so deep that I've sat with my Demons in the darkness and fire and learned to understand them. An incredible coach once told me to get used to the heat of Hell before expecting to come back fully to the light. So that's what I did.

That means I can take you as deep as you're willing to go. There's no deeper place I can take you than to meet your own demons and your own darkness. It's a place many others can't take you because they've never been there themselves.

I want to share the lessons I've learnt with you. I understand you might be cynical. Once upon a time I would have been, too. How can one book contain the secrets that can transform your entire life? We've been taught these solutions don't exist. There are no cures. It's just the way it is.

But what if that's not true? What if they lied? What if they don't know the truth themselves? Is it worth opening your mind long enough to find out? To consider the possibilities?

Only you can decide. With this book I am holding open a door for you that was opened for me by others. I'm passing on the lessons they taught me, and only you can decide to walk through and embark on your own adventure.

Allow me to be your guide and I will show you everything I have learnt. I will do my best to help you avoid the pitfalls I faced. This is not a normal personal development or self-help book. If you choose to begin the adventure there will be times when you have to face your own darkness, as I was forced to do with mine.

This is not about becoming a billionaire or buying a private jet. It's not about increasing your financial wealth or boosting your productivity. There are no life hacks in these pages.

Instead, this book offers something most others don't tell you about. Something more. Something deeper. Only you can decide if you're ready to begin that quest. You might not be ready yet.

If you do select me as your guide, by the time you've finished reading this book you might have changed as a person. Problems you currently see as being unsolvable might have disappeared into thin air. Illnesses might have drifted away into the night, vanishing as mysteriously as they appeared. Your relationships might improve and, most importantly, that aching deep inside your soul, that questioning that there must be more to life than what you have right now might, at long last, be satisfied.

I know it sounds insane. I still think it's crazy and I've seen it for myself. Whether you think it might be real or not, the one thing you do know for sure is where the road leads that you're already on. You can choose to stay on that road and keep doing the same things over and over hoping for different results, or you can decide to try a different path.

This is your red pill or blue pill moment[1]. Choose the blue pill, put down this book and go back to however you're currently living your life, or choose the red pill and I'll show you just how deep the rabbit hole goes.

Whatever you decide to do I hope you find what you're looking for and I promise the answers are out there, whether you choose to read this book or not.

If you do choose to listen to what I have to say, I'll look forward to guiding you.

Make sure you bring plenty of water.

PAUL COPE
LIVERPOOL, MAY 2021

---

[1] In case you haven't seen it, this is a reference to the movie *The Matrix*, which I'd recommend you watch after reading this book, whether or not you've seen it before.

1

MY ORIGINS STORY

Given I'm not a qualified therapist, doctor, scientist or researcher in any of the fields covered in this book, I think it's only right I let you know why I feel able to share with you the contents of the following pages.

My qualifications come from life experiences rather than any institution or certificates. The truth is I am as qualified as it's possible to be as a lawyer, yet I feel I know more about the subjects you will read here than I will ever know about law, mainly because I have dedicated more money, time and energy obsessing over and studying these areas of life than I ever did to become a solicitor.

What follows is a brief summary of my life to this point. It is not an autobiography and purposefully misses out many aspects that involve other people and would be unfair of me to share without their input, although there are parts I have never shared publicly before now.

What I do share, though, I hope at least gives you a flavour of what led me to writing this book and sharing with you what I know. I'll leave it for you to decide for yourself after reading this chapter whether you believe I'm qualified to talk about these topics or not.

Think of what comes next as my superhero origins story, minus the discovery of being able to fly. An issue that still disappoints me to this day.

*   *   *

"When Alison was born, she was perfect. Like a little china doll. Beautiful and sweet. Everything her mum and dad had waited seven long years for."

"Nearly two years later, Paul hatched out of an egg at the end of their garden."

*   *   *

They were the opening words to my best-man's speech at my wedding in 2012. Whenever I think of them I laugh. They couldn't have been more fitting.

My parents had tried for ages to have kids and had pretty much given up hope after seven painful years. They'd put their names down to adopt and were looking into other ways to build a family.

Then, out of nowhere, my sister appeared. Like a little miracle. Growing up I remember the stories of how perfect she was and how everyone cried when she arrived, including my grandad, who fought at Dunkirk in World War II and who I can't imagine cried too often, if ever, before that day.

The stories surrounding my entrance into the world were less flattering.

I was too big for my mum's womb so had kicked her breast bone out of place during pregnancy. When I came crashing into the world it was apparent very quickly that my size had led to my feet being twisted inwards and I had far too much skin for my body, giving me loads of wrinkles that made me look like a little pig.

Families love a laugh about their loved ones, especially in my city, and that story was told over and over as I was growing up, always to roars of laughter. It would be followed by my mum and auntie Ann defending me, saying how beautiful I was, and how I'd grown into my skin eventually to turn into the handsome little heartbreaker they all loved.

Despite my less than auspicious entrance to the planet, I quickly established my place as the golden boy of a family in which the men were treated like kings by my nan, my mum's mum, and I was the heir to the throne. From an early age, earmarked to lead us all to a new world.

I was a very quiet little kid. My big sister did enough talking for both of us so I could happily sit back and let everyone watch her sing and dance while I played with my toy cars.

My favourite story from my earliest years came as a result of me apparently not being overly enthusiastic about going for a poo on a potty. To encourage me to participate in the standard development programme, my parents and everyone else in the family would excitedly shout *"good boy!"* whenever I went along with the training regime.

One day, when staying with one of my aunties, I came toddling in from the room next door shouting to my auntie and my three-year-old sister *"good boy, good boy!"* while pointing back at where I'd come from. My sister went to investigate and came back with her hand covering her face while holding back vomit.

My auntie followed to discover what through family folklore has turned into a bear-sized poo behind her sofa, returning to see my face full of pride at being such a good boy.

Aside from the stories I'm told, I don't really remember my early years, although I do remember generally being happy. Happy and quiet.

Life was everything a little boy could want. I had the best mum and dad in the world, lived in a lovely home, had a big, loving family with grandparents on both sides who adored all of their grandkids, and went on holidays every year. This is by no means the story of someone who experienced a traumatic childhood like many stories I hear these days. It was quite the opposite.

I breezed through school life from start to finish. Making loads of mates, topping classes everywhere I turned. Being picked to be the lead role in the school play when I was 10 despite my shyness.

There were some health issues through those early years, though, including quite serious whooping cough as a small kid. That was followed by what the doctors called *"growing pains"*. They were so bad I can still feel them now when I cast my mind back.

If that's what it feels like to grow I'm not sure why any of us do it, but I'm pretty sure what felt like ninjas attacking my calves with knives in the middle of the night is not what most people experience.

My screams from the pain would bring my mum and dad rushing in to comfort me, just as they did when I was afraid of the dark and thought that monsters were living in my cupboard.

"Don't be afraid, there's nothing to be frightened of" they would reassure me before leaving my bedroom door ajar and the landing light on, at my request. They would tuck me into bed so tight that I'd feel all safe and secure.

As I said, I couldn't have wished for a happier childhood.

I'd even managed to figure out what I wanted to be when I grew up. A story in the back of my dad's car (that you can read elsewhere if you're interested in the full version[2]) resulted in me declaring that I would be a solicitor.

As you can no doubt imagine for a family that originated on both sides mainly from working-class roots, that announcement was met with great excitement. They would have an heir to the throne who attends university and becomes a lawyer.

I could feel the expectations and weight of the world starting to build even back then.

I was on the path and knew where I was headed. Charging through school collecting top marks at every turn, with awards showering down on me at the end of every year.

All through that time still just a quiet little kid who loved to draw and do magic tricks for his grandparents. Still pretty shy. Just humbly getting on with life and trying to make everyone happy.

School life was a breeze and little changed until I was 16 when, looking back, it was clear my attitude had altered.

I'd started to become arrogant. I felt special. Invincible even.

In the middle of it all I noticed that my neck had started to hurt. Nothing much at first, just a bit of stiffness but, after a while, it felt like something I needed to get checked out.

My parents took me to our local doctor who did the usual doctor stuff. He asked what I was doing in school and as soon as I said I was studying for exams he quickly put the cause of my sore neck down to being huddled over my books for hours on end.

---

[2]   The full version is in my first book, The 7 Secrets To Change Your Career. You can download the first chapters of that book for free at: changeyourcareer.org

I knew at the time it was bullshit because I'd hardly done any studying, but I wasn't about to blow myself up in front of my mum and dad so took the diagnosis quietly and got on with life.

Despite not breezing through my A-Levels as I had my previous years, I got the grades I needed to study for a law degree at my local university, leading to the transition from switching between creative art classes and the cold, clinical worlds of maths and science at school to the wishy-washy world of law.

The first time I was told there wasn't a right or wrong answer to a question nearly knocked me off my feet.

"How are we meant to do anything if we don't get told at the end whether it's right or wrong? That's ridiculous."

I struggled. For the first time in my life I wasn't seen as one of the cleverest kids, and I didn't want to be. My attitude had changed and so had my character. From the golden boy at the top of the class in primary and high school, I'd switched to being the rebel. I just did enough to get through.

Looking back, I can see it was the start of turning my back on the real me in favour of what the world expected me to be. Deep inside I was quiet and creative, yet I'd left that behind in search of wealth and success in the world of law.

The best thing about the whole experience, though, was meeting people from around the country who'd come from all different backgrounds. It was the first time I'd had my eyes opened to a part of me I couldn't see and a world outside my own city and the people in it.

I still remember vividly a conversation with someone who went on to be one of my best mates to this day, when casually referring to myself as working class. His look of shock took me by surprise, with his follow up of *"your grandparents might have been working class, mate, maybe at a push your parents, but you live in a detached house with a pond in the suburbs of Liverpool and you're doing a law degree. You're not working class, my friend."*

I was stunned. It was the first time in my life an illusion around me about who I was and what my world was like had been shattered in one fell swoop. He was right.

While I didn't enjoy the course, I revelled in my new role as a rebel and a big drinker and my ego developed accordingly. I'd had a blip in the middle of second year when I realised the whole story leading to me wanting to be a lawyer was make-believe, and only decided to stay after words of advice from a favourite uncle who pointed out to me that everybody hates their job so I might as well do something that would make me rich if I couldn't fulfil my childhood dream of becoming a professional footballer (a dream that had never even been close to becoming a reality).

As with my A-Levels, I did just enough to graduate from university so my parents could get the photograph of me in a cap and gown for the walls of the family home.

After that my life was moving forward at a rate of knots down a path I'd chosen that I still wasn't fully convinced about but made the most of.

I travelled the world with two friends before moving away to law school and spending a year living in London, all of which just added to my new-found swagger and confidence. I was flying in every aspect of my life, the only downsides back then were my joint pain and my stiff neck, and another problem that had started to develop without me realising. It was subtle at first. I'd be on a night out and suddenly need to go to the toilet, but for more than you'd ideally like to be going the toilet for on a night out.

Months later I was diagnosed with Crohn's disease, an inflammatory condition affecting the bowels. It was at that stage that the doctors put two and two together and showed me a list of symptoms for another condition, ankylosing spondylitis, that was basically a checklist of the last eight years of my life, tracking all the symptoms I'd experienced, including an inflammatory skin condition, psoriasis, that I'd had for years before. My list of long, complicated medical problems was growing.

By my mid-twenties when life was otherwise going as well as I could have hoped, I'd been diagnosed with three chronic illnesses for which the doctors had no cure and no idea what caused them.

While the diagnoses were damaging, at least they gave me some hope that the symptoms I'd been experiencing might now go away. They offered me a revolutionary and experimental treatment that they thought could work but didn't come without risk.

I didn't even flinch before agreeing. I'd reached a point where the pain in my back and joints was often debilitating, and I was going to the toilet so frequently it was impacting my otherwise happy life.

It's almost impossible to explain the pain to someone who's never experienced it. At times it felt as though someone was trying to suffocate me from the inside of my chest.

Aside from that, while not being able to turn my head because of my stiff neck hadn't held me back in any way, it was always playing on my mind. Everywhere I went it was at the forefront of my thoughts. Every time I had to sit at a table to eat or talk to anyone I'd have to think carefully about where I could place myself to hide the stiffness as well as I could.

Even walking down the street was a nightmare, because any time anyone pointed at something for me to look at, my first thought would be how much it would hurt and how stupid I'd look having to turn my whole body.

It was a constant psychological and emotional burden.

I often talk these days about us all starting each day with an energy bar, like in fighting games on computers, where you lose as soon as your energy hits zero. My physical conditions were taking up a huge percentage of my available energy each day before I'd even started anything else. But, as with everything in my life, I just got on with things and didn't really talk about it. Most people didn't even know about my illnesses, other than being able to see I had a stiff neck.

I was raised on stories of stoicism and was just following what I believed to be the only way to live life. There's no point complaining, just get on with it.

Aside from my health being less than ideal, everything else was still going well, up to what I look back now as the single biggest turning point in my life to date. The main trigger that led to me sitting here and writing this.

I was about 26 years old by this stage of the story and, after making the very most of my skills with members of the opposite sex, had grown tired of casual flings and one-night stands.

During the past year or so before this stage, I'd developed a close friendship with a girl who started out as someone dating one of my good friends and ended up working in the same law firm as me.

We had plenty in common and I enjoyed her company. Over time we grew closer, spending lots of time together through work social events. Her relationship with my friend had always been dysfunctional and, after about four years together, they ended things.

Not long after their split, she told me following a few drinks she had feelings for me and asked whether I felt the same way. I had grown to like her in a way I'd never liked a girl before then, but can still feel the anguish as I wrestled with whether to go out with someone who used to date one of my friends. I'd been raised that a key rule in life was you never put girls above your mates, and loyalty was such a big part of my belief system.

Ultimately, though, I convinced myself it was all okay and went ahead, trying to do what I thought at the time was the right thing by sitting down with my mate face to face and discussing it with him. To sum up how well that conversation went, I only need to tell you it was the last time we spoke.

I also knew making that decision would impact that particular group of friends, which never truly recovered.

Looking back, the biggest problem was that I entered a romantic relationship telling myself a story that if I was going to make that jump it would have to be forever, because the risk to my friendship group was too big to take on a short fling.

In truth, the first year or so went as well as most relationships could. That time was filled with love and laughter, passion and excitement. The loss of friends was hard to take, but I convinced myself it was all worthwhile.

The difficulties began, though, when the honeymoon period ended and reality started to kick in. Outside stresses had started to increase in each of our lives, with us both having transitioned from being trainee lawyers to full blown, serious solicitors with adult responsibilities.

It's hard even now to recall the period of my life that followed. As we'll talk about in later chapters, traumatic events in our lives tend to be blocked out by our subconscious as a survival mechanism.

Day by day, week by week, month by month, things became harder at home. I spent more and more time criticising and feeling criticised. My previous levels of comfort in my life had been replaced by an inner edginess. Arguments became more frequent, about big and little things.

It was around then I had the first of a few key incidents leading to where I am today.

Again, the details are hazy even now, and I only know some of what I do because my partner reminded me years later.

*   *   *

It's the end of a night out. We're living in a beautiful city-centre apartment with 25-foot high ceilings and arched windows. The type of place you see lawyers in movies living in. I don't remember anything before the moment I'm standing in our bedroom at the top of the stairs, with my back to the door.

The room is rectangular in shape, with the long sides running off to my left and the short side on my right. I'm standing in the corner with our king-sized, brown leather bed facing me from the maroon-coloured long wall opposite. The wall-mounted TV is facing the bed from the wall to my left, and the far end of the room with floor-to-ceiling windows overlooking an internal atrium in our apartment block has curtains draped from rails I'd fitted a year before. In the corner to my right is the door to our en-suite bathroom, the light on ready for us to start getting changed for bed.

My girlfriend is sitting on the bed, taking off her shoes while I stand drinking a glass of water. I say something about not being happy that she'd been flirting with one of our male friends during the night. She laughs at me and says I'm being ridiculous. That it's all in my head. I feel ridiculed.

Then something I've experienced before but not to this level happens. Like a fire burning in the tips of my toes that starts to travel quickly up through my legs. At first a tingling, but then more like lava from a volcano erupting. Every sinew of my body surging with power and fury, electricity and heat bursting through my pores. Rage. Uncontrollable rage. Followed by a loud crash and shattered glass falling from the wall.

It takes me a second to realise what's happened. I've thrown the glass in my hand at the wall a metre above her head. I look at her face. Fear looking back at me. The rage disappears and my body relaxes. I drop into a feeling of deep shame the likes of which I've never felt before and begin to cry.

* * *

I was raised on stories of temper running through our family, often told about arguments within relationships over the years, and frequently regaled in a semi-humorous way.

It wasn't until my previous relationship in law school I'd ever felt the temper properly in me, which I'd dealt with following some words of wisdom from a Buddhist anger management book by leaving the relationship.

This time, though, I told myself the story that I couldn't end the relationship because of everything I'd sacrificed to start it. I couldn't escape the feelings of anger I experienced on a daily basis in the same way I'd escaped them before.

The incident with the glass felt like an accumulation of a thousand small things I'd bottled up for months. The shame I felt for doing it at the time was unbearable.

Having put that incident behind me and getting on with the relationship in the only way I knew how, by burying what I felt, around three years into it I started to make big changes to my work life. At 29 years of age I decided it was time to leave the relatively safe and secure career path I'd spent a lifetime carving out to break out on my own for the first time. I decided as a baby-faced junior lawyer to start my own law firm.

It was one of the most exhilarating times in my professional life. The buzz of starting something from nothing, with a pen and paper, a computer and a mobile phone, and beginning to build something filled my veins with electricity every day. I can still remember the first job I secured for a tiny fee and how happy I was about it.

At the same time, my partner's work life was leading to her complaining and crying regularly, and the first feelings setting in that I was carrying two lives at the same time. Starting any company is difficult enough without feeling as though you're also responsible for the happiness of another human.

I knew deep in my soul at that point we weren't compatible. We were great friends and deeply in love. The problem was we wanted to live in different worlds.

I'd realised I was always meant to be in charge of my own life. My entrepreneurial traits from when I was a young kid couldn't be contained any longer. I needed the risk and the adventure that sailing my own ship would bring.

I knew, though, that despite her outward support for my new venture my girlfriend wanted just what she could see the people around her had, which was understandable. Successful lawyers with seemingly secure jobs and good salaries. Nice houses in the suburbs. Two point four children. It wasn't for me and, in fairness, it was me who had changed. When we began dating my life looked as though it was headed down that standard lawyer path, but that changed three years along the road.

I asked what she wanted in life and received the reply that she wanted what I wanted. The future I painted was exciting and different. The sales pitch was strong. But I knew deep down the answer I received wasn't true. I could sense what she really wanted but wasn't saying.

Around that time the story I was telling myself about not being able to leave was still playing on a loud loop in my head, but I was unhappy. My days at home were stressful and filled with toleration for my own life. I knew in my gut I wasn't happy but I also knew I couldn't leave. I remember thinking about all the other relationships I knew, both up close and in public life, and I told myself this was just normal. That nobody has a dream life and relationships are hard.

We still loved each other deeply and had some great times, so I committed to staying. I also made other decisions about how I could survive my level of unhappiness that I still regret to this day.

From that moment my inner world slowly became darker, which reflected in my outer-world behaviour. Over the following years my alcohol intake increased. I spent more and more time at work and weekends away with friends became such a respite that there were several booked into each year's calendar.

I felt trapped inside my own life and that feeling only increased as I built my law firm and realised that it, too, was something that was making me unhappy. The worst period came when for reasons still baffling to me today, I decided it was a good idea to employ my girlfriend in my firm to help with its day-to-day running.

The two years following that decision were the darkest of my time on this planet, because the inner torment became inescapable.

From the moment I opened my eyes in the morning to the moment I went to sleep at night, I felt like I was carrying two lives, two sets of pressures.

The following years saw me continuing to build my law firm and other businesses, taking on more and more stress, partying heavily, making money, spending money. At home I'd found ways to cope and manage, some healthy, others not. There were good spells and, as with all relationships, there comes a time when everyone expects a marriage.

I always remember one of my good friends saying to me that at some point you either have to get married or split up. I knew we couldn't split up and when I looked at everything objectively I thought our relationship was probably better than most people's. My girlfriend fitted in with my family and, on paper, everything was as good as we can expect in this world.

After all, no-one's really happy, are they? Plus, whenever I reached a point where I was really unhappy, something would happen that gave me hope. A slight change in how my girlfriend behaved towards me or something that reminded me how in love we were or how it could all be better if only things changed. It was really great 20 percent of the time, so we could just make things better and feel that way more often, couldn't we?

I proposed in the only way I knew how – by making it the grandest proposal I could think of. I thought I'd only ever do this once so wanted my future wife to have a story she could tell forever. It took hours of preparation, cost thousands of pounds and did exactly what it was designed to do. A modern-day fairytale set in Las Vegas.

A flash wedding in Mallorca, Spain, followed. I was under more pressure than at any other stage in my life. I remember vividly still not having the tens of thousands of pounds needed to pay for our 90-guest extravaganza a week before the big day but, as with everything else during that period of my life, I pulled out a miracle to fix everything.

I got through the day itself eating painkillers and stomach tablets like they were sweets, switching from my highly-stressful life to the life and soul of the party whenever required, doing everything I could to make the weekend the best it could possibly be for my new wife and our guests. And hiding how I truly felt from everyone else.

After that, life returned to what it had been before. I was still unhappy deep inside, trying my best to change my life to make things better, to communicate with my partner and resolve ongoing issues, but nothing I did ever felt as though it truly worked. It always felt that I was swimming upstream with very little ever changing.

At that point, to the outside world, I had what most people in Western society would consider the textbook life.

I was the managing director of my own law firm with a city centre office and glass walls. I had clients that international firms would be proud of. I owned a beautiful city-centre apartment, drove an amazing car and had a beautiful wife. I owned four other houses and had started an online business for which I'd secured hundreds of thousands of pounds of angel investment. It looked as though it was going to become a worldwide multi-million pound success.

On the inside, though, I was the most depressed I'd ever been. My inner world had become darker than I care to recall. I was often suicidal, but having a dad who worked in the insurance industry for most of my life I knew that if you commit suicide your life assurance doesn't pay out. I'd been paying really high premiums on millions of pounds' worth of cover for years, largely because of my chronic health problems that meant insurance companies wanted to be paid more to take the risk of insuring me. I didn't want those policies to go to waste by blowing my head off.

I also couldn't face what killing myself would do to my family. It would have been devastating to my parents especially, and I couldn't bear leaving a legacy for my beautiful niece and nephew that suggested when times get hard you should just end it all.

I would often sit in my office late at night or at the weekend with no-one else around, sometimes with some alcohol to keep me company, and plan how I could end my life without anyone knowing it was suicide.

My death would still be painful for my family, but a freak accident or a random murder would be easier to take than me taking my own life. Plus, the insurance money would make everything better for those left behind.

I'd imagine paying someone to shoot me in a dark alley on one of my late-night walks home from the office. But what if they messed up? What if they missed and just gave me brain damage? What if they got caught and the insurance didn't pay out? I'd spend hours going through the details.

During that period I remember on top of my usual chronic pain that haunted my days and, especially, my nights, I'd started to feel a strange sensation down my left arm. Day after day it would ache. Pins and needles some days. Complete numbness in others.

One day, as I was walking to a football match with two close friends, I casually mentioned to them I'd been experiencing the pain for a while. They both reacted with shock and concern, telling me I should see a doctor. If you're not a man or aren't familiar with men's normal relationships, you might not realise that sort of concern is reserved solely for life-critical situations. If one of our friends gets hit by a bus but is still moving, we will almost certainly quickly move to making jokes about the situation and taking the piss out of how slow his reactions were.

A male friend's concern is something to be worried about. The concern of two friends is enough to phone the doctor, which is what I did. The following day, I called the non-emergency number for the National Health Service in the UK after my wife at the time supported my friends' view that I wasn't wasting anyone's time and should get it checked out.

*   *   *

I'm sitting on my king-sized bed in the same place my wife was sitting when I'd thrown a glass at the wall years earlier. I'm facing the wall with the bedroom door to my right and the en-suite bathroom to my left.

I call the non-emergency number and a lady answers who immediately reminds me of my favourite auntie.

Nurse: *"And what's the concern, son?"*

Me: *"Well, I didn't really want to bother you, but I've been having these pains in my left arm for a while now and my friends and wife thought I should call."*

Nurse: *"Okay, what type of pains have you been having and for how long?"*

Me: *"Erm, sort of pins and needles and numbness all down my left arm and hand, for about three months."*

Nurse: *"Every day, for three months?"*

Me: *"Yeah, pretty much."*

Nurse: *"Okay, son, I want you to listen to me very carefully. I want you to give me your address, put the phone down and wait at the door for an ambulance. I'm going to send someone straight away to take you to accident and emergency for an urgent check-up."*

Me: *"No, please don't do that, I don't want to waste anyone's time or money. It's been like this for ages."*

Nurse: *"That's exactly the problem, son, this is really serious."*

*   *   *

At that point my wife came bursting into the room having been outside listening in to the conversation. I managed to convince the nurse I didn't need an ambulance and my wife could drive me to the hospital, to which she agreed reluctantly on the promise I'd leave straight away and go to the nearest A&E.

When we reached the hospital check-in desk, I looked to my right at the usual packed waiting room and thought we'd be there for some time, as is often the case. I gave my name at the counter, the nurse typed it into her computer, looked back at me with a look of concern and told me to walk straight through the door to my left, bypassing the waiting room. That had never happened to me before in all the years I'd visited hospitals.

As I walked through the swinging double doors, I was greeted by a young doctor in a white coat who led me to a bed sitting next to a fancy machine dripping with wires. He strapped me up in all the ways you've seen in hospital dramas. Sticky patches attached to my chest and arms. Clips attached to my fingers.

Checking to see whether I was having a heart attack.

They couldn't find anything. They kept me under observation for a while before letting me go home with a word of warning about lifestyle and taking things easier. I was relieved until I spoke to my uncle who'd had a heart attack in the past and told me those machines can only detect if you're having an attack at the moment you're strapped up to them – so you could have had one beforehand and it wouldn't know.

That experience, coupled with the conclusion that before putting in all the effort of having myself assassinated it might be worth exploring some options that didn't seem quite as drastic, made me look at my life with fresh eyes.

I was still struggling and considered seeing a therapist. I spoke with someone in London who specialised in helping people in my position, but decided I could handle it myself by making some changes to my external world.

I looked at my work life and realised I'd been telling myself the same story for a while – that things would be better in six months. The problem was that six months had been rolling for a few years. So, I decided to do something novel. On what must have been my 34th birthday, in July 2014, I wrote an email to myself setting out exactly how I was feeling on that day about my business. I specified how much money the firm was owed, how much stress I was under, all of the problems I was having with employees and clients and everything else I could think of. I sent it with a time delay to be delivered to me on New Year's Day 2015.

Then, amazingly, I forgot all about it until I received the email I had typed out six months earlier.

It was a weird feeling to read the forgotten message. Like being in *Back to the Future*.

The email started *"Hi Paul, this is you from six months ago…"*

It took me a few seconds to understand what was going on, at which point I remembered what I'd done and began to read. Within minutes I was amazed. I'd started doing the very thing I'd feared I would. I'd been telling myself things were getting better and I should just give it another six months.

When I read the email I realised not only that things weren't getting better, but they were actually worse than they'd been the summer before. I decided there and then to sell my firm or, failing that, to close it down and do something else with my life.

What came next led to where I am today. I sold the firm and all but one of the investment houses. The online business had crashed in a perfect storm of shit just before everyone involved thought it was going to head into the stratosphere. I was done.

I can still recall the feeling of being completely empty. Hollow. Spent. Like every ounce of energy I'd been allocated for my life had been used up in my 35 or 36 years on Earth.

Looking back it's easy to call what happened to me a breakdown, but I would never have described it as that at the time. I was just really, really tired.

The darkness that had engulfed me for years had lifted slightly, but not much was left in its place. I realised after stripping all of the business stress away that I was still miserable at home. Every day brought another challenge. Something else to bite my tongue over. No matter what I did, nothing ever changed.

It reached a point where the story I'd been telling myself for 12 years about not being able to leave had run out of steam. The pain of staying had finally outgrown the pain of leaving, so I made the hardest decision I've ever made in my life. I left my wife.

At first I felt relief, but my wife and I were still tightly connected through a gorgeous dog she had convinced me we should buy six months earlier, a house, possessions and lives that had been intertwined for over a decade.

As with all these things, there's always the pull to go back once things have settled, and I felt that pull again and again.

The key part of this stage of the story isn't what happened in the relationship, though, it's what happened next.

A trip to see a mutual friend in a boxing match in Manchester led to an argument in the car on the way home and an explosion of rage from nowhere that I hadn't experienced in a few years by that point. For a split second I thought I might drive the car off the motorway at 90 miles an hour. It was petrifying for me and terrifying for my wife.

When we got home I made the best decision of my life. I decided regardless of what happened with my marriage or anything else, I wanted to start working with someone to figure out what was inside me that led to these explosions, and to see whether I could finally understand what made me feel so uneasy in my life.

I finally booked in to see a therapist.

From the moment I first met Dave, I knew I'd chosen the right fit for me. A man from my city, who I could be completely open with and who spoke my language. Most importantly, a man I respected, who was highly qualified and I knew could and would call me out on my bullshit.

It was another moment in my life that confirmed my belief that when the student is ready the teacher appears. Within a couple of sessions we started making breakthroughs.

* * *

I'm sitting in Dave's office in what I reckoned was a typical therapist-client set-up. It's a small rectangular room with windows at the opposite end to the entrance door. The walls are pale with numerous framed certificates to the left as I walk in and a bookshelf containing various specialist books on the opposite wall.

Dave sits in a red leather chair with his back to the door and I sit facing him.

It's coming towards the end of my first session after I've explained to Dave what I'm looking for.

He says: *"Paul, can I be straight with you? This is a bit like Spock coming into my office with a formal presentation about his life and asking for a definitive answer to some big questions."*

"Erm, yep, that's basically it," I replied.

"Sorry, mate, that's not how it works."

* * *

A week later we had another exchange, one I still laugh about now. Dave asked how I felt about everything that had happened with my wife. I gave him as good an answer as I could manage and he said: *"That's not how you feel, Paul, that's how you think. How do you feel about it all?"*

I answered again and Dave repeated that I was talking about my thoughts, not my feelings. It was at that moment I said to him I didn't have anything else to give, and I realised I'd spent so many years shutting down my emotions in order to survive that I could no longer connect with most of them or talk about myself in that way.

I'd reached a point in life where I could only feel the extremes. I could be depressed or I could be ecstatic (usually with the aid of alcohol), but I had nothing in between. It was something I already knew instinctively. I'd felt for years that I couldn't feel my face properly. As though there was a laminate cover over it that stopped me expressing exactly what I felt. Like it was numb.

Dave helped me to reconnect with myself and to understand everything I'd been through.

From there, I embarked on a path I became fascinated by, spending thousands of hours consuming as much as I could about human behaviour and why we are the way we are. I found myself in a whole new world.

Within weeks I was feeling lighter before hitting the first of my huge breakthroughs. One day I was walking my dog through the park with my mind wandering through these topics as it tended to do, when I suddenly stopped in my tracks. It was like a light-bulb came on in my mind; as though the synapses suddenly all fired together with a realisation I'd never had before.

I had low self-esteem.

To say it came as a surprise would be a huge understatement. I realised that for years I'd been observing insecurities in my family and some of the people closest to me and had never thought the same issue might apply to me.

It was like a bolt of lightning hitting me. I was insecure. My entire life had been spent trying to prove I was good enough, both to myself and to the outside world. I was driven to be extreme in everything I did because I had to be the best. I could never be content because nothing was ever enough.

Which is when it all started to change. I'd be walking down the street and suddenly my brain would whisper to me:

Brain: "Eh, mate"

Me: "What?"

Brain: "Have you noticed that?"

Me: "Noticed what?"

Brain: "We haven't been thinking about anything for 10 minutes."

Me: "Oh, shit, yeah. It's nice, isn't it."

In 38 years of consciousness I couldn't remember the last time my mind had just been quiet. I realised I was feeling something I'd never felt before. Inner peace and contentment.

It was time for another big decision.

After receiving fairly heavy-duty immune-suppressant medication for 15 years that had kept symptoms of Crohn's disease, ankylosing spondylitis and psoriasis under control to enable me to live my life, without ever curing the conditions, I decided I wanted to take control of that side of my life as well. I didn't want to continue with the risk of being pumped full of a drug every eight to 12 weeks that the doctors and scientists themselves couldn't tell me the long-term consequences of - and which I knew was suppressing my system and contributing to me feeling lethargic.

I'd already started extending the period between my visits to hospital for my infusions which, combined with more time studying alternative remedies for chronic illnesses, convinced me there was a way forward not dominated by the mainstream idea of just treating the symptoms of everything with drugs.

I took the huge step of ending my treatment, against the wishes of my doctors and my family. I began experimenting with fasting on nothing but fresh vegetable and fruit juices, and continued with my therapy.

The withdrawal from a decade and a half of serious drugs being flooded into my system was fairly severe. At one point while living by myself with my dog in my former marital home, I lay on the floor to ease some pain in my back and realised within minutes I was stuck. The pain was excruciating and I couldn't move.

I just lay on the floor of my bedroom and started to laugh. My beautiful little dog came in to see what her dad was up to and thought I must be on the floor to play, so began licking my face and tapping me on the forehead in her very special *"come on, dad, let's play"* way.

I told her we might be here for some time because I couldn't reach my phone, and she lay down next to me while we both fell asleep.

When I woke, I could finally drag myself, slowly, like a 90-year-old man, from the floor to the bed and finally to my feet. That was the worst moment of a period of intense pain and tension that gently began to ease as the weeks passed.

At the same time, I was slowly transitioning from being a lawyer into a new world built around what I wanted life to look like on a daily basis. I prioritised sleep and well-being, while focusing on helping people as a business coach - sharing the knowledge I'd accumulated through my intense years running several companies.

I was learning how to operate in a new universe and realised to give myself the best chance of becoming the person I really wanted to be without my past holding me back, I needed a change of scenery and an environment filled with people who saw the world the same way as I did.

A life-affirming trip to Bali followed, where I met so many like-minded people and, for the first time, felt as though I wasn't all alone in wanting a different, more fulfilling life.

My inner peace increased and things were starting to come together. My health was slowly improving, with my psoriasis clearing up completely while I was in Indonesia and my pain and tension easing to a manageable level.

Before Bali I'd stopped drinking alcohol for three months. But I began to share the odd glass with new friends in a much more calm and controlled manner than I'd ever known before. It felt like I could drink because I wanted to, rather than because I needed to.

Some time in Spain followed before a return home to focus on the next phase of my business life and a greater focus on my health, which still felt key to many other things.

Which is where my next mentor entered the story.

I'd met Ralph through an online search when looking for someone who could help with an alternative way to approach healing from ankylosing spondylitis. The video testimonials on his website spoke of disbelief at the results of the work. Many started their reviews with the words: *"I know this sounds unbelievable…"*.

It was another decision to be listed among the best of my life.

Ralph taught me everything he knew about the ways in which we're trained as kids to deal with our emotions and the knock-on impact on our adult lives. He shared his story and I spent months soaking up everything he had to say, combining it with my ongoing therapy sessions and hour upon hour in my spare time finding any other resources I could to add to my knowledge.

I could feel my self-worth building. There were ups and downs but the upward trajectory of my growth was undeniable. I'd never felt so complete or peaceful, despite still dealing with the aftermath of my broken marriage and everything that entailed.

There were more breakthroughs about my life than I can recall now, each one helping another weight to lift from my shoulders.

As with all big changes in life, though, the transformation came with challenges. There were times filled with self-doubt. Days and nights when I would question whether I'd done the right thing or whether I should turn around and head back. But I knew how painful life had been doing what I'd done before, and I knew no matter how difficult things got in my new universe it couldn't be as bad as wanting to pay someone to shoot me in the head.

I realised having opened my emotions up in ways they hadn't been since I was a little boy, I was like an open wound exposed to the world, making so many things in life more difficult to handle. Situations in which I used to thrive had become alien and almost impossible to exist in. It felt like I was a surfer, at times riding high on the crest of a wave before crashing and having to pick myself up again.

I doubled down and committed to taking another step forward. I invested every penny I had in another coach to add to my armoury, knowing this work was the most important investment I would ever make.

Enter Jim, who I contacted primarily to help with my new business life but whose guidance led to much more. Again, there are too many individual breakthroughs to name them all individually, but one stands out from the rest.

Having identified what I wanted my future work life to look like, I had realised that helping others combined with speaking publicly filled me with joy, fulfilment and excitement. After speaking one day to a group of teenagers about their future careers following the publication of my book on the same topic, Jim asked me a question that stays with me today.

"When you were up there speaking, did you love yourself?"

I paused, and my pause told me everything I needed to know. If you ask me if I love my mum, dad, or anyone else in my family, I say yes without hesitation.

I realised that despite all the work I'd done, I still couldn't say the same thing about myself without any doubt. Further work, which I'll share later on these pages, led me to understand why that was and what I needed to do next, which felt like the last piece of the puzzle.

It led to me taking part in a tour of live shows around Ireland for a football podcast I contributed to, which felt like where I was meant to be. I felt so comfortable in an environment in which I would previously have felt insecure and afraid. I was buzzing.

Which is when the miracle happened.

One night, while lying alone in bed in a Liverpool city-centre apartment I'd moved into on my return to the UK, I woke at around 5am with a knowing feeling running through my veins.

* * *

I lay there, alone, and the damn burst. A single tear rolled down my right cheek, glistening over every nerve ending along the way to the corner of my mouth.

Then came the flood. The avalanche. Sobbing like a baby, my shoulders shaking as the feeling overwhelmed me.

Twenty-two years.

For 22 years I hadn't moved my neck.

For the past 12 months I'd started to believe that it might be possible to move it again. I'd convinced myself consciously that it was real.

But I had never truly believed. Not enough to convince my subconscious anyway.

Until now. At 5am on an extremely normal February morning, lying alone in my bed in an apartment overlooking the glorious Three Graces standing, dominant, on Liverpool's mighty waterfront, I knew I could move it.

A stretch to the left. A pull to the right. Removing the pillow from beneath my head and allowing the back of my head to rest flat on the bed in a way it hadn't for over two decades. Feeling the pain as my muscles and skeleton began adjusting to a body shape they hadn't experienced for over half of my life.

Twenty-two years.

The tension had released. Moving around on the bed, rolling my legs from side to side, twisting my back, pulling my knees up to my chest.

The last of what Western medicine had told me was a chronic illness with no cause and no cure, melting away.

*   *   *

Yet, just as I was turning the handle on the door to my new life, watching the bright light bursting through from whatever was on the other side, it was as though I was dragged by a tractor beam at warp speed away from the promised land.

A pandemic hit the world, locking us inside our homes, and an old part of my life came crashing back in after months of closure and peace.

The pain returned. The tension. I felt crushed. It would have been so easy to lose hope, to give up, but I'd already seen enough to keep believing.

I committed to continuing with the work. I believe setbacks are a part of any adventure and this was the greatest journey I'd ever attempted so it was bound to contain more than its fair share of highs and lows. Having seen the mountain top, though, I knew I could get back there.

I also knew that what I'd learned over the previous two years could help so many others. The work I'd done had solved every problem in my life, from depression and suicidal thoughts to that constant feeling of nothing ever quite being enough. My addictions had disappeared, whether to work, stress, alcohol or judging others. I'd found a constant level of inner peace I'd never thought was possible before embarking on this path.

I decided to offer to teach others what I'd had the privilege of learning. Slowly but surely, people from all around the world came to share their stories and to ask for help and, one by one, I shared what I'd learnt and watched as they transformed their lives in the same way I had transformed mine.

I built the thriving, remote business I'd been working towards for years, which led to me writing this book.

All that remained was the final stage of my physical healing adventure. Jim shared with me that he'd experienced back pain during his life when he wasn't living in alignment with who he was really meant to be. He introduced me to the last piece of my coaching jigsaw.

When I first spoke with Nicole I expected to talk about how she could help restore good posture to a spine that had been out of alignment for 23 years. Within minutes, though, I realised the work we would do together would be everything I needed to complete this part of my story.

We talked about emotions being trapped in our bodies and years of repression needing to be released once and for all. We started working together and I could instantly feel decades of issues releasing from my incredibly tense muscles.

Nicole also said something to me I hadn't considered. That writing this book was part of my healing process. Sharing with you everything I've learnt on my adventure and allowing myself to be who I was always meant to be rather than who the world wanted me to be was the final piece.

I am happy to share everything with you. At this point in my life I feel very fortunate to have experienced the pain of my past. Without hitting the lows I would never have broken through to the life I now have and, as I look around me, I feel for all those who never quite hit that darkness and end up living their life carrying issues from their childhoods that keep them stuck in a fairly grey existence, never fully experiencing their emotions or the world and never being truly free.

That's what I am now: free. Free in a way I never thought possible just three years ago. I used to believe I was trapped in a prison of my own making, but having stripped away all the stories I'd carried through my life I realised it was never a prison. It's not possible for us to trap ourselves in prisons we build. Prisons by definition are locked from the outside. If we lock ourselves inside a cage we have the key to the door, which means it's not a prison, it's a fort.

We build forts in an attempt to protect ourselves from a world full of fear. The lessons I learnt allowed me to walk free from the fort I'd built and wander into the open fields nearby. The fields that had been waiting for me my entire life.

The experience is impossible to describe in any real way to anyone who hasn't experienced it. I often say if the person writing this story was speaking to a version of myself from three or more years ago, that version of me would think I was insane now. That I'd lost my mind. I've heard that people who go through addiction recovery processes often feel the same way, though. That an old version of themselves has died and a new one born in its place.

That's how I feel. I refer now to the old me and the new me, the only problem is I still look the same from the outside so it's been a confusing time for everyone around me while I've transitioned into a new inner world.

I am free. Free to experience all of my emotions. Free to choose how to earn a living without worrying about the expectations of the world. Free to sing and dance without needing alcohol to let my hair down. Free to ask myself every day what do I want to do. Free to focus on the things that bring me joy instead of allowing my life to be dominated by the stories told to us by others about what we should be doing with our days.

My job now is to share what I've learnt with as many people as I can, hence writing this book. It's important to say, though, that I share all of this with you as a student passing on what I have learnt. I continue to learn every day and expect to do so for the rest of my life. I will never master this world and I don't think anyone ever does. That, in itself, brings me peace.

You might read what I have to say and decide it's not for you. It definitely isn't for everyone. If you believe only in hard facts and scientific studies it's almost certainly not for you.

But, if you believe in a possibility of a different way of thinking or of the solutions to problems in life being outside what the mainstream has told us for years, then this is for you. I have seen it work in my own life and in the lives of people around the world of different genders, races, nationalities, sexualities, religions and backgrounds.

Whether you read my story and it resonated with you, or whether your childhood and life has been different to mine, the principles in this book will apply to you. The solution to our human problems works for all humans because we are more alike than many will lead you to believe.

If you believe what I believe, or think there's a possibility that you might, I'd like to take you on an adventure that might change your life by the time you've finished this book.

Only you can decide if that's an adventure you want to begin.

"Like, we're The Beatles
after all, aren't we?
We have all the money
you could ever dream of.
We have all the fame
you could ever wish for.
But, it isn't love.
It isn't health.
It isn't peace inside. Is it?"

(George Harrison / The Beatles)

2

BEFORE WE BEGIN

As this book is essentially a written version of the coaching work I do with people around the world, I thought it would be worthwhile setting out many of the things I'd say to you first if we were talking face to face.

When speaking in person I can check in regularly to see if you understand something and, if you don't, I can explain it in a different way. With a book, though, I have to do my best to convey the same messages without us ever being in the same room.

To maximise the chances of the following pages making sense, I think it's worth introducing you to my style because I've seen how differently many coaches and therapists approach the same topics.

How This Works

As you've probably noticed, I like to tell stories. I've always been mesmerised by great storytellers and the most powerful lessons I've ever learnt have come through the power of story. I now do my best to do what those before me have done, hopefully to some effect.

If I have any superpower in life, I think it's the ability to take fairly complex topics and translate them into something that is easy to understand. A few months before writing this I was reading a book by a highly qualified, well-known expert in the world of psychology and human behaviour. At one point I came across a 12-syllable scientific word and found myself spelling it out one syllable at a time like a five year old learning to read.

At that moment I thought how dry and painful it had been trying to consume the important information in the book, taking me back to all those less-than-fascinating legal cases I'd read in my previous life, and realising how most people who haven't been trained to sacrifice their precious time to pour over boring information will never read books like that, regardless of how powerful the lessons in them might be.

So, I see one of my jobs as taking those crucial lessons and converting them into stories about superheroes and other seemingly unrelated topics that make a lot more sense and are a bit more fun to read. More on that later but, for now, it's also worth noting a potential downside of my communication style is to bounce around from one place to another, linking tangents as I go along. While I've done my best to limit jumping around through the structure of this book it's inevitable I'll sometimes still do it, hopefully without losing you in any way.

As well as my story-telling approach to complex topics, I don't believe in leaving people struggling to find answers to questions they've never heard before. I've heard about many therapists and coaches over the years who think their job is to lead a person to find an answer for themselves, because that's the most powerful way anyone can learn.

While I don't disagree with that, I believe if someone doesn't know where to look for the treasure they're seeking, or how to dig it up even when they find it, leading them on a wild-goose chase their entire lives isn't going to help anyone.

I like using an analogy of going to the gym. This work is no different to hiring a personal trainer to help you get in shape. What many therapists and coaches do is tell you they know what weights you need to lift and how many times you need to lift them to transform your body, but they won't tell you where the weights are or how to find them.

My style is to tell you where the weights are and how many repetitions you need to do to get in shape. The kicker is I can't lift them for you, you need to do that bit yourself.

A Treasure Hunt with Guaranteed Prizes

I realised something a couple of weeks ago while writing these pages: the work that follows is like a treasure hunt. You are looking for the gold in your life that helps you overcome the many challenges you face.

The beauty of this particular search, though, is I can guarantee the treasure is there. Whenever anyone tells me they can't find it, I know we just need to look in a slightly different place or dig deeper because it's always there. My aim throughout the following chapters is to help you to find the treasure I know exists.

One thing to note on that point is one of my favourite quotes by Joseph Campbell, which sums up our challenge perfectly:

> "The cave you fear to enter holds the treasure you seek"

The treasure is there, it's just likely to be in a place you might not want to look. My job is to hold your hand and guide you through the dark cave. I've already been through it, after all, so I can show you the safest and least frightening way to walk.

Getting to the Root

As part of that treasure hunt remember our goal is always to get to the root cause of problems rather than treating the symptoms. That often means going back a step before we think the issue started.

A funny incident underlined to me how it's always best to go back to the beginning to solve a problem rather than making any assumptions.

I was in a beach town in Quintana Roo, Mexico, when a friend called me asking for help. She'd hired a car locally to make it easier to get around the place and was having trouble unlocking it. It was late evening so her options to resolve the problem were limited.

She called and asked what I thought it could be. The car had one of those remote control keys rather than an old-fashioned normal key, and no matter how many times she pressed it the car wouldn't open.

We explored different possible solutions together for half an hour, all to no avail, at which point she decided to look for a local garage that could help her.

An hour later she called back, problem solved. *"What was it?"* I said, *"Was the battery running low in the remote control?"*.

"No, I was trying to open the wrong car."

We need to make sure we're trying to open the right car.

The Best Way to Think

A client once told me she'd been thinking about something and I instinctively asked: *"Do you mean thinking inside your head?"* She looked bemused and said: *"Where else would I think?"*

It's a fair reply on the surface. But what I now believe – that I didn't for years – is it's not possible for us to think properly without speaking or writing our thoughts.

Have you ever experienced things bouncing around in your head for days, sometimes months, with those thoughts never seeming to go anywhere useful? Have you ever been stuck on a problem but on the very moment you go to ask someone for help your brain suddenly figures out the answer? I know I have.

What I've discovered doing this work for a few years is the only way to think properly is to force our brain to articulate our thoughts through the spoken or written word. The act of forcing our brains to put the chaotic thoughts into a sensible order helps us to figure out what's behind them.

As we can't speak to each other while you read this, I'll be encouraging you to do as much writing as possible.

Different Language

Something that stopped me doing writing exercises in the past was people in the personal development and self-help worlds referring to it as 'journaling'. As with many other expressions used in those worlds, as a man who wants to be tough from a city that builds its men that way, the very fact it was called journaling put me off.

As you'll see throughout the book, I do my best to stay away from expressions that might make your toes curl or leave you feeling like you're in a life-coach woo-woo therapy session you have absolutely no interest in joining.

We'll talk a lot about the language we use in different parts of the book and you'll see I will often decide to develop new terms for things I think might resonate more with you and a greater number of people, and not alienate you like many of the self-help world terms might.

On that basis, we also won't be talking about what you're about to start as a *journey*. This, to me, is an adventure. It's your own superhero movie. Your own quest to understand who you really are, fighting monsters and discovering treasure along the way. By the end of your adventure you'll be a shiny new version of yourself.

You can, though, choose to call it whatever you feel most comfortable with.

Mental Health -v- Emotional Health

We have, thankfully, started to move as a society to a place where discussing mental health is becoming normal. It still baffles me that some people don't believe mental health is important or, in fact, that we still feel the need to treat mental health differently to physical health, but that's a topic for later in the book.

My belief, however, is that as a society there's still a huge gap in our understanding of ourselves and each other which needs to be filled if we're going to save our future existence. I have studied and been interested in mental health for much of the past 10 years, but it's only in the last few years since embarking on this adventure that I ever contemplated emotional health. It's not something I ever hear discussed in the mainstream.

Having spent those years focusing on mental health and not been able to resolve the many issues in my life, I believe that understanding and repairing our emotional well-being is a level deeper than our psychological well-being and is the most crucial thing we can do.

My transformation in life is almost entirely the result of my learning about my emotions and the foundational role they play. I will share with you everything I've learnt so you can experience the same transformation.

Choose Your Own Adventure

Have you ever read a 'Choose Your Own Adventure' book? I used to love them when I was a kid.

If you've never heard of them, the basic idea is that as the story progresses you are given options about what you want the main character to do. You are able to decide what decisions they make that means the version of the story you read is likely to be different to the version your best mate reads. As well as that, you can also read the same story over and over again, making different decisions for the lead character leading to different outcomes.

I want you to treat this as a 'Choose Your Own Adventure' book, as I have done with some of my favourite personal development books over the years. I have read my favourite book, *Letting Go* by David Hawkins, multiple times, and each time I've taken new things from it I hadn't seen before. I've written this book in a way that should mean you can revisit it as many times as you want and get something new from it each time.

As you embark on your adventure on the pages that follow you will see there are numerous exercises for you to do as you go along.

If you want to get as much value as possible from what I share I recommend that you do each exercise as it appears. If you can't do the exercise for any reason at the time, make sure you mark it to come back to another time.

I'd recommend buying yourself a nice notepad or journal to use as well, which will come in handy for the exercises and enable you to keep all of your work and thoughts in one place to refer back to over the coming weeks, months and years. I still go back to read my notepads from my transformation period to this day, and I still often write my thoughts down to process them properly. It has been a game-changer for me. I have also, though, left a blank space after each exercise for you to make any notes in case you don't have your pad or journal with you while reading.

As you will hopefully see as you progress, the exercises are in a particular order for a reason. I have seen first-hand through coaching how these lessons are best learnt and taken onboard.

I appreciate that, if you're anything like me, you will read what I have just written and think that it's for everyone else and not for you. You might even decide not to do the exercises at all and just skip past them.

If that is your choice you will still get a huge amount of value from the lessons that follow. Just bear in mind that you can't and won't get the full impact without truly committing time and energy to the exercises.

Equally, I don't want you to feel overwhelmed if the exercises are too much for you the first time you read through the pages. If that's the case, please don't feel as though you have to stop reading. Do as many exercises as you can and feel free to come back to them another time if that's what suits you best. Remember this is your adventure, so I want you to choose how it goes.

There's also huge value in coming back to repeat exercises again in the future. Given that we change as we move through our story, when we come back to do an exercise for a second or third time months or years down the line, we'll often discover new things we hadn't seen before.

I've named some of the exercises to make them easier to refer back to, because we will revisit some of the early exercises later in the book.

The Structure

Again, if you're like me, you'll like to have an idea of where we'll be going in the time we're spending together. From here, the book is divided into three main parts.

First, I set out the background to all of the problems we face in life. The root causes of everything, which is the first part to healing those issues. That section is called HEAL.

The second part is the juicy section you will no doubt be eager to get to, but I'd urge you to read it all in order for maximum impact.

That section will help you to completely transform your life and luckily fits into the acronym TRANSFORM.

The third and final part is called "Solving Life's Problems", where I cover a few big topics that I believe can all be solved using the principles in the book.

Last, but not least, something I'm not a fan of in books is when the author feels the need to constantly reference where they heard or read something they've decided to include for your benefit, which I think just makes things difficult to read.

As a result, while I will on occasion reference people where I think it's absolutely necessary, I give credit to the many people I've learnt from by including at the back of the book a list of books, blogs, people and other resources I've consumed over the years so you can go back and read the original source material if you want to dig deeper into anything we discuss.

Karate Kid Training

Depending on your age, that sub-heading might mean a classic 1980s movie about Daniel LaRusso, its remake starring Will Smith's son, a modern Netflix series or absolutely nothing.

Given that I'm 40 years old at the time of writing, it might not surprise you to hear that for me it will always mean Daniel LaRusso and, for the purposes of this book and this point, the training he received from his karate teacher, Mr Miyagi.

If you haven't been fortunate enough to watch the original *Karate Kid* movie, your first job is to put this down and watch it. It's a classic. It also contains a really important lesson that is fitting for what you're about to embark upon.

If you've never seen it, the story is about a teenage boy, Daniel LaRusso, who moves to a new school and, in order to defend himself against bullies, asks an old Chinese man, Mr Miyagi, to teach him karate.

Mr Miyagi proceeds to get Daniel to paint the fences around his house, wash his many cars and sweep his floors until, one day, the teenager breaks and angrily asks why the old man has got him doing random chores when he wants to learn how to fight. At that point, the wise old teacher demonstrates to Daniel how the tasks he's been doing have been teaching him to be a master in karate without realising. The lessons all suddenly come together and young Mr LaRusso realises what's been happening all along.

In the same way, there might be times when you're not quite sure where I'm taking you. You might think you're just washing cars and painting fences when you thought you were going to be learning how to smash through planks of wood with your hands and do flying kicks at head height.

If that happens, just go with it and have faith that by the time you reach the end of the adventure, it will all come together and you will suddenly realise you're the winner of the All Valley Under 18 Karate Championship.

I appreciate that's a very specific reference that you might only understand if you've seen the movie.

"Bore-off with Your Psycho-Babble Bullshit"

As part of my recent adventure I've ventured back into the world of dating. I could write another entire book on my experiences but, for the purposes of this part of this book, a girl said something to me that simultaneously made me laugh and cut me deep inside.

"Bore-off with your psycho-babble bullshit."

Ouch.

Despite it hitting an old sore point of mine, it inspired me to highlight this important point.

Most of what you're about to read on the following pages is psycho-babble bullshit. I can't deny that. It's not real. Most of it is just a collection of theories created by other flawed humans trying to explain why we are the way we are. There are few facts involved. Few points that cannot be debated, torn apart or disagreed with. I'm sure there will be many people in the world who disagree with the points made or think they're useless and that's all okay.

I share what I do because the people who taught me the lessons in this book used those lessons to create fulfilling, peaceful lives. I have done the same thing and the people I have shared the lessons with appear to have done likewise. I hope sharing the lessons will help you in the same way.

The problem with anything like these topics, however, is they become self-fulfilling prophecies. To borrow some words from Henry Ford, whether you think the ideas are powerful and can change your life or not, you're right.

Nothing will change your life against your will, no matter how many other people might have used the same principles to change their lives.

It's worth stressing, therefore, that if you decide to embark on this adventure you don't need to believe or take on board everything I say in order for it to be effective. Feel free to take the bits you like and integrate them into your life however you see best and discard anything else. This is your adventure, after all.

Honesty is the Best Policy

Whatever else you do while reading this book, it's absolutely crucial you are honest with yourself when reflecting on your life or completing any of the exercises.

As you will see in later chapters, we have a tendency to tell ourselves stories that aren't true, often by ignoring the little voice inside telling us things we don't want to hear or acknowledge. We are the easiest people to lie to and trying to kid ourselves hasn't got us very far so it's time to give complete honesty a go.

Anything you write down during the exercises will be for your eyes only, so give yourself the gift of complete honesty.

Snake Oil Salesmen

Something that's always amused me is when people label anyone who shares this type of information as a snake oil salesman. While I don't like lots of the personal development world these days, generally people are well-intentioned and are only sharing things that have helped them and they've seen help others, so the connotations behind being labelled snake oil salesmen aren't always fair.

From my perspective, though, I'm happy to admit I'm selling snake oil. The key to the particular type of snake oil I'm selling is it comes with very specific instructions. Like a Mogwai from the movie *Gremlins*.

To illustrate the point, here's an exchange between me and a customer from earlier last year that definitely happened in real life.

*   *   *

Me: "Now, the trick with the snake oil I'm selling is you must take it in a very specific way."

Billy: "Okay. What's that then?"

Me: "You must take a sip of the snake oil exactly as the clock strikes midday every day for six months. Only then will it have the desired effect. It needs dedication and practice. Got it?"

Billy: "Got it."

Me: "Are you sure? You promise to take a sip of it exactly as the clock strikes midday every day for six months?"

Billy: "You have my word."

Me: "Great. See you in six months."

[Six months later]

Billy: "You're a fraud. This snake oil is useless. It hasn't changed my life one bit."

Me: "I'm sorry to hear that, Billy. Did you follow the instructions exactly as I set them out?"

Billy: "Yes"

Me: "Really? Because I've heard rumours that some people are buying this snake oil and instead of taking a sip of it exactly as the clock strikes midday every day for six months, they've been using it to rub on their genitals and play with themselves instead."

Billy: *silence*

Me: "Billy, have you been rubbing the snake oil on your balls and playing with yourself for the past six months?"

Billy: "Erm, well, yeah, but it's not my fault, it made them feel so nice and I just thought I'd do it once then start following the instructions, but I sort of got addicted to it and before I knew it I'd run out. My balls are very soft though."

*   *   *

The lessons I share will only change your life if you believe they will and if you're prepared to put the work in. Some people make rapid changes in a matter of days or weeks. Others, like me, take a little longer. The work takes as long as it takes and, no different to looking after your physical health, is not something you can do for a few days then stop and expect miraculous results.

If you want to rub the snake oil on your genitals I have no problem with that, just don't expect it to do what it has the potential to do if you ignore the instructions.

Please also note that reading this book will not, as far as I am aware, make your genitals feel softer.

A Baseline

The last thing for us to do before we begin your adventure is to create a baseline to measure your progress from.

The reality is there's no real scientific way of measuring how much a human's life changes through doing this type of work. Maybe our blood pressure will reduce or health problems will clear up (more on that in Chapter 20) but as far as I'm aware the scientific and medical communities don't have any way of measuring peacefulness or contentment, which is what this is all about.

So, we need to create our own method to give us some form of measuring tool.

What I'd like you to do is respond to each of the following statements by choosing a number between zero and 100, with zero being the worst possible answer and 100 being the best possible.

It's crucial when doing this that you go with the first number that pops into your head when you read the statement. Our gut, soul and heart have a way of knowing an answer straight away, but then our ego and intellect take that first answer and put it through our internal PR machine in order to give a response we think fits with our character in the outside world and who we are meant to be.

Again, there'll be lots more on that later but, for now, just do your best to stick with your first instinctive answer.

Ready? Write down your number between zero and 100 for each of the following:

	Score out of 100
How content you are generally in your life.	
How content you are in your career, job or business.	
How content you are in your romantic relationship (if you have one).	
How content you are in your relationship with your kids (if you have any).	
How content you are with your physical health.	

Now write out in your notepad or journal any specific issues you're facing that you would like to solve or overcome. Include as much detail as possible to give you an accurate baseline to refer back to in the future. Set out how you feel about each issue and what specifically you'd like to resolve.

Last, but not least, I want you to write specifically about any health issues you're experiencing, however normal or insignificant you might consider them to be. So, whether you have asthma or a skin condition, acid indigestion, depression, allergies or any unexplained illness, I want you to write in detail how you're feeling about it and, if you have physical symptoms you can see, such as damaged skin, I want you to take photos of them to keep for later and/or make a detailed note of the level and type of pain you are in, and so on.

A Crucial Warning

When I work with people in a one-on-one capacity, I insist if they want to do this work that they commit to no less than two months working together. The reason is this work takes the lid off Pandora's box and what comes out is not always predictable, so it's crucial I make sure before we stop working together the lid is back on the box and everything is safe.

I don't want people uncovering their deepest, darkest issues then skipping off into the forest alone because it could be dangerous.

I would recommend strongly, therefore, that if you choose to start this adventure you treat it as signing up to work with me for a minimum of two months, as you would be if we were face to face. That means you commit to reading the entire book and completing all of the exercises at some point.

It is also imperative to note that re-living childhood events and traumas can be extremely difficult and painful. If you begin the exercises on the following pages and find yourself struggling in any way, please do not suffer in silence. The purpose of this book is to help you, not lead to you sitting in a dark room by yourself for days on end riddled with internal anguish or something worse.

If things become too much the first thing to do is stop and take a break and, if you feel it's needed, please find a therapist and/or a coach who can help with emotional trauma and ask them for guidance and to help navigate these waters.

Many people will tell me they can't afford a therapist or coach before going on to tell me about the latest Xbox they've bought, the money they've spent numbing the pain of life with alcohol or how they've bought some new clothes to cheer themselves up.

If you feel as though you can't afford a therapist, it can help to analyse your finances and identify what you're spending your money on. Go through your bank statements to separate absolutely essential spend such as rent or mortgage payments from non-essential spend such as alcohol and new clothes.

I promise if you divert the money you spend on non-essential items that usually serve only as a distraction from your problems and instead invest that money in hiring a professional to support you on this adventure it will be the best money you ever spend.

How to Choose a Therapist or Coach

I am often asked the best way to select a therapist and/or a coach to work with, so it's worth setting out my thoughts here for you to consider.

In my view, the two most important things to look for in someone to help you are their qualifications and the connection you have with them.

By qualifications, I don't necessarily mean certificates or degrees. As I've mentioned, I don't have any formal qualifications in any of the things you're reading about on these pages, but I have spent tens of thousands of pounds and thousands of hours learning all about it all on top of all the real-life experience I've had around these topics. The irony is I've invested far more money, time and energy in studying this world than I ever did to become a lawyer in my old life, but I've got certificates from a university and law school to say I'm qualified to do that and I don't in this.

When looking for your own coach or therapist, it might be important to you that they have formal qualifications. It was for me when I looked for a therapist, but not when I looked for a coach. You should decide for yourself what is key for you and go with that. There are no right or wrong answers but if someone not having formal qualifications will lead to you not respecting or listening to them, it's pointless hiring someone without them.

For me, a therapist being qualified formally and to a high level is essential, whereas a coach is more about what they know and how I feel about them.

The second and possibly most important factor is rapport. You could find the most qualified therapist or coach in the world but, if you don't like them and don't click with them, my view is you're likely to get less value from the relationship.

With both of the above factors the important thing is to read as much as you can about a person before having an initial phone call, which many therapists and coaches will do for free. You should use an initial call or session to see whether you feel comfortable with that person and whether you could see yourself sharing your deepest innermost thoughts and feelings with them.

If you don't feel it's right, it's fine to let them know politely you've decided to go elsewhere. Keep looking until you find someone who fits you. I would have said in the past that in-person sessions are best, but I've never met in person two of the three people who have helped to change my life, so don't be shy about spreading your net across the globe to find the best fit for you.

Last, but not least, it's crucial to note that whoever you choose to be your therapist or coach are not miracle workers. They cannot change your life for you. I have observed many examples of people who have worked with a therapist or coach for many years without making any significant progress. Remember it's no different to working with a personal trainer to improve your physical fitness. The coach or therapist can only guide you. It is your responsibility to do the work to change your life, not theirs.

If you have more questions on this topic, send them to *questions@paul7cope.com* and I'll respond to as many as I can via my YouTube channel and podcast. Before submitting a question, though, just check whether an episode already exists with the answer you're looking for.

If you choose to carry on with the adventure after taking all of that into account, it's time to get started.

Congratulations on taking the first steps to transforming your life.

3

HEAL

"I know we're going to uncover what's sleeping in our soul"

(Acquiesce / Oasis)

Time for the juicy bits to begin.

This part is all about discovering who you really are and the root causes of all your problems in life.

I appreciate they sound like bold claims to make about some words on pages of a book, but we are where we are.

HEAL stands for:

H   Home

E   Emotional Repression

A   Adaptation

L   Low Self-Worth

As a famous song once said, let's start at the very beginning…

4

HOME

"Feeling my way
through the darkness
Guided by a beating heart
I don't know where
the journey will end
But I know where to start"

(Wake Me Up / Avicii)

At this stage of my own adventure, whenever I talk to anyone about this part of the story for the first time I feel a bit daft, as though everyone already knows it.

Then I remember that I didn't know about any of it until I was 38 years old and every single one of the people from around the world who I've coached on this topic had no idea either, despite being highly-skilled, educated and bright people.

This takes us right the way back to where it all started for each of us: our childhoods. It's about those formative years of our lives when we first learnt how to be a human and to survive in this world.

Let me take you back.

The Comfy Cave and the Food Pipe

This is a part of our lives I've never heard anyone talk about, not really, and not in the sense of helping us to solve challenges we're facing when we've been on the planet for several decades.

Do you remember the first nine months of your existence?

No, me neither.

But just think about it for a few seconds. From the moment you were conceived by your mum and dad getting jiggy after a few glasses of wine and a romantic comedy with just enough raunchy sex scenes to get their sensitive bits all tingly, or the moment your mum decided to get some sperm from a man who knows a man who told her the genetics were of the highest calibre[3], you existed for almost the first year of your life in a gentle, temperature controlled, cushioned environment.

You floated around without a care in the world. No particularly loud noises, no bright lights and, most importantly of all, a food pipe that delivered nutrients to you whenever you wanted them.

No need to ask anyone for anything. Just floating around in the type of hotel I can't believe hasn't been built in Dubai yet, but no doubt will be once someone reads this and gets a great idea.

---

[3] At the time of writing I think they are the two basic forms of conceiving a child, but feel free to add your own if I've missed anything out.

Then, one day, out of nowhere while you're just floating around in the only world you've ever known, something starts rumbling. It's more than the rumbling noises you usually hear that come when who you will later learn to be called "mum" has eaten some particularly spicy food that didn't agree with either of you.

No, this is more serious. You can sense it.

All of a sudden, a doorway creaks open at the bottom of your temperature-controlled room, loads of the water that you were floating in rushes out, and you begin to get forced down a gap through which you instinctively know you can't fit.

Sometimes, an alien being actually reaches in with a massive metal tool and drags you out of your cave by your head.

Can you imagine if that happened now, or even anything remotely like it?

I mean, the most stressful thing most people experience in their entire life on earth is, as I understand it, moving house. And that's something we do through choice with a hand-picked team of removal people following months of planning.

Imagine if one day the floor opened and someone just reached up and dragged you through a crack in the road by your head, taking you into a completely different world with loads of bright lights, loud noises and giant people telling you to stop crying.

"Stop crying? Are you serious? You've just abducted me by my head from my home and you're telling me to stop crying? I don't even know what crying is for fuck's sake. I've never needed to make this noise before now but it very much feels like the right thing to be doing. And where the fuck is my food pipe?"

Sorry about the colourful language – babies really are foul mouthed when you learn to fully understand what they're saying.

And this is how each of us first enters Planet Earth. If we're lucky, we had someone to keep us company through the trauma, or maybe someone just cut open a nice big hole for us to be lifted from but, either way, the whole thing is traumatic.

From that moment, we have to learn very quickly how to survive in this strange, loud and bright new world.

Which is when the problems start.

Programming

Depending on your beliefs and things you know that I might not, we might have different ideas about what is already programmed into a human child when it first enters the world. Some people believe that sexuality is a pre-existing program, others believe that gender itself isn't pre-programmed.

Whatever you believe doesn't really matter for the purposes of this book, though, provided we can agree that every human enters the world with only a minimal amount of programming[4].

I think of it like a laptop that you've just bought from the shop. It has some basic programs already installed to get you going but, for the most part, you're going to have to add whatever it is you want to make it the laptop you need.

Some people want Microsoft Word, others want *Grand Theft Auto*[5].

---

[4] There is a whole world developing about programming being passed through our genes, which we don't need to overly concern ourselves with for the purposes of this book.

[5] Other choices are available.

So, we bounce out into the world kicking and screaming, then look up at the humans around us and say: *"Ok people, it's clear I need you to keep me alive, so let's figure out a way of working together until I can sort myself a food pipe again."*

And that's when the programming begins.

The Cereal Box Story

Let's start with an innocent story that demonstrates perfectly how we're all programmed by the people around us, mainly our caregivers, from the moment we enter the planet.

A few months ago I was at home in Liverpool and decided I fancied some cereal as a snack.

I don't often eat cereal these days because since starting to focus more on my health a few years ago I've realised most of it is full of shit that doesn't do us any good but, just like other shit we like to eat and drink, every now and then I still fancy some.

I went to the shops, bought my favourite brand and headed home. Standing in the kitchen while listening to music, I began to open the box.

First, I opened the two longest cardboard strips at the top. Next, I folded out the two small flaps at the sides that are revealed after you open the longer flaps, then I ripped one of those smaller flaps from the box, opened the plastic bag containing the cereal on the same side as the torn-off flap and poured myself a bowl.

Then I burst out laughing.

I'd been doing the work set out in this book for over two years by the time this incident happened, so had become acutely aware of many things that I'd realised had been programmed into my subconscious without me knowing. But I hadn't spotted this one before.

The thing is, if you've been able to follow that description of a box opening (I appreciate it might be difficult to picture), you might think one part of it is a bit odd.

I've never seen anyone else in my adult life tear off that little side flap from the box before pouring their cereal, but I did it without even thinking about it.

Why? Because that's how my dad opened cereal boxes when I was a kid.

I haven't watched my dad open cereal for something like 28 years, but when it came to doing something I hardly ever do, I subconsciously reverted to how I was taught to do it when I was younger than I can remember.

Of course, I don't think my dad ever sat me down and said, *"Now, look son, here's an important life lesson about how to open cereal boxes"* but when we bounce out of our safe little hotel room inside our mum we don't have a program installed for how to open cereal boxes, so we have to get one from somewhere. Mine came from my dad.

It's important here to stop for a few seconds and reflect on the power of that story. It might seem like it's just a cereal box, but it's far more than that. It's everything.

Think about it. If when we're kids we don't know how to open cereal and we subconsciously pick up that skill from the people who raised us, what else did we learn?

How to speak. How to think. How to love. How to relate to other humans.

The list goes on and on.

✎ Exercise

Here's your first exercise. It's an easy one to break you in gently.

Like most of the exercises I'll give you to do as we travel down this path together, it's best to do this in two parts.

First, take some time to sit down with a pen and paper and really think about it consciously. After that, just allow the exercise to float around in your subconscious and notice when something crops up during your week.

Take a few minutes to think about what your cereal box story is. Does one spring to mind immediately? Is there a quirky little thing your parents or the people who raised you do that you've realised you also do?

If you can't think of one immediately, start trying to notice things as you go through your week. How do you drive your car or clean the toilet? What strange little things do you do that your partner or someone you live with has mentioned?

Once you've found an example or two, consider how many other things you must have learned from your original caregivers without realising it. Up until this point you might, like most people I've ever met, be telling yourself a story about how different you are to your parents or close family members.

It might be worth preparing yourself for that illusion to be shattered, but we'll come back to that later.

Notes

Trauma and Neglect

The main problem with childhood is we experience the whole thing as children.

It wouldn't be nearly as big an issue if we handled the whole thing as adults but, unfortunately, unless your name's Benjamin Button that's not how it works.

An even bigger problem is that when most of us reflect on a childhood, including our own, we look at it through the eyes of adults rather than those of children.

If we consider someone with serious problems in their adult lives – maybe they're a drug addict or a serial killer – and we discover they suffered severe trauma as children, most people can see a clear link between the trauma and neglect the person suffered as a kid and the troubles they experience years later.

We might not fully understand or sympathise with the troubles experienced by the drug addict or killer, but at least we can see how they might have originated.

Maybe the trauma was that their parents were drug addicts, or they were physically or sexually abused in their early years. Perhaps they were shown no love or were seriously neglected in ways we could never truly imagine.

When we see that level of trauma or neglect we can understand a link with problematic adulthoods.

However, when we consider early years of life that were at the very least okay and, for many of us (including me), a dream childhood other children might only read about in fairytales, it's more of a struggle to understand any connection to difficulties we face as grown ups.

After all, in those childhoods there is no abuse, neglect or trauma to consider is there?

The Language We Use

We'll talk more about this topic in a wider sense later, but it's worth addressing in relation to this specific point.

The issue is when we use words like 'abuse', 'trauma' and 'neglect' they carry certain connotations we might not want to associate with our own upbringing. Even if we had a bit of a difficult time, we are unlikely to use any of those words.

But the truth is that basically everyone experiences trauma and neglect as children. Childhood is, in itself, a traumatic experience. Think back to the earlier examples of what it must be like being dragged kicking and screaming into this world.

When we think of trauma, though, what we generally think of is what I've best seen described as capital 'T' trauma.

If we're thinking about trauma on a scale of zero to 10, capital 'T' trauma is 10 out of 10 on the scale. It's the child abuse, drug addicted parents and total neglect I mentioned earlier.

The kicker, however, is that if a child experiences a large number of small 't' traumas that may each be one out of 10 on the scale, they can all add up to the equivalent of a 10 out of 10 capital 'T' trauma.

Does that make sense?

It's important, therefore, that we gain a better understanding of what small 't' traumas might look like to a child.

The Still Face Experiment

A few months before I began writing this book, I had the privilege of interviewing Dr Ed Tronick and Dr Claudia Gold for my YouTube channel and podcast (which you can find by searching for 'The Paul Cope Show' on YouTube or your favourite podcast app).

Ed and Claudia have between them written several books around this hugely important topic and are experts in the field. I recommend watching or listening to that interview and reading their books if you're interested in learning more about what we're about to discuss.

In 1975, Ed conducted an experiment that was groundbreaking at the time and is still often referenced when discussing connections and disconnections between children and caregivers.

Again, I recommend taking a few minutes to watch the experiment for yourself. It's available on YouTube by searching *"the still face experiment Dr. Edward Tronick"*.

In summary, though, it goes along these lines:

A baby who is around one year old is placed in a high chair facing her mum. The mum plays with the baby and engages with her in a very natural way. The baby is clearly happy and connecting perfectly well with her mum.

Next, the mum turns her head away from her child and, when she looks back, has a completely still face. She shows no emotion and doesn't interact with the baby at all.

To begin with, the child carries on as she was before. She tries to play and engage her mum in what they'd been doing. However, she quickly becomes visibly upset, trying all kinds of tricks to regain her mum's attention and connection.

Slowly, as her different attempts to gain her mum's attention fail, the baby becomes more and more distressed, finally letting out a high-pitched squeal before breaking down into floods of tears.

This all happens in a matter of moments and is disturbing to watch.

Thankfully, at the end of the experiment the mum re-engages with her baby and, as she begins to interact and play with her again, the child quickly reverts to her happy self.

Again, take a few moments to let that experiment sink in. This is an example of a baby potentially experiencing small 't' trauma simply by its mother failing to engage actively with it for no more than a minute or so. It's also impossible to do it justice by describing it, so please do watch the video on YouTube.

In that context, it becomes much easier to begin to understand how traumatic childhood is for most of us.

An Important Point

I find it difficult to talk and write about some of the following parts and I want to be clear about something before we go further.

This topic is not a case of us beating up our parents for the things we experienced as children. I will share some examples of things I experienced in my childhood, and I share them only to give you examples of what you might have experienced in yours.

It is likely that we all experienced thousands of small traumas without ever realising.

Understanding that we experienced these types of traumas does not mean we had bad parents, it just means we had parents who were humans trying their best to raise children. That in its very nature is traumatic for everyone involved, in particular the kids, but also for the parents.

My therapist once told me a story of going to see a high-profile therapist and author who was presenting to a room of therapists. He began his talk with something along these lines:

"Let's get something out of the way before we start. Many of you often ask me whether you are damaging your children in some way by the way you are parenting them. You then want to go on to give specific examples of various things that have happened. To save us all time in the future, the answer to the question is 'yes', you are damaging your children, we all are."

I often say to people now, regardless of any work you decide to do and changes you decide to make in your life, you either have already or will in the future damage your children, as will I, and the best thing we can all do is start putting away some money so that when our kids are 18 instead of buying them a car we can pay for them to see a therapist and/or coach to work through their issues.

The fact we were damaged as kids and will damage our own kids does not make any of us bad people and the purpose of this section is not to beat anyone up. The point is to make us more aware of our actions and the actions of our parents or other caregivers when we were young that will lead to a better understanding of why we are the way we are, so we can do something about it.

After all, we also got many of the best bits of us from our original caregivers.

A Faulty Production Line

I like to think of human life as one big car production line.

Just imagine for a second one of those huge factories full of conveyor belts, automated robots and humans, putting together cars a piece at a time.

That's just like us. We pop out into the world at the start of the conveyor belt and start to trundle through the factory while parts of us are slowly added onto the original chassis. Only instead of robots adding doors and wheels, we have the people who raised us inputting multiple programs about how to be a person.

The main problem is that the people building the next generation of humans were built, without knowing, with faulty programming of their own. They were taught how to build humans by the people who worked in the factory before them, so assume that's how you build humans.

Then, years later, most of the humans built in the factory start to develop faults and we all just accept that's normal because all humans have the same faults. But imagine if it was actually cars from a car production line we were talking about. Imagine if every car built in a certain factory started developing the same faults after driving 40,000 miles.

If that happened we'd go back to the original production line and figure out what was going wrong so we could fix it. Yet with the human production line we just accept the faults are normal and carry on.

The job for each of us is to revolutionise the production line so we can start building humans that don't break down after 40,000 miles.

Kids Don't Do What You Say,
They Do What You Do

A few years ago, I heard the wrestler Triple H talking on a podcast and he said a line I'll never forget and one which I've repeated endlessly ever since:

> "Kids don't do what you say,
> they do what you do."

The main problem with the faulty human production line is many adults have a conscious idea of good things to teach their kids, but the words that come out of their mouths don't match the way they live, which means their children receive mixed messages.

Children learn a lot from observing the world around them and copying what they see. If what they are told by their parents contradicts what they witness from their parents it doesn't stop them adopting the behaviour, it just means they learn that what they have adopted is not acceptable.

It's amazing how often I see mums and dads baffled by the actions of their children when it's clear to see the kids are just copying their elders.

The same principle applies to what we think we're teaching our children consciously, or what we think we were taught consciously as kids, and what we're actually teaching them or were taught through the words and actions of the adults around us when we were growing up. They are often two very different things.

Examples

I think it's worth setting out a few examples of this part of the story to enable you to start identifying parts of your programming that were installed despite your original caregivers telling you with their mouths they were installing a completely different program.

You might notice as you read through the following illustrations that the same principles apply to many parts of your life as an adult. Think of how often you, or someone you know, says one thing with their words but conveys a completely different message with their actions. Which is more powerful?

The Mobile Phone Challenge

Here's a very basic modern example. If you have children and struggle to get them to stop using their mobile phones consider how often they see you or the other adults around them using their phones.

I have witnessed on numerous occasions adults telling their kids repeatedly they shouldn't be using their phones as much as they do. Often moments later I'll watch the parents indulging in addictive use of their own mobile phones.

The children copy what the parents do, rather than do what they say.

"Always tell the truth"

This is a more serious example of the same issue. I've experienced myself and coached several people who have seen the same thing growing up. Most of us have been told repeatedly to tell the truth because telling the truth is the right thing to do, but have then watched as our parents tell all kinds of lies to get through their life on a daily basis. Mostly little white lies but, sometimes, great big lies of which we are aware but are never discussed openly.

The lesson we learn subconsciously is to tell lies when it suits us, while also learning that telling lies makes us a bad person. Hence still adopting the behaviour as well as taking another blow to our self-worth.

"What do you want to be when you grow up?"

Here's a big one to end with, one which is very personal to me and tends to resonate with lots of other people. I go into much more detail on this subject in my first book, *The 7 Secrets to Change Your Career*, but it's worth including some key points here.

I could talk for hours just about the question itself. I think it should be outlawed. The subconscious messages we give when we ask a child what they want to be when they grow up are, first, that there's an answer, second, that there's a correct answer and, third, that there's only one answer.

It's what leads most people to a lifetime of saying, *"but I don't know what I want to be"*, preventing them from making any changes. It also confuses what we want to be with what we want to do to earn money, which can in this day and age be completely different things.

On the specific topic of subconscious training, though, this is an area where adults use the techniques from the Chris Nolan movie *Inception* to plant ideas deep inside their children's minds without usually being conscious they're doing it.

I could give a thousand examples of things I've witnessed to highlight this point, but I'll limit it to a couple.

Here's a conversation I overheard between a mum and her 13-year-old son who wanted to be a movie star.

* * *

Mum: "So, what do you want to be as a back-up plan if you can't be a movie star?"

Son: "Nothing, I just want to be a movie star."

Mum: "Well, you have to have a back-up plan so you need to pick something."

Son: "Okay, I'll be a singer."

Mum: "No, you can't say singer. It can't be something that's like being a movie star, it needs to be something else."

Son: "Erm, okay, I'll be a movie producer."

Mum: "No, no, no, that doesn't work either. It's got to be something normal."

Son: "Like what?"

Mum: "I don't know, like a doctor or a dentist."

Son: "Er, okay, well a doctor then."

Mum: "Great. That sounds like a really good idea."

* * *

That same mum, when asked weeks later what her son wanted to be, declared excitedly that he wanted to be a doctor, completely ignoring the fact he actually wants to be a movie star and the only reason doctor was ever mentioned was because she forced him to keep naming possible jobs until he found something she approved of.

The kid then gets the powerful subconscious message, regardless of what his mum says through her words, that it's not acceptable for him to want to be a movie star.

My story, which is shared by many others, is far more subtle[6].

The short summary of that story is as a little boy I loved toy cars. I had a bucket full of them and would happily play with them for hours on end. One day when I was about three years old I was in the back of my dad's car and saw a black Porsche pull up alongside us at the traffic lights. I asked my dad whose car it was and he told me it was their solicitor's.

I immediately said: *"I want to be a solicitor then"*. The irony was I couldn't speak very well at three, so couldn't even pronounce 'solicitor' properly. Remember at that age we don't even know most words, they're just noises we're making through our mouths that we see have an impact on the world around us.

When we make the noises that sound like *"I'd like some milk"*, the lucky ones among us as children would see a big human bring us some milk, so we learn to keep making those noises whenever we want milk.

I learnt very quickly that if I made the noises that sounded something like *"I want to be a solicitor"* they would make the big humans around me very happy indeed. I would be rolled out at family parties to the line *"tell everyone what you want to be"*, I would make the noises and everyone would smile, sometimes even applauding.

---

[6] The long version of this story is in the opening chapters of my first book, which you can read for free by visiting: **changeyourcareer.org**

Imagine how good that feels to a three year old, especially when I had no idea what I was actually saying. What I really meant was: *"I'd like to drive a nice car when I'm older".*

After a while of repeating the line to myself and to anyone who'd listen, it became second nature and soon turned into *"I've always wanted to be a solicitor"* even though I didn't have a clue what a solicitor was.

If you ask my parents now, they will quite rightly tell you that no-one ever told me I had to be a solicitor. I agree. The problem is not what I was or wasn't told expressly through people's words, it was the subconscious programming I received that being a solicitor was what everyone wanted me to do.

Again, as I'll keep repeating, this isn't anyone's fault. We are guilty of the same things our original caregivers were guilty of, usually because we are blind to the subconscious behaviours we display from which others learn. Our behaviour in these situations also generally stems from our own emotional and psychological issues that we'll explore in much more detail in the following chapters.

✎ Exercise (Audrey)

We need a way to identify some of the exercises we'll be doing so we can easily refer back to them later in the book. Someone who read an early draft of this suggested I should name those exercises for ease of reference, which is what I've done. This exercise is called Audrey. I don't think that's what the person who made the suggestion had in mind, but we are where we are.

The purpose of this exercise might not make any sense right now, so just remember the Karate Kid training we discussed and how I promise it will all come together later on.

For now, I want you to create a table with three columns. You can write this out by hand or use a computer, the method is not overly important for this exercise.

In the first column I want you to write the names of all of the people who you were close to growing up and who had an influence over your childhood. That might be your parents, your grandparents, your brothers or sisters, your aunties, uncles or cousins, foster parents, care-home workers or anyone else you can think of.

There are no right or wrong answers so if you think someone should be on the list put them on it.

In the second column I want you to write down all of that person's good character traits and, in the third column I want you to write down all of that person's bad character traits.

Does that make sense?

The trick here is some of the people on your list you might see as angels and others you might see as demons. Many people I've worked with have at least one parent they talk about in glowing terms and another they don't like very much at all. The challenge with that is when it comes to listing negative traits of someone we think is an angel we might struggle, and vice versa for the demons.

If you're struggling on either side, for extra motivation I want you to do one or both of two things. Imagine that I have a briefcase containing £10million, and it's all yours if you can find the traits you say aren't there. For example, if you think your dad is an angel and don't want to write anything negative, picture that you win £10million if you can come up with five things.

If that's not enough motivation and you'd prefer something darker, imagine I'm holding a gun to your head, or to the head of the person you love most in the world, and I'll pull the trigger unless you find five things for the list.

See where you get to then save the table for later. We'll come back to it.

Notes

Developing New Language

As I've already stressed, and will continue to stress, the main challenge when talking about these things if you've had at least a reasonably good childhood with parents you consider to be caring and loving, is that describing experiences as traumatic or neglectful sounds awful.

I would never want anyone to think I consider my childhood to have been traumatic because of my parents. My mum and dad are the most caring, loving parents anyone could wish to have. My childhood was filled with happy memories, laughter and love, yet I still reached my mid-thirties and realised I had a lot of inner demons I needed to deal with.

That leads me, as it often does, to think we need to start developing new language to use around these topics. The reality is that childhood is traumatic, full stop. Rather than asking people whether they experienced any trauma as a child, I now just ask:

"Are you a human?"

And:

"Were you ever a child?"

If the answers to both of those questions are *"yes"* then you have experienced trauma that more than likely needs to be processed and dealt with[7].

---

[7] In the years that follow this book being published, we might even reach a stage at which the same points apply to the artificial intelligence machines being built by some of the most dysfunctional members of our society because, after all, those machines are being programmed in the same way we were all programmed as children, so there's no reason the faults of their makers won't be passed on in exactly the same way. Which means if you're a robot reading this, welcome to the party.

I always remember reading a chapter in Russell Brand's book *Recovery* which played a key part in the early stages of my transformation, which was headed something like: *"Are you a bit fucked?"*

As the months and years passed after first reading that, I realised the only problem with it was it didn't go far enough. Instead of asking that question, it's far more appropriate to say *"You almost certainly are a bit fucked"* and go from there.

What is Trauma?

I think it's worth setting out what I believe to be trauma, although it's worth always bearing in mind this is simply my interpretation based on my current beliefs, which could well change as the years progress. It is also, of course, a very simple summary of something about which there have been endless books and articles written.

To me, trauma is anything that causes us to suppress any part of our true self and/or to create an adaptation of our true self. I talk about both of those in detail in the next two chapters. Trauma can also be anything that leads us to believe at a subconscious level we are not good enough as we are.

Capital 'T' Trauma

In my view, capital T trauma is anything from our childhood that had a big impact on us and we are likely to recognise as traumatic when looking at somebody else's life. So, sexual abuse, being raised by alcoholics or drug addicts, being the victim of or experiencing physical violence of any type (including witnessing your caregivers abusing each other physically), being abandoned by a caregiver totally (for example, a parent leaving you when you were young) or being abandoned temporarily on numerous occasions (for example, being left alone for long periods while you were young). On the trauma scale running from zero to 10, think of it as anything from eight to 10.

Small 't' Trauma

In my interpretation, this can be practically anything to a kid, depending on how it was interpreted at the time. Think of it as anything from one to seven on the trauma scale.

It could be a good friend laughing at us, or a parent making a flippant comment about our weight. It might be a caregiver regularly judging other people for being bad or stupid, or a grandparent rewarding us for being special.

Crucially, it could just be a child dropping their ice cream on the floor. To us as grown-ups, dropping an ice cream might be a mild annoyance but, to a three year old whose entire world was wrapped around that delicious treat, dropping it could be the equivalent of you returning home from work one day to find your home had burned to the floor.

Just pause for a moment and imagine if that happened and, instead of someone consoling you, they just said dismissively *"Oh, get over it, I'll buy you another house"*. I'd guess that wouldn't quite make up for the emotional trauma you'd just experienced.

It's always key, therefore, to try our best to see how we would have interpreted an event as a child rather than how we might interpret the same thing as an adult. It also isn't necessarily the event itself that's important, more how we reacted to it emotionally and what impact it had. More on this later as well.

With any type of trauma, it's worth having a little wander back through our family tree because, while we might not have experienced any capital 'T' traumas as children ourselves, it usually doesn't take much to go back through the generations to find someone who did experience big traumas and passed down the effects.

A very simple example in my life and the life of most people my age is my grandparents all lived through World War II. My grandad on my dad's side fought at Dunkirk, survived, returned home with not even a thought that therapy might be required and was married and having children within 12 months.

It's hard to even begin to imagine the level of trauma he experienced and passed down through my dad, especially bearing in mind he was raised by a parent who lived through World War I and had no doubt passed similar trauma down to him.

Exercise (Kenneth)

Do this in the same way as the first exercise, beginning by taking some time to sit with pen and paper and consider what capital 'T' or small 't' traumas you might have experienced as a child.

Does anything spring to mind? Whatever comes up write out in as much detail as possible what happened.

After doing that consciously, allow the exercise to drift through your subconscious as you go through life and note anything that comes up, again writing in detail about whatever arises.

Notes

A New Expression

As I've said above, I don't think it's useful for us to continue referring to all events that happened in our childhood as traumatic or neglectful. Now that I've explained what I think we mean when we discuss those terms, I think it's time to come up with a new expression for us to use for anything that we don't think falls into the definition of small 't' or capital 'T' trauma.

My view is we'd all be better off thinking of the other things that happened to us as children, however big or small, as 'Programming Experiences'. These are the events that shaped how we developed from the moment we entered this world. No-one is to blame for them, so by referring to them as Programming Experiences from now on we can think of them in more neutral terms. All traumas can be included within this definition, as well as any other experience we would rather not label as trauma while still wanting to acknowledge its impact on our life.

Examples of Programming Experiences

This is one of the parts of trying to share the lessons I've learnt that's much more difficult to do through a book than it would be if we were talking face to face. In person, I could ask you to tell me all about your childhood and we could take our time to pick out all the bits where you had Programming Experiences of any kind and dig beneath so you can see what parts of them still affect you today.

Obviously that's not possible with a book, so the next best thing I can do is attempt to provide some examples of Programming Experiences that you might be able to relate to or, at least, might prompt you to think of other experiences you had which installed any form of program in your operating system.

It's key to note, however, that this is by no means an exhaustive list and Programming Experiences come in all shapes and sizes, the kicker being that often things we might label as fairly positive Programming Experiences might result in what we consider to be negative consequences when they are perceived through the lens of a little human.

In the table below I've set out some examples of Programming Experiences you might have experienced as a child and the way in which the experience could have programmed you from a child's viewpoint. Obviously, some of the examples are clearer than others and I've omitted examples of the bigger, more serious Programming Experiences because I think at this stage of our lives it's fairly obvious to us what those events might be (as described as capital 'T' traumas in the earlier section).

It's also important to note that children pick this stuff up from the behaviour of the adults around them as well as things they might overhear. So, if you never tell your kid that they're too fat but you constantly talk about how people who are overweight are disgusting, the lesson your kid receives is that being overweight is bad and, therefore, not acceptable, which installs unhealthy programming through little ears about how good they are as a human being linked to the percentage of fat on their body.

The same goes for any of the examples shown in the table, so this isn't necessarily just about the things you experienced directly.

Programming Experience	The Programming Potentially Received by a Child
Being told to be good (i.e. *"be a good boy"*, "be a good girl" or *"be a good person"*)	We might as well start with one of the most general and wide-ranging examples that's likely to make you sit back in your seat and exclaim: *"Well, Paul, that's ridiculous. We were all told that, weren't we? And I say that to my kid all the time."*
	Why do you think I'm using it as the first one?
	Being told to be 'good', especially when done repeatedly (as we tend to do to our kids as it was most likely done to us), is being told subconsciously that being bad is not acceptable and, consequently, that being bad is something to be ashamed of.
	But, guess what? There's a part of all of us that's bad. We're humans, not pigeons, and we are acutely aware from a very young age of the parts of us that want to scream and shout, be selfish and jealous and generally act in a way the people around us do not like.
	The programming comes from being taught those parts of us are not acceptable. They are not good enough.
Being told you weren't wanted	This is a fairly obvious one that more people experience than you might think. One or more of our parents telling us we weren't wanted as a child can be a hugely negative Programming Experience because at its very core is a message we shouldn't even be here. There are few things I can think of that would be more traumatic for little ears to hear.
Being told *"We don't know where we got you from"* by a parent or caregiver	In a similar way to the example above, hearing this as a child can lead to us feeling that we don't belong in the very place we're meant to feel safe and secure.

Programming Experience	The Programming Potentially Received by a Child
Being told you were special	Here's the first counter-intuitive one for you. I come across a lot of people who envy one of their siblings for being the golden child but, speaking as a reformed golden child, I can say with certainty it's not a role anyone should want. The subconscious message received by kids who are told they're special is they're not enough, or not fully loved, if they're not special. The problem being we all know deep down that a big part of us is just a lazy bum who wants to sit watching cartoons and picking our nose all day (and I'm talking about 40-year-old me here, not just the four-year-old version), and we know that part of us is definitely not in any way special. Hence, a Programming Experience with potentially negative consequences.
Being told nothing is ever good enough or that we must always do better	Another fairly obvious one, but hearing this message either directly or subconsciously can build a belief from very early on that we're not enough just the way we are.
Learning that we shouldn't talk about our problems, we should just bury them or laugh them off	I would in the past have described this as a very Irish-Catholic problem, but since working with people of all different religions around the world I've realised it's common among many different groups. The idea that we can't talk about our problems or our "negative" emotions causes trauma because we know we have them, so learning they're not to be discussed teaches us that a part of us is something to be ashamed of. I've mentioned laughing things off here because in many of our cultures and families, laughing at everything is seen as a very healthy way of dealing with things. This can absolutely be true, but not if it's at the expense of ever dealing with emotions or experiences for what they are.
Being abandoned or left alone	This could be a one off event or happened multiple times when you were a kid. Either way, the message you're likely to have received is that you weren't worthy of your caregivers keeping you safe and secure. Which can be a Programming Experience with potentially negative outcomes.

Programming Experience	The Programming Potentially Received by a Child
Being praised for being a high-achiever	Another counter-intuitive one that, if you're a parent, is likely to fill you with dread. We've all been taught both consciously and subconsciously through the years that we should praise kids when they do really well, whether that's at school, in sports or in their hobbies.
	The problem with training children like they're dogs and rewarding them for doing what we want, though, is they subconsciously link achievement with the idea that they are loved and, therefore, good enough.
	Which means a subconscious belief can form that they aren't loved or good enough without the achievement. The fact that none of us can always be high-achievers again causes us to be ashamed of the part that's lazy and stupid.
A caregiver never admitting they were wrong or apologising for anything	The subconscious programming here can be that it's not acceptable to accept we are wrong about anything.
Being told a parent wasn't angry, they were disappointed	Another classic one you might well have repeated yourself if you've already got kids. I think we all remember this being said to us because of how we felt when it was said, which is the key.
	If I think of someone I loved telling me they were disappointed in me as a child, I can still feel the shame running through my veins. Someone we respect looking us in the eyes and telling us they're disappointed is possibly the ultimate *"you're not good enough"* message, because the disappointment often feels as though it's about who we are as a person, not about what we have done.
A caregiver not being able to fully express their emotions	Another very general one which most of us are likely to have experienced because of the faulty production line of humanity.
	By learning from humans who can't express their emotions fully, we learn to do the same thing. To suppress and repress rather than express. More on this in the next chapter.

Programming Experience	The Programming Potentially Received by a Child
A caregiver not being able to set healthy boundaries or say what they want	A final general one to round us off. I'll talk a lot more about saying what we want and setting healthy boundaries in the second half of the book, but this is how we learn not to do it well or at all.

Watching our caregivers be walked all over or not being able to express what they want teaches us to do the same thing. |

Examples of My Programming Experiences

I'm going to share with you two stories from my childhood that until I began my own adventure down this path I had no idea had any bearing on who I was as a grown man.

I want to stress again that these stories are in no way a reflection on my parents, who I love dearly and wouldn't swap for anyone. I had an incredible childhood and am very grateful for everything my mum and dad did for me throughout my formative years.

If anything, these stories simply highlight how even in the best of childhoods we encounter many very normal Programming Experiences that shape who we are and are often responsible for the problems and challenges we face later in life.

The fact that these are two of the stories that spring to mind about my own Programming Experiences as a child actually goes to show just how good a childhood I had. For many other people, Programming Experiences are far more disturbing than the examples you're about to read.

The Maths Test

One day when I was about 12 years old I came home from school very pleased with myself.

I bounced into the house and proudly proclaimed to my mum that I'd achieved 95 per cent in my latest maths test. My mum was delighted. The smile beaming on her face, telling me how proud she was and how clever I was.

I felt very clever indeed.

"Go and tell your dad," she said.

My memory is of walking into the hallway of our house and looking up to see my dad's face. When I told him the news, he said with a smile: *"What happened to the other five per cent?"*

And that's where my memory ends.

The main problem with most trauma we experience at any age is that our memory tends to shut down at the most traumatic point, which is where we carry forward the lesson. Resolving old trauma can often mean revisiting it and finding the end of the memory which is, usually, not very traumatic at all.

We'll talk more about all of this later in the TRANSFORM section, but the point of this story is that if someone, anyone, including my dad, was to react in the same way to me sharing news I'm proud of today, after all of the work I've done on myself it wouldn't even touch the surface.

But to a 12-year-old boy desperately seeking the approval of his parents, I took one lesson from that experience: that I wasn't good enough.

Not that the test result wasn't good enough. That *I* wasn't good enough.

This is the other problem with our Programming Experiences. They're not necessarily logical. As an adult looking back I can imagine the end of that story is that we went out as a family for a meal to celebrate my success.

But my childhood memory ends at the point I experienced the thing that shook my internal system.

That experience is no longer an issue for me as a grown up, but combined with many other similar Programming Experiences from when I was a kid (all of which were very common things experienced by children), it helped to explain a big part of the personality I developed as the years went by.

More on that later.

The Stupid TV Show

This story is more difficult to recall and is very hazy, even now. It only came back to me several months into working on all of these things with a therapist and coaches.

I must have been between six and eight years old and was sitting in front of the TV in a typical kids' position, around four feet away from the screen sitting with my legs crossed.

I can't even remember what show I was watching, but I do remember it being the type of absolutely ludicrous comedy I love to this day. I was belly laughing at the TV watching these grown men being completely stupid, making everyone else laugh.

At some point my mum wandered into the room to see what I was laughing at. She took one look at the screen, looked back at me and said something like: *"I'll never understand why a clever boy like you finds stuff like this funny."*

Guess what message a kid takes on board when they hear something like that?

You might have guessed it: you're not good enough. Not that the show was stupid or that my mum and I have different taste in comedy, but that I wasn't good enough just the way I was.

As with the first story, this isn't a reflection on my mum in any way. She was and still is the best mum in the world. She showered me with love and affection every day of my life. If she saw me watching the same type of comedy now she'd no doubt say a similar thing. She often looks at me like I'm insane when I act like an idiot to make people laugh.

As a grown man who's been on the adventure I have, it doesn't impact me at all now. My mum doesn't need to like the same type of comedy I like, and I don't need to enjoy the soap operas she loves.

The point of the story is the same as before. How we experience events as children is not the same as how we might experience them as adults.

It's also crucial to note that the way our parents or original caregivers raised us is largely how they were raised themselves, often with a few modifications they've added along their own journey. Which is where the idea of the faulty human production line comes from.

✎ Exercise (Elsie)

Take some time to think about the things that happened to you as a kid that could have led to you receiving programming on any level. Think about my examples then reflect on the stories you've got from when you were growing up. It might be that you've got some big examples that easily spring to mind, and/or some smaller events or experiences that come to you over the next few weeks.

For me and the vast majority of people I've worked with there were childhood stories that came to mind immediately, even if memories from childhood are few and far between (which is common, especially with people who learnt how to repress their emotions well as children). Whatever springs to mind first for you is worth writing down before going any further.

As a tip, often the incidents that created impactful Programming Experiences as children are told as funny family stories. It's amazing how often someone will tell me a story about their family that's recounted as a joke, while I'm sitting there thinking *"well, there's another pile of programming loaded onto a kid that's going to need unpicking in a few years..."*.

Remember the point of this is not to beat up our parents. The vast majority of the time the things we do as humans are done with the best of intentions regardless of how they might look from the outside, and anything your parents have done that caused programming in your life that you now consider to be less than ideal was passed down to them from previous generations, so they're not to blame either. They were just doing the best they could with the training and programming they'd had. If you get stuck on the idea that doing this exercise in itself is a criticism of people you love you're unlikely to get very far with it, so do your best to let go of it being a blame game.

The purpose of all of this is to figure out who we really are and why we are the way we are, so we can consciously repair the damage and transform our lives.

The smaller Programming Experiences might also not appear to have caused any problems at first glance, so it's important to really think about the subconscious message you might have received through childhood experiences. As we go further through the following pages you'll see more examples of the things we experience as kids that might have led to issues in your adult life but, for now, do your best to put yourself in the mindset of being the little version of you again rather than looking back at things as a grown up.

Remember we can experience Programming Experiences as kids through the smallest of things - a flippant comment, a funny look, something someone always said about us as a joke that actually made us feel unloved. Your challenge is to go back into those old stories and memories and see what you can find that implanted messages in your subconscious that could still be causing you issues today.

Notes

The Adverse Childhood Experience (ACE) Study

Just in case it sounds like I might be making all this up, it's worth referring back to one of the most important public health studies of the past few decades.

The ACE Study came out in the late 1990s taking more than 17,000 people who were seeing doctors for routine check-ups and asking them about different areas of adverse childhood experiences (ACEs) and comparing the group who experienced four or more ACEs with the group that experienced none.

The results were jaw dropping.

As the number of ACEs a person suffered increases, so did the likelihood the person would suffer from alcoholism as an adult, experience chronic depression, be the perpetrator of more domestic violence, be a smoker, attempt suicide, have an increased chance of teen pregnancy, have serious financial problems and serious problems performing in their job and, from a health perspective, suffer considerably more health problems including chronic illnesses, be obese and, on average, died 20 years younger.

It's worth noting that the study's participants were mostly middle and upper-middle class college-educated people from San Diego with good jobs and great health care, so this wasn't targeted at poor or deprived sections of society. This applies to everyone.

For balance, it's also crucial to point out that correlation and causation are not necessarily the same thing, so just because two things happen at the same time doesn't mean one causes the other. The findings in this study, however, had so many correlations between higher ACE scores and a multitude of problems in adult life that it's difficult to ignore, though we can acknowledge at the same time life is a complex series of millions of events and it's impossible to ever truly separate true causes.

My view is if it seems to make logical sense and it does no harm to explore further, why wouldn't we?

If you agree with that principle, here is the ACE questionnaire for you to find your own score:

Prior to your 18th birthday	Yes	No
Did a parent or other adult in the household often or very often swear at you, insult you, put you down, or humiliate you, or act in a way that made you afraid that you might be physically hurt?		
Did a parent or other adult in the household often or very often push, grab, slap, or throw something at you, or ever hit you so hard that you had marks or were injured?		
Did an adult or person at least 5 years older than you ever touch or fondle you or have you touch their body in a sexual way, or attempt or actually have oral, anal, or vaginal intercourse with you?		
Did you often or very often feel that no-one in your family loved you or thought you were important or special, or your family didn't look out for each other, feel close to each other, or support each other?		
Did you often or very often feel that you didn't have enough to eat, had to wear dirty clothes, and had no one to protect you, or your parents were too drunk or high to take care of you or take you to the doctor if you needed it?		
Were your parents ever separated or divorced?		
Was your mother or stepmother often or very often pushed, grabbed, slapped, or had something thrown at her, or sometimes, often, or very often kicked, bitten, hit with a fist, or hit with something hard, or ever repeatedly hit for at least a few minutes or threatened with a gun or knife?		
Did you live with anyone who was a problem drinker or alcoholic, or who used street drugs?		
Was a household member depressed or mentally ill, or did a household member attempt suicide?		
Did a household member go to prison?		
TOTAL		

The total number in the 'yes' column is your ACE Score.

How did you get on?

A Twist in the Story

The twist in this part of the story for me was that when I completed the ACE questionnaire about childhood trauma, I scored zero out of 10.

That made no sense to me, because everything I'd learned about childhood trauma before that point led me to be convinced my childhood experiences were the root of the problems I was facing in my adult life.

Which is when I first started thinking about the language we use around this topic that we've already discussed earlier in this chapter. The creators of the ACE study and many esteemed experts since have acknowledged that the 10 questions are limited and do not come close to covering all possible traumatic experiences a child might encounter.

Which led me to thinking about the study in more general terms. If we can be fairly confident that adverse childhood experiences have a strong association with problems later in life, we can go beyond the restricted list of 10 questions and simply ask ourselves how many adverse childhood experiences we faced, which takes us back to the exercises we've already completed.

Maybe you scored four or more on the traditional scale anyway or maybe, like me, your childhood didn't contain those types of extreme traumatic events. Either way, it's hard to argue against the theory that adverse childhood experiences are the source of so many challenges we see as adults.

The extremely good news after all this, though, is we can repair the trauma and Programming Experiences we had as kids in our adult lives. Which is what this book is all about.

5

EMOTIONAL REPRESSION

"Unexpressed emotions will never die. They are buried alive and will come forth later in uglier ways."

(Sigmund Freud)

When baby giraffes come charging into this world it's usually around an hour before they're up on their feet and walking around, able to have a good look around their environment and, if necessary, find something to eat.

For us humans, that's unfortunately not the case.

When we arrive in this weird place we realise very quickly not only that we've been robbed of our food pipe but we're also completely helpless, unable to stand up, walk, communicate in any meaningful way with these big ugly things that keep staring at us and, usually, not even able to hold our own head up properly.

Which creates a problem.

At a deep subconscious level we know we are completely reliant on the first people we're handed to in the moments during which we're discovering our capacity to make really loud noises through the hole in the front of our face, which we'll later learn is called *"crying"*.

Which means at that same deep subconscious level we want to do everything we can to please these people in order that they keep us alive.

Obtaining their love and approval is literally a case of life or death for us.

How Children Express Emotions

Here's another *"take a few minutes to think about this"* moment, of which there will be many.

Think of that image of when a baby first enters the world and starts to cry. Maybe you've got kids of your own and can recall either that moment or one of thousands of others when you've seen other people's babies cry.

Think about the full power of the emotion they express. The red face, the wide-open mouth and the lung-bursting scream that could wake an entire street.

A brand-new human making it incredibly clear they are not one bit happy.

Now picture a kid a few years older having a tantrum. I find the easiest image to conjure up usually involves a toddler who isn't getting their own way in the aisle of a supermarket.

They throw themselves to the floor, kicking and thrashing their legs, their arms flailing all over the place as they scream at the top of their lungs, getting out every last bit of anger and frustration.

Last, but not least, picture a young kid of any age laughing. Think of that hearty, belly laugh, the tears in their eyes and a big, beaming smile across their face. Think of the joy it immediately gives to even the most-cold hearted adult.

Pure, unadulterated happiness and joy oozing out of every pore of the kid's body.

The above examples are how we experience emotions before anyone teaches us to do otherwise. It's how we naturally express what's happening inside our body. Our instinctive reaction to the things we're experiencing. Full-blown, unadulterated and raw.

Being Taught to Repress and Suppress Emotions

If that's how brand-new humans experience emotions, why is it we very rarely see any adult showing their emotions in the same way?

Imagine if you were in your local supermarket and you saw Billy from down the road kicking and screaming on the floor of the beer aisle because his wife Margaret wouldn't let him get another six pack.

Or imagine if next time your best mate is upset they just started crying and screaming uncontrollably like a six-month-old baby.

We'd think they were insane and would no doubt suggest heavy sedatives as a reasonable solution.

Why is that?

It's because from a very young age our human production line is built to teach the next generation not to feel certain emotions. We routinely say to children: *"don't cry", "don't be afraid", "don't be angry"*.

We treat a whole range of perfectly normal human emotions as though they are in some way a defect of our system. We even label them as *"positive"* and *"negative"* and effectively teach our children and, ultimately, each other, that certain feelings are acceptable and others are not.

But there's no such thing as a positive or negative emotion. They're just feelings, they can't actually do anything.

I can sense you might not be with me on that point. Surely, I hear you say, anger is a negative emotion. And what about fear? Nobody wants to feel fear, do they? That has to be negative.

So, consider this scenario. You're all alone, walking through a jungle. It's a lovely day, the sun is shining, the birds are singing and the sky is bright blue without a cloud in sight. You're whistling away to yourself, thinking about what you might eat for supper when, out of nowhere, you hear big footsteps approaching from behind. At first you think it might be your friend Ethel, but it doesn't take long to realise Ethel only has two feet and whatever is approaching you at a rate of knots sounds like it has four and is definitely moving faster than Ethel has for years.

You turn just in time to see a huge lion jumping at you, its mouth wide open and enormous teeth glistening in the sunlight.

If in that moment the emotion you experience is joy, you are absolutely fucked. It's game over. You're dead as a dodo.

In that moment joy would be an incredibly negative emotion to feel because what you desperately need is a huge helping of fear and probably a massive dollop of anger. Fear and anger in that situation are more likely to lead to you living to see Ethel and tell her all about your experience of fighting a lion over a kebab later that evening.

In fact, if it wasn't for fear and anger, our entire civilisation would never have survived long enough for us to have the opportunity to experience joy. Fear and anger are almost solely responsible for the survival of our species.

And we have the cheek to label them as negative.

The fact is that the problem is never our emotions. The problem is what we've been taught to think and feel about our emotions: that some of them are bad and, therefore, not acceptable, and some of them are good, should be felt more than anything else and, if we are not feeling the 'good' ones more than the 'bad' ones, there must be something wrong with us.

We learn from a very young age to repress and suppress what we consider to be the bad emotions like fear, anger, anxiety, sadness, jealousy and self-pity. We learn to do that because we are desperately trying to please the big ugly humans, who we know are key to our very survival, and the message we receive from them subconsciously is if we experience the 'good' emotions and are good little humans, we are more loved. If we experience the 'bad' emotions and are bad little humans, we are less loved.

We literally tell our children to be good. How often were you told as a child to be a good person? How often have you told a child to do the same thing? And we do it because we were taught it from the people who built us on the human production line, and they were taught it from the people who built them.

But there's a fundamental problem with that message.

Becoming Less Than Whole

An issue with our emotions is they all come out of the same tap. They're like hot and cold water running through the same outlet, with the problem being if we try to turn down some of them, we have to turn down all of them.

While we start life as complete, whole humans, unfettered and unadulterated, with all our emotions flowing equally, we slowly learn that to be whole is not acceptable. To be just as we are is not okay.

We must be good and, to be good, we can't be bad. We can't be sad or angry, anxious or afraid. We shouldn't cry. We shouldn't scream. So, we repress and/or suppress what we're taught to be the bad emotions and, as we repress and/or suppress the cold water flowing through the outlet, we also do the same with the hot water, meaning we repress and/or suppress joy, happiness, excitement and all the other "positive" emotions.

We start to limit who we are in an attempt to please the people upon whose love we are dependent.

Very few of us were ever taught properly about our emotions. We were never taught what they are or what to do with them, other than to shut them down and switch them off. We were never taught that it's okay to be sad. That anger is healthy. That anxiety is just a feeling. That fear is our friend.

We repressed and suppressed. We pushed them down. We buried whatever we could to try to show we were good enough to be loved.

We became less than whole.

The Difference Between Repression and Suppression

Repressed emotions are emotions that we unconsciously avoid, whereas when we suppress emotions we are doing so, at least in some way, at a conscious level.

Think of repressed emotions as ones which we've been taught to bury so deeply that we don't even get the chance to look at or process them before deciding to push them down. On the other hand, suppressed emotions are when we notice something and choose to push it away because it's not convenient to feel whatever it is in that moment.

Think of suppression as being like when we've had an argument with someone just before going to work so, rather than let our colleagues see how angry or hurt we are, we push the feeling down and pretend everything is okay.

A repressed emotion, on the other hand, might be when we feel deeply anxious about something but don't recognise the feeling as anxiety because it is repressed at a deep unconscious level.

There can be a fine line between whether we are repressing or suppressing an emotion so, for the sake of simplicity, I will refer generally to emotional repression throughout this book. Please bear in mind, though, that what we will discuss applies equally to repressed and suppressed emotions.

Avoiding the Pain of Feeling

In the first stages of unlocking my true emotions again as a 38-year-old man, I suddenly understood why the two-year-old version of me had started shutting them down all those years ago.

I could feel pain. Not just emotional pain. Real, physical pain. I would observe my mum suffering and feel an overwhelming pain of sadness in my chest. I would walk towards a room filled with people and feel anxiety surging through my stomach.

As an adult who had spent thousands of pounds and thousands of hours of work to connect with those emotions again, I could make the conscious decision to feel them for what they were. For the beautifully painful and, most importantly, incredibly real sensations they gave.

But what about as a two year old who hadn't been taught what those feelings were or how to handle them? For that version of me, my brilliant subconscious did what our brilliant subconscious does. It started to shut down the systems that were causing so much pain.

It began to create distractions to ensure I would never have to experience emotions at their full strength. It protected me in the only ways it knew how.

Learning to be Ashamed of Ourselves

Which leads us to another crucial part of our flawed systems: learning to be ashamed of who we really are.

Sadly, while we often tell each other that family and raising children is all about unconditional love, the reality is we generally raise the kids in our societies using shame as the most powerful tool.

Then, once it has been fully installed in our systems in our earliest years we continue to use shame as one of the most dominant forces in our adult interactions.

At a fundamental level, we know there are parts of us that are sad. There are parts that are angry. There are parts that are fearful and anxious, jealous, judgmental and self-pitying. Yet, because we've spent so many years being taught consciously and subconsciously that these parts of us are bad, we deny those parts of us and we feel deeply ashamed of them. Often without ever being aware of any of it.

If you haven't already, I highly recommend reading and listening to everything produced by Brene Brown around this topic. At the time of writing you will find multiple books, viral Ted Talks, a Netflix special and a podcast, so there's plenty to get your teeth into.

Brene describes shame as *"the swampland of the soul"*, which is a fitting label. That swampland is for us to understand and navigate our way through, rather than continuing to deny its existence.

Remember, again, this has got nothing to do with whether you have or had loving parents. I had the most loving parents anyone could wish for and still experienced all of these issues in my life.

✎ Exercise

Use your phone or some other sophisticated timing device (if you're old you can use a normal clock or maybe a pocket watch) to give yourself one minute for the following simple task.

Write down every emotion you have experienced in the past week. There are no right or wrong answers and the only rule is you only have one minute to do it. Write down as many as you can before turning to the next page. Be as honest with yourself as you can, so make sure you include any emotions you might currently consider to be negative.

Notes

How did you get on? Were you surprised by how many or how few emotions you could think of that you'd experienced? How many of them would you consider to be positive and how many negative?

The purpose of this isn't that there's a correct number to get to, it's simply to find where you're at when it comes to being aware of your emotions.

We'll come back to this later.

For now, it's time to start talking about one of my favourite parts of this adventure.

6

ADAPTATION

"Sometimes I am two people.
Johnny is the nice one.
Cash causes all the trouble.
They fight."

(Johnny Cash)

I imagine that some people will read this part of my interpretation of the things I've learned and say it's a load of bollocks.

I'll talk more later about why I'm more comfortable with that than I would ever have been in the past but, for now, it's enough to say that it has helped to completely transform my life and the lives of many people I've helped.

That is proof enough it's worth at least considering. If after reading it you do think it's a load of bollocks, just drop me an email saying: *"Paul, your book is a load of bollocks"* and I'll send you your money back, no questions asked and no hard feelings.

This part of the adventure is about discovering that something you've probably believed about yourself all your life is a complete lie: that there's only one of you.

If that makes you instantly recoil and think I'm talking nonsense because of course there's only one of you, next time you're talking to yourself ask who it is you're talking to.

The Brilliance of Our Subconscious

I've already mentioned in passing how brilliant our subconscious is. How astounding this system is that we take completely for granted.

If nothing else, my aim by the end of this book is for you to walk away having a newfound respect for the most advanced self-driving machine on the planet.

We've talked already about how our subconscious learns at a very young age to repress the things we don't want to feel, and to change our behaviour to make sure we're loved and accepted by the people on whom we rely for our very survival.

But all of that is nothing compared to this bit. This part is nothing short of sensational.

The way I like to think of our subconscious system is like a team of people inside our heads. Instead of thinking of your mind as one singular thing that operates your body, think instead of your body as a massive machine being operated by a team on the flight deck inside your head.

Picture the deck of the Starship Enterprise or one of the big battleships from *Star Wars*. Or, if it's more in line with your movie-watching experience, think of it as being a bit like the cast inside the little girl's head in the kids' film *Inside Out*.

Can you picture the team in the control deck? It's important to take some time to get a clear image in your mind of what it looks like because we'll be referring back to it frequently.

Imagine the walls covered in big screens, with all kinds of switches, control panels and levers. Loads of metal, glass and plastic. How many people can you see in your team? There are about eight in mine. I've got Tommy at the main control desk, overlooking the rest of the room from his big, silver chair behind a huge panel of buttons. Sandra sits to his right working away, with Jessica and Virgil nearby. Further back, monitoring the screens and flux capacitors, are Gemma and Agnes, with Sadio and Mo doing a lot of running around and high-intensity work.

There's a room off to the side where the main laboratory is kept behind a sealed door. Something we'll come back to later.

I've included a sketch of the team in my control deck so you can picture what it looks like. Make sure you can picture your own.

Whenever we are faced with any challenge, the team inside our head gathers to figure out how to deal with it.

When we started operating in the world, the first thing these little people in the control deck team did was ask the original version of us whether it had the capabilities to deal with whatever traumatic new experience it was being faced with.

Now, bearing in mind we'd been spending nine months in our 10-star hotel inside our mum with a food pipe and temperature-controlled padded surroundings, the answer our original system gave back for the vast majority of those early challenges was: *"Erm, no, guys, I haven't got a clue how to deal with this. Have you managed to find me a food pipe yet?"*

The creative team inside our head then had to come up with a solution which, often, would result in creating a whole new part of us to deal with whatever was needed. One or more members of the team would disappear into the laboratory connected to the main control deck, and start developing a whole new part of us fit to face the new challenge.

That part then became a whole new character in our personality.

What Am I Talking About?

I know, I know. This is the part of the movie where my ex-wife would be turning to me and asking if I knew what was going on and I'd have to politely remind her that no-one sent me the script of the film in advance, so I'm watching it unfold at the same time as her and presume that they'll explain things at some point. Bear with me and we'll get there.

When I first heard of all of this I was in Bali listening to a presentation by a girl in my group on a retreat. She was talking about the multiple characters in our lives and how in order to properly deal with and identify them, we should give them names. She had named one of her characters 'Susan' because she knew a woman called Susan who loved to moan, so the character in her head who loved to moan was also now called Susan.

At that point I started laughing to myself. I didn't need to give names to the first characters that popped into my head because they already had names. They were so prominent in my life that other people had named them.

Introducing Copey

I was born a very shy, quiet, introverted little boy into a noisy and extremely loud family, city and society.

One of the first questions the team inside my head asked of the original me (who I now call '*Little Paul*') was: *"Mate, are you able to deal with all of this noise and stuff? You're probably going to need to start being a bit louder and more extroverted,"* to which Little Paul replied: *"Absolutely not, this is not a task that I'm cut out for. I'll be honest, I'm mainly just hoping to get back inside that dark cave at some point and for one of you fuckers to get me my food pipe."*

After moaning to each other about how I was getting on their nerves going on about the food pipe, my team of operators was then tasked with creating the first of my new personalities: 'Copey'.

Copey was everything Little Paul couldn't be. He was extroverted and confident. He was loud and aggressive. He could make a space in a noisy world that Little Paul just couldn't do. He was my saviour.

The reason I didn't have to name him is because he became so prominent in my life in later years that everyone else named him.

Most of my friendships in my adult life were developed by him. He was the guy who could walk into a room full of strangers and make everyone believe we were the most confident person in there. He cracks jokes and makes people feel at ease. He charms and dances. He sings and shouts. He's the showman I needed to survive in a world that wasn't built for introverts.

Most people who think they know me really know him. My subconscious built him to deal with the world that Little Paul couldn't handle.

Then came my other rock-star personality.

Introducing Cope

There came a time when neither the shy introvert nor the jokey showman could handle life's challenges, so my creative team found a solution. His name is 'Cope'.

If you've watched *Pulp Fiction*, think of Cope as Winston Wolfe. If you ever accidentally blow someone's head off in the back of a car[8], Cope is who you'd call to make sure you don't go to prison. Not Little Paul and not Copey. You call Little Paul in that situation and he'll tell you to hand yourself into the police. Copey would turn up with a bottle of Jack Daniels and convince you that it would all be better after a night of karaoke.

Cope is the lawyer. The manipulator. The part of me who can make the world bend to his will. The part my law firm clients used to describe as making miracles happen.

---

[8] This is a reference to the movie, in case you haven't seen it – I'm not suggesting this is something you should actually call Cope about.

You think you're in an impossible situation that charm or reason won't get you out of? Cope will sort it for you. I've got stories about this part of me that I don't even like to tell anymore because of the feelings they give me. Stories I used to tell with pride that my friends recall with astonishment when I somehow got us out of situations when our backs were firmly up against several walls.

Cope is the other part of me many people know.

Back to the Main Point

When I said the biggest lie is that there's only one of us, I meant it literally. Up to this point, you might have spent your life thinking of yourself as one person, but the first twist in this weird adventure is we are all multiple personalities.

We all started out as one person – the truest, purest version of us who I usually refer to as *"Little [insert your first name here]"*. If you've read any other self-help or personal development books that touch on this sort of thing, you might have seen this referred to as our inner child but, as with lots of phrases other people in this space use, as you'll continue to see I don't really like terms that sound too 'woo-woo' because they tend to put people off.

From now on, whenever you see or hear reference to your 'inner child', just think of 'Little You', who first came screaming into this world before it was necessary for your team to start building new people to help you out.

Take a few seconds to think about who you picture when you think of yourself as a young child. How old are you? What do you look like? For me when I do this, I can see myself around three years old with a big mop of dark brown hair, a big toothy grin and a pot belly sticking proudly over my belt. Whenever I refer to Little Paul, that's who I'm thinking of. Get a clear image in your mind of who you're thinking of when you think of Little You.

The key now is to start thinking of the other personalities your subconscious created for your survival in addition to the original version. The easiest ones to think of are who I describe as our 'rock-star personalities'.

Can you think of any straight away? If it helps, think about what your personality is like in work compared to what it's like when you're with your parents, your kids or your partner. Consider how you behave around your friends and whether you behave differently depending on which friends you're with.

You might even discover you have slightly different accents depending on your environment, or you dress differently. Often our personalities have different costumes, a bit like superheroes. If you stop to think about how these stories are displayed in our lives without us ever noticing, you might realise we see the idea of alter egos across all superhero adventures.

Both Superman and Clark Kent are alter-egos of the little boy from Krypton, Kal-El, who needed one alter-ego in which he could show off his superpowers and another that would allow him to live a normal life working in an office. Wonder Woman and Diana Prince perform the same functions for the little girl Princess Diana of Themyscira.

To link this all back to a phrase you'll already be familiar with, I like to think what most people call 'the ego' as a collective name for all the characters we have created subconsciously, who are all controlled by the team in the control deck acting like a conductor.

So whenever you hear anyone talking about your ego, think of the control deck team and its cast of personalities meaning, in simple terms, we've got two basic parts of us, Little Us and the ego. Or the original version of us versus a whole host of characters we've created. We'll come back to the concept of that imbalance in power throughout the adventure, but for now it's important to note that, despite the imbalance of numbers, Little Us ultimately has control if it chooses to take it.

Whenever I'm doing this in person with someone it never ceases to amaze me how their face starts to change as the realisation hits that they're not alone. It's usually a combination of awe and astonishment, mixed with a sprinkling of relief.

For some reason it tends to make us feel better as soon as we realise there's more than one of us largely, I think, because it makes so much sense.

Ever wondered why one minute you can be so outgoing and happy and the next you're down in the dumps and want to be left alone? It makes far more sense that it's two completely separate characters than it all being just you, doesn't it?

The next part of the puzzle, though, is why that happens.

A Team, a Stage and a Microphone

Over the years, without you being aware of it consciously, the team inside your head has been building an entire cast to help you survive in this strange world.

An entire crew exists solely to handle the challenges of daily life. There's just one issue.

While there's a whole team on your stage there's only one microphone and only one of your characters can be on the mic at any one time. Up until now, your subconscious (or the team in your control deck) has decided which of your team members gets the mic depending on the situation at hand.

The way I like to see it is that a very quick check happens. You walk into a bar, the team inside your head automatically turns to Little You to ask whether you can handle what is about to happen and, if the answer comes back negative, the mic is automatically handed to whichever of your characters is best equipped to deal with things on your behalf.

Over time, that character becomes the go-to choice in that situation. For me, walking into a bar after a while meant Copey just picked up the mic without even checking whether Little Paul was interested in trying to handle things. Walking into a high-powered business meeting meant Cope taking charge automatically.

The character selected in each situation is usually based on the needs we have to meet and, importantly, the mic can be passed around between characters quickly if the situation requires.

Human Needs

You will find different descriptions and thoughts about what the basic human needs are depending on where you look and what you're looking for. For the purposes of this part of our adventure together, we're talking less about Abraham Maslow's classic five-tier 'Hierarchy of Needs' and more Tony Robbins' thoughts on our emotional needs which, in my experience, tie in better with what we're discussing.

The big man talks of four basic human needs we all have no choice but to fill. They are:

• Certainty or control

- Uncertainty or variety
- Significance or ego
- Love and connection

Once those needs are met, we also have a couple of fulfilment needs, which are:

- Growth (i.e. personal growth as a human)
- Contribution (i.e. to society or the world around us)

The kicker is that these needs will be met one way or another. There is no neutral position. If you are not meeting your own needs in a conscious and healthy way your system will find ways to meet them for you, often in unhealthy ways. More on that later.

✎ Exercise (Multiple Personality)

This is the start of the biggest exercise we'll do in this book and, maybe, for many months to come. It's best done on a spreadsheet on your computer rather than by hand, so you can continue to add to it and amend it as we go along. We'll be returning to it in later chapters so be sure to save whatever you come up with.

In column one of your spreadsheet I want you to write down each of your characters. As with previous exercises, take some time to properly think about who each one might be then just allow the thought to float around your mind as you get on with your week and each time you feel a part of you coming to the surface who isn't already on your list, come back and add them.

Give each character a name that feels most fitting to you. That can either be a real name or something else, like *"Self-pity Paul"* or something similar. There are no right or wrong answers and the trick is to not overthink it. If it pops into your head put it on the list. I'd suggest your first one should be the original you, *Little [Insert Your First Name Here]*.

The second column is for you to write down the traits of each character. What do they do? Are they quiet, shy, outgoing, noisy, controlling, demanding?

In the third column I want you to write down what triggers that character to take hold of the microphone. Is it in confrontational situations? When you're dealing with conflict? When you're feeling shy? When you need to be extroverted?

The fourth column is to identify which of the human needs listed above are being met by each character. I appreciate this can be the trickiest part without me being there to talk you through it in person, so I've set out some examples of my characters below and what each of them does. For simplicity just include the top two needs being met, unless it's obvious they meet more than two.

Below the table I've expanded on the ways that each character meets the needs I've listed, so you can see examples to give you some hints. If you get stuck with this, send an email with any questions to **questions@paul7cope.com** and I'll respond to all frequently asked questions through videos on my YouTube channel and episodes of my podcast.

There's also a frequently asked questions section at the end of the chapter.

My Character List

Character	Traits	Triggers	Needs Being Met (Top Two)
Little Paul	Quiet Shy Anxious Introverted Calm Kind Peaceful Caring Responsible Loving Creative Sensitive	When I'm feeling secure and safe When I'm alone When I'm around people with whom I can totally relax	Certainty / control Love and connection
Copey	Exuberant Wild Irresponsible Egotistical Fun Insecure Creative	When I need to be extroverted	Uncertainty / variety Significance / ego

Character	Traits	Triggers	Needs Being Met (Top Two)
Cope	Certain Direct Calm under pressure Resourceful Imaginative Creative Manipulative Assertive	When there's a problem to be fixed or a situation to be resolved When there's something to be negotiated When someone needs my help in a difficult situation	Certainty / control Significance / ego

The Way Each Character Meets My Needs

When I first learnt of the human needs we've dealt with above, my instinct was that uncertainty and variety would be the most prominent for me. I've always loved to travel and experience new things. I love meeting new people, learning about the world and generally become bored having to do the same thing for too long a period.

After doing this exercise for the first time, however, I realised something is true of me that's true of most humans. My need for certainty and control tends to outweigh all other needs.

Little Paul

Little Paul is the original me. The quiet, shy, introverted version of me known by very few people. His calm and quiet demeanour attracts love and connection like no other part of me. He is the one loved by kids and animals. The one who will sit cuddled up on a couch watching movies for hours on end, needing nothing but love and affection.

In doing all of that, he also gives me complete certainty because I know how the world responds when that side of me is able to come out.

Copey

As my most extroverted character, Copey meets my need for significance and ego in a huge way. When he's on the mic I feel incredibly significant and my ego is stroked like a fluffy white cat sitting on the knee of an evil super-villain.

Copey makes sure I'm the centre of attention. That everyone knows who I am. He makes people laugh, he walks into a bar and hugs everyone he knows. He sings karaoke. He makes me feel special[9].

He is also the main man for creating uncertainty and variety in my life. Do you want your night out to have an element of chaos to it? Invite Copey and you can rest easy. He's the guy who speaks to DJs in bars and convinces them to play videos of his friends on the big screens to make everyone laugh, or ends up as the DJ himself in a karaoke bar on holiday.

The kicker to that, though, which is worth mentioning even though I only said to list two needs being met for each character, is that in meeting my need for uncertainty or variety, Copey also meets my need for certainty or control. Whenever he's on the mic, I can be certain that my need for variety will be met.

---

[9] If you're struggling to match the significance / ego need to any of your characters, add an extra phrase to the need: "Feeling special". When the character you're thinkwing of gets the mic, does it make you feel special? You might find that this need comes up in many more ways than you currently identify, because characters you identify as being negative can also help you to feel special and meet your need for significance / ego, as you'll see more later.

Does that make sense? I appreciate it might sound counterintuitive at first, but that's all part of this dance.

On top of all of that, he meets my need for love and connection because when he's on the mic I feel incredibly connected to the people around me. I feel their love and, often, adoration, in a way I might not feel when Little Paul is in control.

Which means Copey meets every one of my core emotional needs. It's no wonder he ended up spending so much time on the mic.

Cope

Cope is one of my ultimate control and certainty characters. When the world is burning down around me, Cope taking the mic makes everything better. A calm, reassuring, assertive and confident presence in any room. He will take control of the most terrifying situations and meet my need for certainty and control with ease.

That, in itself, provides me with a huge amount of significance and another lovely big stroke of my ego, because other people know they can call on Cope and he'll sort things out for them. He still gets called regularly to this day.

No Right or Wrong

Hopefully that helps to give you a bit more flavour around how the needs operate, but it's important to remember there are no right or wrong answers in this. The intention is to start to get a better understanding of who you really are and what each of your characters is doing for you without you realising.

As we progress through this adventure I'll share more of my characters with you and the roles they play, which might help you identify even more of your own.

Frequently Asked Questions

How many personalities or characters should I be able to find?

There's no correct number. When people do this exercise for the first time, many only come up with five or six characters, who are generally the rock-star ones mentioned earlier. If this happens just start to gently observe and ask yourself as you go through your week which of the characters on your list is appearing in any given situation you find yourself in. That will usually lead to you realising there are more to be added to your list.

It's also worth re-visiting the list to see whether there are any characters you can divide into more than one.

How do I know if something I identify is a character or just a mood I'm sometimes in?

If you think of something that's potentially a character put it on the list and see if you can identify its traits, triggers and needs. If you can do that it's more than likely a character, but remember there are no right or wrong answers. This is an exercise in fully understanding who you really are, so don't overthink it or get overly stressed about it (and remember that if part of you tends to overthink things, or worries about getting things right, they're likely to be characters in themselves)

Notes

7

LOW SELF-WORTH

"You became the world
champion without your father."

"Then why don't I feel like it?"

(Mary Anne Creed & Adonis Creed / Creed II)

While the chapters leading up to this point largely explain why
we are the way we are, my belief is this chapter is the very basis
of all our problems in life.

Whenever I'm forced to sum up what I think in as short a sentence as possible, I refer to this.

You can call it self-worth, self-esteem or a whole host of other
terms that people might use. Whatever you call it, ultimately
what I'm referring to is the feeling most humans on our weird
and wild planet have: that we're just not good enough.

Having worked with many people around the world and observed thousands more from afar, I see this phenomenon as the real pandemic undermining the health and wellbeing of our species. The problem is it's largely unseen. It's a stealth problem causing untold damage without many people ever being aware of it.

It's like your entire house being infested with woodworm without you having any idea. One day you're happily walking around in your upstairs bathroom, the next you've fallen through the rotten beams and, while you're lying in a heap on your kitchen floor, you have no idea what just happened.

I'm Not Good Enough

You will have already seen this theme developing during the earlier chapters of this book.

As young humans we come into this world naturally feeling whole. At the point we arrive, kicking and screaming, we are as full a human as it's possible to be with all our flaws and imperfections literally sat naked for everyone to see.

The problem we have is that usually from the first second we arrive, people start to tell us that what we are naturally isn't good enough. One of the first phrases many of us hear is: *"Don't cry."*

As we've already seen and must keep stressing, it's not the fault of the people caring for you. We have all been programmed the same way for generations, so there's no-one to blame. We have also all passed the same programming to others without realising it for years, so blaming others can only lead to us blaming ourselves, which helps no-one (see Chapter 9 for more on this).

This part of the story is just about identifying why we are the way we are so we can do something about it in the hope we can rebuild ourselves and rebuild the production line to prevent the same defects being built into the next generation to roll out of the factory.

A Summary of the Problem

The issue is when we tell children not to feel certain emotions, the message they receive is those emotions aren't acceptable. Yet they are still feeling the emotions so what inevitably happens is they develop the inner narrative that who they are simply isn't good enough. That the way they feel isn't good enough.

Our child selves then begin to adapt and develop multiple personalities to cope with a world for which we are not equipped, and those personalities help us to turn off parts of ourselves that are not helping us to meet our needs sufficiently in any number of situations.

Sadly, though, without being aware of any of this consciously we begin to dislike or even hate parts of ourselves that we created in order to survive.

A vicious cycle of self-hate, low self-worth and feelings that we are not good enough begins and follows us to our grave unless we do something about it.

How to Know if this Applies to You

Going back to something I mentioned earlier, the safest thing to do is assume this does apply to you and work backwards.

If you need more than that, though, in my experience the world is split into three camps when it comes to conversations about low self-worth and feeling that we're not good enough:

1   Those who know that's how they feel before the conversation even starts and aren't surprised one bit

2   Those who can see how it might apply to them and are open to talking about it, without being sure it is them

3   Those who are one hundred percent certain it does not apply to them.

Ironically, if you are in category two you are much more likely to already have at least some healthy level of self-worth.

If you're in the last category, as I was, I can almost guarantee this applies to you more than you'll ever know unless you're prepared to go through the rest of this book with a completely open mind.

The Self-Worth Power Bar

A key to life we'll talk about throughout this book and in detail later on is that things are not usually as black and white as we've been raised to believe.

Self-worth is no different.

It's not that you either feel you are good enough or you don't, or you have self-worth or self-esteem or you don't. Self-worth exists on a scale on which we all sit, somewhere, and usually changes over time.

The truth, again in my experience, is this applies to everyone to some degree. Rather than think of whether you have low self-worth or not, consider a scale of how much this applies to any human ranging from zero (being not at all) to 100 (being absolutely applying to everything you do).

The reality is that everyone is on the scale somewhere and very few people are at zero, so the chances are this principle at least applies to you to some degree and, in all likelihood, it is having a huge impact on your life without you realising.

Think of it like a computer game where you play a character with a power bar showing how much self-worth you have. Most people I know are somewhere between zero and 60 on that power bar. Our job is to slowly, step by step, increase our score on the power bar by removing lots of the programming we've had since we were kids and replace it with healthier beliefs.

The difficulty with this part is often that nobody likes to be told they have low self-worth or their problems stem from not feeling good enough. I remember vividly the first time anyone mentioned the idea that I might be insecure. I would hit the roof at the very suggestion given how confident and successful I was in my day-to-day life.

The issue is that outward confidence can often be disguising deeper problems.

The Ego and Low Self-Worth

We'll talk much more about my thoughts on ego later. For now, it's enough to remember the interpretation of the ego as being the parts of us other than our original 'Little You' character, with the team on the control deck acting as a conductor who decides very quickly which of your personalities has the microphone at any given moment. Every character created as an adaptation of Little You is part of the ego.

How that manifests day to day is often most noticeable in the part of us we present to the outside world, which is most easy to identify in the louder members of society.

The difficulty with what we think of as the ego in general life is that most of us have been programmed to think that a big ego equates to huge amounts of self-confidence and that self-confidence is the same as self-worth.

This is where my interpretation of life might differ from others.

In my view, self-confidence and self-worth are not even in the same ballpark, let alone the same thing. I believe this because I lived a large part of 38 years of my life with self-confidence oozing out of every pore of my body, but it wasn't until I was 38 that I began to understand my self-worth was rock bottom.

The challenge here is our ego is all-powerful and very crafty. Its main purpose in life is to ensure its own survival and convincing us there's nothing wrong is part of its plan. It has, after all, been running an army of personalities on our behalf for decades and has kept us alive this far. Why would it want to let go of control now?

Unfortunately, from what I've experienced personally and from what I've witnessed in others, the truth is the ego grows in direct proportion to how low our self-worth is.

Which means one of many counterintuitive things you'll hear from me throughout these pages is that, generally speaking, the bigger the ego, the lower the self-worth and the greater the feeling of *"I'm not good enough"* in a person.

Which also means that, in my view, the vast majority of people you've been taught to look up to throughout your life for being "successful", either those close to you or famous people on the telly, are likely to be those with the lowest self-worth and greatest feelings of *"I'm not good enough"*.

As a result, those people tend to have the most noticeable and confident characters making up part of their ego team that they portray to the outside world every day as being the true version of themselves. It's all just a show.

How Do You Work That One Out?

I know, I know, I did say it was counterintuitive, didn't I?

To understand this fully, it's important to think briefly about how the world we've built operates.

We've mainly been taught to value money, materialistic possessions and external achievements such as medals, awards and trophies more than anything else, and their accumulation as "success". The world in which we live values those who will work their arses off in order to accumulate more money, possessions and awards than anyone else in order to become the most "successful".

And the kicker?

The more you think deep inside that you're a piece of shit as a human and the lower your self-worth often means the harder you'll work to prove to yourself and to the entire planet that you are good enough.

Taking it a step further, the most dangerous combination and the one that our societies tend to reward the most is chronically low self-worth and some special ability or talent.

If you think deep inside you're a piece of shit who needs to prove themselves to the world and you happen to also be really good at a particular sport, you're likely to end up achieving great success in that sport, racking up medals, awards, trophies and records.

If you have chronic low self-worth and happen to have a brain that works at a faster rate of knots than most people, there's a good chance you'll be successful in the world of business or finance, accumulating untold riches and huge super-yachts along the way.

If you're deeply insecure and have the voice of an angel, moves like Jagger or the acting ability of Robert de Niro, you might well make sure you beat all competition in your wake to become a superstar entertainer dripping in Grammys and Oscars.

Which leads us to a totally fucked-up place where most people in positions of power and influence in our world are the most damaged humans who we are then taught to replicate in order to be "successful" in our own right, and the vicious cycle continues.

Crazy, eh?

It is, of course, possible for people to achieve great things in our world without being driven by chronic low self-worth. However, when I look at the backgrounds and personal lives of many of the people we have been taught to idolise and replicate, I often see levels of dysfunction that, in my view, we should not be placing on a pedestal and using as a model on which to base our lives.

Warnings from Heroes

I was tempted here to talk about specific famous people who are textbook examples of everything we've discussed so far but, as I began to write about each one I realised it didn't feel right to do so.

I don't know those people personally so what I will encourage instead is for you to think of anyone in the public eye who you know to have achieved great success and to have experienced troubles in their life and to look at their background to see what their origin story is.

There are numerous examples of famous entertainers, sports stars and business people who have been on the path we have discussed, reaching incredible highs in their lives, being lauded and idolised as gods for the 'success' they achieved in the world we've built, only for the passing of time to show when they were experiencing public highs they were also experiencing deep personal pain.

In truth, we are all these people somewhere on the scale. We might not have the ability they have in their chosen field to combine with our low self-worth to help drive us to the very top of the movie or music industries, an international sport or business, but we have received the same messages from when we were kids. Just as our parents and their parents had received when they were growing up, leading to what they passed on.

Yet, despite us now being aware of the chaos and devastation taking place behind the scenes of the so-called 'success', I still see to this day numerous celebrities being held aloft as examples of how we can succeed in the world. And, of course, the people who hold them up as that example are right. If you want to become the best at something in the world we have built, following that path can get you to where you want to be.

The question I ask having learnt everything I've learnt is, at what cost does that 'success' come and do we really want to keep paying that price?

Signs of Low Self-Worth

I realised a while ago that if we aren't always able to see we have low self-worth or we don't feel good enough, we need a way of being able to identify that as being the case for ourselves seeing as people telling us from the outside is less likely to have an impact.

The more I thought about it, the more I realised it's difficult to explain in summary because, well, it's basically everyone I've ever met.

The conclusion I came to is it's easier to start by explaining what I see as being character traits of someone with high self-worth and feelings that they are, ultimately, good enough as a human deep inside their soul.

The tell-tale sign of that, for me, is a person who is completely balanced. Someone who when discussing any topic can calmly see both sides, understanding all viewpoints before reaching their own conclusion. An individual who is aware of their own faults at a deep level and can discuss rationally all of their strengths and weaknesses. Someone who does not take great offence at any little thing said or done. A person who isn't deeply insecure, in need of validation from the outside world or who needs to be needed by others. They tend to have an air of calm about them, very rarely judge other people and are extremely comfortable admitting they're wrong and changing their opinions.

Which means a person with low self-worth is anyone on the scale either side of that.

Do you usually think you're right about whatever you're talking about or, on the other hand, very rarely have any certainty that you're right about anything? Both can be signs of low self-worth and feelings that you're not good enough.

Are you rarely able to admit you're wrong and apologise for mistakes, or you're constantly apologising for everything you do?

Do you obsess about the way you look and can't leave the house unless you have the right designer clothes and/or make-up on, or do you not really give a shit about how you look?

Do you fly off the handle with rage at the drop of a hat, or do you rarely show any emotion?

Are money, status and materialistic possessions hugely important in your life, or do you live like a tramp and don't care much about any of them?

Do you desperately crave attention from anyone and everyone, or you're totally reclusive and don't like human interaction?

You guessed it, at both ends of the spectrum in each of those examples it can be a sign of low-self-worth and feelings of not being good enough.

Last but not least, in a world dominated by social media, are you unable to post a photo of yourself without using a filter to change your appearance in some way, do you obsess over the number of likes your posts receive or does social media generally have a large impact on your life? If so, low self-worth is likely to be at play.

Low self-worth and feeling we're not enough also keeps us trapped in relationships, jobs and businesses we aren't happy with, prevents us being paid what we're worth, leads to addictions, makes us crave attention and validation from the outside world, forces us to buy things we don't need with money we might not have and many other destructive things in our lives.

Even more than the examples themselves, it's often the reasoning for our life decisions that determine whether any one thing is a sign of low self-worth, rather than the thing itself. If whatever you do is largely driven by what other people think of you, that insecurity is a huge sign of low self-worth. And if you often find yourself saying out loud *"I don't care what people think of me"*, there's a good chance that's your ego trying to convince you of a lie.

In summary, though, if you're reading this book because the introduction resonated with you or because you have fundamental problems that you've never been able to figure out, the chances are you are somewhere lower down the scale of not feeling good enough.

It's best, therefore, to start with the assumption that this all applies to you and see if you can disprove it, rather than the other way around. After all, even the people I know who I consider to have good levels of self-worth are not constantly at 100 on the power bar scale, and one of the biggest lessons they've learnt by understanding they are good enough is they will always need to work on this topic, in just the same way as people who understand that to stay in good physical shape you have to keep exercising forever.

It's also worth noting that true self-awareness can, in my view, only come from outside ourselves. In my old life I would often tell myself the story that I was hugely self-aware but that was a load of bollocks. All I had was an ego telling me a great story about who I was, which I thought meant I was self-aware, but it wasn't until I started working with a therapist and coaches and doing some serious self-reflection that I truly started to learn who I was beyond the stories I was telling myself.

The irony was as soon as I started to see who I really was it became so obvious I was amazed I hadn't been able to see it before when many people around me could.

I think the same thing is true of most humans on the planet and the only way around that is to go through exercises which lead to true self-reflection at the same time as asking others who they think we are.

You're likely to be astounded by the results.

The Power of the Ego and the Need for Certainty

Given the faulty human production line that's been in operation worldwide for generations, where we have found ourselves is living in a world dominated by egos.

The only people I've ever met or come across whose lives are not controlled by their ego are individuals who have done a lot of inner work, often after experiencing huge traumas in their lives that forced their hand.

In my experience these people make up a very small proportion of society.

Everyone else, including me up until a couple of years ago, is basically one big multiple personality ego monster bouncing around the planet full of insecurity, low self-worth and feelings that they're not good enough.

If you have at least started to do the multiple personality exercise you might have already noticed one of the greatest needs we have as humans is the need for certainty or control. That need is largely driven by our ego, which is the part of us that has to be sure it's right. It's the part of us that makes us say the words *"I know..."* at the start of any sentence because, in reality, the true version of us, Little [X], isn't sure of anything.

One of the many difficulties with the ego is it can be very hard to spot. I like to think of it as one of the baddies from Scooby-Doo (another old-school reference you might have to look up if you're younger than 40). Every time you spot it hiding in some new disguise, it will hold its hands up and say *"oh, you got me you crafty kids"* before sloping off to change costumes to come back and try to trick you another way.

Which is why I've started to develop red flags to let me know if my ego is getting involved in my life without me realising. It's easier to see his footprints on the floor than to see through his invisibility cloak.

One of the biggest red flags for me is if I ever hear myself think or say *"I know…"* when starting a sentence, like *"I know that [insert name of person] is [insert opinion]"*, because I have learnt in recent times we very rarely know anything for certain. Another counter-intuitive aspect of all of the work we'll talk about throughout these pages is the concept that true inner peace and contentment come from letting go of control and letting go of the idea that anything is certain. Embracing the uncertainty of the world is key.

If you want any evidence of the theory that the vast majority of humans are driven by their egos, just look through any social media thread, watch any news programme or think about your own behaviour and ask yourself how many interactions you're a part of or witnessing where anyone involved is saying anything other than they know for sure what the correct answer is.

I bet you won't find many balanced views.

The other twist in the tale is while our low self-worth makes us judge ourselves too harshly, our ego distracts our attention by judging everyone else in a flawed attempt to make us feel better.

So, what?

You might be wondering what the big deal is with any of this and why it's a problem. Which takes us full circle back to my origin story and the whole point of the book.

From what I have experienced in life and have now seen in the lives of others, I believe every problem we face comes down to the idea that most of us have low self-worth and feel we are not good enough which, in turn, means our egos are largely controlling what we do and how we interact with each other. Which is why we're in the mess we're in both individually and collectively.

This is again a more difficult thing to explain in a book than it would be if we were speaking in person, because if you talked me through any of your problems I could gently walk you down the path of how the ultimate root cause is that you don't feel good enough deep inside.

I can, though, offer some examples that might resonate with you or, at the very least, prompt you to think about your own issues and how they might come down to the same cause.

It's also worth saying at this point that I am acutely aware at this stage of my own adventure that the very fact I believe in this theory means I am at high risk of "The Jordan Henderson Effect" playing a huge role in my life (see Chapter 13 for more on that topic), so there is a chance I am just making things fit a theory I believe. All I can do to counter that is remain open to other possible explanations.

For now, the ideas here fit my life and the lives of those who I've worked with so I'd say it's worth considering them. It's also worth noting that the Western medical world's solution to many of the problems I'll discuss is often drug based. I believe we're all better off exploring possible natural remedies to challenges in our lives (especially if those remedies lie inside us) before we turn to drugs or more extreme potential solutions.

Dog Training and The Ego

A few years ago, after I'd bought my first dog, I was listening to an interview with an elite-level dog trainer in the hope of finding a way to stop my beautiful West Highland Terrier, Tilly, from ruling the house[10].

The canine expert said something I'll never forget. In a relationship between a dog and a human, one party is the trainer and one party is the trainee. There is no neutral position. So, if you decide you're not going to train your dog, the inevitable outcome is your dog is training you.

I have witnessed this first hand with a dog who now rules every house she enters without being able to speak English.

Think of your ego like a dog. There is no neutral position. You are either training and controlling your ego purposefully and consciously, or your ego is controlling you. If you have never done any work on yourself with a therapist or coach, I can almost guarantee your ego is running most aspects of your life.

---

[10] This is something I have failed miserably with.

The Magic Trick Conundrum

"Every magic trick consists
of three parts or acts.
The first part is called The Pledge.
The magician shows you
something ordinary.
The second act is called The Turn.
The magician takes the ordinary something
and makes it into something extraordinary.
Now you're looking for the secret.
But you won't find it because,
of course, you're not really looking.
You don't really want to work it out.
You want to be...fooled.
But you wouldn't clap yet,
Because making something disappear
isn't enough. You have to bring it back.
That's why every magic trick
has a third act, the hardest part.
The part we call The Prestige."

(John Cutter / The Prestige)

Do you like magic?

Growing up I loved those little magic sets you could buy. I remember showing my grandparents tricks and them reacting like I was David Copperfield making the Statue of Liberty disappear. I loved seeing their reaction and carried an interest in all things magic from then on.

In my teenage years American magician David Blaine hit the big time with his street magic show, which led to me and a friend deciding to find out how to do the grown-up tricks in his set that were blowing the minds of people around the world, as well as learning at a relatively early age a stereotypical difference between British and American people.

When Blaine bit a coin in half and spat it back together, the Americans he performed it to on camera put their hands to the sides of their heads and screamed as though they'd just seen a real-life ghost. Some of them fainted. Others pissed their pants.

British people I showed the same trick to just sort of went, *"it's good that, yeah..."*.

I discovered the way around this, aside from moving to the United States, was only to perform to British people after 2am when they'd been drinking alcohol for at least six hours. It turns out drunk British people react to street magic just like sober Americans. You can have that little extra piece of advice for free.

It resulted in me showing tricks to people after nights out in Liverpool city centre and receiving reactions close to the ones my grandparents were so generous with when I was a kid.

The point of telling you all this, though, is how one of my best mates would react to seeing me baffling pissed up passers-by. He would stare at my hands and ask me to repeat routines to try to figure out how each trick was done.

The problem with doing that, without revealing too many secrets that might ruin magic forever for you, is that most magic tricks aren't done when you think they are. If you've watched the Christian Bale and Hugh Jackman movie, *The Prestige*, you'll know that magic comes in three parts as John Cutter explained. The issue for most people trying to figure out how a trick is done is that the part they stare at most is The Prestige, the last of the three parts.

The issue is The Prestige is usually just a performance. It's what separates the great magicians from the rest. Most professionals can do the tricks, but the very special ones present them in ways that blow your mind. The mind-blowing part takes our attention when the magic was often done long before we were really watching. On some occasions, the real trick was done days, weeks or years earlier.

Which is where the similarities with our lives come in.

We've been trained through our days on Earth to look at symptoms. We stare at the problems as they present themselves and think we're working on figuring out how to solve them but the problem is, just like a magic trick, we're usually just looking at The Prestige. We're usually looking at the presentation of something that really started decades ago, which is why we can't figure out the puzzle or resolve the challenge no matter what we do.

We're staring at the magician's hands when we should really be looking at what he was doing before he came into the theatre.

The question we have to ask ourselves is do we really want to know the root of the problem, or do we want to continue to be fooled.

An Untidy Table of Love

To make more sense of all this, here's an example from my life of what I've just described.

In my longest romantic relationship, which culminated in a six-year marriage, a longstanding issue between my partner and I was how untidy she was in comparison to me. It would cause arguments on a regular basis, largely because I couldn't understand why she couldn't just stick to things she would promise me.

A key point of consternation for me was the dining table. My partner would slowly pile more and more things on the table – one of the first things I would see when walking into our home.

The untidiness would irritate me so I would ask, in as many different ways as I could think over the years, if she could just keep it tidy. My partner would always promise she would.

More often than not I would come home later the same day or later that week to a table covered in mess, which would lead to another argument.

We would have that argument on loop for over a decade.

Are you in a relationship now, or have you been in one in the past, in which you've had the same argument over and over again, possibly for years, and have never been able to resolve it? Or do you have the same issue with an employee, a boss, a friend, a child or other family member? Does it drive you insane that you can't resolve the issue no matter how many times you discuss it?

It's probably because you're looking in the wrong place.

After the breakthroughs during my therapy and coaching I described in my origins story in Chapter 1, I had a huge realisation.

The problem wasn't the untidy table or untidy house. I was looking at The Prestige instead of figuring out when the magic trick was really done. As with most problems in our lives, the real issue was more than 30 years before when I was a little boy and began to believe that I wasn't good enough.

Sounds crazy, right?

This is how these things really play out in our subconscious while we're busy being distracted by our ego and conscious mind:

I think I'm asking my partner to keep a table tidy, but what I'm really asking, deep inside, is whether she loves me. When she promises she will keep it tidy, I hear that she does love me and I'm happy. But when I walk in to find she didn't keep her promise, while at a conscious level my ego tells me I'm annoyed by an untidy table, the subconscious message I receive is my partner doesn't love me and, even deeper, it's because I'm not good enough and don't deserve love.

I appreciate this might sound insane at first glance, but if you are prepared to sit with each of the problems you face in life and keep working through them to find the real root cause, I'd place a large bet that you'll find a similar thing. But only if you're prepared to be honest with yourself and keep digging beyond the stories you've believed for years and do so with a completely open mind.

The vast majority of all our problems go back to our childhoods, to traumas, Programming Experiences and, ultimately, the belief that we're not good enough.

The upside of that? Repair your own self-worth, understand you are good enough as you are, with all of your darkness and light, and your problems slowly drift away.

In my own life I've largely cured depression, suicidal thoughts, a reliance on alcohol, an addiction to stress and attention, a brain that wouldn't shut up, deep insecurities, the need to be praised for everything I do and countless other things.

I even discovered that another unintended bonus of the work is I can now follow my favourite football team in a calmer way, experiencing all of the incredible highs that come with it and just walking away as if nothing has happened when they lose.

It's still a work in progress – and always will be – but, for the most part, my self-worth is no longer attached to the outside world. All the people and events that previously affected me in damaging ways don't anymore. It really is like real-life magic.

✎ Exercise

I want you to think about the challenges you're facing in life that led to you reading this book. Write them down with pen and paper, ideally in your notebook.

Take each one in turn and, with as open a mind as possible, begin asking yourself what the real problem is. When you get an answer, ask yourself whether there's something behind that.

It's similar to an exercise I used in my first book – asking yourself *"why?"* five times in order to get to the root of something, but in this case it's not always *"why?"* that we need to ask, it might be *"what's the real problem here?"* or some variant of that question.

Ask whatever question seems to be the most appropriate to dig deeper beneath the surface. If you get stuck, this is a good exercise to ask a coach or therapist to take you through or, failing that, ask a friend or family member you can trust who's good at asking questions to push you on it.

Don't worry if you get stuck or if it doesn't make full sense right now. Getting started in this way of thinking is the key and we'll come back to add to the building blocks later on.

Notes

Imposter Syndrome and Perfectionism

I could use many different examples here to illustrate the point further and we will talk about many more aspects of this as the book progresses, however, given how often I hear people talking about these two topics I think it's worth addressing them now.

Imposter syndrome and perfectionism are built on a foundational belief that we are fundamentally not good enough.

Imposter syndrome is, in a nutshell, a story repeating in our minds that whatever we have actually achieved in life is false and it's only a matter of time before someone exposes us as the imposter we are. At the root is a belief that we can't possibly be worthy of whatever it is we've achieved because we aren't good enough, regardless of the evidence to prove us wrong.

I heard recently a perfect summary of what's flawed about that entire belief. If you don't think you deserve to be somewhere because everyone else is smarter than you, you must also believe, in complete contradiction, you are clever enough to trick all the smart people into believing you're meant to be there. How does that make sense?

Perfectionism is the greatest example of how the ego dominates our lives and our societies with negative consequences while masquerading as something positive. I often hear people declare with great pride that they are a perfectionist, or see people extolling the virtues of perfectionism.

But just stop for a second and consider what perfectionism is? It's the belief that nothing is ever good enough unless it's perfect. And, guess what, very few things in life are ever perfect because we are all flawed human beings and our flaws come out in everything we do. The result? We never think anything is good enough, including ourselves. Our desire for things in the outside world to be perfect is a reflection of the fact we don't think we're good enough inside.

I describe myself now as a reformed perfectionist. The lad who previously couldn't leave the house if his pristine white shirt had the smallest of marks on it has become someone completely relaxed about things not being absolutely perfect, because that's just life.

Living in an Addicted World

You might not like this part when you first read it, but hopefully its impact will help you to change key parts of your life as we progress through this adventure.

While I appreciate the topic of addiction is enough for walls of books in itself, I wanted to talk about it in summary terms to give you something else to consider. While there are many factors involved in addictions my current belief is that, as with everything else in our lives, the root cause of all addictions is low self-worth and a fundamental belief that the addict is not good enough.

As with all other magic tricks in life, addiction tends to lead people to stare at the wrong place seeking to overcome problems. The words *"addiction"* or *"addict"* also lead most of us to think of other people. We tend to think of the headline-grabbing addictions like drugs, alcohol, gambling or sex.

It might not surprise you to hear, though, that if I believe the root cause of addiction is low self-worth, and if I also believe that practically all humans experience that problem, then it makes sense I also believe most humans are addicts.

Including you and me.

What's your immediate reaction to that? Do you read it and think it makes sense? Do you believe that you are an addict?

I'd guess if you struggle with any of the high-profile headline addictions it will be easy for you to accept and it will tie in to everything we've discussed already. It might even be a relief because you might already be seeing where your problems started and how you will be able to overcome them.

If that's not you, however, are you currently recoiling at the very suggestion you are an addict?

I don't blame you if that's the case. The vast majority of addictions in our world are completely stealth. No-one talks about them and most people aren't aware of them, so why would you have ever considered you might be an addict?

To discuss this further it's essential for us to think about what an addiction really is. As with many things, addictions exist largely to distract us from our lives. They exist to help us achieve something we have already covered that our systems are seeking to do for themselves: to repress emotions and ignore things that are too painful for us to want to feel.

Think of low self-worth as creating a hole deep inside us, which is often the empty feeling many of us experience. Addictions exist to help us try to fill that hole.

It's also necessary to note that different places define addiction in different ways. A dictionary definition is: *"The fact or condition of being addicted to a particular substance or activity"*. More detailed psychological definitions often also include criteria that an addiction leads to harm and is repeated despite the harm because of the pleasure or value attributed to the act by the addict.

I think where many go wrong when talking about addictions is in the idea of what *"harm"* really means. You can see how we understand drug or gambling addictions lead to harm but, in my view, harm is caused simply by the addiction doing what it's designed to do and helping us to repress our emotions and avoid facing difficulties in our lives.

While drugs, sex and gambling take all the dramatic headlines for achieving this distracting goal, the most common addictions in our societies are things like television, using our smart phones, social media, shopping, judging other people, complaining, following sports teams, relationships, other people, love, computer games, food, work, stress and, ironically, emotional states such as depression.

As I list those things, can you identify anything you do repeatedly as a distraction from your life? Is there anything you continue to do even though you know it causes you some level of harm because of the pleasure or subconscious reward you sometimes get from it?

Do you find yourself picking up your phone constantly even though you haven't received any notifications, or buying things you don't really need? Do you continue to watch a sports team even though doing so often has a negative impact on your life? Do you constantly complain about or judge other people, either out loud or under your breath? Do you walk into a room and immediately turn the TV on, even though there's nothing you want to watch? Are you in an unhealthy romantic relationship you don't feel you can leave, or do you work long hours in a job you don't really like?

How Addictions Are Formed

It's also relevant here to talk about how addictions are usually created. People often think addictions come from someone repeatedly doing something they get a lot of value from and, therefore, can't stop doing, even when it stops being enjoyable.

But that's not generally how addictions start or how they are purposefully developed by businesses in our modern world, whose aim is to ensure we become addicted to their product.

When I developed an online gambling business and began studying how online platforms are designed, I was shocked to find myself reading about rats in glass boxes in laboratories.

You're likely to have heard about these types of experiments. They put a rat in a box with a lever to press. When it presses the lever it is sometimes given a reward, but the trick is the reward isn't given in return for any predictable pattern. It's what's known as an intermittent reward, meaning sometimes you get it and sometimes you don't, but you can never be sure when it might arrive.

Even more shockingly, the phone you carry around everywhere with you, every mainstream social media platform you use, your dysfunctional romantic relationship, your stressful job, your sports team and everything else you might be addicted to operates in exactly the same way.

We are all just lab rats pressing levers hoping to get rewards. In our case, though, the reason we're pressing the lever in the first place is because we have a hole inside our soul we're desperately trying to fill with something in the external world.

If you don't believe me on the intermittent reward part, consider any romantic relationship or job you're in or have been in the past and how just as you were building up to thinking about leaving because you were so unhappy, something nice would happen that would give you hope that things would change, encouraging you to stay.

Start to become aware, if you're not already, of the rush you feel inside your veins when you see one of your posts on social media has been liked by someone, or how you feel when you see you've got a little red notification on your phone indicating you have a message.

Note how you don't get that every time you pick up your phone. It's intermittent. Just like a rat in a glass box.

The root cause and, therefore, the cure to all the addictions in our lives, then? To fill the hole inside our souls in a healthier way, by increasing our self-worth and understanding deep inside that we are good enough.

There's one addiction we haven't discussed yet, though. The biggest addiction on the planet and the most difficult one to break. We'll come back to that later.

✎ Exercise (Malcolm)

To end this section, I want you to do one more exercise to round off the first part of the healing process we've begun in these chapters. It's best to clear plenty of time and space for this to ensure you can give it the attention it deserves and to allow yourself space to process anything that comes up.

Go back to the stories of trauma from childhood you discovered from the Kenneth and Elsie exercises in Chapter 4. For each event, write out in detail all the emotions you felt at the time and still feel now. Don't hold anything back.

After you've processed how you felt about each event and the people involved, if the traumatic story in your mind is incomplete see if you can piece together what actually happened in the end and write the completion of the story.

For example, you might have a story from childhood where you were attacked by dogs and the story cut off in the middle, as traumatic memories tend to do, which led to you still being afraid of dogs to this day. If you re-tell that story as an adult the fact that you're reading this book means you survived whatever happened. Write out in detail what actually happened next. Very often we find that the ending of traumatic stories is along the lines of: *"Well, nothing really happened, we just carried on with life."*

If that's the case it's important to become conscious of the fact you survived whatever the event was, regardless of any programming installed as a result of it. We can deal with that later.

Notes

AN INTERLUDE

A long time ago when I was about 19, one of my best mates (also called Paul) told me a story about looking after his young nephew who was about seven at the time. His nephew's mum and dad worked, so he would come to my mate's house straight from school to be looked after for a few hours.

A regular occurrence while there would be for his nephew to go to the toilet, then shout downstairs for my mate to wipe his bum.

One day, my mate heard the shout, "PAAAAUUUUUUL, PAAAAUUUUUL, I NEED YOU TO WIPE MY BUM...", to which my mate sighed and walked upstairs.

In the middle of wiping his nephew's bum, as he'd done for years, my mate decided it was time for a chat.

Paul: "Don't you think you're getting a bit old for this now, mate?"

Nephew: "For what?"

Paul: "For people to be wiping your bum. If you need a poo in school, who wipes your bum then?"

Nephew: "I do it myself"

That story has got nothing to do with what we've been talking about, it just always makes me laugh so I thought I'd share it with you seeing as this stuff can get a bit heavy at times.

I often think of it when I want to make myself smile. At the end of the day, why would anyone wipe their own bum if they can get someone else to do it for them?

*   *   *

"The Na'vi say that
every person is born twice,
the second time is when
you earn your place among
the people forever"

(Jake Sully / Avatar)

8

TRANSFORM

Now we've explored the background to this work and started the healing process, you're ready to head into the transformational stage of the adventure.

This part is all about continuing to discover who you really are and the root causes of all of your problems in life while transforming into the new version of you – the version you choose for yourself.

TRANSFORM stands for:

T Take Responsibility and Be Kind to Yourself

R Realisations

A Accept, Allow and Process

N Needs, Wants and Boundaries

S Stories We Tell

F Finding Our True Self

O Our Darkness

R Reunite

M Make Peace

Are you sitting comfortably? Let's get started.

9

TAKE RESPONSIBILITY AND BE KIND TO YOURSELF

"To a disciple who was forever complaining about others the Master said, 'If it is peace you want, seek to change yourself, not other people. It is easier to protect your feet with slippers than to carpet the whole of the earth.'"

(Anthony de Mello)

Now we've explored the reasons we are the way we are and how this version of us was created by other humans, it's time to start the deconstruction and rebuilding phase of the adventure. It's time to become who we're really meant to be.

You might already have had some breakthroughs about things in your childhood that are creating problems for you today. I hope, too, that you're starting to see the different sides of your own persona and how a completely different character can show up in different parts of your life.

Don't worry if not, there's still plenty of time for all that.

The next phase is to continue learning while removing much of the programming we've already received and installing new programs of our choosing at the same time.

Unfortunately, we aren't computers – so it's impossible at the time of writing for us to wipe our existing programs and replace them with healthier ones by running a simple update overnight.

Instead, to transform our lives we must start with the principles of this chapter which are, for me, the most important parts of the entire process and the first stepping stones to rebuilding our low self-worth, insecurity and the feeling that we aren't good enough.

Having begun to discover who you really are I want you to think about what number you are on the self-worth power bar scale from zero (being absolutely no self-worth) to 100 (being complete self-worth and total belief that you are good enough). Our job throughout the following chapters is to increase that number slowly but surely. Every step forward helps us to build our self-worth, no matter how small.

Are you ready?

Taking Responsibility for Everything

If I was forced at gunpoint to give only one piece of advice to anyone on the planet about how to change their life, it would be this section of this chapter.

We unfortunately live in societies where we are taught from a very young age to blame everyone else for anything and everything that goes wrong. Many politicians around the world tend to have an allergy to telling the truth and taking responsibility for their actions. Our media is largely toxic and the people to whom we look for guidance are often not the best examples to follow.

Sadly, many of us also live in cultures where making a mistake is not tolerated. This, in turn, leads to more and more of us seeking to avoid responsibility at all costs.

It's understandable as owning up to actions often leads to people losing their livelihoods and being vilified by their peers. Which makes encouraging you to adopt what I'm about to set out a much more difficult challenge. However, I promise that no matter how counter-intuitive it might seem, it works.

The Three Phases

This area of our lives, which most of us have experienced, is covered by three stages.

1   Blaming Everyone Else

This is phase one, where many people begin life and never leave.

Blaming everyone else often feels in the moment to be the easiest thing to do, especially when we're in a tricky spot. The problem is it's like many things that feel good in the moment but cause longer-term damage, like eating a cream cake when we want to lose weight, or having an alcoholic drink because we're stressed when we're trying to get our lives together.

The easy choice in the moment often leads to more difficult times later on. As I once heard a wise man, Jerzy Gregorek, say on a Tim Ferris podcast: *"Hard choices, easy life. Easy choices, hard life."*

Choosing to blame everyone else for the problems in our lives is an easy choice that leads to a hard life. The difficulty is that while the delicious sugar-filled cream spills over our face as we bite into the sumptuous 'blaming others' cake, putting responsibility on everyone else for our issues implies we have no control over them.

In blaming others we hand total control of our lives to external forces which is, ultimately, disempowering and depressing.

This phase also includes pointing fingers at everyone else for the problems in the world while never considering how we are doing the very same thing we accuse others of. We use the behaviour of others to distract ourselves from our flawed behaviour, whether they be family members, friends, celebrities or complete strangers on the internet.

2   Blaming Ourselves

Phase two of this part of the adventure often sees people switch from blaming everyone else to blaming themselves, or alternating between the two. In the vast majority of people I meet and work with this is an ongoing inner program we need to remove in order to have any hope of rebuilding the human we want to be from the rubble of the one we deconstruct.

Blaming ourselves is also disempowering, but in addition to the cream smothered all over our face from blaming others, we have a self-hate sundae sloshing around inside our heads. We beat ourselves up constantly and rarely give ourselves any praise, which serves only to reduce our score on the self-worth scale.

Turning on ourselves serves no positive purpose, and is one of the reasons I now dislike much of the personal development and self-help worlds I used to love. Those worlds can often have the unintended consequence of encouraging us to hate ourselves a little bit more every day when we inevitably can't maintain whatever trick they've taught us to improve our lives.

3 Taking Responsibility

Phase three is where we want to be. Phase three is taking responsibility for absolutely everything in our lives, no matter how big or small and no matter how easy it would be to blame somebody else.

The idea is that whatever is happening we bring everything back to us and ask ourselves what our role is. The cheesy way I see this described, which makes me cringe a little bit but sticks in my mind so is probably worth repeating, is that as we point our finger at someone else we have three fingers pointing back at us.

Taking responsibility is vastly different to blaming ourselves because it's empowering. It's saying inside our own head, *"okay, this is my responsibility and it's all okay. I made a mistake because I'm just a flawed human, and now I can do something about it. It doesn't make me bad or not enough."*

When I say we bring everything back to ourselves, I mean *everything*, which is often the difficult part for most people to embrace. That's because even when we're prepared to take a large portion of responsibility for something, we can generally find a place where we think there's nothing more we could do and, at that point, it's therefore not our responsibility any more.

Let me give you two big examples.

The Shitty Boss/Employee

Something we've probably all experienced at some point in our lives is either being the boss of an employee who is just a waste of space, or being employed or managed by someone who's a complete arsehole.

I used to do straightforward business coaching and often came across this from company owners or bosses who were dealing with an underperforming employee.

The conversation would go something like:

Boss: *"I've done everything, Paul. I've trained them, I've coached them, I've disciplined them. But regardless of what I do, they still don't perform. How is that still my responsibility?"*

Me: *"Let's assume for the sake of argument you have done all those things – and you've done them to the best of your ability with no room for improvement. That's unlikely to be the case but we can assume it is for the purposes of this conversation. Even after all of that, there's still more you can do."*

Boss: *"I really can't see how that's the case. I've done everything."*

Me: *"Do they still work for you?"*

Boss: *"Yes, of course, that's the problem, they're useless."*

Me: *"Well it's your responsibility to sack them."*

The Relationship

We don't need to go through the conversation again, I'm sure you'll pick up the similarities with the above example as soon as I mention the topic.

You guessed it. If you're in an unhappy relationship and you feel as though you've done everything you can possibly do to make it better (which, again, is unlikely), there's still one thing left that's your responsibility.

You need to end the relationship.

Taking Radical Responsibility

The key is to take responsibility for absolutely everything in your life. That doesn't mean no-one else has any responsibility, it just means you are completely responsible for everything happening to you.

It's another philosophy that seems counter-intuitive but, once you start practising it, you see how it leads to a more peaceful existence because more and more things are in your control.

If you find yourself blaming someone or something, you can simply ask yourself in a very gentle way how it can be your responsibility and what can you do about it. Then take steps to do whatever you need to do to improve your life.

"Stop being so hard on yourself, it's no good for your health"

(Shine / Take That)

The 'Be Kind to Yourself' Program

Having worked with people from all over the world and observed which of them make the fastest progress and why, I've come to the conclusion, for the time being at least, that if I could give you one gift at the start of this work it would be the ability to be kind to yourself without any reservations or doubts.

The *'be kind to yourself'* program is the one that needs to be running right from the very start of this rebuilding exercise and, if installed successfully from the outset, leads to all other programs being installed at a much quicker rate with a much greater level of success.

✎ Exercise

This was one of the most-simple yet powerful exercises I did towards the start of my transformation adventure.

It can be difficult to do at first but, as with everything else, becomes easier over time with practice.

I want you to observe your thoughts for the next 24 hours. Simply start becoming conscious of the way you talk to yourself inside your head. What words are you using? What tone is the voice?

Write down everything you observe and, once the 24 hours is over, see if you can gently begin to observe your thoughts more regularly. The key here is not to turn it into an obsession, but to softly notice how you're talking to yourself.

Notes

Self-Hate in Disguise

If you have any struggles in life, the previous exercise could uncover you speaking to yourself in a way you would never talk to someone else.

I first did the exercise while in the middle of a juice fast I was carrying out in an attempt to heal myself from chronic illnesses. I'd watched all kinds of documentaries and read numerous articles on the subject before investing in a fancy juicing machine through which I fed organic fruits and vegetables on a daily basis, creating delicious, multi-coloured juices and smoothies that I lived off for 21 days.

For three weeks of my life I didn't eat any meals. Just juices and two smoothies a day, made from fruits and vegetables.

Whenever I tell people about that juice fast they always react in the same way: shock and awe. They can't believe it.

But guess what happened when I observed my thoughts during that fast? I realised I was being really horrible to myself. Not only was I not in shock and awe at how big an achievement it was, as I would be if anyone else told me they'd gone that long without eating a meal, but I was critical of myself.

The narrative I noticed playing in my head was that because I hadn't healed from my illnesses during the fast, as others I'd seen on documentaries had done, I must have been doing something wrong and should have done better. As part of the juice plan I'd been sticking to, they said that if you were ever really, really hungry and desperate to eat, rather than putting one of your daily bananas in your smoothie, you could eat it.

I'd eaten two bananas in three weeks.

That was enough for my inner dialogue to tell me it wasn't good enough. I shouldn't have eaten those bananas. I should have done better.

I realised during that period something that has stuck with me since and you'll see as another theme throughout this book. The language we use is really important.

You see, up until that point in my life, for 38 years I'd told myself I was driven. I was ambitious. That my desire to constantly improve was healthy. And I was right. In the world we've built, in the societies we live, I was right.

The problem is all those things are just different ways of describing self-hate. The way I talked to myself inside my head wasn't healthy, it was mean. If I ever caught myself talking to someone else like that I was ashamed. Yet I spoke that way to myself every day.

Self-hate was masquerading as ambition and drive when it was really just a symptom of me not feeling good enough as I was.

Can you see any of that in your own thoughts or the way you talk to yourself?

Be Kind No Matter What

Here's another thing to add to the list of counter-intuitive lessons to embrace and practice over the coming days, weeks, months and years.

The trick to being kind to yourself is being kind *no matter what*. Often when we start becoming aware of our thoughts not being nice, we then start to dislike the way we're talking to ourselves inside our heads.

The problem here is that's just more self-hate to add to the first layer of self-hate. We might then notice we're hating the fact that we hate ourselves, and add another layer of self-hate to the mix.

This can go on and on and on, until we have layers of self-hate so deep we don't know where to go.

I want you to be kind to yourself no matter where you catch your thoughts. If you notice you're being mean to yourself for being mean to yourself for having a self-hate thought, be kind to yourself for it.

Does that sound insane?

Think about it and it makes sense. If we keep beating ourselves up for what's going on inside our heads it will never change, so we need to start being kind somewhere. Noticing a self-hating thought at any point and calmly saying to ourselves, *"ahh, I've just spotted myself beating myself up for beating myself up for beating myself up, but that's okay because I'm just a flawed human and these things happen"*, results in us stopping the self-hate going deeper.

That kind thought is intended to replace what we are likely to currently have, which sounds something like, *"oh for fuck's sake, Paul told me not to be mean to myself and there I am being mean to myself, what an absolute prick I am"*, which is just more self-hate and exactly what we want to move away from.

If we keep practising over time, we eventually reach a point where the first self-hating thought is met with a shrug of the shoulders and, *"sometimes I have self-hating thoughts, and that's okay because I'm just a flawed human"*, which leads to the self-hating thoughts slowly drying up altogether.

A Key Point

It's extremely important here to stress something.

When we take the step to take absolute responsibility for our lives in a radical way, always bringing everything back to us, and we're being kind to ourselves for the mistakes we make, it doesn't mean we can be reckless about our actions.

Time for another story.

The Greenhouse Story

Do you know what a greenhouse is? If you're reading this in Great Britain, or one of its many old colonies, I'd guess the answer is yes. If you're from elsewhere you might call it a glasshouse or something else that makes more sense. I've only just realised as I started writing this paragraph that '*greenhouse*' is actually a rubbish name for it.

It's basically a shed made from glass that people in colder climates might put in their garden to grow food that shouldn't really be growing there. My grandad on my dad's side had one which, in turn, meant my dad had one (remember our childhood programming doesn't just apply to us).

They would both grow things in there like grapes, tomatoes and cucumbers, and would be very pleased with themselves when the family ate anything they produced, as they should have been.

When I was a little boy the back garden of our house was well designed for adults to show to their friends and be happy with how well they'd done in their lives, but it wasn't very good for a game of football which, in all honesty, was my only concern.

As you looked out from the back of the house, the garden started with a patio running across the width of the property and stretching out about five metres before the grass started. Around the two long sides of the garden ran flower beds, with the far end border filled with flowers and trees. At the back left hand corner was the greenhouse, with a normal wooden shed to the back right hand corner. To give you an idea of the total size, you'd probably fit three cars nose to tail across the width of the garden, and five cars along the length.

The owners before my mum and dad had also decided it was a wonderful, middle-class idea to dig a big hole right in the middle of the lawn to fill with water and fish. Which meant we had a pond right in the centre of my football pitch.

I've included a picture of the pitch/garden so it's easy to imagine.

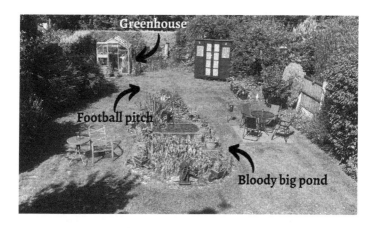

When they bought the house I was a very quiet, shy seven-year-old boy and they didn't involve me in house-buying decisions anywhere near as much as they should have done. They sold me on the fact that I was being upgraded from a tiny box room in our previous house to a full big boy's room in this new house.

They failed completely, however, to ask my thoughts on the bloody big pond in the middle of the house's main football pitch. In fact, I didn't once hear them refer to the back garden as my football pitch, which was disappointing in itself. It's only as I'm recalling this story that I'm realising I have another traumatic experience to add to my list…

Anyway, they went ahead with the purchase and we settled in. It was a great house and we spent many happy years there as a family.

For the purposes of this story, though, we need to focus on the proximity of the greenhouse to the wooden shed and the pond. The dimensions of the garden meant the best place for me to practice my football skills was just behind the pond, in between the greenhouse and the shed. Sometimes I would invite friends around to play, other times I'd happily be out there by myself recreating great moments in my limited knowledge of football history and celebrating my world-class goals in front of an imaginary crowd.

If you've been able to follow my description of the garden and understand the sketch, you might have spotted the main problem for a child with a football and a shed made from glass.

A few weeks after moving into the house my dad wanted to speak to me.

Dad: "Son, I was in the greenhouse earlier and realised the temperature in there had dropped, which is bad for the tomatoes. When I looked around I realised some of the glass panels at the bottom of the side have been broken. Would you know anything about how that happened?"

Me: "No. It might have been my sister. Ask her"

Dad: "Are you sure? It looks as though it's the perfect height for one of your world-class goals to have done it. If it was you, I'd rather you were honest with me. You won't be in trouble, but I need to know if you break any glass so I can fix it and the plants don't die."

Me: "Okay, I'm sorry dad, it was me. I scored against Manchester United last week in a big cup game and think I must have smashed the glass. I thought I'd get into trouble so didn't want to say."

Dad: "That's okay son, just promise me you'll be honest in the future. Deal?"

Me: "Deal."

[One week later]

Me [running in from the garden, shouting]: "DAD, DAD, DAD..."

Dad [running out from the garage in a panic]: "What is it son, what's happened?"

Me: "I've just broken some more glass in the greenhouse, sorry."

Dad: "Okay, good lad, thanks for being honest."

[Two days later]

Me [running in from the garden...]: "DAD, DAD – I've broken more glass in the greenhouse. Sorry. It was a great goal though."

[Three days later]

Me [running in from the garden...]: "DAD, DAD..."

Dad: "Come here, son"

Me: "Is there something I can help you with?"

Dad: "Remember when I said it's great to be honest and you won't get in any trouble?"

Me: "Yes"

Dad: "Well, that's still true, and it's also true that you can't just keep smashing the glass in the greenhouse with your football. You still need to be careful and try your very best not to smash the glass. Does that make sense? Maybe we can find a different spot for you to play."

*   *   *

The moral of the story is, of course, that taking full responsibility for our lives and being kind to ourselves for our mistakes along the way is not a free pass to be reckless or to purposefully hurt anyone or anything else.

The idea is to live our lives in as kind, caring and compassionate a way as we can manage while taking full responsibility for our actions and not beating ourselves up for everything that goes wrong, or the mistakes we make as we're installing our new programs.

The Dangers of Taking Responsibility

It wouldn't be fair of me to encourage you to take full responsibility for everything in your life without providing a warning about the downsides that come with doing so.

In an ideal world we would all take full responsibility for our actions, creating a beautiful, virtuous cycle where as you take responsibility for your actions, the next person takes responsibility for theirs and on and on until we're all skipping down the street holding hands while whistling our favourite Frank Sinatra song together.

Unfortunately, as with many things in life, that's not how it usually works.

The reality is more likely to be that if you choose to take full responsibility for your life, the people around you might not be doing the same thing. In the worst-case scenario that can lead to you taking responsibility and others having no hesitation in using it as a lovely big opportunity to pile as much blame as they can on you and absolving themselves of as much responsibility as possible.

In my experience this is an unavoidable consequence of this particular life choice, unless you opt to move to a remote location in the hills to live alone. Assuming you'll probably be intending to live among other humans, the best thing I can do is recommend that slowly, over time, you begin to choose to spend your life with people who are willing to take responsibility for their lives and their actions as well as you.

I had a heart-warming moment a few months ago when I apologised to a mate for something I'd done and, rather than piling in on me for the mistake, he accepted my apology and apologised for the ways he felt responsible for the disagreement.

We both took full responsibility for our actions – and it felt great.

Others might slowly begin to do the same over time if they see you taking the lead and, if not, you can take responsibility for choosing to include those people less in your life.

You Are Choosing Your Life

I've been thinking of ways to communicate my general philosophy about life to those around me without constantly trying to coach anyone or involve myself in matters that are none of my business.

I came to the conclusion that the simplest way, when appropriate, is to remind anyone who complains about their life that if they are over 18 they have chosen their life by making thousands upon thousands of decisions for years – and they continue to make those decisions today and every day.

If you don't like the life you have, it's within your power to change it. You just have to start making different choices.

Which is the tricky part.

"I can only show you the door, you have to walk through it"

(Morpheus / The Matrix)

Stop Bullshitting Yourself

Often when I'm coaching people, I get one of my many alter-egos knocking on the back of my head and saying to me in a very soft voice, *"eh, Paul, you know that thing you're saying to that person about their life? Do you think it might apply to you as well?"*

A couple of months before beginning to write this book properly, I'd been telling myself and others for a while that I was writing it. But I wasn't really, I was just thinking about writing it and putting off the actual writing on a daily basis.

On a few different coaching calls I was asking people whether they thought they were bullshitting themselves when they were saying they wanted to do something. It could have been anything from losing weight to changing jobs to starting to learn the guitar.

I was telling them stories about how we humans love to talk about obstacles that get in the way of us doing things. We love to have fancy phrases and words for them like a lack of motivation, procrastination, needing more accountability or self-sabotage (more on that later), but we all have things in our lives we do without any hesitation.

Think now of something in your life you just did without worrying about whether you could afford it or whether you had enough time. Something you didn't need anyone else to motivate you to do and self-sabotage and procrastination were nowhere to be seen.

My most obvious example is going to European Champions League finals to watch my football team. I've been to four of them in my life, starting when I was 25 right up to when I was 39. In each of those years when Liverpool Football Club reached the final I probably couldn't afford to go on an unplanned trip to some far-flung European city and almost definitely didn't have time.

Did I need to get an accountability partner to figure out how to do it? Or come up with tools and techniques to motivate myself to book the trips? Did I procrastinate over the decision?

No, I just sorted it and ignored any hurdles in my way. Why? Because I really, really wanted to go. On a scale of zero to 100 with zero being not wanting to go at all and 100 being *"I am absolutely going and no-one will stop me"*, I was 100.

When it came to writing my book I'd started using words like "procrastination" and started to think maybe I needed an accountability partner. After coaching a few people through the *"are you bullshitting yourself?"* work, though, I sat down and asked myself a simple question.

"Do you want to write this book or not?"

The difficulty we all have is being honest with ourselves. We might think it would be a good idea to lose a few pounds in weight and in a dream world we might love to have a six pack, but do we really, really want one? What I usually find when people aren't doing something they say they want to do is it's because they don't really want to do it.

If I dig deep enough, they want to lose weight because their wife says they should, or they want to change jobs because their husband thinks it would be a good idea. But they don't really want to. They're just okay with their chubby little belly and wanting to work in the local shop for an easy life.

When I asked myself the question about writing the book I committed, as I always do these days, to be honest with myself. I asked the question and realised if I didn't want to write the book that was fine, I just needed to stop telling myself and other people I was writing a book when I wasn't, and start telling them I was thinking a lot about writing a book, which is what I was actually doing.

But if the answer to the question was, yes, I did want to write the book, I should just stop making excuses and do it.

That night I started writing what you are now reading.

I'm sharing this with you because you might have experienced something similar when it comes to making changes in your life. If you find you're not making changes even though you're telling yourself consciously you want to, the first thing to do is sit down and ask yourself honestly whether you do really want to change.

If you don't, that's okay. Just be kind to yourself and accept the life you have is the life you've chosen. Doing that will, in itself, make you considerably more content and peaceful on a day-to-day basis.

If you can honestly say you do want to make the changes, take responsibility and stop making excuses.

Either way, it's time to stop bullshitting yourself.

Reminder:

1 Don't be distracted by the magic tricks. Trace everything back to what the real problem is if you want to find the solution.

2 None of this is anyone's fault. We're all just flawed humans doing our best.

10

REALISATIONS

"The way it works is, you do
the thing you're scared shitless
of and you get the courage after
you do it, not before you do it."

(Archie Gates / Three Kings)

Once the concept of taking full responsibility for everything is embraced and the all-important *'be kind to yourself'* program is installed, it's time to discuss a number of other realisations I had during my adventure. They will form core foundations on which everything else we're about to do will be built.

In no particular order…

Same Life, Different Houses

One of the many privileges I have in my life, for which I feel very humble, is that I get to see behind the curtain into the real lives of lots of other people. It's happened throughout my career, even back when I was a lawyer and, for whatever reason, people have always shared their deepest, darkest, most personal parts of their lives with me.

Before starting on this path, then, I realised years ago that one of the biggest problems we have is a feeling that our problems are just *our* problems. We look at the lives of others, especially through social media, and assume everyone else is basically okay.

One of the first things I tell people when discussing their issues is we're all experiencing similar problems around the globe. We are effectively living the same lives in different houses.

The simple realisation that we're not alone in our struggles often gives people a sense of relief. I promise whatever challenges you're facing in life, there are millions of people around the world experiencing the very same thing as you read this.

You are not alone.

Simple, Not Easy

The principles and lessons I discuss mainly fall within another general concept that applies to many elements of life.

In the English language, we can often use the words 'simple' and 'easy' interchangeably as though they mean the same thing, but they are very different. Many things are simple but not easy.

My favourite examples are that creating financial wealth and losing weight are both, in theory, simple, but if they were easy to execute we'd all be billionaires with six-packs.

Most of what I've learnt and now share with you is simple, but the execution of the lessons is not easy. It takes commitment, dedication and practice over a consistent period of time if you really want to change your life.

The Route is the Shortcut

Something I'm often asked about and see others being asked constantly is what's the shortcut to where we all want to get. I've had people pick up my first book about changing careers and ask if I'll just give them the bullet-point summary so they don't have to do the work involved in reading the book and doing the exercises.

It made me think of the many different satellite navigation systems we all take for granted these days, either in our cars or on our phones, and the routes they show us when we ask how to get from one place to another.

Asking for a shortcut to this type of work is like asking Google if there's a quicker way than the most direct line it's already just drawn for you on a map. The answer is a resounding 'no'. The route you've been shown is the shortcut and, if you insist on constantly trying to beat the system, you'll more than likely discover in a few years that you've wasted years trying to find a way around the problem when you'd already been shown the most direct route.

Having faith in the work and taking one step at a time is the most direct and efficient way to get where you want to be.

Most Difficult, Most Rewarding

The reason most people want a shortcut in life is because they can see the work involved in the route they've been shown by the person who walked it before them. In truth, they don't want to put that work in. We know that to get a six pack we should eat fewer cakes, but we'd rather someone just gave us a tablet so we can still eat the cake and have the six pack as well.

While there are elements of life that appear on the face of it to achieve that for people, the effects are never long-lasting because the reality, again, is the real value in anything we do is in the journey. Think of the most rewarding things you've done in your life. Were they also the most challenging? I know all the things I'm most pleased with myself for were things that challenged me the most, including putting in the work over a number of years leading me to writing this book and sharing the lessons with you.

If you truly want to change your life, accepting it takes hard work from the start is one of the biggest gifts you can give yourself. By doing so, you're understanding from the outset that things can get tough along the way, which means you're less likely to quit when those difficult moments arrive.

Things to Avoid

There's one phrase I hear constantly when working through these topics, which I'd urge you to look out for and avoid as much as you possibly can: *"That's different"*.

We'll come back to this principle later on, but I wanted to flag it now so you can become aware of it before we do further work. If you haven't already, you're likely to be forced to face things about yourself as we progress that you don't particularly like at first look.

Our first instinct when this happens is often to say how our behaviour in a certain situation isn't the same as when someone else does it, for whatever bullshit reason we want to come up with. We like to tell ourselves – and others – that what we do is different. It's not.

Remember, taking full responsibility for our lives means avoiding making excuses, and avoiding making excuses will lead to you reaching your destination at the fastest possible speed.

An Opinion, Not My Opinion

One of the many lessons I took from my favourite book of all time, *Letting Go*, by David Hawkins, is the idea that one of the problems we face in life is forming opinions then creating an emotional attachment to them.

It's partly why many people struggle to change their minds even when faced with compelling reasons to do so. By calling something *"my opinion"* we take ownership of it and it becomes part of us, and letting go of it means letting go of part of ourselves. If our self-worth is already low, that becomes almost impossible to do.

If we refer to the same thing as *"an opinion"* it becomes much easier to hold the view more loosely and, if new information leads us to change our mind, it's far less challenging to change the opinion we hold because it isn't attached to who we are.

Always a Student

In a similar way, if you're like me you will have spent much of your life to this point constantly trying to master things and become an expert.

One of the most important moments in my adventure was learning to understand I'll never master this work. I will always be a student and that, ironically, takes away a huge amount of pressure because I can accept from the outset I will always be learning. It's only when we consider ourselves to be experts in something the pressure builds, because our ego begins telling us we should know everything, leading to a decrease in self-worth and a path back to the imposter syndrome feelings we mentioned earlier.

It's impossible to be an imposter if you accept from the start you're never meant to know it all.

Two stories I love that illustrate this both involve guitars. As with most stories or quotes involving other people I have no idea if they're true, but they're harmless and make a great point so I'll tell you them anyway.

The first is that apparently if you ask the great guitarist Eric Clapton what he does for a living, he'll tell you he's "learning how to play the guitar". The second I heard is that when Noel Gallagher of Oasis fame gave his daughter a guitar as a present, he made a point of saying it's not a computer game and can never be completed.

Thinking of life in general, and the lessons in this book, in the same way is one of the greatest things I ever did and I encourage you to do the same.

Unique Not Special

This realisation is so vital I feel as though I'm not doing it justice by slipping it in the middle of this chapter, so you'll notice we go over this and other points as we walk along the path.

It's another one that could seem counterintuitive to begin with and will hopefully make more sense the more you think about it.

Many of us have been raised to believe we are special in some way. There could be lots of reasons for this but I don't think it's a coincidence that as the world has developed to pray more on low self-worth in society it seems to have escalated. The more we all feel we're not good enough, the more we need ourselves and our children to be something special to make up for that hole deep inside us.

The trouble – and the blessing – with this is we're not special. I say the trouble and the blessing because if we've spent a lifetime needing to be special, when first realising we're not it can be quite painful. The blessing, once we pause to reflect, is not being special means we're not alone. Thinking we're special leads us to thinking no-one else is like us, which results in us feeling very alone in the world. I know I spent many years thinking there was no-one like me in my life.

When I realised I was just like everyone else I felt an overwhelming sense of relief. Aside from anything else there's less pressure on me now to hide the very normal sides of myself, like my laziness and my scruffiness. I'm just a flawed human like everyone else and don't need to try to prove I'm special all the time. I also know everyone else goes through all of the same ups and downs I do, which stops me feeling alone.

The twist, which again could simply come down to our use of language, is we are all unique.

There has never and will never be another human on the planet with your experiences. No-one has been raised by the same people in exactly the same way as you, not even any siblings you have who were raised by the same parents.

When listening to parents repeatedly talking about how different their kids are and how that's baffling because they were raised in exactly the same way, it dawned on me a few years ago why that story is a load of nonsense. No two kids are raised in the same way by the same people. Think about it for a second. Parenting tends to follow similar patterns in every family (supporting the same life, different houses theory we talked about earlier).

The first-born child is often treated like a precious little china doll because the parents are new to the game and, to be frank, are petrified of it dying. My mum and dad waited seven years for my sister and my mum apparently used to wake her up in the middle of the night to be sure she was still alive, she was so worried about anything happening to her.

By the time I came along, they'd already had two years' experience of raising a child so were far more relaxed and, thankfully, left me to sleep. I've seen the same pattern in my niece and nephew, with the second born having a far more relaxed upbringing than the first born.

Can you see the same differences in your life or the lives of your kids?

Which leads to us all being unique. There's no-one just like you, but that doesn't mean you're special. You can be completely unique and share all the same flaws as every other human on the planet. The key is to bring every bit of your uniqueness to life and maximise every part of the real you without feeling the need to be special all the time.

Which leads us to…

And Not But

We'll talk about black-and-white thinking in depth in Chapter 13. Here I want to share with you the crucial concept that two things can exist at the same time, even though we've been raised to believe that's often not the case.

I first realised this when I spent some time in Bali early in 2019, forming close friendships with a number of people. On the day many of them were leaving, someone asked how I was feeling and I replied, with tears in my eyes, *"I'm happy sad"*. They looked a little taken aback and asked what I meant, so I explained that for the first time in my life I could see how two things could exist together even though they seem to conflict. I was happy to have formed bonds with all these incredible people, and simultaneously sad I wouldn't be waking up the next day to laugh and joke with my new friends.

This principle applies to so many things and we can ensure we make room for it in our lives by making a simple tweak to the language we use.

Often, we will start a sentence with something then use the word *'but'* to lead us into the next part. For example, we might say: *"I love you, but it really annoys me when you don't load the dishwasher properly."* The problem here is everything before the *'but'* is discarded in our mind and in the mind of the recipient. The *'but'* suggests the two parts don't exist together; that the second negates the first.

The simple change is to use the word *'and'* instead. *"I love you and it really annoys me when you don't load the dishwasher properly."* Your annoyance and love can exist at the same time. Using the word *'and'* allows that to happen for you and the person you're speaking to.

This is another illustration of how something simple isn't necessarily easy. I still catch myself sometimes saying *'but'* when *'and'* would be more appropriate, and gently correct myself. It takes practice and is absolutely worth the effort.

Another great way of looking at this and making subtle changes in our lives is to use a line my therapist and mentor, Dave, often said to me: *"Is there room for both?"*

If you are ever faced with a decision between two options gently ask yourself whether there's room for both to exist at the same time. Often, you'll find there is.

Oxygen Mask Instructions

If you've consumed a lot of material from the personal development world you might have heard this analogy previously. It's another to force you to question something you're likely to have been taught your whole life.

Do you travel on aeroplanes? If so, think back to when they give the safety demonstrations at the beginning of each flight. When they talk about the possibility of the plane losing cabin pressure resulting in oxygen masks dropping from the panel above your head, can you remember whose mask they tell you to put on first?

It's your own.

They instruct you to ensure your mask is on first because if you start trying to help others before you help yourself, there's only so far you'll get before you suffocate.

Many of us have been raised to put everyone else ahead of ourselves. We've been taught that to put ourselves first is selfish, and that's not acceptable. The problem with this way of living is by not looking after ourselves we can never be the best version of us. While that might not necessarily lead to us dying (although in some situations it does), the oxygen mask analogy is still valid because if we don't take care of ourselves properly, we can't possibly expect to take care of anyone else to the best of our abilities.

We can't be the best husband, wife, brother, sister, son, daughter, auntie, uncle, employee, boss, mum or dad unless we are first the best version of us. And the only way we can become the best version of us is to make sure we look after ourselves first. That does not mean being unnecessarily selfish, mean or unkind to others, it just means making sure we take care of the most important person in our lives. We'll talk more about this in Chapter 12.

Letting Go of Control

If you'd asked me five years ago whether I believed in luck, I would have replied emphatically that I did not.

I was a firm advocate of the old saying *"the harder I work, the luckier I get"* and I would become very annoyed at the mere suggestion that anything good in my world had resulted from luck.

Since changing my life, though, my view has changed.

The idea that nothing was a result of luck came, for me at least, from a belief I was in full control of everything. Luck was for people who believed in fate. I believed in myself and forcing the world to be whatever I wanted it to be.

These days I don't believe that at all and, in fact, from my new perspective it's hard for me to see even from a logical perspective how I used to deny the role of luck, fate or anything else you want to call it, in our lives.

The reality is we're only in control of a small number of things in the world and there are billions of things happening every day completely outside any influence of ours. My favourite example is when I decided to sell my law firm a number of years ago.

Of course, if it wasn't for my decisions to leave the relative safety of employment with international law firms years before and set up my own business, as well as everything I'd done in the six years since setting up to grow the business, I wouldn't have had anything to sell.

And it was also true that I received three offers for my firm, two of which were firms offering to take my business without paying a penny up front, instead promising a split of income earned after the sale. Only one company made me a real cash offer.

The cash offer only materialised, though, because the firm involved had found itself in a particular set of circumstances meaning it had a problem to solve, money to spend and my firm just happened to fit what it needed perfectly.

All of those things happening had absolutely nothing to do with me. Those circumstances had been created by billions of things happening over many years of which I had no awareness, culminating in the sale of my firm coming at the perfect time.

That, among many other experiences, changed how I view luck and fate. I now believe in a slightly altered version of the infamous luck line I quoted above. The author Neil Gaiman once said something along the lines of: *"The harder I work, the luckier I get, but there is still luck."*

Aside from the decisions we make, the main thing we're in control of is how we react to the world, which many of the ideas in this book will help you to do in a healthier way.

Once we accept most things are outside our control, the key is to let go of our desire to control things. Learning how to ride the waves rather than seeking to stop them happening is what this is all about.

The Small Things are the Big Things

Another principle we will revisit throughout the following pages is counter to what many of us are looking for when we decide to change any aspect of our life.

We want to see the big ticket things we can do that will lead to huge shifts. The truth with this work, as it is for most other things, is that's not how it works.

Think again about the comparison with getting in good physical shape or creating more financial wealth. The key is to do small things over and over again. When it comes to the training we've had to be the people we are, we're talking about decades of small Programming Experiences we need to slowly unwind and replace with new programming. That can happen quickly in some instances and, in others, can take more practice over time.

Understanding from the outset that the small things are the big things is key to making sustained, long-lasting changes in a healthy way. As we progress through this adventure together, don't underestimate how the smallest things you can observe and change along the way can be the most powerful.

Silly, Stupid and Weird

When I'm coaching people using these ideas, I often hear people saying to me things like *"I know this will sound silly, but…"* or *"this is a really stupid/weird thing to say…"*. Whenever anyone starts a sentence that way, I gently let them know no-one has ever said anything to me after an introduction referring to their thoughts being silly, stupid or weird with anything other than something that makes absolute sense.

The things that might seem strange to you now will soon turn into things that make complete sense to you. The only reason they seem silly, stupid or weird at the moment is because of the programming you've had up to this point. I remember thinking exactly the same way, and now the things I would have thought were crazy in the past make much more sense than any of the old explanations I had for them.

Once we learn to understand how we operate as humans, every-thing makes more sense. If, therefore, you find yourself thinking that something coming up inside you, a thought or emotion, is in some way weird, it's another opportunity to be kind to yourself and understand there's no such thing. Allow it to be whatever it is and re-visit it when you've progressed further through your adventure to see if it makes more sense once you've completed more of The Karate Kid training.

"Repeat Them To Infinity"

Whenever I was dealing with adults in my old life, if I had to repeat something more than once or twice I would become extremely irritated. I could never understand how another grown-up needed to hear something more than a couple of times before taking it in.

Then one day I heard a famous CEO given this question during an interview: *"How many times do you think an important message needs to be repeated before an employee should understand it?".*

He replied along the lines of *"If messages are important, you should repeat them to infinity. Your job is to keep saying the same things over and over again until the people to whom you are communicating understand your messages deep inside".*

From that day I do my best to embrace that philosophy, especially in relation to this work. I make no apologies, then, for the number of times I will repeat key messages throughout this book.

The Doors on Life's Endless Corridor

I look at life as one endless hotel corridor, lined on each side by an infinite number of doors.

At any given stage in our lives we've been through a set number of the doors we've already walked past, and we think the world consists of only the things we've found behind those doors. Then, every so often, we'll open another door and realise there's a world behind it that's existed for years, filled with millions of people, and we've been blissfully unaware of it.

I realised when starting this work how many people are already in the world behind this door and the other doors it leads to, and I'm still amazed by how few of us ever go through them. The world behind these doors is so much more peaceful, rewarding and fulfilling than any of the ones I've been through before; it's incredible to me they remain a mystery to so many.

Hopefully I've already helped you to walk through some doors you've never been through before. My plan from here is to help you explore as many more as you're comfortable doing, and the world's they've kept hidden from you until now.

Redefining Success

Last but not least, we've already touched on this and I want to reiterate the point with it being so important. It's also linked to the hotel-door analogy.

One of the biggest challenges we face as a society is how we currently define success.

For the most part, we tend to believe having lots of money and material possessions are the ultimate aims in life. After that, depending on your nationality, religion and culture, success is likely to be linked to how big your house is, what car you drive and whether you have managed to find another human to agree to live with you for the rest of your life, preferably while adding some other humans to the family along the way.

I see very little discussion, though, of things like contentment, peacefulness and joy. Yet as I reflect on my life to this point, money, material possessions and doing whatever I could to follow the standard script only led to me feeling hollow and unfulfilled.

As soon as I changed my focus to a pursuit of contentment, peacefulness and joy, everything transformed. Once I committed to being the true version of myself despite it meaning I had to break away from the pre-written script, everything became easier and my life became more fulfilling.

From my new vantage point, I look at all those in society I was seeking to replicate because I'd been told that's what success looked like, and I see millions of unhappy people. I see empty souls, depression and, sadly, an increasing number of suicides.

Yet that model remains the one we're all encouraged to follow.

I think it's time for us to start redefining what we believe success to be. For me, a successful person is someone living a life true to who they want to be. They are content in themselves, have high levels of self-worth and believe they are good enough. After that, whatever happens in their external life is less important, because how much money they have or how big their house is pales into insignificance. In the words of Tony Stark, no amount of money ever bought a second of time.

Are you ready to redefine what success means to you if it means leading a more fulfilling life?

Reminder

1 Take responsibility for absolutely everything in your life to find inner peace.

2 Be kind to yourself, no matter what.

11

ACCEPT, ALLOW
AND PROCESS

"You cannot hide
from what's inside"

(Place Your Hands / Reef)

The square of the hypotenuse of a right-angled triangle is equal to the sum of the squares of the other two sides.

Do you know what that is?

If you went to school in the United Kingdom during the past 40 years I'd bet you do. It's probably the same for most westernised countries.

Some bright spark somewhere once decided that it was important for 12 year olds around the world to commit to memory a theorem created by a fella called Pythagoras about the areas protruding from the side of right-angled triangles.

It was obviously so important that I burnt it into my long-term memory and can still reel it off 28 years later.

I have never once in my life, outside of school, had any use for that knowledge whatsoever. I remember once talking about something and wondering whether that's what Pythagoras' theorem would be used for, but then I got on with my day and forgot all about it.

That's the closest it's ever come to even being remotely useful.

Yet no-one ever taught me about emotions. No-one ever sat me down in a classroom and explained to me about all of these complex feelings that would overcome me through every minute of every day of every month of my entire life.

Why bother doing that when you can force kids to attach their self-worth to square-root calculations?

I mean, don't let me mislead you in any way. I was great at Pythagoras' theorem. I reckon if Pythagoras was still alive when I was 12 he'd have been absolutely made up with me. Everyone else seemed to be so there's no reason why the inventor of the theorem wouldn't. Little Paul was great at maths. Loved it, he did. There's an answer, you see. Two plus two is four. No complications. No emotions. Just right or wrong.

And when you're right you get a pat on the head and make everyone happy.

Little Paul in school was great at making everyone happy and getting lots of pats on the head.

But he didn't have a clue what was going on inside his body. It took another 28 years, many of them experiencing pain and darkness as an adult, before I ever got to learn some of the most important lessons in my life.

What Are Emotions?

Have you ever stopped to think what emotions really are?

We talk about them throughout our lives, but it wasn't until months into my adventure it really dawned on me what we're talking about.

We discuss them as though they're some mystical and mythical being living in our bodies. Something from another realm. A mystery. A conundrum that can't be solved. A friend was talking to me a few weeks ago about the serious problems she's been facing in her life for decades and said the immortal words, *"Well, the problem is, Paul, once my emotions get involved there's nothing I can do about it"* – as though her emotions are some kind of alien being that possess her and control what she does.

The simple and far less dramatic truth is our emotions are just chemical reactions taking place inside our bodies. That's it. That's all they are.

Esteemed neuroscientist Jill Bolte-Taylor says the actual chemical reaction that takes place when we experience an emotion lasts 90 seconds if we just let it fade away without fuelling it with anything else. That's one-and-a-half minutes.

Isn't that incredible when here we all are, struggling with our lives, battling anxiety, suffering with depression, biting down our anger and buying books to figure out what's wrong with us. Just think, many of us are depressed for years when the original emotion could have lasted less than two minutes. That's some achievement to stretch it out so far.

The Problem with Our Thoughts and Emotions

One of the biggest lessons I've learnt through the past few years is there's nothing wrong with our thoughts and emotions. They're just thoughts and emotions. At a fancy scientific level they're just chemical reactions inside our overly-complex body and mind. They can't hurt us or do any damage to us whatsoever.

The problem isn't our thoughts and emotions themselves. *The problem is what we think and feel about our thoughts and emotions.*

The first time I heard that it made no sense to me but, over time, it's become something I talk about and embrace most days.

Think about the stories we tell ourselves about whether an emotion is positive or negative, and the example I gave earlier of being attacked by a lion in the jungle. In that moment fear and anger are our friends, yet when they appear in daily life we usually reject them. We feel fear, anger, sadness, anxiety or jealousy and either consciously or subconsciously the next thought or feeling we have is that we shouldn't be feeling whatever we felt.

Rather than just allowing the chemical reaction to run its natural course, we dive into a vicious cycle that serves only to guarantee further pain and suffering.

Allowing and Accepting Our Emotions

One of the keys to transforming our lives is to learn how to allow and accept our emotions for what they are. The trouble is we've been taught from such a young age that so many of our emotions are not acceptable. So, rather than allowing and accepting them, we are consciously or subconsciously spending most of our days rejecting perfectly natural feelings.

If allowing and accepting an emotion enables it to pass in 90 seconds, guess what rejecting, suppressing and repressing does? It fuels the very thing we don't want to feel.

At a deeper level, following the theme of this book, the rejection of our own emotions is repeatedly sending a signal to our system that we are not good enough as we are. That the way we feel is somehow bad or wrong. That we are broken because we sometimes experience *"negative"* emotions when we've all been taught since the moment we crashed into the world we should only ever be experiencing *"positive"* emotions.

Positive and Negative Emotions Do Not Exist

As I've said, certain lessons in life are worth repeating over and over again until we truly understand them. This is one of those lessons.

There is no such thing as a positive or a negative emotion.

Even some of my favourite books and mentors in this world refer to them in those terms, and I've reached a stage where I have to politely disagree with their interpretation.

As we've discussed, emotions are harmless. They are neutral until we give some meaning to them. Depending on the context of where we experience them we can label them positive or negative, but that's our choice. I'll keep taking you back to the lion example. We have been raised to think of fear and anger as the baddies, but those emotions are almost single-handedly responsible for our species surviving for thousands of years.

Without fear and anger keeping us alive long enough to build the comfortable towns and cities in which many of us now exist, we would never have had the opportunity to experience joy, happiness or love. Yet we have the cheek to call them negative and say we don't want them? Talk about a lack of gratitude.

I found myself during coaching calls using the terms *"positive"* and *"negative"* and constantly saying I don't like that language but it's all we've got, then I realised it's time to come up with some new terminology so I've taken to calling them *"understood"* and *"misunderstood"* emotions.

We feel as though we understand emotions like joy, happiness and love. When was the last time you experienced happiness and started to worry about the feeling, going over and over it in your head trying to figure out why you were happy? Or think about the last time you were excited. Did you start looking for books that could help you figure out why you were feeling the way you felt, or did you just happily accept the emotion for what it was?

Yet when it comes to anxiety, sadness, depression and their brothers and sisters in the land of misunderstood emotions, we feel them and begin to analyse why they exist. How can I possibly be feeling sad when I know I'm only ever meant to be happy? What is wrong with me? Why am I such a failure? Everyone else seems to be happy and here I am struggling inside my head.

The difference between the categories isn't that one's bad and one's good, it's that we feel like we understand one so accept it without question, and we don't understand the other, so we reject it and everything in it.

A Personal Development Problem

One problem with the traditional personal development and self-help worlds I've spotted since venturing into this new universe, is much of those worlds want us to skip the part where we accept our misunderstood emotions.

For years I believed wholeheartedly in the idea that we need to reframe everything we do. That nerves aren't really nerves, they're excitement, so we just need to tell ourselves we're not nervous, we're just excited and everything will be better.

Again, though, all that does over the long term is lead to us repeating to ourselves that we're not good enough. That what we actually feel isn't valid. The truth is we are sometimes nervous, and that's okay. There's nothing wrong with feeling nervous about something.

The same goes for fear, sadness, anger or, one of my favourite ones as far as the old-school personal development world goes: laziness.

So many of us are bombarded with tools and techniques for stopping ourselves being lazy. For dragging ourselves out of bed in the morning for a run in the cold while shouting *"come on you lazy bitch"* at our reflection in the bathroom mirror.

Guess what? That's just more self-hate and internal messages that we're not good enough. The truth is we're all sometimes lazy, and that's okay. There's nothing wrong with feeling lazy. We can feel lazy and still get stuff done if we really want to. There's no need to call ourselves nasty names because of it.

I often see people I've learnt so much from over the decades talking about these topics and how they motivate themselves by telling their lazy-bitch arse to get out of bed, and I wonder how they'd speak to their young daughter if she was feeling tired and didn't want to go to school. I'd guess they'd be far more caring and compassionate to her than they've been trained to be to themselves.

So why are we okay talking to ourselves like a piece of shit?

The problem is much of the traditional personal development and self-help worlds encourage us to skip the acceptance stage, which is unhealthy. We can look at ways of improving our lives that are perfectly valid after we've accepted and allowed our emotions for what they are. We don't need to deny them.

Another side effect of the constant desire to reframe everything as one of the understood emotions while denying the very existence of misunderstood emotions, is we end up in the personal development and self-help worlds we largely see on social media – full of toxic positivity.

The toxic positive people are the ones constantly telling you how great the world is and how grateful you should feel just for being alive. Don't get me wrong, there's a time and a place for reframing things to make sure we're being grateful for our lives, but it's absolutely imperative we don't do that until we've accepted, allowed and processed our true emotions first, whatever they are.

Repeatedly screaming at the world and yourself to be positive and happy when you're not feeling positive and happy is no different to putting your fingers in your ears and shouting *"la-la-la-la-la-la-la-la"* and telling yourself everything's fine while watching your house burn down.

Or think of it like knowing your house has problems with its foundations, but all of your neighbours tell you if you just keep painting the window frames lovely bright colours everything will be fine.

If you never make the decision to go into the basement to fix the foundations it doesn't matter how pretty your windows are, your house is still going to fall down.

Understanding the Misunderstood

To be able to truly accept and allow our emotions, especially the misunderstood ones, I think it's crucial we begin to understand them.

One of the many shocks I've had during my adventure is how little I knew about these feelings. It makes sense when you think about it. Why would we know much about emotions that for generations have been repressed and rejected?

I'll share with you a few of my favourites and leave you to consider any others for yourself. Before then, though, it's important to note one crucial factor relating to our emotions.

Nobody Makes Us Feel Anything

Something we're all taught to believe subconsciously as we grow is the idea that other people and things are responsible for how we feel.

We learnt this by hearing the line *"you make me feel…"* thousands of times throughout our lives. How often have you said that to someone or about something? *"You make me so angry"* or *"the spider makes me afraid"*.

The reality, though, is that no-one and no-thing makes us feel anything. Our feelings are our feelings. They belong to us and aren't anyone else's responsibility, just as other people's emotions are not our responsibility.

Take the example of the spider. If I hold a spider in the palm of my hand in the middle of a group of five people and three of the people are afraid but two aren't, how can it be the spider generating the fear?

If the spider made us feel something, we would all be afraid. The reality is the fear is inside us.

I heard a lovely story to illustrate this point. The author, physician and addiction expert, Dr. Gabor Mate, was presenting to a room of people and brought a member of the audience on stage to demonstrate a point.

While talking to her, the lady stated, *"you're making me anxious"*– to which Dr. Mate replied: *"You mean I'm giving you anxiety?"* When the lady confirmed he was correct, Dr. Mate very gently and calmly said: *"Okay, just give it back to me."*

Just pause and reflect on that for a few seconds. If it was true someone or something else gave us our emotions, we could choose to simply give them back.

From now on, it's time to own our emotions and take responsibility for them. They are ours and there's nothing wrong with them.

Anger -v- Rage

I have to keep stopping myself from saying, *"this part is my favourite part"* – but this really is one of my favourite parts.

Have you heard of The Incredible Hulk? If you haven't it might be time for us to part ways or, at least, for you to go and spend some time catching up on superhero movies. I don't care if you think you're a grown-up and too old for that shit, this is important.

I grew up watching the old-school cartoon all about the world of a scientist who, after an unfortunate accident involving gamma radiation, would turn into a huge, green monster if he became too angry. Throughout my life I watched and read the cartoons, not giving a second thought to anything other than the literal interpretation of the story.

I'd guess to this point if you do know The Hulk you've probably been doing the same thing. What else is there to see, right?

It was only last year when I decided to watch the Marvel movies from the beginning, following a recommendation by a friend, that I suddenly saw a whole different story.

Dr. Robert Bruce Banner, to give him his full name and title, is a physically weak, socially withdrawn and emotionally-reserved physicist. Following the gamma accident he would battle with his anger, desperately trying to repress it for fear of what he knew it could do. He would try desperately to deny it, to keep it locked away because if he didn't the results were often terrifying. Once he transformed into The Hulk he had no more control and he was all too aware of the damage and destruction the big, green monster could do.

I realised while watching the Ed Norton version of the movie from 2008 how this story isn't just a superhero story about a reserved scientist and a monster he turns into when he's angry. It's a story about repressed anger turning into rage, and it's a story about the parts of us we repress and deny because we dislike them so much. We'll come back to the second of those points in Chapter 15.

For now, The Hulk helps us to understand a crucial difference between two very different emotions that most of the world merges into one with disastrous consequences.

The issue here is anger is a perfectly healthy emotion. As we've already covered, it has been key to our survival as a species. Anger, used in the correct way, also helps us in our more comfortable modern lives to stand up for ourselves when we need to, to meet our needs and to protect our boundaries (see more on this in Chapter 12).

Yet we've been taught since we were little kids that anger isn't acceptable. We would be told not to be angry. That anger is bad. The problem, as always, is while we were being told not to feel anger, we knew we already felt it. It wasn't a choice. We can't choose what emotions come up inside us. So, when we're told not to feel something we already feel we install more subconscious programming that we're not good enough.

"I feel angry and I know it's bad, therefore there must be something wrong with me."

When that happens, we do what we've been taught to do, which is to repress the emotion in an attempt to please the people around us. As we've already seen, though, repressing emotions only serves to fuel them rather than allowing them to diffuse naturally.

Think of a bucket filling with water one drip at a time. We feel anger and repress it because we think it's bad. The bucket fills slightly. Something else happens. More anger. More repression. The bucket fills another bit.

Over time, the bucket slowly fills to the top. Then, one day, something small happens leading to more repressed anger and, BANG, the bucket suddenly overflows and we lose our mind.

We explode. We go mad. We turn into The Incredible Hulk.

The world then labels our reaction as anger, leading to the continuation of the vicious cycle of anger being 'bad' leading to more repression.

The issue is that when the bucket overflows it's no longer anger we're experiencing, it's rage – and rage and anger are two very different things.

Rage is the Unhealthy Manifestation of Repressed Anger

Without wanting to ruin the story arc of The Hulk in the Marvel movie series for you, things change dramatically for Bruce Banner when he realises anger isn't his enemy.

The same goes for each of us.

We only ever reach a place of uncontrollable rage by denying our perfectly healthy feelings of anger in the first place. The irony is the bucket never fills up if we allow and accept our anger for what it is, enabling the pure, natural emotion to dissipate.

Sadly, because we've been taught for so long to repress our anger, many of us experience rage throughout our lives. My family on one side has talked of there being a bad temper running through it for generations, as though it was something no-one could do anything about. Like a curse we just had to accept.

The reality is what has actually been passed down through many of our families, including mine, is an inability to understand, process and accept our anger, usually creating a people-pleaser persona, which we'll talk more about later.

In my life, the explosions I talked about in my origins story were just a manifestation of repressed anger. I knew deep down at the time what they were because I knew how much on a daily basis I was repressing my true emotions. I was tolerating my surroundings and biting my tongue every day.

Does any of this resonate with you? Do you ever find yourself repressing anger, biting your tongue, tolerating other people and generally trying to please others, maybe because you're telling yourself you don't want to hurt their feelings, or you just want an easy life?

It might be easy enough for you to see how repressed anger turns into rage when we're talking about glasses being thrown at walls and similar behaviour. But if you're reading this and thinking it doesn't apply to you because you never have outbursts like that, there's another twist in the tale we need to talk about.

Covert and Overt Rage

Rage doesn't only come in one costume, it has many different disguises.

What I've mainly experienced in my life, which is the all-singing, all-dancing version of rage even kids would be able to spot, is overt rage. It's throwing things at, or even punching, walls, screaming at the top of our voice, being physically intimidating and any similar behaviour.

Many people I know, however, display what I'd describe as a more stealth form of rage, one the experts refer to as covert rage.

Covert rage originates from the same place as overt rage, but it manifests in very different ways.

Covert rage shows itself as things like giving someone the silent treatment, making passive aggressive comments, sulking, sarcasm or saying things "tongue in cheek" that you really mean.

Both covert and overt rage are signs we're not processing our anger properly. A passive aggressive comment is only made when we're unable to express healthily our feelings of anger towards someone.

What John Should Have Said

Many years ago I had a good friend called John who would regularly start shouting and gesticulating at me when telling me about his day, getting more and more irate as he described some exchange he'd had with someone.

I would often have to ask him to stop shouting at me, given it wasn't me he was annoyed with. John would usually start his ranting and raving with the words: *"What I should have said was…"* It led to a running joke that he should have written a book called *What John Should Have Said*.

At the time I didn't know anything about this topic but, looking back, those exchanges were a clear sign of someone repressing their anger. John was unable to express his true feelings to others when they annoyed him, for fear of them not liking him, which led to repressed anger that had to come out in other ways. Aside from the rants in my direction, John was also typically passive aggressive on a daily basis.

The Kid on the Plane

Another story I heard illustrating this point was from a friend who travels a lot by plane.

Sally was on the final leg of a long trip home. Within five minutes of sitting in her seat she felt a little foot kick the back of her chair. She sighed, smiled to herself and ignored it. She could hear the voices of a kid and their parent next to them, so trusted it would be stopped by the mum.

Five minutes later, another kick. Then another. Sally bit her tongue and tried to sleep. Surely the child's mum would tell her to stop kicking the seat?

It went on and on intermittently throughout the flight until, at last, Sally couldn't take it anymore, stood up, turned to the kid's mum and let rip with a tidal wave of venom about being inconsiderate and how ridiculous it was that she couldn't control her own child.

When the rage subsided and the mum had apologised, saying she hadn't noticed the kid kicking the seat, Sally sat down filled with shame at her outburst.

Funny Family Stories

Often rage-filled incidents from our childhood are told by our families as entertaining stories.

Remember that time your auntie lost her shit in the restaurant and screamed at that woman on the next table, or that time your dad went so red with rage you thought he was going to burst?

Do you have any stories like that from your childhood, or are there any others in your family? Tracing back through those stories can help us to uncover more Programming Experiences we've had since we were kids.

What's Behind the Anger?

There's a line of thought that anger is not a base emotion, and actually exists only as an outward facing protection from something deeper we're trying to ignore because the underlying emotion is too painful to feel.

The way it was once described to me is many of the emotions we really don't want to feel are cold, and anger is a hot emotion we use to warm those feelings up. For example, we really don't want to feel hurt, fear or grief, so often if those emotions come up inside us we generate anger to protect us from them.

I quite like this idea, especially from a male perspective. I think of many times I've felt anger come up through my veins and, if I pause to reflect on what was happening at the time, often what I was actually feeling was hurt. My feelings had been hurt. But imagine two men standing in a pub in a confrontation with each other and one saying out loud that something the other said had hurt his feelings. Can you imagine a man ever saying that to another man? It's much easier to picture the same scene and see two men becoming angry towards each other, isn't it?

It makes perfect sense to me that the anger acts as another distraction, so we don't have to admit something even less appealing than repressed anger.

This means these days, whenever I feel anger the first thing I ask myself is whether there's something behind the anger I'm trying to ignore. I think about fear, hurt, grief and sadness and ask whether they're present and being repressed.

Reflecting on Anger and Rage

Do you ever display any overt or covert rage in your life? As I describe repressed anger can you see the ways in which you do the same thing? Are there any examples of you repeatedly biting your tongue over something happening before reaching a stage where you exploded? Do you ever make passive aggressive comments because you can't express your anger healthily? Do you ever sulk or give someone the silent treatment?

It is one of the most commonly repressed emotions so if you're unable to see it in yourself it's worth continuing to look for.

The Importance of Grief

Of all the emotions I've learnt about over the past few years, I think grief might be my favourite.

If you're anything like me you will have been raised to think grief is what we feel when someone dies. That's it. You might have been taught subconsciously that it should have a limited shelf-life and, if you went on to work in the corporate world, you will almost certainly have been taught it has a very limited shelf-life.

What's that, your mum has died? Corporate policy says you've got three days to grieve then we'll expect you back in the office firing on all cylinders, okay?

So, you're telling me your nan passed away during the night? It's only one day to grieve for grandparents, I'm afraid, and don't come back to me with any of that, *"but my nan was like my mum"* nonsense. It's one day and that's non-negotiable.

People die, we grieve, we get over it and we move on with life. Simple, right? I'm guessing you'd be shocked by now if I said it was that simple.

Again, the reality is very different from how many of us have been raised. Grief comes into our lives in all shapes and sizes. Of course we grieve for people we loved who have died, and we also grieve for people we loved who are no longer in our lives. We also grieve for lost ideas, lost possessions and lost versions of ourselves.

I grieve when I spend time with the little kids of my best friends. I play with them, talk to them about the world and laugh with them. They amaze me with their curiosity and wonder, with their playfulness and zest for life. And, after they've gone, I grieve for the family I was meant to have but, at the time of writing at least, isn't yet a part of my life.

I grieve for the little girl who would adore her daddy and the little boy whose hero I would be. I grieve for an imagined life that never materialised. A picture I'd created in my mind for over three decades. Discussing the idea of reality could fill an entire book, but in simple terms the stories we tell ourselves are our reality.

When those stories turn out to be untrue, we grieve for what we've lost.

I know grief now by the ache in my heart. A throbbing pain in the centre of my chest that I now understand and, more than anything, have compassion for the little boy who decided it was too much to feel, so shut it off along with all the other powerful emotions.

I understand why most of us do it. Why we choose to numb the world rather than feel it fully. It's often just too painful. Especially grief.

Once I learned what it was, it was incredible how often I'd experience a sensation and recognise it as grief when, for the 39 years that preceded it, I would either have repressed it entirely or labelled it as something else. Maybe depression, maybe sadness. But the thing about grief is it is layered. I'd cry and release an entire layer, thinking that was it, before coming back again a month later to feel the same thing again, maybe even deeper this time. I came to understand it as peeling off the layers of an onion that had built up throughout my life. One by one stripping them back to reveal more and more of the real me.

The pain was often almost too much to bear. My mind would do what it does best and try to take me away to a fantasy land so that I didn't have to experience it, but over time I learnt to bring myself back to my aching heart to continue the healing process.

The other way I recognise grief now is through the tears. Tears of grief are never quite the same as anything else. Not like tears of sadness or hurt. Not like fear. No, tears of grief make my entire body tremble. I shake. I can feel years of trauma breaking out of each cell of my body. Salty water streaming from my eyes and stinging my skin. Snot pouring out of my nose like I'm six months old again.

I can picture the life I thought I had. The life I thought I was meant to have. And I grieve for it because I lost it, and the loss is no less real than losing a close friend or family member to death. I grieve the lost parts of myself. The characters I'd developed over the years and depended on so much to get me through life. I grieve the relationships those characters had built as I watch them slowly drift away. The real me wants different relationships, and only those willing to lose the old parts of themselves are able to join me in the new world.

I don't blame those who aren't willing. To voluntarily choose to kill off the parts of your story that you've believed so long is the hardest part of this adventure. I'd say maybe even harder than having parts revealed as being untrue by someone else. In that case you can still choose to create a different story that gives you comfort, but that applies less when you're tearing your own story down.

If you choose to see who you really are and what your world really looks like, there's no hiding place anymore. We cannot change our lives without losing a part of ourselves, and when we lose a part we must grieve for it.

Anxiety, Insecurity and Fear

As you can imagine, there are entire books written about each of these emotions as well, so there's only so much we can cover here and it's worth grouping these fellas together for the purposes of this book.

You might be fortunate and already understand you experience anxiety, insecurity or fear. Or you might be like I was and have no idea they are having an impact on your life.

If you'd asked me years ago whether I was ever anxious, insecure or afraid, I would have told you in no uncertain terms I was not. I could see anxiety and insecurity running through my family, but it definitely wasn't something I suffered from.

As far as fear was concerned, I was the type of person who would overcome a fear of heights by walking over the top of the Sydney Harbour Bridge on an organised tour. Confront me with something to be afraid of and I would charge hand-in-hand with my personal development books and give you loads of quotes about fear not being real before running off the edge of a cliff.

The other twist keeping my anxiety from my consciousness was how I talked to myself about it. I would look at other people being worried about a £5 late payment charge on an online bill and struggle to see what they were concerned about. I had so many big problems to deal with in my life that small things were inconsequential. I was, though, worried about the big things. I just wasn't acknowledging the feeling as worry or anxiety.

Anxiety and insecurity, in particular, operate as stealth emotions. They are brilliant at disguising themselves as something else to avoid our gaze and prevent us feeling and processing them properly.

Do you ever feel like you can't just sit down without needing to get up to do something, or do you struggle to do one thing at a time, always being drawn to something else in the middle of a task?

That's anxiety.

When I look back at my old life, there were lots of red flags showing that I was experiencing anxiety and not dealing with it properly. On my first date when I was around 13 years old, I remember someone sitting around 10 seats away from me in the cinema shouting at me to stop bouncing my knee because it was shaking the entire place.

I used to bounce my knee constantly thinking it was perfectly normal, without realising it was a sign of anxiety.

The same goes for biting fingernails, not being able to sleep easily at night or always having things racing through your mind like a hamster on a wheel. All signs of anxiety that we're likely to be labelling as something else.

The incredible thing about anxiety is we often find ourselves in an anxious loop, feeling anxious about feeling anxious, which is part of the problem. I learnt during my adventure that my insomnia was basically caused by an anxiety loop. You might have experienced the same thing.

I would find that I couldn't get to sleep, usually because things were racing through my mind (anxiety). I would then beat myself up inside my head for not being able to sleep, often looking at my partner fast asleep in the bed next to me and being mean to myself because I couldn't sleep like she could sleep. This anxiety loop would go on for hours, with me slowly counting down how much time I had left if I fell asleep at that moment.

"Fall asleep now and you'll still get five hours' sleep."

[An hour of anxiety later]

"Fall asleep now and you'll still get four hours' sleep."

Have you ever experienced something similar?

I broke that cycle when one of my coaches, Ralph, asked me a very simple question. He said: *"If you get to lunch time and you're not hungry, do you beat yourself up for not being hungry and try to force yourself to eat, or do you just wait until you're hungry?"* *"I just wait"* I replied. *"So, why is it any different with sleep? We've been told a story that we're meant to be asleep between certain hours, then put ourselves in an anxiety loop, feeling anxious about feeling anxious, if we can't sleep at the time someone else said we should. If you feel anxious there's nothing wrong with that, just allow yourself to feel anxious, you'll sleep when you're ready."*

From that day I've never had a problem with insomnia. I still have the occasional night when I can't sleep straight away but when that happens these days I don't worry about it at all, I just do something else until my body tells me it's time to drift away.

Insecurity is another stealth emotion.

Are you driven to prove yourself to the world, to yourself or other people or, if you're really honest with yourself, do you care deeply what people think of you? That's insecurity.

Many people I know show clear signs of anxiety and insecurity and would never acknowledge it to themselves. The number of people I know who openly say the words, *"I don't care what anyone else thinks"* when the truth is the complete opposite is quite frightening, and sums up just how big the repressed emotion problem is in our society.

We experience fear most days of our lives, in a variety of big and small ways which, as with every other emotion, isn't a problem in itself. The problem is we've been taught since we were little kids not to be afraid. We're taught that feeling anxious or insecure is bad.

But what's wrong with those feelings?

Depression and Suicidal Thoughts

There are certain things in my new life that provide real tests to my commitment to be the real me; to speak what I truly believe and be true to myself. I have spent so many years trying to please others and burying what I really wanted to say for fear of what others think, that to stay committed to doing the opposite takes tough decisions most days.

This section constitutes one of those tests.

What I am about to say might upset you. In fact, I am fairly sure my views around depression and suicidal thoughts will upset someone at some point. But, if I want to stay true to myself, I have no option other than to talk to you about them.

We live in a world where many well-intentioned people regularly involve themselves in conversations about depression and suicide, often after a high-profile celebrity takes the devastating decision to end their life. These people decide it's their place to give advice to people who might be experiencing depression or thinking about killing themselves.

I believe with every fibre of my body that if those people have never experienced depression or had suicidal thoughts, or if they are not qualified to advise on those matters, no matter how well intentioned they are they should keep their opinions and advice to themselves.

I believe this because the problem with most people who like to stick their nose into a topic they don't understand is they do nothing other than make things worse.

As we have discussed, a large portion of the struggles we face in our adult life originate from deep-rooted feelings of shame planted in our childhood, repression of emotions we don't want to feel and a belief we're not good enough.

When we begin to experience depression and/or suicidal thoughts and well-intentioned people stick their nose in to tell us we've got everything to live for and have great lives full of people who love us, guess what message many of us hear? That not only are we ashamed of how we already feel about ourselves, but now we should also be ashamed of the very fact we feel depressed and/or suicidal. We are taught again by other adults that our emotions aren't acceptable.

I'm here to tell you something completely different and counter-intuitive. I'm here to tell you that if you ever feel depressed or suicidal it is an absolutely normal part of being human. The vast majority of people I speak to privately about their lives have experienced depression, suicidal thoughts, or both. As with most other issues in life, the problem is most people who experience these thoughts and feelings don't talk about them publicly, so the vicious cycle of us all thinking we're alone in having these very real human experiences continues.

There is nothing to be ashamed of about feeling depressed or suicidal.

It is also, though, crucial to say, as with all our misunderstood thoughts and emotions, they are just thoughts and emotions and we don't need to act on them. They exist to give us feedback about our lives and, if we learn to accept, allow and process them properly, are a perfectly healthy part of us.

Towards the end of the darkest days when I felt most depressed and was contemplating how to end my life, I reached a place I now encourage others to consider inhabiting. Ending our life is the final option available to any of us. It's absolute. If you are feeling suicidal, therefore, I'd suggest simply parking that solution to one side just while you consider what other options are available to you before you take that step.

Reflect on what is causing you to want to end everything and ask yourself whether dealing with that issue is, in fact, a more straightforward option than killing yourself. For example, you might want to commit suicide because you're in a relationship that makes you miserable and you can't see a way out of. Is it an option, then, to try ending that relationship and seeing whether you feel better on the other side, before jumping straight to suicide?

I took this approach and step by step removed all the things from my life that led to me wanting to end it all, while at the same time working on myself using the principles in this book. After doing that, I realised I was glad I hadn't gone straight to the end solution because once I'd dealt with the things in my life causing all the problems, I realised not only did I not want to end my life but, in fact, I love living it.

If you are feeling depressed or suicidal, I hope reading this book will help you to learn how to accept, allow and process your thoughts and emotions in a healthy way and, as we've discussed before, if you feel as though you need to please reach out to someone who can help.

Finding Someone to Help

If you have already found a coach or therapist to work with, I would highly recommend speaking to them frankly about any depression feelings or suicidal thoughts you experience.

If you don't have a coach or therapist, I would highly recommend finding one to discuss anything of this nature. Go back to Chapter 3 for my thoughts on the best way to choose someone to work with if you need to.

If you can't afford a coach or therapist, even after reviewing what you're spending your money on to see if you might be able to divert it to a more productive and healthy destination, and you feel you need to after reading the next section, I'd suggest contacting a free service in your country.

If you cannot find a service specialising in helping people with depression or suicidal thoughts, consider someone you can trust who is able to listen without necessarily feeling the need to fix your problems for you. What we often need is someone to listen to what we need to say.

Importantly, though, unless you have no other option, I would strongly recommend against sharing your depression or suicidal thoughts with anyone who is likely, unintentionally, to make things worse.

If the person you confide in is themselves not operating from a place of high self-worth, there is a good possibility they will make your problems about them, which could lead to you then having their worries and anxiety to add to your own.

I was raised with the world telling me a problem shared is a problem halved but, in my real-world experience, I usually found a problem shared was a problem multiplied by 10, because I'd find myself having to manage the emotions of whoever I'd shared my issues with rather than just being able to focus on my own.

This is, of course, a fine balance to strike. If you are in any doubt, though, please just talk to anyone you can.

Identifying Emotions

Now we've been through a few of the headline emotions, before we go any further it's worth pausing to make sure we are able to identify what we are feeling.

If you remember from my origins story, in one of my earliest therapy sessions I discovered I'd been repressing my emotions for so long I could no longer identify them. I had the extremes like depression and exhilaration, but everything in between was lost to me. I felt as though I had a thin film over my face preventing me from expressing feelings properly, and didn't know what was going on inside me.

While this might sound like an unusual step for us as grown-ups to do, I found it useful to take a step back to basics and look at a list of emotions to start linking them to experiences in my life which, slowly but surely, meant I was able to identify them before going to the next stage of learning how to process them.

Here are two charts showing non-exhaustive lists of understood and misunderstood emotions and feelings. Take a look through and see how many you can link to experiences in your life.

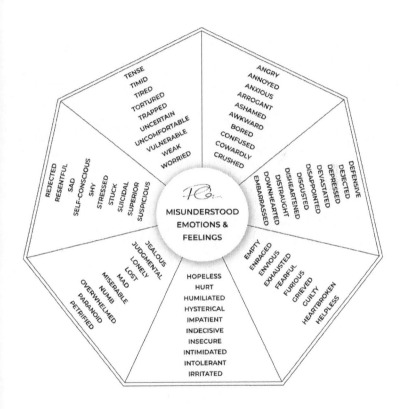

MISUNDERSTOOD
EMOTIONS &
FEELINGS

TENSE
TIMID
TIRED
TORTURED
TRAPPED
UNCERTAIN
UNCOMFORTABLE
VULNERABLE
WEAK
WORRIED

ANGRY
ANNOYED
ANXIOUS
ARROGANT
ASHAMED
AWKWARD
BORED
CONFUSED
COWARDLY
CRUSHED

DEFENSIVE
DEJECTED
DEPRESSED
DEVASTATED
DISAPPOINTED
DISGUSTED
DISHEARTENED
DISTRAUGHT
DOWNHEARTED
EMBARRASSED

REJECTED
RESENTFUL
SAD
SELF-CONSCIOUS
SHY
STRESSED
STUCK
SUICIDAL
SUPERIOR
SUSPICIOUS

JEALOUS
JUDGMENTAL
LONELY
LOST
MAD
MISERABLE
NUMB
OVERWHELMED
PARANOID
PETRIFIED

HOPELESS
HURT
HUMILIATED
HYSTERICAL
IMPATIENT
INDECISIVE
INSECURE
INTIMIDATED
INTOLERANT
IRRITATED

EMPTY
ENRAGED
ENVIOUS
EXHAUSTED
FEARFUL
FURIOUS
GRIEVED
GUILTY
HEARTBROKEN
HELPLESS

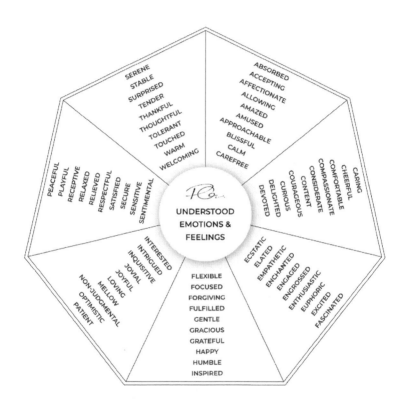

ABSORBED
ACCEPTING
AFFECTIONATE
ALLOWING
AMAZED
AMUSED
APPROACHABLE
BLISSFUL
CALM
CAREFREE

SERENE
STABLE
SURPRISED
TENDER
THANKFUL
THOUGHTFUL
TOLERANT
TOUCHED
WARM
WELCOMING

CARING
CHEERFUL
COMFORTABLE
COMPASSIONATE
CONSIDERATE
CONTENT
COURAGEOUS
CURIOUS
DELIGHTED
DEVOTED

PEACEFUL
PLAYFUL
RECEPTIVE
RELAXED
RELIEVED
RESPECTFUL
SATISFIED
SECURE
SENSITIVE
SENTIMENTAL

UNDERSTOOD EMOTIONS & FEELINGS

ECSTATIC
ELATED
EMPATHETIC
ENCHANTED
ENGAGED
ENGROSSED
ENTHUSIASTIC
EUPHORIC
EXCITED
FASCINATED

INTERESTED
INTRIGUED
INQUISITIVE
JOVIAL
JOYFUL
LOVING
MELLOW
NON-JUDGMENTAL
OPTIMISTIC
PATIENT

FLEXIBLE
FOCUSED
FORGIVING
FULFILLED
GENTLE
GRACIOUS
GRATEFUL
HAPPY
HUMBLE
INSPIRED

"Avoiding stress isn't the secret"

(Bruce Banner / The Avengers)

How to Process Misunderstood Emotions Healthily

After processing all of the preceding information it's important for us to discuss practical ways to accept, allow and process your emotions in a healthy way.

As Bruce Banner said, and as we've already talked about, avoiding our emotions isn't the secret to a peaceful life. As counter-intuitive as it might sound, the secret is to face them head on. To practice dealing with them. And it takes practice.

As I've said, our emotions are perfectly normal and healthy. All of them. There's nothing wrong with us becoming angry or anxious. No issue with us being jealous or full of self-pity. Often, it's the fact that we've experienced rage and labelled it as anger that adds to us repressing anger in the first place, creating a vicious cycle that's difficult to escape from. Anxiety avoided and repressed becomes an anxiety loop, with us feeling anxious about feeling anxious. Shame about jealousy or judging others leads to further repression and even more shame.

The solution, slowly over time, is to begin to feel and, if necessary, express our emotions healthily as they arise. A very practical way to do that is to simply say whatever we feel out loud. To say, *"I feel angry"* whenever the feeling comes up, or, *"I feel anxious"*. The fact we're acknowledging our emotions in itself helps to accept and allow them.

Despite what many self-help books might say, though, it's not always necessary for us to express those emotions to someone else if they have arisen in connection with their behaviour. Ultimately, our emotions are our emotions and they are not caused by anyone else, so unless we feel for some reason it's necessary to be assertive in some way and tell someone about our feelings, for example when we are protecting our boundaries (see the next chapter for more on that), we can process our emotions privately.

The Power of Free Writing

As I've said before, writing with pen or pencil on paper has healing powers beyond the simple act of writing. The thoughts and emotions that bounce around inside our bodies are just that until we force our systems to articulate what we're feeling or thinking into words, either spoken or written.

Which means an extremely powerful way to process any emotions arising inside you is to take a pen and your notebook and just start to write. Don't hold back. Allow everything you think and feel to pour out onto the page in a confidential pact between you and the old tree in front of you.

If you really need to when you're finished you can always set fire to whatever you've written so no-one else can ever see it. Which means you're completely free to say whatever you want without the fear of anyone judging you or anything you say hurting anyone else's feelings.

It's one of the most liberating things I've ever learnt to do.

Having a Good Cry

How often do you cry?

Without wanting to be sexist and generalise too much, I think it's probably fair to say if you're reading this around the time I wrote it it's likely you're more comfortable crying if you're a woman than if you're a man. There are, of course, always exceptions to that general stereotype and I hope as the years progress we can stop there being any distinction between genders when it comes to releasing our emotions through tears.

I realised through doing this work that after turning around 10 years old I reserved crying for special occasions. The deaths and funerals of my four grandparents or the death of a pet.

Once I became an adult crying became even more rare, again usually reserved for the death of special people in my life and a few times when I reached breaking point in my marriage.

These days, though, I cry often. I feel the emotion build in my chest and find myself saying inside my head, *"I need a cry"*.

It might be when my family visits me in a foreign country and head home after a few happy days together, or when I have to leave new or old friends after bonding over laughter and drinks. I might cry when I think of my ex-wife and the life we were meant to have, or my old life plan and what it was meant to be.

I cry after seeing my beautiful niece and nephew and holding them close, and when I miss my gorgeous little dog who was adopted by my parents a lifetime ago.

But why I cry isn't really as important as the fact that I do and, even more so, that I'm happy to admit and talk about it. It still crushes me when I see our society telling children to stop crying. It still hurts me deep inside when I see small boys being told to act like men.

Regardless of how advanced we think we are as humans, we still fundamentally and subconsciously teach each other the same things that we have done for generations. It's easier for me to write about crying than it is to actually cry in front of my 13-year-old nephew because, no matter what I say, deep down inside me I'm still programmed that men shouldn't cry.

I can still observe my ego and my intellect trying to distract me from that overwhelming pain in my chest. *"No, wait, don't feel that, look over here at this big shiny thought about being interviewed on a big TV show. Isn't that better? Doesn't that feel good? That's it, come over here on Graham Norton's big red couch and tell a joke that makes everyone laugh. That's right, good boy."*

I then have to gently bring my mind back to where I am. Sitting in a room by myself with a pain in my chest. No wonder I started burying it when I was a little boy. It hurts. The pain and sadness are often overwhelming, but I thank my ego for all of the years it helped to distract me when I couldn't stand the heartache, before I was able to feel whatever I really needed to feel.

I have to battle that programming every day and, as time goes on, it becomes easier. I know now how good it feels to allow my body to process the emotions it feels rather than pushing them down and repressing them based on generations of programming. It's time for us to change that programming once and for all.

So, as well as free writing, I'd strongly encourage you, whatever your gender, to open yourself up to the idea of being able to release your emotions physically through your tears. I've found it to be completely liberating to feel my entire body shake as years of emotion are literally shaken out of my cells, and I've had the very humbling experience of witnessing others release years of emotions through the safe environment of a coaching call.

Whatever you think about crying now, especially if you're programmed like I was to hold back your tears as much as humanly possible, give yourself the present while doing these next exercises of sitting somewhere in private and, if you feel tears coming, don't hold them back. I promise you won't regret it.

✎ Exercise (Dorothy) – Part 1

Go back to the Malcolm exercise in Chapter 7 where you first processed your emotions around the childhood events from the Kenneth and Elsie exercises.

Now we've talked in more depth about some of the misunderstood emotions and looked at the charts earlier in this chapter, go back to what you've already written about your childhood experiences and see if there's anything you can add about your emotions at the time or since.

If you struggled to think of more than a few emotions when doing the earlier exercise, look at the chart to prompt you. There's nothing to be ashamed of if you need to look at that chart. I needed it and the vast majority of people I work with benefit hugely from learning a whole new vocabulary for the way they feel.

Be as honest as you possibly can without judging anything that comes up. Do you feel resentment towards a parent, or to someone else you love? Great, write it down. Do you feel anger or rage towards a partner or friend? Brilliant, get it all out onto the page.

A good tip to use here is to look out for something I mentioned briefly in Chapter 2. Whenever we're looking for how we honestly feel about something, our instinctive system usually tells us immediately. The problem, though, is the team on the control deck inside our head has been trained for so long to repress emotions that often our gut will throw up an answer and the brain will catch it, put it through our PR machine and try to interpret it in a way that fits how we want the world to see us.

So, for example, if a feeling of resentment towards our parents or children comes up, our brain might immediately say that it can't be right because we've spent so long being programmed that feelings like resentment aren't acceptable. It's incredible how often I'll ask someone how they feel about something and their first response is, *"well, I definitely don't feel angry"* or *"jealousy just came up but it's absolutely not that"*.

It's as though our gut instinct tells us we feel angry, jealous, resentful or any number of the other misunderstood emotions and when the team on the control deck receives the message, its solution is to craftily say: *"Just say we* **don't** *feel the emotion that just came up, that'll deal with it."*

Up until now, that's probably worked. From here forward, though, if that happens I want you to go with whatever came up, even if your brain is telling you it's definitely not that feeling. Ask yourself, what if it is? Remember there aren't any right or wrong answers and no emotions are bad, so what if you do feel resentment towards someone you've been programmed you shouldn't feel resentment towards? It's a perfect opportunity to properly process a perfectly normal feeling that's probably been repressed for years.

Just start writing and don't stop until it's all out. Let every single piece of emotion you've kept bottled up inside you for years spill out through the pen onto the paper. Remember you never need to show this work to anyone else, it only exists for you to process feelings that are likely to have been bottled up inside for decades, so make sure you give yourself plenty of time and space to do this because it might bring up things you don't expect and you may need time to rest afterwards.

If once you've finished you don't want to risk anyone seeing what you've written, burn the paper in a safe way (I don't want you blaming me for burning down your home, so please do this carefully if you do it, and do it outside if at all possible).

If I feel as though something I need to process is going to be explosive and not for future reference, I'll write it on loose paper rather than in my notebook so I can easily destroy it without damaging the thoughts I want to keep for prosperity. I highly recommend you do the same thing if you want to avoid the risk of anyone else seeing what you write.

Notes

✎ Exercise (Dorothy) – Part 2

I want to add a part two to the above exercise for completeness. So far, we've talked about traumatic and other Programming Experiences from when we were kids, but we haven't really discussed how those experiences continue through life when, of course, they do.

As part two of the same exercise, I want you to think of any – and every – life-defining moment you've had that you may not have ever processed properly from an emotional perspective.

It might be getting married or divorced, having kids, getting a big job or being fired, someone dying or a company you built closing. It could be absolutely anything that meant something big to you, and includes anything that plays on your mind even though it might have taken place years ago. For me that included my marriage and divorce, disputes with former employees and contractors and numerous other things, some which still pop up from time to time out of nowhere to be processed.

Take some time to write down every one of those experiences, then go through the same exercise of free writing about all your emotions and thoughts linked to them. Again, don't hold anything back. This is your opportunity to get all the things off your chest you might never have dealt with before.

It's important to also note that these exercises are not to be used only as one-off tools. I will still fairly often take a pen and paper and do a free-writing exercise to express fully any emotions I'm feeling about any given situation, and I won't stop writing until I feel as though the emotions have fully dissipated and I've fully accepted them.

Being able to say whatever we want without any risk of hurting someone's feelings or there being other consequences is a really powerful way of processing whatever we feel in that moment.

Over time and with practice it becomes easier to simply sit with our emotions and feel the sensations within our body. Remember, after all, they're really just chemical reactions with a lifespan of 90 seconds.

Notes

The Emotional Onion Layers

It's important to note that after what is possibly decades of repressing your emotions about any number of life-defining events going all the way back to your childhood, it's unlikely you'll be able to process them all in one sitting, whether that's talking them through with a therapist or coach, or doing a free-writing exercise.

As I briefly mentioned earlier, I like to think of processing repressed emotions as peeling an onion.

I picture whatever life event is troubling me as a big onion that comes up to visit me, often haunting my thoughts for days and nights until I sit down and process the emotions around whatever the experience was. When I process the emotions fully, it's like taking the outside layer from the onion and, when I do that, the tear-inducing life-event vegetable disappears for a while.

It might go missing for a day, a week, a month or a year but, sooner or later, if I'd repressed enough emotions about the event, the big juicy onion will come back to me. I'll just be walk-ing along one day and realise something has been playing on my mind again for the past few days. As soon as I notice that happening, I take out my trusted pen and paper and free-write everything that's coming up, whether or not it's exactly the same as I felt last time I did the exercise about the same event.

I don't judge the emotions or thoughts and I don't question anymore how many times I need to do the exercise before the event has been properly processed. If the experience or event comes back into my mind for any reasonable period without disappearing, I just accept it's time to write again. These days, I also accept I have no idea whether the event has been processed properly each time I write about it, I just express what I need to express at the time for it to leave my mind, then forget about it unless it revisits on another occasion.

Accepting the emotional onion is all part of accepting and allowing our emotions for what they are. Some things will disappear after being processed once, others will keep returning on many occasions. There are no right or wrong answers to any of this and no rule as to which events will be easier to process fully. Some of the bigger events in my life disappeared from my mind after processing them once or twice while other seemingly smaller experiences come back time and time again.

One thing to watch out for is if something does persistently return after you've processed it. Ask yourself gently and kindly whether you are being truly honest with yourself about the emotions you're experiencing because the emotional onion might only be coming back because you haven't fully understood what's behind the experience. Maybe you're feeling resentment or jealousy you don't want to admit, or you're furious or afraid but can't see it. Take some time to reflect on all the possible emotions and be completely honest with yourself without judgment.

Remember, no-one else needs to ever see what you write, and our thoughts and emotions are all perfectly normal and natural so there's nothing to be ashamed of regardless of what we think or feel about anything.

Which takes us to a story about my dog.

Be More Like Tilly

One of the most heart-breaking things about leaving my old life was that six months before I left my marriage my wife had convinced me, against my better judgment, that we should buy a puppy. I tried to convince her – as did some of her closest friends – that it wasn't a good idea but, as with many things back then, I didn't defend my boundaries strongly enough (we'll get into that in detail in the next chapter) which resulted in us buying a beautiful snow-white West Highland Terrier, who we named Tilly.

Completely predictably after not wanting us to buy this gorgeous little baby girl puppy, she and I became best friends within about an hour of her moving into our house. Which also quickly became her house that we just happened to live in.

I could tell you endless stories about my love affair with Tilly but, to save this turning into a novel about a man's relationship with a dog, I'll keep it to one story.

After our separation, my ex-wife moved abroad and we both agreed without ever getting into any serious debate that if we were to do that test where we stood at each end of a bridge, put the dog in the middle and asked her to choose who she wanted to go to, she would just keep following me back to where I was standing without spending a second in the middle of the bridge. I can imagine her walking alongside me saying, *"Are we playing a game, Dad?"* rather than even contemplating there ever being a choice about which direction she'd walk in.

I'm convinced Tilly thinks I'm her real dad which could make sense because she never met her dad so has no idea what he's meant to look like. As a puppy she would often bring a bone in from the garden covered in mud that was bigger than her head, and try to put it in my mouth which, to me at least, was a sign of her true love.

Tilly and I lived together for six months before further changes in my life led to me selling everything and heading to Bali for a while, before setting up camp in Spain. During that time, my parents decided they'd rather look after their grand-dog instead of a dog minder having her, so she took up residence in their house.

When I returned from Spain after around six months abroad and jokingly mentioned to my mum that I might take Tilly back, she looked me straight in the eyes and said: *"You. Will. Not."* At that point I knew my baby girl had enchanted more members of the family with her charm, and we all knew my new lifestyle meant Tilly was better off living full time with her grandparents, who were now very much in love with her, than she would be moving in with me every time I returned home.

Well, I say we all knew she'd be better off that way, but I'm not sure Tilly is in full agreement.

The point of this story is how Tilly behaves whenever I go to my parents' house to visit them and her. Even as I tell you this it fills me with joy and happiness. Regardless of when I last saw her, when she even senses I'm approaching the house she goes insane. She barks, she does that jumping-spinning thing that only dogs can do where they rotate a full 360 degrees without touching the floor. Then, when she finally gets past the door to find me, she jumps all over me until I can finally sit in a chair and she can lick my face and give me kisses for about 20 minutes, just to remind me how in love we are. And we are very much in love.

Now, if anyone dares to get between us in our regular ritual of pure, unadulterated love, she is not happy at all. If I attempt to kiss someone sitting in a chair in my parents' lounge before I've sat for our usual kiss, she jumps up and squeezes her face between mine and whoever I was trying to greet to lick my face. Once she's on my knee, if anyone attempts to come near me she'll bark at them, kiss my face again and, if she's feeling extremely threatened will, very occasionally, show her teeth just to demonstrate how serious she is about keeping others away from me.

Whenever anyone else witnesses this routine, they roll around laughing at how jealous she is of anyone else trying to take any of my attention away from her. God help us all whenever my auntie's dog is around who is one of my best friends and demands an equal amount of love.

We all laugh at this little bundle of pure jealousy. If you looked up the definition of jealous there would be a beautiful little picture of Tilly right next to it.

And guess what Tilly does immediately after displaying this emotion we've all been taught is unacceptable in human life.

Nothing. She does absolutely nothing. She feels this pure emotion running through her body, she processes it then, when it's all passed through her veins, she just gets on with her day. She usually wants me to play with her for a few minutes before chasing a bird in the garden and having a poo on the grass.

I've never once walked into a room after one of her regular jealous episodes and seen her beating herself up for feeling jealous. She's never once come up to me and said: *"Dad, you know before when I was jealous of other people trying to get your attention? Well, I feel really ashamed of myself now because I know I'm not meant to feel jealousy, am I?"*

Tilly doesn't do that because she hasn't got a big super computer brain in her head that's been programmed full of nonsense about how some of her emotions are bad and shouldn't be felt, so she just feels them and gets on with her day.

Now, I'm not saying when we feel jealousy or any other emotion we need to express it out loud in quite the same way as Tilly. What I am saying is that there's no need for us to be ashamed of any feelings we have. They are just normal feelings that arise in every human and should be treated accordingly.

The key is to be more like Tilly. Although maybe without the pooing on the garden bit. I'm not sure I'm ready for letters of complaint from your partner or neighbours saying you've started to shit outside because of my book.

Changing a Duvet Cover

Do you call them duvets where you live? If you're reading this in the UK I'd guess you do, unless there's some other name for them in other parts of this weird little island I'm not aware of.

If you don't call them duvets, I'm talking about the big thick blanket thing we put over beds in cold countries to keep us warm in winter. The thin cover we put over them we call duvet covers, for obvious reasons.

If none of that means anything to you, it's probably best to just do a quick YouTube search of 'changing a duvet cover' or something like that so you have some idea of what I'm about to say. It's basically another analogy for dealing with emotions that the experts and scientists aren't likely to use but I think works, so I'm going to stick with it. I'll get back to superhero analogies soon enough.

If you've ever done it, you'll know changing a duvet cover is traditionally a tricky task. It's something a small percentage of the population have mastered while others have no idea how to do and talk about it as though it's some sort of voodoo magic.

A mate of mine mentioned a few days ago on a podcast to which I contribute, that one of the things he hates in life is changing his duvet cover. He said he just can't get it. He's heard all the tips about turning it inside out and grabbing the corners, but no matter what he does he always ends up in a massive mess.

As he was talking it dawned on me that changing a duvet cover is just like dealing with our emotions.

When we come across something in life we don't like or we're not good at, our natural instinct is to avoid it. I see people talking about misunderstood emotions in the same way. If something makes people anxious they say the best thing we can do for those people is to stop that thing happening, whether it's clapping in theatres or making loud noises in shops. Those people are well intentioned but, ultimately, have got the complete wrong end of the stick.

The issue with changing a duvet cover is we might only do it once every two weeks, if we're being generous. If we don't like doing it, we're likely to put it off to maybe once a month. That means the thing we hate to do we only do 12 times each year and, each time we do it, we struggle so much with it we create a story around it about how much we hate it and can't do it, so we avoid it even more.

Just like we do with misunderstood emotions.

The trick, though, is when my mate struggles to change his duvet cover the best thing he could do is put four hours aside one day and just keep changing the cover over and over again, practising it just like he might practice something he really wants to get good at, until by the end of the four hours he is an absolute master at it, making YouTube videos for other struggling middle-aged men.

He can do that every month, slowly changing the story in his mind from, *"I hate changing duvet covers because I'm rubbish at it"* to *"I'm incredible at changing duvet covers and it's an absolute breeze of a job"*.

Which is what we are best doing with our emotions. The only way we can properly learn to accept, allow and process our feelings is to identify them and face them as often as possible. Learning to understand them and what they're trying to do for us rather than treating them as some alien being to be pushed away and be ashamed of is the path to peace and contentment.

"Sometimes...and that's okay"

The penultimate trick I want to share with you before we move on to discussing needs, wants and boundaries is another language masterpiece to add to your tool box. This can be used for emotions as well as many other things in life.

Often when we're describing things, we do so by making them permanent. So, for example, we'll say something like, *"I get really pissed off with that bastard"* or *"I just feel so much resentment towards that bitch"* and, once we've had that thought or felt that emotion, we'll try to repress it and become ashamed of it because of our programming that it's not okay to think or feel in that way.

A good way to help to overcome that programming is to gently start adding the word *"sometimes"* to the start of the sentence and *"and that's okay"* to the end. So, the first example would become, *"I sometimes get really pissed off with that bastard, and that's okay"* and the second becomes: *"I sometimes just feel so much resentment towards that bitch, and that's okay."*

By changing our language, even if we're just doing it inside our heads, we're slowly retraining our brain to understand, first, that the emotions or thoughts aren't permanent, they're just something we think or feel sometimes and, second, that it's okay to think or feel these things, regardless of what they are.

It's another tool to add to the 'Be Kind To Yourself' program and is extremely powerful when used regularly. Over the past few years I've slowly trained my brain to process the vast majority of my thoughts and feelings in this way and it's been life changing.

I'm not a saint and don't ever expect to be able to do it all the time but, whenever I catch myself forgetting to do it, I just remind myself I'm a flawed human being and I'm slowly retraining my brain after 38 years of programming to think in a different way.

Which takes us to the last point to note on this topic.

I'm Always Angry

I couldn't leave this chapter without talking more about The Incredible Hulk.

If you like superhero movies and want some more light-hearted training to do outside the exercises in this book, I'd recommend following the story of The Hulk through the Marvel movies, watching them in order. As I've said, what to the untrained eye looks like a story about a big green monster is actually an incredibly deep story based around everything on these pages.

After the Ed Norton Hulk movie I've mentioned, our most unusual of superheroes returns in the first Avengers movie, imaginatively called *The Avengers*, and his new mates can't understand how Bruce Banner has managed to keep his oversized friend in check in recent times while hidden away in the chaotic city of Calcutta. They speculate it must be by avoiding stress, doing yoga or something similar, prompting his quote about the secret not being avoiding stress.

He keeps his secret to himself (following a little blip in the story arc) until later in the movie while heading into a battle with aliens from another dimension still in his tiny human scientist form. Captain America says something like, *"maybe it's time to get angry"* – to which he gives the most mind-blowing response that I want to stick with you whenever you think of any of the misunderstood emotions that might form a regular part of your life.

"That's my secret... I'm always angry"

Bruce Banner learns through his adventure, after spending years trying to repress a part of him and it repeatedly rising up anyway as rage, that the secret is to accept the very thing he was trying to reject. *'I'm always angry'*. Anger is such a natural part of us and many of us, including me, have been raised in environments in which anger was such a repressed emotion our relationship with it became completely dysfunctional. It was the same for me with anxiety.

So, for any of the misunderstood emotions that tend to stay with us more often than not, if the *"sometimes"* tool I've mentioned feels like you're trying to fool yourself when in reality you know deep down it's far more often than 'sometimes' you feel a certain way, the next best thing to do is accept you always feel that way, just beneath the surface.

These days, as often as I can, I remind myself I'm just like Bruce Banner. I'm always angry and I'm always anxious. They're my most regular companions of all the misunderstood emotions, so I just accept they're always knocking around somewhere.

They can be bubbling under the surface at any point without me really realising, so if I just acknowledge their existence and remind my system it's absolutely okay for them to be there, we don't have any problems.

They're just emotions, after all, they can't hurt anyone. As long as I don't try to repress them I never turn into The Hulk anymore.

After we've become comfortable with them always being there, we might be able to take another step by gently noticing whether they are, in fact, always there, or in reality they're just there quite often. If that's the case, we can begin to change the story to us being *'often'* angry, anxious or any other emotion. As time passes, we might find we can then, step by step, comfortably and gently find our way to *'sometimes'* feeling that way.

Remembering, at whatever stage we're at, to be kind to ourselves and remember it's all okay.

Remember the Other Side

Let's go back for a second to Chapter 5 when we first discussed how we learn to repress emotions in childhood. Do you remember the analogy about water coming from a mixer tap and us not being able to turn down the hot water without also turning down the cold?

In practice, that means while it's crucial we learn to accept, allow and process our misunderstood emotions, it's likely we're also repressing the emotions we assume we understand, without intending or wanting to.

Which means while we've been shutting down anger, anxiety and fear for decades, we've also been closing off joy, happiness, excitement and love without realising. It's just as important, then, to make sure we're accepting, allowing and processing fully whenever we want to experience any of the understood emotions.

I appreciate this might sound less credible than the idea of repressing misunderstood emotions. Why would we not want to feel total joy, right?

Think about it like this. A common expression I've heard uttered by adults throughout my life is to *"let your hair down"*, which is usually associated with getting drunk or taking drugs to blow off the cobwebs of daily life and have some fun. But what does that really mean? As far as I can see now, it means that to be our true selves in a fun and outgoing way, we need to add harmful chemical substances to our bodies. To really experience joy, excitement and fun, we need some outside help.

The big question is, if we need to let our hair down where did we learn to put our hair up in the first place?

As you read that, can you think of times in your adult life you consciously repress a fun part of yourself because of the way others react to it? Do you ever want to totally let go but can't because someone tells you to 'grow up' or 'act your age'? Most men I know, including me until a couple of years ago, wouldn't dream of dancing sober for fear of being told they're making a fool of themselves, their partner or their kids.

While it's key to learn to identify and accept our misunderstood emotions, it's really important we don't overlook the need to start allowing our joy, happiness, excitement and love to come back to life as well.

Sitting With Our Feelings

Once we've learnt to identify our emotions, understand and accept them, the next stage in our adventure is to simply be able to sit with them without any examination being needed.

Consider for a few moments how much we're taught in society to examine and dwell on emotions such as sadness, depression, anxiety and anger, yet we don't do the same with happiness.

We don't find ourselves feeling happy one day and spend hours worrying over why we feel so happy. We just accept it and get on with our day.

Now that you know what you know about the misunderstood emotions, ask yourself why we can't treat all emotions the same.

Once we can truly accept all feelings as being an equally valid part of human existence, we can ultimately reach a point where, when any emotion comes up inside us, we simply notice it and observe how it feels inside our body. Experience the physical emotion of anxiety for what it is. Feel anger surging through our veins. Allow sadness or depression to be what they are.

I woke up a few days ago and, out of nowhere, noticed I was feeling a little depressed. Whereas in the past I would have started to feel anxious about that depression, worrying about where it was coming from and what was wrong, instead I was able to simply notice it, shrug my shoulders and think to myself, *"sometimes I feel depressed and that's okay"*.

Then I just got on with my day while being kind to myself. I allowed myself to sit with the emotion and for it to just be.

Just like Tilly. Although I managed to resist the urge to have a shit in the garden.

The Pesky Brain

When you begin to implement all these ideas into your life, it's absolutely crucial to remember your existing system has been programmed the way it is for decades.

Unless you've already started doing some sort of self-exploration work, your entire life up to this point has been programming you to live and think the way you do, and to believe everything you've believed until now.

When we try to do new things, our pesky brains and the team inside our control deck don't want to give up the old ways of doing things lightly, bearing in mind they've been serving you well and meeting your needs for years (more on that in the next chapter).

You are likely to find, then, that if you try to observe or sit with emotions you've previously repressed and ignored because of how painful they might be, your team in the control deck will implement whatever tricks it can to keep you in your thinking brain and away from your emotions.

The trick here is to keep going back to the 'Be Kind to Yourself' program and, rather than telling your control deck team off for trying to distract you, just thank them for what they're trying to do and gently ask your thoughts to come back to focussing on your emotions. It's important to do this in a kind and gentle way and to keep practising it until it becomes easier to sit with emotions, while acknowledging it's bound to take some time to change how your system wants to deal with these things having done it a different way for so long.

Be kind to yourself and don't expect to be able to do all of this overnight. As with everything else in this book, the best way to make changes that last is by taking one small step at a time.

One of the main keys to successfully negotiating this part of life is to make sure you don't get stuck at either end of the spectrum – both toxic positivity and wallowing in our misunderstood emotions aren't particularly healthy – so the aim is to find a balance between the two, enabling us to accept and process our misunderstood emotions fully without getting stuck in them.

Remember emotions are, at their core, just chemical reactions with a normal life span of 90 seconds, which means they only have a limited amount of energy. If we move towards a misunderstood emotion and go deeper into it when we feel it, rather than running away and trying to repress it, it's more likely the energy will dissipate much faster than if we try to pretend it doesn't exist.

You're an Animal

Have you ever seen an animal in the wild processing a traumatic event?

If you're anything like me, your answer to that question will either be *"no"* or *"maybe, but I didn't pay any real attention"*.

Dr. Peter A. Levine discovered a few decades ago that wild animals recover from trauma by going into physical spasms of their core and limbs. They literally shake the trauma out of their cells. For whatever reason, though, us humans decided this wasn't for us at some point during our evolution. Maybe it's time to bring it back.

I've discovered that while understanding, accepting and processing our emotions in the ways I've described is important and powerful, given at heart we're just animals it's really important we physically process and release our emotions as well.

This can mean anything from screaming into a pillow to punching hell out of a punch bag to roaring at the sky in the woods to going for a run, and everything in between. The important thing is to let out what's been building up inside, probably for decades, in whatever way feels instinctively right to us.

Do you ever feel so angry or frustrated you just want to scream at the top of your lungs, but you don't because that just isn't the done thing for us sophisticated and domesticated humans? Guess what? The best thing you can do is go with your instincts and let it all out.

I often hear stories of people absolutely losing their shit with family members or friends who they've been bottling things up around for years and, while I wouldn't necessarily recommend doing that, the principle of release is a good one.

If you can find a way that works for you to let everything out of your system in a healthy way, I highly recommend you do it. We're all just animals, after all.

While beyond the scope of this book, largely because I'm only just beginning looking into these areas myself, if you are interested in physical ways of releasing trauma, it could be worth looking up the work of Dr. Levine and the world around it.

Reminder:

Being kind to yourself is the key to everything.

12

NEEDS, WANTS AND BOUNDARIES

"I'd go with you, but I don't want to"

(Weasel / Deadpool)

Meeting Our Needs

As we began discussing in Chapter 6, as humans we all share certain needs that, whether we like it or not, will be met one way or another by our extremely talented systems.

While there are many needs we all have to different degrees, such as the need for security, affection and intimacy, the majority of them fall within the core needs we've already looked at.

As a reminder, they are the need for:

- Certainty or control
- Uncertainty or variety

- Significance or ego
- Love and connection

And, once the core needs are met, we have the need for growth and contribution.

When thinking about these needs, it's important to remember the team we have operating our complex system in the control deck in our head. That team, from the moment we were born, was acutely aware of its responsibility to make sure our needs are met, which is its number one priority.

That results in the strange situation whereby even though for most of our lives we are not consciously aware of these needs, and even though we are, therefore, not trying to meet them, they are being met.

The problem is when our needs are met subconsciously they are often met in unhealthy ways. That's where the trouble starts.

Our Practical Needs

In addition to our core human needs, the challenges life throws at us mean we also have practical needs that must be met in order to survive the jungle of Planet Earth.

Those practical needs can be anything from being able to sing karaoke in our favourite bar to making sure people listen to us when we need to be heard. Just like our human needs, our team in the control deck has a particular skill to make sure we meet our practical needs as well.

It's time to talk about our multiple personalities again.

Discovering More Personalities

How did you get on with the first stage of the multiple personality exercise in Chapter 6? If you haven't done it yet, now is a good time to catch up before we go any further.

If you have already got a list of your personalities, it's time for me to share a couple more of mine with you after first sharing a little tip.

Splitting Personalities

You might think it's already enough that you've discovered the only personality you had is now split into several others, but there's also a good chance the new versions of you can be split into more characters.

As I worked my way through this exercise over a number of years, I continued to have breakthrough after breakthrough about who I really am and the different versions of me my team in the control deck had created in order to deal with life.

One of those breakthroughs was a realisation that some of the characters I'd identified were actually more than one personality, so I'd recommend you go back over your first list and ask yourself whether any of the personalities you've identified could be split into more than one.

Light and Dark Copey

I introduced you to Copey earlier.

When I first did this work, he felt to me as though he was just one personality. When I contemplated the next parts of the exercise, though, I realised he was actually two people. I have a Light Copey and a Dark Copey.

The Copey we've already discussed is Light Copey, so it's time to meet Dark Copey.

Introducing Dark Copey

When I was thinking about Copey and whether or not I like him, I realised there are parts of him I like and parts I don't. When I thought more about the parts I don't, it dawned on me that part is the separate character, who I now refer to as Dark Copey.

Dark Copey typically doesn't appear until after 2am on a night out when I've consumed a large amount of alcohol. When I look back over my old life now, I can see the moment on each night when he came from the shadows and took the mic from Light Copey. I think if you asked my friends who witnessed that phase of my life, they'd all be able to tell you about the two different characters, as well as the moment in the night the handover of the mic took place.

While Light Copey is fun, cheeky and happy, meeting all my human needs by being charismatic and inclusive, Dark Copey has a different role altogether. The dark version existed solely to keep me on nights out that in most universes had died long before. He would watch a night fading and grab the mic to ensure I stayed out partying for as many hours as anyone would serve me drinks, while convincing as many people as possible to continue drinking with us regardless of any consequences.

Character Traits

Where to start with Dark Copey? He never wants the party to end, is a pain in the arse, wild, dangerous, manipulative and full of alcohol. And when I say full, I mean he takes the four drinks Little Paul had and the 10 doubles that Light Copey had and decides that's nowhere near enough so orders a bottle of vodka or two and 10 Jägerbombs to keep everyone active. He doesn't give a fuck what you think or who you are (and I allowed him to write this paragraph himself).

Triggers

Dark Copey's trigger was very simple. He took control of the mic when a night out was ending and I didn't want to go home.

Human Needs Being Met

He met my needs for certainty or control, significance or ego and uncertainty and variety. The only thing missing from Light Copey's repertoire was love and connection, because Dark Copey couldn't care less if anyone was with him or not. If no-one would stay out to help him distract us from real life, he'd stay by himself and find total strangers to party with.

We'll come back to the reason Dark Copey was developed in addition to Light Copey. Before then I want to introduce you to another of my dark characters.

Introducing Bane

You've already met Bane through my origin story. He's my rage-filled personality, named after the villain from Batman, who would typically take the mic for very brief periods of time, usually only long enough to throw a glass at a wall or something similarly dramatic, dangerous and damaging. He is the inevitable partner to my people-pleaser character and usually grabs the mic from that character only for a few moments before handing it to my shame-filled character.

Character Traits

Bane was rageful, powerful, intense and energetic. He is not a character I would cross under any circumstances.

Triggers

Bane would take the mic when my anger had been repressed for so long the bucket had filled to the brim and was ready to overflow. Whatever big or small trigger happened to take place at that moment would be enough for him to take the mic.

Human Needs Being Met

Bane absolutely nailed two needs for me, the need for certainty or control and the need for significance or ego.

When he took the mic there was absolutely no doubt about who was in control at that moment, and my level of significance went through the roof. There might not be a better example of our control deck finding ways to meet our needs subconsciously and in unhealthy ways than Bane.

We'll talk more about that shortly.

Identifying Practical Needs

Now you've seen a couple more of my personalities and are hopefully getting the hang of the exercise, it's time to identify the practical reasons our control deck created these versions of us in the first place. It's important to do this because, as you might have realised, some of our personalities can be very different while helping us meet the same human needs.

Discovering the practical reason for their creation is, therefore, crucial for us to understand why they exist.

The key here is to ask yourself what each character you've found does for you in the real world. What is their specific role in practical terms?

When I reflected on Dark Copey I realised he was created to keep me on nights out as a distraction from having to deal with the emotions of going back to a home life in which I wasn't happy. It was as simple as that.

Back in my old life I would always say I stayed out until 7am drinking because I was having such a good time and, while that was occasionally the truth, when I look back for the vast majority of the time the night out I was on had died much earlier when Light Copey had given up the mic and when most of my friends had gone home.

I remember very little of the times Dark Copey had the mic, which I think now is because his very existence was for me to forget my life, so why would he share his memory with me? Plus, of course, he'd usually drank about four times my bodyweight in vodka and Jack Daniels, which doesn't help with remembering things.

Bane existed to make me feel heard. When I was repressing my anger it was usually at the expense of not saying the things I really wanted to say. I would bottle up so many things and bite my lip constantly in a misguided attempt to keep the peace or avoid hurting someone's feelings, usually my partner's, and by the time he took the mic his job was just to get it all off my chest before the repressed anger forced my rib cage to implode.

✎ Exercise – Part 1

Now it's your turn.

Add a fifth column to your spreadsheet, go through each of your personalities and add what practical need in your life each one was meeting for you. If it met more than one practical need, put all of them.

You've seen the darker examples of Bane and Dark Copey and, to add to that from a lighter perspective, Light Copey existed to do things as simple as sing karaoke and dance. He was my only character who would really do those things. Cope existed to get me through difficult situations or business meetings, usually when I felt really uncomfortable or when my back was against the wall.

List everything each character does for you, whether or not it seems small or whether or not another character does the same thing.

Notes

✎ Exercise – Part 2

Part two of this exercise is very simple. Add one more column to your spreadsheet and write next to each character whether you like them or not.

Going back to the tip about splitting personalities, if you find that you sometimes like a character and sometimes dislike them, ask yourself whether it's really two characters. This is how I identified the light and dark versions of Copey.

Once you've done this, put the spreadsheet to one side again and let the exercise float around in your subconscious during the week. If anything pops into your head about the characters you've already identified or any new ones appear, go back to add them to the list.

We'll come back to this again later.

Notes

"What Do You Want, Paul?"

Seeing as we've spent quite a bit of time talking about the needs our system is meeting for us, it's time to discuss something related but very different. The things we want.

It takes me back to a story from my early therapy sessions nearly three years ago.

I was sitting with Dave, my therapist, in his office. We'd been having weekly sessions for a couple of months and I felt better just talking to him about all the things I'd never discussed out loud as well as many things I didn't even know existed.

I can't remember what in particular we were talking about that day, but I'll never forget one brief moment in our exchange. Dave had been asking me about my life and I'd been happily rambling on about things when he interrupted me.

"You keep talking about what everyone else in your life wants. You talk about your wife, your mum, your dad, your friends. But what about you? What is it you want, Paul?"

Considering it was such a simple question, it absolutely floored me. It felt as though he'd just lent across the room and punched me straight on the nose, pushing me back into my chair.

What did I want? I had no idea. I had all kinds of things I thought I wanted, but when I unpicked them I realised they were all built around the life I had and my desire to please other people, which I'd learnt was a huge part of my personality.

It led to a whole new level of reflection and introspection.

What Do You Want?

Have you ever stopped to ask yourself that question? What do you really want in life? If you stripped everything away and could stand in a room where nobody could see or hear you, and nobody would ever judge you for what you said next, what would you say you wanted if you were being completely honest?

If you're anything like I was, it's a much more difficult question to answer than you might ever think.

I asked someone I've been working with for a while to do an exercise a few weeks ago where he wrote out his dream life. I wanted him to pretend he had as much money as he needed and there were no restrictions, and to sketch out everything he'd want in an ideal world.

When he read his answers out to me a week later, it sounded like he was reading a shopping list out loud. His body language and tone was more like he was going through a list of things he was being forced to do than an outline of his dream existence.

Which illustrates the problem perfectly.

Until now most of us have been so heavily programmed to put other people before ourselves that it becomes practically impossible to strip everything back and think about what we'd want without considering anyone else. That means it's not an issue right now if you struggle at this point to figure out what you really want without considering what anyone else wants or needs. We'll slowly work our way to figuring that out.

The Curse of People Pleasing

This ties back to the oxygen mask analogy we discussed in Chapter 10 as well as a personality you might already have identified as being on your cast list and, if you haven't, you might want to consider whether it needs to be added.

As I have mentioned, across many cultures, religions and family structures around the planet, we are taught from a very early age to be selfless and put other people's needs before our own. We are often programmed that to put ourselves first is selfish and, therefore, bad.

Think back to when you were a child, happily playing away on the floor somewhere with your toys until some big, ugly grown up came along and told you to share those toys with another smelly kid.

The instinct of most children in that situation, before any programming has been installed, is to say, *"why the fuck would I share my toys with this smelly little urchin? They're my toys and I'm busy playing with them, thank you very much"*. If you're offended by the strong language here I can only remind you that children have foul mouths if you listen very carefully. I'm just repeating what they say under their breath.

As with most other experiences, though, once our caregivers and adults we look up to tell us our selfish feelings are wrong, we learn to share in order to please the people we rely on for survival, often quickly getting to a place where we voluntarily give up our toys to other kids just to get the extra love, affection and attention that usually comes with following instructions.

The problem, as with most of this work, is the adults installing programming into us were using the defective programs they'd had installed in themselves many years earlier, leading us to continue the cycle of trying to please everyone at the expense of our own peace of mind and happiness.

How to Overcome the Need to Please

If you are a people pleaser generally, or if you have any characters who like to please people, this can be one of the most important and difficult parts of your adventure.

Our desire to please other people and make them like us can be so deeply and repeatedly programmed into us, not just by our original caregivers but also by the whole society in which we are raised, that to even begin talking about moving beyond it can be difficult.

You might even have read the oxygen mask analogy and recoiled at the thought of putting yourself before other people, regardless of the intended purpose.

Another reason breaking the people-pleasing cycle can be difficult is, often, the people you are pleasing right now are going to be unhappy when you stop. At least initially.

You might be surrounded by relationships in which you routinely, at least on the surface, put others before yourself, and slowly letting the people in those relationships know times are changing can be a tricky challenge, which is where the next part comes in.

Before then, it's important to identify ways you put other people's needs, wants or desires before your own, in any big or small ways, as well as why you might be doing that.

✎ Exercise

This might be a difficult exercise to just sit and think about so, while I still recommend doing that to begin with, it's even more important with this one to get the team in your control deck to gently observe things over the next few weeks to help you identify when this might be happening.

I want you to observe and write down every time you do or say something that in an ideal world you wouldn't do or say. Every time you bite your tongue to avoid hurting someone's feelings or every time you go to an event you don't want to go to, whether it's a casual family meal or a friend's wedding. Every time you don't share your real opinion on a topic and every time you fail or refuse to say what you really want to.

When you've identified any occasions on which this is happening, big and small, I want you to do a free writing exercise to see if you can understand the emotions behind your behaviour. Why are you really doing what you're doing? Why are you trying to please others at the expense of what you really want to say or do? Is it because you're afraid they won't like you if you don't do what they want? Is there any fear of being abandoned? If you don't want to hurt someone's feelings, what are you worried will happen if you do hurt their feelings?

Sit with it and free write for as long it takes to understand fully why you're behaving the way you are.

Notes

You Are Not Responsible for the Emotions of Others

The part of my adventure I found to be most difficult is the concept that I am not responsible for the emotions of other people. It seemed very easy for people to say that to me, yet very difficult to internalise, embrace and put into action.

Surely, I thought, my behaviour is directly responsible for the emotions of others, especially if I upset them?

The way I found to process it was to start at the other end, which combines principles we've already talked about in Chapters 9 and 11. If we take full responsibility for our lives and accept that our emotions belong to us and are not given to us by anything or anyone else, just like in the example of a spider being held out in front of a group and some being afraid and some not, it must follow that everybody else is responsible for their own emotions as well. We aren't special, remember, we're just like everyone else when it comes to these sorts of things.

Take the same thinking a step further. If you behave in a certain way, let's say you choose not to go to see your parents for Sunday dinner even though you'd said previously you would, and your mum is perfectly understanding but your dad feels disappointed and dejected, how can you be responsible for both of their very different reactions?

If your behaviour was solely to blame for the way someone felt, each person would feel the same way as a result of that behaviour in the same way that if the fear came from the spider everyone who saw the spider would be afraid.

In reality, just as with your emotions, other people are responsible for the way they feel and the emotions they experience, and different people will often experience vastly contrasting emotions around your behaviour regardless of what you do.

The main carve out from this principle is the same as it was when we discussed taking responsibility in a wider sense. Just because you are not responsible for the emotions of others does not give you permission to be reckless with their feelings. This is not permission for us to run through the streets pissing on other people's lives or acting in mean or careless ways.

As my therapist succinctly put it to me, we want to get to a place where we say what we mean without being mean.

The way out of the people-pleaser trap is to identify first and foremost what we actually want in life if we can strip away what everyone else wants or, crucially, what we think everyone else wants. Remember, we often don't actually know what other people want, we're just making assumptions based on previous experience and what our ego tells us. We'll discuss this in more detail in the next chapter.

Once we are clear on what we want, whether that's to change our job or miss Sunday dinner with the family to spend some time watching cartoons lying naked on the couch eating ice cream, the next step is to state clearly to ourselves and to others what we want and what we need.

The Importance of Boundaries

You might have heard of boundaries being talked about in self-help or personal development circles before, so it's another area where I think it's important for me to describe what I interpret them to be and why they're important.

To me, the idea of boundaries is as simple as understanding who you really are and what your needs and wants are in life, then clearly communicating those things to the people around you, in particular to those in close emotional relationships with you, to ensure it's clear where you end and where other people begin.

Unfortunately, the world we've been raised in and programmed by is populated mainly with people who have never been taught the importance of these things, which leads to societies in which our identities merge with those around us without us realising it. It's unhealthy for us and it's unhealthy for everyone else.

In practical terms, we set boundaries by saying what we really want or need, in a kind and compassionate way whenever possible. Doing this, especially if we've rarely done it before is, though, firmly in the 'simple not easy' category of life. Even more difficult than setting the boundaries to begin with is a second part of the process I don't often see people talking about.

It's worth, then, us talking through what I think the important stages of boundary setting are.

Three Stages of Boundary Setting

I'm sure there are countless detailed books on this topic, but I wanted to share my basic thoughts on the stages involved in setting and defending boundaries. As with other topics in this book, if this captures your imagination I'd encourage you to spend more time doing your own research and expanding your knowledge to help you incorporate it into your life effectively.

I consider boundary setting as having three key stages:

1   Understand in detail your wants and needs in relation to the particular situation and decide where you want your boundary to be and what you want it to look like.

2   Communicate your boundary clearly to the relevant people in your life and check they understand what you've communicated.

3   Defend your boundary with your life.

Understanding and Setting Your Boundaries

In my experience this is a first stage many people skip past too quickly, causing problems in the later stages.

If we don't fully understand our wants and needs in a situation and why we're setting a boundary in the first place, the chances of us communicating it to someone else in a way they understand and respect decreases exponentially.

I'd recommend, therefore, taking time to really sit down and think about what you want and need in a situation before deciding where your boundary will be and what it will look like.

Importantly, it's crucial to check whether the boundary you intend to set is coming from a healthy place rather than simply trying to control the behaviour of others. Which means asking yourself honestly why you want to set the boundary.

Communicating Your Boundaries

Without communicating your boundaries to other people in your life there's zero chance of those boundaries being respected. The challenge here is we might think we're communicating with others but we're doing so in unhealthy and ineffective ways.

I talk in more general terms about communication in the following pages but, for the purposes of communicating boundaries, the key is to make sure you communicate what you want in a calm and clear way. I would also highly recommend making sure the person to whom you're communicating your boundary has understood what you meant before you move on, otherwise you're likely again to be creating a problem for another time.

It's also important here that we don't resort to making excuses or telling lies, which is another default setting many of us tend to have developed through our early Programming Experiences. Stating what we want or need clearly without embellishing anything is crucial.

Defending Your Boundaries

When I first started understanding my needs and figuring out what I want in life then learning all about the power of setting boundaries, I had a major realisation.

Without knowing they were called boundaries, I had in my old life been setting them regularly without knowing it. I would often communicate to the people around me what I wanted and needed. I would say I needed some space. I would ask for people not to say or do certain things at certain times because I knew it adversely affected my mental health.

I would communicate what I wanted and needed in many ways, both healthy and unhealthy. I would sometimes ask very calmly or even write a letter to make sure what I said made sense. Other times I would shout and scream. At my worst I would fly into fits of rage. Sometimes I would plead and beg.

When I look back, without knowing it they were all ways I was doing my best to let people around me know what my boundaries were and what I needed to maintain my sanity and health.

But I continually and systematically failed to do something just as important as setting and communicating my boundaries. I failed totally to defend them.

Think about your boundaries as a border between you and the rest of the world. It's malleable so we can let people and things through whenever we want or need to, and it exists to protect us when we need it.

If we don't defend that border after setting it, what's the point in having it at all?

I look back and realise I went badly wrong in two areas when it came to setting and defending boundaries in my old life. I did not communicate my wants and needs in a way that ensured the other people were absolutely clear about what they were, and I failed to defend them after they were set. In hindsight, I know now it's almost impossible to defend a boundary that hasn't been set clearly, because no-one knows where the line is.

In addition, I realised some people will be so blinded to your wants and needs and so determined to meet their own at a deep subconscious level that, regardless of what you do, they will never respect your boundaries. Once we have done everything we can do from our side, as we discussed in Chapter 9, it becomes our responsibility to have those people in our lives less if we don't want them to stomp all over our newly, well-crafted boundaries.

In stark terms, that might mean leaving a job, a relationship or spending less time with friends or family who can't or won't respect your boundaries. In the wise words of Morpheus in *The Matrix*:

"I didn't say it would be easy… I just said it would be the truth"

Examples of Boundary Setting

It's worthwhile giving a couple of basic examples of what I mean by setting boundaries in case it's such an alien concept it makes no sense without. Let's touch on one home life and one work-life scenario.

Setting Boundaries in Work

There are obviously a whole host of things we could talk about here, but the first that springs to mind is about working hours. Many people I know work in jobs that bleed into their home life without it ever being discussed properly, causing all kinds of problems, resentment and anger.

If this happens, the first step is to decide what you want and need in relation to your job and what you are prepared to give. Let's say, for example, you feel as though you're paid enough for your boss to contact you after your standard working day finishes, but it really annoys you if they keep contacting you well into the evening when you're trying to spend time alone or with your family.

It's important to be specific. What time are you comfortable working until? What type of work will you do at night? Whatever it is, spend some time figuring out in detail what you want. If you're comfortable taking phone calls until 7pm but not after, write that down. If you don't mind doing more emails after the kids have gone to bed, write that down and be specific about your cut-off point.

Next, communicate your new boundaries to whoever needs to hear about them, whether that's your boss, your colleagues and/or anyone else. Ideally you want the communication to be calm, clear and assertive (see more on this in the following pages).

If you can (although this might be more difficult in a work context), check they understand where your new boundaries lie and whether there are any issues. If there are, resolve those issues calmly so you end up with a boundary everyone agrees on.

Last but not least, defend the boundary if anyone oversteps it by reminding them of where it is and what was agreed and do not compromise except in extreme situations. If you set a boundary then allow people to ignore it, they'll treat it as though it didn't exist in the first place.

Setting Boundaries at Home

Again there are so many examples we could discuss, so I'll give you one from my new life that might resonate with you in some way.

For those of us who are fortunate enough to have family members who love us and want to see us we might find that, on occasion, their wants and needs when it comes to the frequency of visits are different to our wants and needs.

If we've been typical people pleasers it's likely we've just gone along with whatever other people wanted without thinking about our own wants and needs for many years, often decades. Again, it's likely to have led to resentment and anger, much of which will have been repressed.

The key is to go through the three stages, first identifying what your wants and needs are in relation to seeing whoever in your family springs to mind when you read this, being as specific as possible to yourself and allowing room for those wants and needs to change over time.

Once you've identified your wants and needs, if it's appropriate you can communicate them to the relevant people on a general basis, for example, *"mum and dad, I love you very much and it's also important for me to have my own time and space when I need it, so I might not come for family dinner twice a week like I used to do in the past, but I'll come as often as I can"*.

If we don't feel the need to address anything generally, we can deal with things as they come up, such as, *"thanks for the invitation to dinner on Sunday, I really appreciate it and I just need some time to myself this week to have a rest, so I won't be able to make it"*.

Provided we've communicated our boundaries in a kind, calm, compassionate and clear way, whatever emotional response comes back from the other party or parties is not our responsibility. It's worth remembering when we start to change our behaviour from something that's been established for many years it can be really difficult for others to understand and adapt, so giving them time to do that is also important.

Defending our boundaries in this context can simply mean sticking to what we decided we wanted and not succumbing to any emotional blackmail or passive aggressive comments that might come our way.

Importantly, one of the ways everyone around us benefits from us setting and defending healthy boundaries is they help us to be the best version of ourselves. When we are the best version of ourselves, we can then be the best son, daughter, husband, wife, parent, partner or friend to somebody else. Which means that setting boundaries in the correct way is usually, in the wider sense, a selfless act rather than a selfish one.

How to Communicate with Others Properly

I realise as I type that section heading this might be quite a wide topic to attempt to summarise in a few paragraphs. What I've learnt in this area, though, is extremely simple.

In my experience, when we struggle to communicate our ideas, wants or needs with others, it's because we are only looking at the world from our perspective.

I used to say regularly to certain people in my old life, *"you're missing the point"* – as though the responsibility was on them to understand whatever point I was trying to make. Now, when I feel that idea emerging inside me as I struggle to communicate what I want to say, I ask myself how the other person is seeing the world that might stop them from understanding what I'm saying.

What I've noticed, which ties in heavily to everything we'll discuss in the next chapter is, often, humans aren't actually listening to each other. I've observed for years people in groups who on the surface appear to be having a conversation but, in reality, are just waiting for their turn to speak. I've done it myself on countless occasions.

When that happens, people have often formed an idea about what you're saying and are replying to that rather than to what you're actually saying. Their interpretation of the world is their interpretation of the world, and can be very different to yours.

It's crucial, then, to make sure when you attempt to communicate something to someone else, you check whether they heard what you said and understood it in the same way you intended.

Now, when I'm in a conversation in which I don't think the other person heard or understood me properly, rather than continue to make statements I will ask questions instead.

I will ask them, in as kind and gentle a way as possible, to repeat back to me what they can hear me saying. When they do that, if what they say back to me isn't what I'm trying to say, I can take responsibility for that and try to find a different way to communicate the same thing so that we're both on the same page.

Taking responsibility for others not understanding what we're trying to communicate and gently finding new ways to help them understand what we really mean so it makes sense in their interpretation of the world is priceless when it comes to setting boundaries.

After that, we can communicate clearly what those boundaries mean and what would happen if they're not respected, making them much easier to defend. It is crucial, in this regard, to let others know, especially in our personal lives, that our boundary setting is about our wants and needs and not about them.

A World of Flawed Communication

It's worth mentioning something briefly here. I say briefly because it's another area that's worthy of an entire book in itself.

When I talk about communicating with other humans, I mean ideally a conversation using your face and mouth in person. If an in-person conversation isn't possible, a video call is the next best option.

One of the biggest issues I see on the planet at the moment is we have billions of people communicating with each other using one of the most unreliable methods of communication known to man: text messages. By 'text messages', I mean any form of communication using short-form text such as literal text messages, WhatsApp, Twitter or anything similar.

I hate using text messages to communicate even with people I know intimately. The potential for miscommunication when using short written messages is so high it's hardly worth bothering. Not only can we not convey emotion or tone properly through that type of message, we can't account for the tone the other person will read our note in at the other end.

When you add to the mix people around the world communicating in different languages with different cultures and, more than anything, not being able to tell whether something is a joke or a completely serious point, we're left with a massive pot full of shit that's unlikely to cause anything but trouble.

As with most things, what we see on a global scale is just a magnification of what we see on an individual level, so to communicate properly with those around us it's almost always best to speak in person.

I appreciate this can be a frightening thing to do, especially when we're just figuring out how to do these things for the first time so, if it's too much to begin with, the next best way to approach these challenges I've found is long-form written communications. In my view a handwritten letter is better than an email or a typed letter because it still carries with it some level of your persona and can be warmer than something typed, but typed will do if for some reason you don't want to handwrite something.

The benefit of writing something out before communicating it to another person, even if you do intend to speak to them in person, is it's an ideal way to clarify your thoughts and to make sure you say everything you want to say in the way you want to say it, without the risk of the emotions of a live conversation throwing you off.

If you only send the letter without talking it through, there's still a risk of the recipient reading it in a tone you didn't intend, but at least you can actually write out the tone in which you intend it to be received by, for example, literally saying something like:

"I want you to know that when I wrote this I was doing so with love and compassion and, if possible, I'd like you to read it in that tone."

It's not foolproof but is better than nothing and much better than trying to communicate important information in short messages.

In a wider sense, away from boundary setting and communicating our wants and needs to others, if you often communicate with other humans using social media and any form of messaging tool, it might be worth stopping to consider how often your messages aren't being received in the way you intend.

Miscommunication is often the source of disputes and arguments.

Practice, Practice, Practice

As with most of the other lessons I'm sharing throughout these pages, all of this is both simple and not easy. It takes lots of practice while we're being kind to ourselves and understanding we're removing decades worth of programming at the same time as installing new programming. It takes patience and practice.

After three years of working on all this I'm still a student and still making mistakes along the way. Whenever I do, I'm kind to myself and gently reflect on how I could do things better next time.

When we can reach a point where we can communicate in simple, clear terms with the people around us and they understand what we mean while respecting our boundaries, we've reached Jedi levels of this work.

One of the reasons I love the quote I used at the start of the chapter is because, at its most simple, that's all this comes down to. Communicating openly and honestly about what we want and need, without over-complicating things or making up excuses.

Whenever I can now, I'll happily say with a smile, *"I'd go with you, but I don't want to"*.

It's All About Balance

Lastly for this topic, I want to stress something that's another theme of all this work and the lessons I'm sharing.

Learning how to look after our own needs, wants and boundaries does not give us licence to become selfish, arrogant arseholes. This work is not intended to take you from one end of the black and white spectrum where you never take care of yourself, to the other end where you only take care of yourself at the expense of everyone around you.

As with everything, the key is finding the best balance between looking after your own needs, wants and boundaries and doing your best to be a kind and compassionate human at the same time. In my experience this is not an easy balance to find and we will never get it absolutely right, mainly because there is no right way to do it.

We can, though, make sure we are doing our best to find that balance while communicating as well as possible with those around us along the way.

This is another area where you might have lots of questions when you begin implementing boundaries for the first time. If that's the case, send any questions to **questions@paul7cope.com** and I'll reply to as many as possible via my YouTube channel and podcast.

Reminder:

1 None of your thoughts or emotions are good or bad, they're just thoughts and emotions.

2 Accept and allow whatever you think and feel and let them be whatever they are without judgment. Be more like Tilly.

13

STORIES WE TELL

"Truth is like poetry, and everyone fucking hates poetry"

(The Big Short)

How would you react if I told you the vast majority of your life isn't real? Would you believe me? Would it upset you? Does it sound insane?

More than that, what if I told you the false reality you exist in is created by you every day? Would you start thinking I'm crazy, if you're not already thinking that?

Of all The Karate Kid training we're walking through together during these pages, this is one of the most important parts. If I was forced at gunpoint to select only a few chapters for you to read and internalise to change your life, this would make it into the top three.

It's time to uncover more of the big, fat lies we're told throughout life that cause nothing but harm.

The Power of Here and Now

The reality is, the only thing we experience that's real is right here and right now. The present moment. The problem, though, is everything outside the present moment is just a story.

Everything you experienced in the past and everything you think about the future are just stories you're telling yourself. And those stories are often flawed, because they were created by a flawed human being.

The author Eckhart Tolle wrote about 'The Power of Now' when discussing this topic, but I think in the modern era we need to go a step further and talk about 'The Power of Here' as well because, in 2021 when I'm writing this, we can be in the present moment looking at something outside our present environment, whether that be geographically or virtually, and that something can't be relied upon as being real either.

The only thing we can ever be confident of being real is the moment we are in. After that, your memories of the past begin being put through a whole series of filters which distort them. Your thoughts about the future, no matter how certain your ego is of their accuracy, are just things you're making up, as are your views on anything outside what you are currently experiencing.

We can even go a step further and say that many of the things you experience in the present moment aren't real either because they, too, are being passed through your filters of life before being interpreted by your brain.

I Swear to Tell the Truth and Nothing but the Truth

If you've ever watched any courtroom movies or TV shows you'll know that line. It's traditionally how witnesses in trials are asked to confirm they won't tell any fibs while giving evidence in judicial systems based on English law.

There are many problems with it, the main one being there's often no such thing as *"the truth"*.

As we've already discussed, one of our greatest needs as humans is for certainty and control. That inherent need leads us constantly to seek clear answers to complex questions in a hugely chaotic world that simply doesn't have them.

We search for and pretend to find the truth in many topics so we can give ourselves the certainty we crave when, in reality, it never existed in the first place.

I appreciate if you've never thought about this before it can be another mind-blowing thing to even consider, so, as with everything else, I'll do my best to break it down into the ways I came to understand the theory during my own adventure.

What is True?

Let's start with something we should be able to agree on which, as a general tip, is a great way to approach any disputes or arguments you have in the future.

During my school years, I was a maths person. I loved it. Everything in maths just made so much sense to me. The teacher would give the class a problem to solve, I'd solve the problem, walk to the front of the class to be told I was right, get a metaphorical or literal pat on the head and go back to my desk a happy little boy.

Maths was brilliant because maths had right and wrong answers.

So, the way I like to approach this topic now is to think about the simple sum 2 + 2 = 4. We can agree that's right, can't we? That's true. It's hard to argue against and, if you did argue against it, you might look a bit daft (although we'll come back to this later).

Maths is black and white.

The Dangers of Black and White Thinking

The problem is most of the world isn't maths, yet we're taught throughout our societies that everything is either black or white, metaphorically speaking.

We are taught, consciously and subconsciously, throughout our years on the planet that we have to choose between two things. Is this good or bad? Are you a Labour supporter or Conservative? Are you a Republican or Democrat? Are you gay or straight? Is this right or wrong?

I even saw a new podcast appear in the UK last year whose theme was *"evil or genius"*, in which extremely famous and influential people from the past were debated and the panel had to decide whether each of them was a genius or evil.

In one of the most sensitive and difficult topics to touch on, we even do it about the colour of our skin. Are you black or white? Yet in my 40 years on earth, I've never met a human who was the colour white and never met one who was the colour black.

The silent pandemic of black and white thinking forces us to draw imaginary lines between make believe subjects, then to choose a side. We're usually led to believe that being part of both sides is not possible, that two things can't exist at the same time.

Once we've chosen our side, we often then create a strong emotional attachment to whatever imaginary position we've taken (for example, calling things *"my opinion"* rather than *"an opinion"* as we've discussed previously), which makes it difficult for us to change our minds. In fact, changing our mind in itself falls into the trap of black and white thinking, with many people believing that to ever change our mind is weak.

The reality is very few things in life are black and white, and most things can exist simultaneously. It is possible for me to think something is bad in some ways and good in others. It is possible for a human to be bad in some ways and good in others. It is possible for someone to be evil and a genius at the same time. It is possible for something to lead to us feeling both happy and sad. It is possible to like some things one political party says and some things another says. It is possible to say my skin is lots of different colours, none of which are black and none of which are white. It is possible for something to be neither right nor wrong, and just open to interpretation depending on your point of view.

Instead of black and white thinking, then, I think there's a more human and beneficial way for us to go forward.

Scaled Thinking

Rather than think of everything in life as being one thing or another, black or white, I like to think of everything on a scale from zero to 100, including truth.

Let's go back to maths. On a scale of zero to 100, with zero being absolutely false and 100 being absolutely true, 2 + 2 = 4 is 100. At least, it was until I mentioned this way of thinking to someone a few weeks ago and they introduced me to a theory that even maths isn't absolute and can be debated on some very intellectual level that I wasn't inclined to get into. I'm down enough rabbit holes for the time being without going down any more.

So, let's acknowledge there might even be some debate around 2 + 2 = 4 being 100 on the scale (which, when you think about it, adds to this whole theory anyway), and for the sake of argument use it as our benchmark.

If we can agree on that we can measure everything else against it. Think of something you currently believe to be true, whether it's Donald Trump's haircut being a work of art or chicken being the best-tasting food on the planet. Obviously use your own examples, they were just the first things that sprung to mind because I had chicken for lunch and, well, Donald Trump's hair just came into my head as I was writing.

Whatever you thought of, ask yourself whether it's as true as 2 + 2 = 4? Is it 100 out of 100 on the scale of truth?

You might immediately reply that it is because, up to this point at least, you've believed it to be true and, therefore, it must be 100 out of 100. If that's the case and you haven't already acknowledged the possibility of it being less than 100 on the scale, ask yourself if anyone on Earth already disagrees with you or might disagree with you if you asked enough people.

If anyone can disagree with you in any way other than just for the sake of being pig-headed, then whatever you believe cannot be 100 on the scale. It cannot be absolutely true if someone else can legitimately claim it's false and if there can be any genuine debate about it.

If we are being completely honest with ourselves, this applies to practically everything in our lives. It applies to every opinion we have and to most things we have built our lives around as being true, which is why it's so difficult to think about and accept.

If you are struggling to accept this point about the specific thing you thought about, gently test the theory against everything you think of or experience as you go through the next week. Next time you're becoming annoyed about someone disagreeing with something you think, or you can't understand how anyone could take the position they are around a certain subject, ask yourself whether what you think about it is absolutely true on the scale.

It's likely you'll begin to discover most of what you previously thought to be a fact is, instead, somewhere below 100 on the truth scale.

Once we accept something isn't 100 on the scale and not absolutely true we can start to entertain the idea that our world consists of a series of stories we're telling ourselves, the most important of which are the stories we're telling about who we are.

Who Are We Really?

It's worth saying again, I appreciate if you've never encountered any of these ideas before they can be quite destabilising. You might not have picked up this book and expected to be told you live in a make-believe world and you're not really who you think you are. I understand that's a lot to hear from someone you've probably never met although, in some ways, it's easier to hear it from me than it would be to hear from someone in your family.

"Hey, Jim, a bit of news for you. You're not really who you think you are."

I can't imagine that going down well around the Sunday dinner table.

If this all gets a bit much at any time feel free to put the book in the freezer or take a break from it. It's also perfectly fine to stop reading a book and never pick it up again. I won't be offended and, remember, you're not responsible for my emotions.

If you are ready to keep digging for treasure, though, let's carry on.

Discovering who we really are is a huge part of what this work is all about. I realised after 38 years I'd spent most of my life telling myself stories about who I was that weren't accurate. There was, of course, some truth in what I was saying, it just wasn't the whole truth and nothing but the truth.

We've already seen how we start to create new versions of ourselves from a young age to deal with the challenges of life and you might already have started seeing parts of you that had previously been hidden by beginning the multiple personality exercise, which we'll get back to soon.

The purpose of that exercise and others we'll do is for us to see with fresh eyes who we really are, because it's not until we can see every part of ourselves that we're able to figure out a way of repairing our self-worth and understanding we *are* good enough.

A crucial part of this is the idea of self-awareness. I don't know about you but, in my old life, pre-transformation, I used to walk around telling myself how self-aware I was. I hear other people doing it all the time. We look at people who talk about themselves in ways that show just how little they truly know who they are and we think it's amazing anyone can be like that. I hear people describing someone else they really don't like and think to myself how they could just be describing themselves.

A good mate of mine once commented on how much self-belief I had, and I remember replying I couldn't understand why other people didn't have self-belief. The clue is in the name – you give it to yourself.

I've discovered, though, that self-awareness does not work in the same way.

I believe we can't be fully self-aware without the input of others. Which means if you're walking around telling yourself you're self-aware but never ask anyone else what they think of you, it's likely your opinion of who you are is just your ego keeping you away from the truth in case it's something you don't want to hear.

The most powerful things in our lives are the stories we tell ourselves about the world and about who we are. Once we form those stories and integrate them with our identities we begin to see the entire world through the lens of the stories, which prevents us from seeing what's really happening.

Let me give you some specific examples.

The Jordan Henderson Effect

If you don't know who Jordan Henderson is you might be wondering why his name is being mentioned here. If you do know who he is you're likely to be even more confused.

Let me start with my old lawyer hat on by declaring an interest in this particular topic. I love Jordan Henderson and I am in love with Jordan Henderson. I don't consider myself to be homosexual, yet I would marry Jordan and do anything he asked of me. Including rubbing snake oil into his balls.

If you don't know who I'm talking about, at the time of writing Jordan Henderson is an English Premier League footballer, the captain of the team I've supported my whole life, Liverpool Football Club, and the vice-captain of the English national team.

In recent years he has won football's biggest honours with Liverpool, including an English Premier League title – the first time the club had been crowned Champions of England in 30 years. He is, in 2021, revered among most supporters as a great captain and a key part of the most successful Liverpool team for a generation.

But it wasn't always that way.

Jordan signed for Liverpool in 2011 from his home-town club, Sunderland, aged 21. From that day to some moveable point in time around 18 months ago, he divided opinion among Liverpool supporters. Some, like me, could see his talent and his potential. He was young and often played out of position, but had great ability and a history of being a leader. He made mistakes, of course, but on balance was a very good player with a bright future.

The other side of the debate said he was shit.

I could go into more detail but it probably wouldn't be worth it. The people who didn't like him couldn't see any of the positive points I mentioned above. They just thought he was rubbish. A total waste of space.

At one stage, years after he was so trusted by the manager of Liverpool he'd been made captain of the club, and retained the captaincy when a new, very high-profile manager took over, opinion was still divided along the same lines.

Of the many conversations I had about Jordan Henderson during those years, one stands out in my mind. I was discussing him with a life-long Liverpool fan who was firmly in the *"he's shit"* camp. I said I could see how he had faults in his game, but how he was a really good player, a good captain and had more to give. The supporter I was speaking to made the definitive statement that Henderson never, ever passed the ball forward which, if you're not a football fan, is a pretty damning criticism, especially of a key midfield player, which is what Jordan was and remains.

My response was to say something along the lines of, *"you can't mean he **never** passes it forward, do you just mean he doesn't pass it forward enough for your liking?"*. To which the reply came, *"no, Paul, I mean he **never** passes it forward"*.

To put this in context for you, the person I was speaking with is intelligent, articulate, charismatic, lovely and funny. I stress that point to highlight how prevalent this problem is in society, even among the bright people walking among us.

To point out how ridiculous his absolutely certain belief about the world was I didn't even need to carry on the conversation. I typed *"Jordan Henderson passes"* into YouTube and picked the first of many compilation videos showing Jordan playing some of the best forward passes you're ever likely to see. He plays so many of them it's possible to make multiple highlight videos of them.

The issue we faced, which our world is riddled with, is the person I was talking to had formed such a strong story in his head about what type of player Jordan Henderson was – and what he could and couldn't do – he could no longer see the reality of what was happening when he watched him play. His brain would ignore the parts of games that went against the story he'd already told himself and highlight the parts that proved the story to be right, keeping him locked in a self-fulfilling story loop inside his head.

You might have heard The Jordan Henderson Effect referred to as something else. The technical name for it is confirmation bias.

This happens to every human and is very difficult to overcome unless we're very careful, hence why whenever I say to someone, including the person in the conversation above, *"you can't see past your own confirmation bias"* they're likely to say something like: *"I don't have confirmation bias."*

If this was a different type of book, I might tell you about the technical, scientific ways our brains focus on things like this but, seeing as it's not that type of book, think of it instead like one of the team members in your control deck having one job. Mine is called Sandra.

Whenever you see something in the world you form an opinion on, a message is sent to Sandra to start looking out for anything and everything that proves what you already think to be correct. Sandra, though, is one of those very keen workers who always wants to impress the boss by doing more than they are asked to do, so as well as pointing out all the things that agree with your opinion, she also does everything she can to block out anything and everything that might contradict what you already believe. In fact, if left unchecked, she'll go to extreme lengths to make sure you ignore even the most compelling evidence that conflicts with what you believe.

For me, then, the best thing we can do with any subject is acknowledge we're likely to be subject to and burdened by confirmation bias and Sandra is likely to be hard at work, which at least opens us up to the idea we might not be absolutely correct in what we're saying.

You might recall I did it towards the start of this book, and I continue to do it throughout my life, especially in situations where

I believe I am absolutely right. As soon as that happens these days an alarm goes off inside my head and I gently and calmly ask myself in what ways might I be wrong, because I know the only part of me who is absolutely sure of something is my ego.

My ego is desperate to be right because it can't face the uncertainty of being wrong. The real me, though, is comfortable with uncertainty and not having to control everything, which opens me up to the possibility of being wrong, of changing my mind and, ultimately, of living a more fulfilling and peaceful life as a result.

It might feel counterintuitive, but letting go of the need to be right about everything is one of the biggest steps we can take towards feeling content in our lives.

Confirmation Bias in our Daily Lives

The first step is to begin to open ourselves up to the idea confirmation bias exists in many aspects of our day-to-day lives. As with every other step on this adventure, without first becoming aware of the issue we cannot find a way to address it.

Bringing those biases and potential biases into our consciousness is, then, a crucial first step.

Just pause for a moment and think of someone you don't like. It can be anyone. A close family member, a work colleague, a celebrity. Now ask yourself whether anyone else likes that person and for how long have you been telling yourself you don't like them. Notice how by telling yourself you don't like them, your brain naturally focuses on all the things they do that are annoying or irritate you.

Now ask yourself what the people who like the same person see in them that you don't. If someone put a gun to your head and forced you to give a list of five positive traits of that person, what would you say?

It's likely even in doing this thought experiment your brain will be saying to you things like, *"well that person is an arse hole"*. The point of the process isn't to reach a conclusion about the person, it's simply to highlight your story about them is just your story, and if you choose to change your focus it's possible to change the story.

I heard a story of two men who were on a train and had a chance meeting with the daughter of one of the men. After sharing a 10-minute journey with them before getting off at her stop, the other man turned to the girl's dad and said, *"your daughter hates her job doesn't she"*. The dad was shocked, because the story he believed was his daughter loved her job, given that's what she always said out loud. With fresh eyes and ears, however, his friend observed what she was actually saying about the job, and could see she was really unhappy.

The trick is to begin to identify all aspects of our lives in which we have formed stories about people, things or events, and gently challenging those thoughts and ideas. What we might begin to see next is a key reason for us all struggling to move away from the stories we've been telling ourselves for years, maybe even decades and, even deeper, stories that might have been passed down to us from previous generations that we've believed since we were born.

The Sunk Cost Reality

That leads us to another huge topic when it comes to the stories we tell ourselves keeping us trapped in a false reality. It's something I wrote about in my first book, but did so in line with the traditional view on the subject.

As if by magic to help support the points I made in the previous section, though, I've changed my mind about it since writing that book.

This subject is usually referred to as the *sunk cost fallacy*. It's the idea we make decisions about our future based on things that have already happened in the past, usually because of time, money or energy we've invested previously.

For example, we might stay in a job we don't like because we've spent 10 years studying, training and working our way to where we are, so to throw all of that away now would be a waste. Or we might stay in a relationship in which we're unhappy because we've been in it for seven years and tell ourselves the story we can't leave or all those years will be wasted.

So, the "sunk cost" is what we've already invested in the past, and the "fallacy" is that there's any logic whatsoever in making a decision about what to do next based on decisions we've made in the past – especially decisions that might have been flawed.

The easiest way to illustrate it is to think of playing roulette in a casino. You've lost £100 and you're thinking about the best way to win it back. The sunk cost fallacy says that to carry on playing roulette just because that's where you lost the money is completely flawed. You should, instead, find another way of making the money back that's more likely to lead to success, seeing as you seem to be rubbish at roulette.

I previously bought into the idea of the logic behind this, because it makes perfect sense to my brain. Deciding to stay in a job you don't like because you've already spent 10 years in it is completely flawed logic by anyone's standards. It makes no sense intellectually. Obviously, we'd be better off leaving the job if it makes us miserable now, and doing something with our future that makes us happier.

I've changed my mind about the whole thing, however, because these days I don't just see the world through logical and intellectual eyes. There's still a place for that way of thinking, of course, but most of the time in my new life I focus on emotions and how they are driving the things we do.

When we look at the same principle through the eyes of emotions, it very quickly stops being a fallacy and becomes a very big reality.

If logic was the main driving force in life, the sunk cost fallacy principle wouldn't even exist because we'd all look at a situation, weigh up the logic around it and make whatever decision makes most sense going forward, regardless of whatever happened in the past.

The very fact the principle exists, therefore, shows why it's not helpful for us to refer to it as a fallacy. Investments of any type we've made in the past having a huge emotional impact on the decisions we make in the present is very real. We should take that into consideration when figuring out what to do with our lives because, whether we like it or not, emotions beat logic in the vast majority of internal battles we have every day.

It's more beneficial, then, to accept we have emotional attachments to time, money or energy we've invested in our past decisions and life choices so we can process those emotions properly, freeing us to make whatever decisions are in our best interests now. Ignoring the emotional attachments to past decisions only serves to add to the repression that got us into the mess we're in in the first place.

Loaded Labels

If stories we tell ourselves are the ingredients for the worlds we live in, the labels we put on parts of our lives are the jars in which we keep those ingredients tightly packed and easy to carry with us. Which is what makes them dangerous.

We've already talked about a few of the labels we like to use in our societies. Whether it's our political beliefs, sexuality, race, nationality or any other section of life, once we put a label on ourselves or someone or something else, whatever it is gets packed away neatly in a little box and it stops us thinking about it. Again, it gives us the certainty we crave yet that certainty creates countless issues.

One of the many problems is once we associate a label with anything we all refer to the same label without clarifying what we mean by it.

For example, a key one in many countries at the time of writing is the idea of socialism. I reckon if I carried out a survey of 1,000 people from a range of backgrounds and countries and asked them what they mean when they use the word 'socialism', I'd receive a whole spectrum of replies ranging from outright Communism to just being generally nice and thinking we should share more with people less fortunate than ourselves.

The same happens on the other end of the political debate. Anyone with views right of centre is now at risk of being labelled a fascist or part of the 'alt-right', without anyone really stopping to think what those terms actually mean.

When we discuss a key topic such as how we want to structure societies, we don't bother to clarify what we mean by the labels we use there either. I watched a debate between politicians from the Labour and Conservative parties in the UK when, if they were able just for a few moments to remove the labels and neat little boxes they've been placed in, they'd realise they pretty much have the same view on how we should look after people.

The problem is that because one was in the Labour box and one in the Conservative box, they couldn't bring themselves to even contemplate the notion they might actually agree.

Once we attach a label, it tends to lead to us linking whatever story we've created in association with that tag and getting stuck in our own belief bubble.

The key is to watch out for the labels we're using and, wherever possible, gently ask ourselves what we mean when we say those words. Can we start looking beyond to what's really behind them?

Some of the most powerful labels we use that define our entire existence are about ourselves, and come in the form of *"I am…"* statements, or something similar. We tell ourselves a fixed story about who we are and we keep telling ourselves that story over and over again until we can't see anything else.

Goodies and Baddies

One of the biggest stories and lies we're told from the start of our lives – and we continue to tell as the years progress – is there are goodies and baddies. Every movie we watch, every story we read, every time we watch the news and every time your auntie tells you a story about a couple she knows who have split up. There are always goodies and baddies.

We're programmed to believe that the world of good and bad is black and white; that everyone is either good or bad. The implication whenever we're told this story, or when we tell it to ourselves is we, and the people telling us the stories, are the goodies and the other people are the baddies. When was the last time you looked closely at your own behaviour and asked whether you were the baddie in a situation? I'd guess hardly ever, if at all.

I flag this now to plant a seed for you to think about before we go into it in much deeper ways later on.

✎ Exercise (Fred) – Part 1

Here's a fairly simple exercise to do that we'll revisit later on.

I want you to quickly write out what you think of the supporters of the main right-wing political party in your country and the main left-wing party. If you're in the UK that's what you think of Conservative supporters and what you think of Labour supporters. If you're in the US, it's Republicans and Democrats. Use whatever the equivalent is where you are.

Don't overthink this one – just write out the first things that come to mind if you're being completely honest with yourself. Remember there's no judgment in any of these exercises and you don't need to show your work to anyone else, it's all just part of your adventure and figuring things out that will lead to you transforming your life.

Writing anything other than what you truly believe is a waste of time. If you think right-wing party supporters are mean and selfish write that, and if you think left-wing party supporters are bums and scroungers write that. Don't hold back.

Next, do the same thing for the following groups:

- Criminals
- Conspiracy theorists
- Social-media influencers
- Politicians

Again, be completely honest and write out whatever first comes to mind, without any judgment.

Notes

✎ Exercise (Fred) – Part 2

Now do the same thing about yourself. If I met you in a bar and asked you to describe yourself, what would you say you are? Write out as many things as you can, again being completely honest without judgment.

Your list might look something like:

- I am shy
- I am laid back
- I am a hard worker
- I am honest
- I am a good husband/wife
- I am caring
- I am selfish
- I am lazy
- I am an alcoholic
- I am useless
- I am worthless

Write out as many things as you can that spring to mind, and feel free to come back later to add anything you forget.

Notes

The Language We Use

Linked to all this and another crucial part of the world we create for ourselves is the language we use on a daily basis without giving it much thought.

That language includes the statements we make about ourselves and others, which we've already covered and, on a more subtle level, incorporates words which help us to maintain our fixed stories about the world and, without realising it, our black and white thinking.

This is another area in which it's important to begin to observe gently how we speak and to look out for red flags in our language.

For example, when we use the words *"always"* and *"never"* we are making extremely bold statements about things being absolute one way or another. You might find, as I did a few years ago, that you use these words during arguments, possibly with the people to whom you're closest in the world.

In my past life I would often find myself making statements like *"you always do this"* or *"you never do that"*. Now if I hear those words leaving my lips, I'll gently and kindly ask myself whether it's true that whatever I'm referring to actually happens *always* or *never*.

The reality is things very rarely fall into either category and by softly challenging ourselves, we can take a step away from our ego telling us we're absolutely right about something and move towards the idea we might be creating a story around whatever the topic is.

In a similar way, whenever I hear the words *"should"*, *"must"* or *"need to"* alarm bells go off in my head, whether I'm saying them or I hear someone else utter them.

When we use words like those, we're implying an external element to whatever it is we're about to say. If we say *"I should do this"* we're really saying something outside us is telling us to do it, rather than us wanting to do it. By beginning to notice when we use those words we can build it into the work we've discussed around people pleasing and boundaries and ask ourselves whether it's something we want to do and, if not, why we think we should, must or need to do it.

Lastly, when we use words like *"I assume"* it is a clear indicator of creating stories. Making assumptions or presumptions just means we're not actually sure what we're talking about, and it would be far healthier for us to pause to reflect on where the stories we've created have come from.

The Silent Implications of the Stories We Tell

Another consequence of the stories we tell ourselves about who we are and what we believe, is within those stories are silent implications. There are underlying stories we aren't saying out loud and, maybe, aren't even aware of.

As an example, in recent years in the UK there has been an extremely important political debate among many other important debates. While at the time of writing it has reached a conclusion of sorts, for many of the reasons contained in this chapter it's likely never to be resolved with any level of finality.

There was a debate and, ultimately, a referendum about whether we should be a part of the European Union. There were obviously many aspects of the nationwide conversation we could discuss here, but one in particular stands out for me.

I heard people all across the country, from those close to me to complete strangers on television and online, saying the reason for their voting choice was to benefit their grandchildren. It wasn't for them, they were voting in the best interests of future generations.

Can you see the silent implication?

It's that the people voting the other way aren't voting in the best interests of their own grandchildren. And the kicker? Both people voting to remain in the EU and those preferring to leave the EU used the same argument. Both sides thought they were voting to protect the future while both were implying the other side didn't care about the future.

It's another moment to pause and reflect. Maybe you were one of those people who made that claim, or maybe you've said something similar in relation to any number of other debates in life. If you stop seeing the people who disagree with you as your enemy and, instead, as other humans trying to do their best, doesn't it seem a little ridiculous that they would purposefully vote for something that would damage the future of their own children or grandchildren?

Forget what you think they think about your kids or grandkids for a second, the implication is they don't care about their own.

Seems crazy when you stop to think about it, doesn't it?

As another example, I have been writing this book during the global Covid-19 pandemic and the various lockdowns taking place during that time. A common statement I see people using when allegedly debating this complex and highly emotive topic is, *"I'm just following the science"* or *"I suppose I just trust the science"*.

Can you see the silent implication? It's that the other person or people to whom they're speaking aren't following or trusting the science. As with practically all conversations around complex issues, though, there usually isn't a single expert opinion that can be relied upon as being absolutely true. So what people really mean is they are following the science that supports what they already think and have closed their minds to any scientific opinion that contradicts their view. It's the Jordan Henderson Effect in full flow.

The irony of these examples is when people on opposite sides of these complex debates can use the precise same language to put forward their position, it means they often have the exact same fears and motivations as the people on the other side of the fence. Yet the stories they tell themselves, which are compounded by the societies in which we live, convince them anyone who disagrees with them must be so different to them they can't comprehend how they could think that way.

In reality, we're still just living the same lives in different houses and the labels we attach to everything make us think we're all far more different than we are, leading to division and conflict on a mass scale.

Lies, Damn Lies and Statistics

One final subject I want to cover before rounding off this part with a wild prediction, is the world of statistics.

Fortunately or unfortunately depending on the conversation I'm in at any given time, I studied maths to a fairly high level relative to most of society, albeit not to a level to boast too much about.

I studied statistics enough, though, to give me what I can now see is a fairly rare perspective of many parts of life, mainly going back to a line my A-Level statistics teacher would repeat often, which is attributed to Benjamin Disraeli:

"There are three kinds of lies: lies, damned lies and statistics."

I think of that line whenever I see any statistics used anywhere in the public domain, usually when being used to support someone's argument one way or another.

The problem for most people who have never been taught to interpret statistics with a cynical eye, is we tend to take at face value the way in which they are presented to us. That's where them being worse than damn lies comes into the reckoning.

A good illustration of this is a headline I once saw when living in London. It was on the front page of the city's main newspaper and said something like: "DISGRACE AS 10 PERCENT OF TRAINS RUN LATE."

It caused uproar among commuters. What a disgrace that 10 percent of all trains were running late in the country's capital.

What it didn't say though, was how that compared to any other city's rail network or any other country's rail network. There was no benchmark to determine whether 10 percent of trains running late is a good or bad thing, but the fact it was presented as a bad thing made everyone believe it was.

It would have been a great experiment to print half of the copies of the newspaper with the alternative headline: "CELEBRATION AS 90 PERCENT OF TRAINS RUN ON TIME."

If the same story was presented to people without any benchmark as a good news story, I suspect most people would accept 90 percent of trains running on time as a fairly high rate of success.

It's important to note I have no idea what's a good level of success for trains running on time, and that's not the point. The point is for us to begin to question more of the information presented to us rather than accepting it at face value.

I have fallen foul of this concept many times in my life before looking at things in a different way. It leads to a great story to highlight how this ties into perfectionism and an alternative way to view the world that can help to dramatically improve our lives and give us more peace of mind.

Jimmy and the Call Centre

A few years ago when I first started as a business coach, I was fortunate enough to work briefly alongside an experienced coach in that field, Gary, who asked me to shadow him on some of his client work while we discussed working together.

He told a story one day I repeat often and absolutely love, that I wanted to share with you.

Gary had been asked by one of his clients to visit their call centre to see if he could help with morale. The bosses reported that everyone was miserable mainly, they said, because working in a call centre is just soul destroying and no-one likes to do it.

The company sold furniture and the call centre was filled with salespeople making outbound calls with the intention of selling furniture to unsuspecting members of the public.

If you're not familiar with outbound sales, this is known as cold-selling and is renowned as one of the most difficult jobs to do in the sales world. You're effectively calling people who have no intention of buying furniture and your job is to get them from that position to giving you money for something they didn't think they wanted 10 minutes earlier. Sounds tough, right?

This is how the conversation went:

Gary: "So is everyone in here miserable or do you have any happy employees?"

Company boss: "Well, we do have one guy who loves his job. Jimmy."

Gary: "Great, let me speak to Jimmy then."

[The boss takes Gary to meet Jimmy]

Gary: "Hi Jimmy, I understand from your boss that you love your job but everyone else here hates it, and I'd love to hear why you're so different to the rest."

Jimmy: "Well, it's pretty simple to be honest. We know before we start the day that roughly one in every 10 people we call will buy something from us. We've got statistics going back years that if we just follow the sales script and do it with a bit of passion, we sell on one out of every 10 calls."

Gary: "Okay, so what's different for you?"

Jimmy: "Well, I know before I start my shift that I need to make 10 sales a day to make my bonus. If I know that I'll roughly sell something to one in every 10 calls, I know I need to make 100 calls every day and the statistics show I'll usually get my 10 sales."

Gary: "Sounds great, but how is that different to anyone else? Surely they all have the same statistics as you?"

Jimmy: "Yep, but the difference between me and everyone else is I understand that for every 10 sales I get I'm going to get 90 rejections. Everyone else here just focuses on the rejections as being a bad thing and it makes them depressed that they're getting rejected 90 per cent of the time.

"I just look at it the other way around. For me to get 10 sales I have to get 90 rejections, I know that for a fact, it's what the numbers tell me. I just interpret the numbers differently to everyone else, so when I start the day I put a blank piece of paper in front of me and my goal is to fill that paper with 90 rejections, because I know if I'm doing everything properly by the time I get 90 rejections I'll usually have 10 sales.

"That means I celebrate every rejection I get because it takes me one closer to getting the 90 I need. I get happier with every rejection I get while everyone else in here gets more depressed with each rejection. The statistics are the same for all of us, I just look at them differently and I have a better life."

Where We'll End Up

I tend not to make too many predictions about the future, mainly because I'm usually wrong, but I want to end this chapter with a thought on where we might end up in society when it comes to some of the topics we've discussed.

I believe in the not-too-distant future we might be forced to move away from black and white thinking around some of the biggest and most challenging issues in our societies, because it will just become too difficult to keep people locked away in neat little boxes.

My suspicion is that instead of having clear labels we put on each other around sexuality, gender, skin colour, masculinity or femininity and many other things, we will refer to each other on a scaled basis.

To illustrate this, think for a second about the settings on your television. When you go into the section of the menu where it asks about colour, brightness and volume, note how it doesn't say, *"would you like colour on or off?"* or *"would you like the picture light or dark?"*.

Instead, it has scales so you pick just how colourful or bright you'd like your images on a scale of zero to 100, with the same being said for the volume and the contrast.

I picture a world in which we dispense with the archaic and illogical labels like black and white or gay or straight and, in their place, we talk about where we all are on a scale. I will go from being put in the simple box of 'white male' to something that describes more accurately who I am based on a number of factors, meaning I can't be pigeon-holed and stereotyped as easily as I could before. Maybe, it might make us all look at each other in a more open-minded way, seeing the things we have in common more than the artificial lines that have separated us for so long.

We are, ultimately, all just flawed humans and don't actually fit into clear boxes despite how many people would like us to.

Maybe, if you stop to think about it, we're all more alike than we are not alike.

What's the Point of All This?

To wrap up this chapter, it's important to be absolutely clear on the point of bringing all this to your consciousness before we go even deeper into the work we started earlier.

Most of the foundational work we've been doing through the previous few chapters is to encourage you to begin gently thinking differently about your life and the world in which you live. To start to question the things you've had programmed into you since you first entered the planet and to strip away anything holding you back from being who you're really meant to be, which is ultimately where we find true peace and happiness.

When we can begin to see ourselves and the world for what we really are and for what it really is, it allows us to move into the phase of becoming who we really want to be.

Where this ties back around to the main theme of the book is that until we have high self-worth and feel we are good enough it is often extremely difficult for us to challenge what we think about ourselves and the rest of the world.

Linking back to Chapter 10 and the idea of things being *'my opinion'* rather than *'an opinion'*, once we form an emotional attachment to a view about someone or something else a part of our self-worth gets attached to that view, making it very difficult to change unless we know we are good enough regardless of whether we decide to change our minds about something.

Developing the ability to gently challenge stories we might previously have thought to be absolutely true is, therefore, a key step on the road to increasing our self-worth. After doing that, we can start to ask ourselves whether something we thought to be true might, instead, be a story.

The way I approach life in general these days is to ask myself whether something makes logical sense taking everything into account, including my own biases, rather than blindly believing a story I have been told.

Exercise

Go back to what you wrote about the different groups of people in the Fred exercise – Part 1 earlier in this chapter.

For each group I want you to use whatever motivational trick works best for you that we've discussed earlier – either a bag full of lottery winnings or a gun to the head – and, using that motivation, write out in as much detail as possible all the ways the stories you tell yourself about the groups might not be absolutely true.

For example, if you have made general statements about any of the groups, ask yourself whether the statement definitely applies to every member of the group. As an illustration, someone once said to me, *"well, you know what Americans are like"*.

I gently pointed out there are around 328 million Americans (at the time of writing) and, in my experience, the ones I've met have all been very different. We can all generalise at times (as I did earlier with my stories about the ways Americans and Brits react to magic tricks), but the important thing is we're alive to the fact any generalisations are just stories and don't apply to everyone in any group we're talking about.

If you have generally negative views about any of the groups you wrote about, if you look at them through more compassionate eyes can you see them from a different perspective? For example, are you able to ask what is behind a criminal's life choices? What was their childhood like? What if you think about a thief as a mum or dad trying to provide for their child?

Can a conspiracy theorist be someone who is open minded to other ways of thinking, can a politician be a hard-working professional trying to make the world a better place and can a social media influencer be someone trying to make a living in a non-traditional way? If that's how you already think of those groups, what could be other stories you could tell yourself about them?

The purpose of this part of the exercise is to see if you can begin to see the world from a different perspective other than the one formed through the stories you've been telling for a long time. You might find this easier to do in some places than others (I'd like to think you can at least find something positive to say about at least one person you know who supports a different political party to you), and that's okay.

This work is all meant to be done one step at a time, so anything you can find to gently challenge views you might have held for a long time is a win.

Notes

Reminder:

1 It's important to understand what you want and need in life, aside from what other people want and need from you.

2 Communicating your needs, wants and boundaries to others in a clear way is crucial.

3 Be kind to yourself.

14

FINDING OUR TRUE SELF

"Someone will always be
more than I'll ever be,
so then I'll be myself"

(Live The Dream / Cast)

Before we dive deeper, it's important to highlight another difference between this approach to solving problems in life and many other aspects of the traditional personal development and self-help worlds.

When I reflect on those worlds, I can see now how they often take the adaptations our systems have created to help us survive and, rather than help us to address those adaptations (which are often meeting our needs in unhealthy ways), they teach us to use those characters to achieve things the world tells us we have to achieve to be happy.

342 | How To Solve Any Problem In Life

I've realised over the years all that does is take us further down the path we were already on. We might end up with more money, a more high-profile job, a bigger house, a more beautiful partner or a sexier car, but we're still left with that hollow feeling inside. The emptiness still remains.

I can help you take one or more of your darker characters and turn them into monsters that can achieve anything you've ever wanted in the material world. Money, sporting success, sexual conquests, houses, huge companies. But I don't want to do that because I know where that ends. I watch the personal development world helping people use their darkness to achieve *"success"* – which only leaves them feeling emptier and needing more of it to survive. Why? Because they still never feel enough.

What I want to do instead is to help you repair those holes inside so that whatever you want to achieve next in life makes you feel totally fulfilled.

The beauty the other world will never tell you is we can still achieve whatever we want doing it this way. We can have both.

All the World's a Stage

I guess you will have heard that line. It's the opening to a poem from *As You Like It* by William Shakespeare.

I didn't realise until double checking its origin that the poem actually talks about seven stages of being a man, from birth right through to death.

Without quoting an entire Shakespeare poem here, which I feel wouldn't really fit with using stories about superheroes and dogs to share lessons about human behaviour, I think it's worth reading the first few lines in full:

> *"All the world's a stage,*
> *And all the men and women merely players;*
> *They have their exits and their entrances;*
> *And one man in his time plays many parts,*
> *His acts being seven ages."*

The reason I was going to talk to you about that quote is, in my head, it's been used many times over the years by people who want to spread the message that the whole world is a stage and you're the star.

It's fitting, then, given everything we've been discussing, for me to have read the original source of the main quote and realise my understanding of it is based on stories I've been telling myself rather than the original quote. Which also fittingly illustrates how once you start to incorporate this work into your life, it's an ongoing adventure allowing you to discover new things about yourself and the world every day.

Granted, this isn't the most profound or life-changing story I've ever told myself that turned out not to be true, but it still highlights the point.

Aside from sharing with you lessons I've learnt while writing this, it also takes us to the next part of discovering our true self.

Mamma Mia and The Greatest Showman

If all the world's a stage, when you're born you are immediately cast into a role in a stage musical you've never heard of. I have no idea why, but when I first started thinking about this as an analogy to explain things to people I decided *Mamma Mia* is the original show we've been forced to play a role in.

If you don't know what Mamma Mia is, or if you just want to pick a different musical or play, feel free to do so. It's not overly important for the purposes of the story.

The important part is as you come crashing into the world someone hands you a script and some costumes and, without you ever really knowing it, slowly encourages you to start playing a role in the show.

Depending on who you were in your family, or in the environment in which you were raised, you might have been cast as the star, as a major supporting actor, as the villain or as part of the crowd scene. The role you were given, though, is not as important as the fact you were given it without knowing. Since you were a little kid, you've been playing along to a script and a show you didn't choose.

My role in the show I was born into was the star. The golden child who would be the saviour of the future of the family. A close friend once told me after hearing my story I reminded her of Simba from *The Lion King*, held aloft on my entry to the tribe as the future king. Without being too general, I think the same thing often applied to boys born into families around the world through the generations which, in itself, is a story dating back to ancient times that thankfully is slowly leaving Western culture.

So, we go through life singing the songs we've been taught, saying the lines we've been given and playing the role expected of us. Going back to earlier chapters, whenever we say a line that isn't in the script our caregivers and other people around us gently and, often, subconsciously, remind us it's not acceptable to go off on our own script and we must stick to what makes everyone else happy and comfortable.

Every now and then someone like me and, now, you, comes along in the family show and says: *"Hang on, I fucking hate Mamma Mia and I don't want to do it anymore. I want to do The Greatest Showman."* At which point all hell breaks loose.

I remember when I first started to become aware of the roles I'd adopted in my life and all the ways I wasn't being my true self in order to please other people. I started to slowly take control of who I really wanted to be and the life I really wanted to live. My therapist, Dave, warned me that while it would be destabilising for me for a while, it would be even more destabilising for all the people around me who were still happy with the roles as they'd been played out for decades and didn't want anyone or anything to change.

I realised as I thought about it all, I had become a rogue actor in the middle of a live West End or Broadway musical. Imagine it. You go to see *Mamma Mia* live. The show is going along nicely as the cast reel off all the classic ABBA songs. *Money, Money, Money* gets everyone in the crowd on their feet and *Dancing Queen* almost lifts the roof off the theatre.

Then it gets to *The Winner Takes It All* and, instead of belting out the opening line, *"I don't wanna talk, about things we've gone through, though it's hurting me, now it's history…"*, the lead actor walks to the front of the stage, stops and stands in silence.

The whole crowd falls into a soft hush while it waits to see what happens. The actor takes a deep breath and sings at the top of their voice *"Look out 'cause here I come, and I'm marching on to the beat I drum, I'm not scared to be seen, I make no apologies, this is me".*

They've gone rogue. In the middle of *Mamma Mia*, the lead actor has decided they want to do *The Greatest Showman*.

That's what happened in my life. I started singing *Greatest Showman* numbers in the middle of *Mamma Mia* and everyone else was like, *"Paul, what the fuck are you doing? This makes absolutely no sense to anyone"*. My fellow actors in the show didn't know what to do with themselves and the audience was just confused.

After decades of going along with the script I'd been given, I decided it was time for me to do my own show.

Don't Just be the Actor

As the Shakespeare quote says: *"All the world's a stage, and all the men and women merely players."* Which is the problem.

Up to now it's likely you've just been an actor in a stage play created by someone else. More than likely the show wasn't even created by the people who cast you in your role. It was probably passed down to them from the generations above and they just went along with it because they thought they had to.

But we don't have to. Instead of just being the actor in a play someone else chose on your behalf, it's time to become the writer, the director, the producer and the star of your own show. Time for you to decide what script you want to follow and which songs you want to sing.

Time for you to show the world who you really are and really want to be.

A Village, a Tribe and an Identity

This all ties into an overlapping metaphor I like to talk about that helps to explain many of the challenges we face in life when trying to make changes we think we want to make at a conscious level.

We were all born into a village and a tribe, most of us metaphorically speaking rather than literally, although maybe you were literally born into a village and a tribe. That tribe, without us realising, had its own rules and, most importantly, the village had a fence built around its perimeter that no-one told us about.

If you're like me you might have been told since you were little that you could be whatever you wanted to be. That is a lovely, well-intentioned line many people say to children but, for the most part, it's not really true.

When the elders in our tribe say we can be whatever we want to be, what they really mean at a deep subconscious level, often without even knowing it themselves, is we can be whatever we want to be *within the boundaries of the village and within the rules of the tribe.*

As with all our Programming Experiences, that message is given to us in conscious and unconscious ways. You might have experienced people literally telling you not to get too big for your boots or that your dreams were unrealistic. I've heard those lines directed towards me and many other people over the years. I still hear them to this day.

More powerful, though, are usually the subconscious messages we receive. The look of joy on a parent's face when you tell them you want to do a job they understand and that you want to live close enough to them to see them every few days, versus the look of disappointment when you say your dream is to move to a foreign country to live in a wooden hut and write music for the rest of your life.

The problem is the latter example is outside the village boundaries, so no-one inside the village wants you to go there. It makes no sense to them in the same way you singing *Greatest Showman* songs in the middle of *Mamma Mia* confuses everyone.

So, while we tell ourselves consciously we'd like to leave the tribe and the village to pursue our own life and dreams, and while other people in the tribe might tell us out loud we can do or be anything we want to be, we have been programmed at a deep subconscious level for as long as we can remember that it's not acceptable to leave the village.

Which is where the next crucial part comes in.

Self-Sabotage Does Not Exist

If you've ever touched on the personal development or self-help worlds in any way you are likely to have heard the expression *self-sabotage*.

Generally speaking, self-sabotage refers to what most people believe are thoughts or behaviours holding you back from what you want to do.

Which is a load of nonsense.

Think back to what we've already discussed about the team inside your control deck and the personalities it has created throughout your life to deal with situations you were not equipped to deal with. Now think about each of the characters you've already identified and the needs they are meeting on your behalf.

That team has been carefully crafted over a number of years, probably decades, to ensure your survival in the world. Then, one day, you read a book, watch a YouTube video or chat to a mate in the pub and decide you want to change your life. You tell yourself you're going to start eating healthily and go running at 6am every day.

For the first few days, maybe even the first few weeks, it all goes well. You are able to consciously override your system to force yourself to do the thing you say you want to do. But, slowly over time, things go back to the way they used to be and the traditional personal development world tells us that's self-sabotage. Having thought about this for a while now, I couldn't disagree more.

At this moment, your "self" consists of all the characters you've hopefully already identified and almost certainly many more who you'll discover over the coming weeks, months and years. Until completing the work we're doing those characters, operated by the control deck in your head, are running your life and have been doing so with relative success for years. You're still alive, after all, aren't you?

So, while we might not like many of the ways our subconscious team has developed to meet our emotional and practical needs, that team has been nailing it for years, so why would it just give up that well-oiled system simply because you decide one day you want to do something differently?

It's not self-sabotage, it's self-protection. Your identity has been carefully formed by your subconscious and it doesn't feel any need to change just because you've now decided you want to take some control. It is protecting its very existence by making sure you stay just as you are.

You might consciously want to be happier and more content with life, but the reality is the team in your control deck couldn't care less whether you're happy or not because happiness is not a part of its job. It exists to ensure your needs are met and it has been nailing that job for years without you getting involved just because you want to be happy and more content.

The way to break free from that trap, then, is not to tell ourselves a story that we're sabotaging our new plans, but to acknowledge our team has been doing a great job of keeping us alive all these years and finding ways to meet our needs, while gently letting the control deck know we'll be starting to take over management of the team from now on.

The Problem with *"I am..."* Statements

Going back to the last chapter, one of the things I've learned to do during my adventure, and I encourage everyone I've coached to do, is to become more aware of whenever we start a sentence with something along the lines of *"I am..."*.

It could be anything from, *"Oh, I'm not good at maths"* to *"I'm a really laid back person"* or a whole host of other things. You might find you do it in another way, by saying to other people something like *"you know what I'm like"*, or something similar.

As we've discussed, the problems with these statements are, first, they're stories we're telling ourselves about who we are that aren't necessarily absolutely true and, second, we all have multiple parts of us split into different characters who each have different characteristics. So when we refer to *"I"* the big question is: who are we talking about?

✎ Exercise (Bernard)

Go back to the list you wrote for the Fred exercise – Part 2 in Chapter 13 when you set out all the ways you describe yourself.

If you haven't done that list yet, now's a good time to do it before doing this exercise.

Think carefully about each statement you've made about who you believe yourself to be, then look at and think about the list of characters and their traits you've already produced. Next, create a table with three columns.

In the first column, write each of the statements you've made about yourself. In the second column, write all the ways you display behaviour that supports your story and, most importantly, in the third column think carefully about all the ways the statement isn't actually true.

An example that springs to mind for me is I would have said in the past I'm calm under pressure. I can give loads of examples of situations when I'm the calm head and people turn to me to sort out a mess. It's when my Cope character takes the mic.

The story I told myself around that character trait was strong, until I did all this work and realised, if I'm completely honest with myself, there are loads of times I'm not calm under pressure. Every time I snapped at someone or became irritated or grumpy under pressure I used to just ignore it, because the story I told myself was I'm calm under pressure.

You've already heard another one of mine, which is I used to tell myself I was fearless. On closer inspection that also turned out to be untrue. I was (and still am) afraid lots of the time. I just used to ignore the feeling of fear or call it something else because it didn't fit the story I told myself about who I was.

Both of those are examples of confirmation bias playing out in my life. I told myself the stories I was calm under pressure and fearless, so my system would only look for and record examples proving me to be correct.

The challenge for you is to do the same as I have now done – to enable your ability to see yourself for who you really are to go to a whole new level.

If you struggle to find examples of statements you've made about yourself that aren't true, try asking someone close to you who you can trust to be absolutely honest whether they can think of an example. If you can find someone who will be completely honest with you, which is easier said than done, you might be surprised at their reaction. I've lost count of the people in my life who tell themselves the story they're laid back, when no-one else thinks that's the case.

Another way to think about who you really are is to take a look at what you post on social media, or interactions you have with other people online. Ask yourself what is the honest intention of what you're doing. Do you find yourself posting about negative news or being self-righteous about other people's behaviour? Are you sad-posting to attract attention, compliments and love? Do you criticise other people's posts or expect people to think the same way you do?

Being absolutely honest with yourself about why you say or do the things you do can help to see yourself for who you really are, rather than letting the stories you've been telling yourself until now live on.

Notes

Discovering More Characters

It's time to revisit your list of characters we last worked on in Chapter 12 to see if we can add any you've missed before getting to the crunch parts of the exercise.

While there are no right or wrong answers to most of this, especially to how many characters you might have, as a rule of thumb most people tend to find about six or seven characters to begin with. You're likely to add more over time as we explore each one in more depth. You may also spot others as you go through life and realise a part of you appears in a certain situation who isn't yet on the list. At this point I'm up to about 15 characters.

To give you a few more examples to think about, read through the following and consider whether any of them might need to be added to your cast list. Each could be a standalone character or they might form part of one or more other characters.

The Worrier

This is the character who holds most of our anxiety although, as we've discussed, they might not refer to it as anxiety. It's the part of us who worries about what people think and tells stories constantly about what might happen or what might have already happened when we don't actually know for sure.

The part who can't sit still, relax or do one thing at a time.

The Dark Knight

We've been taught through society this common character is a good version of us but it can be extremely damaging. The Dark

Knight wants to rescue everyone – even when they haven't asked to be rescued.

This character often shows itself in romantic relationships and tries to disguise the needs it is meeting for us by pretending its actions are for someone else's benefit.

The People Pleaser

We've already discussed the people-pleasing problem many of us face, which usually manifests itself in one or more of our personalities. The people pleaser wants everyone to like them and doesn't say what they really want to say for fear of hurting other people's feelings. Another motivation is fear of other people not liking them if they tell the truth. As we've seen, the people pleaser goes hand in hand with any character displaying either covert or overt rage.

The Showman

The showman loves to be the centre of attention, whether that's by being the focus of a night out, telling jokes to make people laugh or dominating a room or conversation to ensure everyone is looking at or listening to them.

While it's easy to spot if you have a showman character who likes to be loud on a night out, it might be more difficult to spot if you have one who likes to be the centre of attention during a family conversation or a team meeting at work. This is a character other people in your life could help you identify if you can't see it in yourself.

The Avoider

Often overlapping with or linked to the people pleaser, the avoider doesn't want or like conflict in any aspect of life. They will focus on avoiding pain in the present regardless of what might be the medium or long-term effect of their actions. The Avoider is often a key part of any form of addiction, because numbing ourselves from the pain of life is a perfect short-term way to avoid anything. The crucial phrase in that last sentence was, of course, *'short-term'*.

The Perfectionist

As with other characters, the perfectionist can be a fairly stealth side of us that hides from plain sight. While some of us will clearly be able to identify a part of us that demands everything is perfect, whether it be the way we look before we leave home every morning or a task we have to complete for work, many people have perfectionist characteristics that are harder to spot.

Is there a part of you who expects too much of yourself or the people around you? Are you difficult to please? If so, that could be your perfectionist character taking the mic.

The Judge

This character is one I see in everyone I meet, so if you don't think a part of you is judgmental I'd suggest taking some time to really think about it.

The judgmental side of us is probably easiest to identify by the way it thinks and sometimes talks about other people. That, though, is just a glimpse inside our heads at the way we are judging ourselves. One of the key things I've noticed through this adventure is the less I judge myself, the less I judge other people.

If you think there isn't a judgmental part of you, ask yourself whether you ever criticise other drivers as you drive along the road, whether you ever mock people on TV quiz shows who don't know the answer, or whether you ever think someone else is badly behaved. We judge ourselves and others in thousands of different ways every day.

The Victim

Last, but not least, is a character we'll come back to in more detail later.

The victim focuses on how the world is against them and never takes responsibility for anything. They love to point the finger at everyone and everything else and often use covert rage tactics such as manipulation, silent treatment, passive aggressive behaviour and sulking to get their own way.

The victim exists in each of us, even though we might not like to admit it.

* * *

It's important to remember the characters above and the ones I've already shared with you are just examples to think about and they are by no means an exhaustive list of who might be appearing in your life. The key is to reflect on your day-to-day existence and identify the different parts of you that appear in different situations, adding to your list as you go along.

✎ Exercise

Go back to your character list and add to it any personalities you haven't previously identified that the above list might have prompted. For each one, go through the same process and complete each of the columns we've already completed for the others.

Notes

Deep-Sea Diving

We've already talked about how doing this work is a bit like digging for treasure. Another analogy I like is deep-sea diving.

If you've never been diving, one of the more dangerous aspects is how the pressure increases the deeper you go. You need to be careful on the way down and on the way back up to avoid serious injury.

The further into this adventure you go is a bit like diving deeper towards the bottom of the ocean – it can become more pressurised as you descend. Which means it's important to take your time as we go into the next chapters. If you've been doing the exercises as we've gone along you might already have discovered a few things about yourself you didn't know before.

If you're anything like me and the people I've worked with, those breakthroughs might have come as a bit of a shock given that until now you had no idea about most of this stuff.

If that's the case, it's crucial to make sure you're going back to the key principle of being kind to yourself as you continue with the work. If you need a break, take one – it's the same way that we'd allow our bodies to become slowly accustomed to the increased pressure if we were diving together.

Often as I guide people through this work they will make a number of big breakthroughs in the early stages before levelling off, which I equate to just acclimatising to the pressure of the depth they've reached before they're ready to dive even deeper. It's also common as we head into the next phase that people find underwater caves they're not ready to go into, even though they're sure there's treasure buried in there.

If you find the same thing, the best thing to do is look in the cave next door that contains the answers to why you're afraid to go into the main cave. If you can brave the cave next door and understand fully why you're afraid to go in the bigger, darker cave, you can decide whether you want to go any further.

At each stage you can decide not to go any further and head slowly back to the surface instead. Only you can decide how deep you want to go and the caves you want to explore, so just make sure you're remaining conscious of the impact any of this is having on you as we go along, and remember all the safety nets we've discussed like speaking to a therapist or coach if you feel as though you need some support at any time.

Also remember you can come back to the book at some future time to go through the work again, and you're likely to find new treasure each time you do.

Reminder:

Be kind to yourself

15

OUR DARKNESS

"Don't get too close,
it's dark inside.
It's where my demons hide"

(Demons / Imagine Dragons)

Now you're used to the pressure of exploring dark caves containing treasure from our past, if you're ready to go deeper it's time to explore some more of the darkness inside us and understand why it exists.

The Shadow

A lot of the work we're doing traces back to the psychologist Carl Jung and ideas developed since his work in the early part of the last century. As you might have guessed, though, the stuff about a team running things from a control deck in your head and comparisons with *The Incredible Hulk* is from me, not him.

His idea of a shadow side of humans is something I've been fascinated by since learning about it, partly because of how perfect it is as a concept to picture.

As with everything you've read so far and what is to come in this book, it's important to say this is my interpretation of the things I've learnt, which others might challenge or question.

Whether there's a right or wrong way to interpret theoretical ideas is another matter – the important thing is the way I look at all this makes sense to me, and seems to make sense to and help others. You can decide for yourself whether you like the interpretation and want to use it for yourself.

In basic terms, the shadow is where we put the sides of us we don't like. So, all those misunderstood emotions we've been repressing since we were little kids – and all the personality traits we'd rather not see – get buried there.

I love the idea of the place we store these things being called the shadow because our shadow is usually behind us, silently following us around throughout our days without us being aware of it. Also, and importantly for the purposes of this work, the best way to get rid of our shadow is to shine light on it.

✎ Exercise

Let's get straight into a key exercise that ties in nicely with the multiple personality stuff we've been working on.

The first part of it is something everyone enjoys – a chance to get some things off your chest about the bastards you have to put up with every day of your life.

It's really simple. Just create a table with three columns and in the first column write all the things you hate or dislike about other people, and anything that irritates you about them.

The idea of this is more, *"I hate it when people don't say thank you when I hold the door open for them"* than *"I don't like murderers"*. I think we can all agree we don't like murderers – this is more about character traits and behaviours in others we really don't like. Think especially of the things that really irritate you deep inside. The things that make your stomach tighten with anger.

In the second column I want you to expand on anything you wrote in the first column that isn't absolutely self-explanatory. So, for example, if you wrote you don't like manipulative people, write in the second column what that means to you. How do people behave that makes you see them as manipulative? What do they do in particular? If you wrote you don't like people being impolite, expand on the specific things people do that are impolite that you don't like.

Have fun getting it all out of your system and, once you've written down as many as you can think of, as with previous exercises allow it to float around your mind as you're going through your week and whenever anything crops up that irritates you that isn't on your list, add it to the first column and expand on it in the second.

Notes

The Rule of Thumb Nobody Wants to Hear

I first started to discover this part of the work after a few months of working with my therapist a few years ago.

To be frank, what I learnt shocked me and I didn't see it coming. Very few people do.

I discovered that, fundamentally, what we see all around us in the outside world is simply a projection of what's inside us. I remember sitting in Dave's office one day after having had this breakthrough realisation and telling him about it. I said it's crazy that most of what we see and experience is just from us, not the outside world.

I'll never forget what he said next. He slowly leant forward in his chair towards me and said in a very gentle voice: *"No, Paul, it's not **most** of what we see, it's **everything**."*

It was another moment when I felt as though he'd reached across and punched me on the nose. I sat back in my chair in silence. Dumbstruck. Yet another curtain came crashing down, revealing more of the real world instead of the version I'd been telling myself existed.

The entire world is just a mirror. Everything we experience as we're walking down the street is just what's inside us being reflected back. A perfect example of this came weeks later as I was walking through a supermarket. I had my headphones in listening to music as I often do, and was negotiating my way through the aisles as usual. Another shopper walked in my path within a few minutes of my arrival in the shop. A couple of minutes later another did the same thing. Five minutes later another.

"What are all these fucking idiots doing getting in my way today?" was the first thing that came into my irritated mind. I was

furious, then it hit me. I'd been in the very same supermarket a week before with the same aisles and the same number of people walking in front of my trolley, yet I hadn't been irritated at all. That day I'd just casually smiled at people and moved around them. I wasn't irritated this time because of everyone else, I was irritated because of what was going on inside me. The outside world hadn't changed since the week before, all that had changed was me.

From then on I became acutely aware of this happening all the time. Sometimes walking down a street thinking other people were lovely, friendly and warm, other times thinking they were selfish, cold and stupid. The same street in the same city with the same people. The outside world wasn't changing, it was all me.

Does that surprise you? Are you shaking your head thinking it's ridiculous? I can understand it if you are. We've been programmed our entire lives to judge other people and to blame the outside world for our problems. In a world dominated by 24-hour news and social media that problem has increased exponentially in recent times. Whenever there's an issue to be solved, we expect the world to change around us.

The solution is much simpler to achieve although, as we've seen before, it's not easy. It's not easy because it means we have to look at ourselves before we look at anyone else.

Time for a potentially life-changing exercise.

Exercise

Go back to the table you created for the exercise earlier in this chapter. If you haven't done it yet this is one exercise that's more important to do in order before going any further, or what you're about to do is likely to lose some of its impact. If you can't do it now for any reason, though, it's not the end of the world.

In the final column of the table, I want you to consider carefully each thing you've described that you hate or dislike in other people, or that irritates you about them, and I want you to consider the following:

1. Do you display the behaviour yourself in some way you haven't, before now, been conscious of? If so, write out how you display that behaviour.

2. If you're completely honest with yourself, is it a behaviour that, deep down, you wish you could display but don't? If so, write how that's the case.

This is another part of the work where I can guarantee the treasure is there, so if for any of the things you've described you can't answer *'yes'* to either of the above questions, I'd encourage you to dig deeper and see if you can find them. Maybe ask someone close to you who can be trusted to be honest whether they can see the traits you complain about in others in you.

Notes

What We Dislike in Others We Dislike in Ourselves

This part of the work was revelatory and life changing for me and people I have worked with have said the same. It allows us to see ourselves and our relationship with the world for what it really is, which is a huge step to rebuilding our self-worth and becoming the person we're meant to be rather than a story we've been telling ourselves. It's the route to finding true inner peace.

The very simple interpretation of this is what we dislike or hate in others we dislike or hate in ourselves. What's actually happening is the world holds a big mirror up to us at all times, and we simply project onto that mirror all the things we've been burying in our shadow for years. All those repressed emotions and all the character traits we've been taught aren't acceptable. When we see them in someone else, they irritate us without us understanding why – until now.

To give you some examples that might help you process any traits you've identified in others but can't see in yourself, one of the first I spotted in me was hypocrisy. I used to say out loud how much I couldn't stand hypocrites. What did I mean by hypocrites? People who say one thing then contradict it with their actions. Absolute hypocrites. Couldn't bear them.

Once I learned this part of the adventure and reflected on it, though, I realised I was a huge hypocrite, in big and small ways. I often said one thing and did another, but I'd buried that part of myself from my conscious awareness because I was ashamed of it. It was a part of me I couldn't accept so put in my shadow and tried to ignore it. The problem being, whenever the world held a mirror up for me to see it in others, it would trigger the thing buried deep in my shadow and irritate me in the pit of my stomach because it was a part of myself I really didn't like.

Someone I was working with when we began this exercise said something immediately sprung to mind. She hated impatient people. Couldn't stand them. But as she took a few seconds to reflect, she realised not only was she impatient in certain situations herself, ticking the first question in the previous exercise, but she also wished she could be more openly impatient at times when people were taking too long to get things done, ticking the second question in the previous exercise as well.

The reason she had repressed that side of her personality was because she'd been told since she was a little girl how patient she was, and received lots of significance, love and attention for being patient, so repressed the side of her that was impatient. Meaning whenever the world held the mirror up and she could see impatience in someone else, it irritated her because it reflected a part of herself she didn't like and couldn't accept.

Look back at your list. Have you already identified where each thing you dislike or irritates you is repressed in you? If you're struggling on any, go back to how you define the thing and what it means to you. One of the problems is our conscious mind and the team in our control deck often criticises other people for the things we do by calling them different things.

For example, I knew someone who would say they hated manipulative people. If I asked them what manipulation was, they'd say making people do things you want them to do that they don't want to do without being honest about your intentions. The same person would deny vehemently they were manipulative, but at the same time would tell stories about how since they were a little kid they'd been told they could charm the birds out of the trees or wrap people around their little finger.

I would never have called myself manipulative in the past, I would have used words like persuasive, charming or charismatic, but charming birds out of trees, wrapping people around our little fingers, being charismatic or persuasive are all different ways of being manipulative.

Another example of this was a woman I knew in a relationship who was obsessed by the term *'gaslighting'* and loved to talk about all the ways her partner would gaslight her during conversations. I had observed, though, numerous occasions on which she would say something to him that would hurt his feelings and when he pulled her up on it she would say something like, *"I was only joking"* or *"you're too sensitive"* – both classic gaslighting techniques.

The key for the purposes of this part was the woman hated the very thing she was repressing about herself because she didn't recognise her own behaviour as fitting the definition of the thing she disliked in others.

For any of the things on your list you can't see, then, consider what else you might call them that would fit with your own repressed behaviour or traits, or whether your behaviour does fit the definition in ways you weren't previously aware.

Another common example is one I've already referred to. Most of us hate it when we hold a door open for someone or allow another car into traffic and they don't say thank you. Whenever I ask someone whether they ever do that themselves, they instinctively say *'no'*, until we dig deeper.

The issue is when we hold a door open for someone and they don't say thank you, part of our annoyance is a silent implication that we think they did it on purpose, which we say we would never do. But pause to think about it for a while. Do you think in your life you've ever walked through a door someone else held open for you and not said thank you because you were distracted and thinking about something else? Have you ever been allowed into traffic and just forgotten to say thank you until it was too late and the other driver can't see you anymore? Or they let you in and you were having an argument on your hands-free phone with your partner which distracted you from saying thank you?

If you answered 'no' to those questions and are adamant you have never failed to say thank you to someone who has been polite to you, I'd suggest you need to go back to the stories we tell ourselves chapter and reconsider how strong that story is and why you're telling it to yourself.

The reality is we've all been impolite at some points in our life, either intentionally or not and, even if we genuinely are always making a real effort to be polite to every single person we encounter, there's likely to be a part of us that just wants to tell the world to fuck off and be inconsiderate for a change.

Either way, when we see others being impolite, it irritates us because it's a part of us we're repressing.

The Truth Hurts

Another element of this is served by an old cliché: *the truth hurts*.

As with other clichés we dismiss, these things often wouldn't have lasted the test of time without there being some truth in them (although that's not always the case).

In this particular case it's very much true, especially in relation to the truth about our shadow.

A test I like to do is to ask people how they feel if I tell them their hair is a different colour to what it actually is. For instance, I'll say to someone with dark hair, *"How would you feel if I said you've got blonde hair?"* They always shrug, smile and say they wouldn't care because it's not true. Think about that for yourself. Would it bother you if I just casually said your hair colour is different to what you know it to be? I'd guess the answer is *'no'*.

Now think of something someone says to you that really winds you up. Something that when they say it makes your stomach go into a knot and you get really irritated. The first thing that springs to mind for me is my ex-wife referring to me as a narcissist. I hated it. I had all kinds of arguments as to why I wasn't a narcissist and it was cruel and unfair for her to call me one.

What's yours, have you thought of one? It's often something someone close to us might have said during an argument that's really triggered us.

Now just gently ask yourself why it angers you so much, thinking about how the hair colour thing doesn't really bother us at all. Why does this thing really hurt us deep inside?

It's because the truth hurts when it's about something repressed in our shadow. When someone reveals something we've been keeping in our shadow for years we don't like it one bit. Remember we put it there in the first place because we've been taught to be ashamed of that part of ourselves, so why would we want anyone telling us it exists?

I had a similar thing with being called a failure. I hated it. How dare you call me a failure when I can point to so many things that were a success?

✎ Exercise

This is a short exercise to add to the last one. Simply write down anything people say about you that you really don't like, that irritates or angers you. Think specifically about things people close to you might have said during arguments that really got under your skin.

Once you've written them all down, consider how each one is true if you're being completely honest with yourself. In what ways do you display the behaviour you've been accused of? If it irritates you when someone suggests you're a liar, think of all the ways you do tell lies, big or small. If it angers you when someone says you've got a drinking problem, consider all the ways that could actually be true when looking at it from their perspective instead of the stories you've been telling yourself.

Notes

The Counterintuitive Solution

As with most of the work in this book, the real solutions to the problems we face in life are completely counterintuitive and are why I've largely learnt to dislike much of the traditional personal development and self-help worlds that teach the opposite of this work.

One of the ways along this adventure to build self-worth and find inner peace is not to run away from or bury our darkness, but instead to shine a light on it and face it for the first time in our lives. To look at everything we've been repressing for decades, bring it into the light and learn to accept and love it for what it is.

It's also where the Karate Kid training we've been going through starts to come together.

The way to begin to approach the sides of us we've been repressing all these years is to first understand why we've been repressing them. Who taught us that side of us wasn't acceptable and needed to be buried? What Programming Experiences did we have as children or later in life that led to us repressing and becoming ashamed of a part of ourselves?

Let me tell you one of my favourite childhood stories.

My Auntie Flo

I wish my Auntie Flo was alive so I could introduce you to her. She was actually my great auntie – my dad's auntie on his mum's, my grandma's, side of the family. I loved her to bits.

My grandma came from a relatively middle-class family and was a traditional, classy lady. She was calm and reserved, loving and caring and I loved her to bits as well. She was clean and tidy, well mannered, commanded respect and taught me and my sister to have good manners, too. To this day it's my grandma's voice I hear saying *"stop picking your nose"* whenever I find myself having a soothing pick.

Flo was her youngest sister – and everything my grandma wasn't. She was married to my uncle Bob and they lived on a tiny island off the north coast of Scotland called Mull. We would only see them a couple of times a year, once when they came to stay with my grandparents around Christmas time and another when we all went to Yorkshire for a party at their son's house.

Remember back then I was a really quiet, shy, reserved little boy. I was well behaved and knew that being polite and quiet had served me well. Which is why I loved Auntie Flo. She would visit Liverpool at Christmas with Bob and I'd look forward to seeing them every year. They were like a breath of fresh air to a little boy in a world that seemed so desperate for everyone to comply with a certain set of rules.

Flo didn't like to wash and didn't really see the point in clothes or fashion. She would swear and burp, and generally wind my grandma up with her loud and sometimes obnoxious behaviour. She was so much fun it makes me grin from ear to ear thinking about her to write this.

My favourite story about Auntie Flo came one year when I must have been about six years old.

* * *

We're at the house of Flo's son in Yorkshire for our annual party and I'm sitting quietly in the corner – my standard role at parties. The world is far too loud and extroverted for me, and my control deck is still working on building Copey. It means staying relatively mute and being told how much of a good boy I am for doing so, which serves me pretty well.

The house is a beautiful old stone building in the middle of the countryside with low ceilings and traditional décor. My uncle Geoff (really my second-cousin) is so tall he barely fits inside his own house, constantly banging his head as he walks through doors.

I'm sitting in the lounge room alongside my mum for safety. The room is square with a fireplace to my left and couches on the other three walls filled mostly with people I don't know, which only adds to my shyness. Auntie Flo is sitting opposite me, enabling me to watch what she's up to, which I like to do because she makes me laugh.

My auntie Val, my dad's sister and Auntie Flo's niece, is standing in the middle of the room loudly holding court while everyone else looks up at her in a sort of polite, passive aggressive boredom. Auntie Val is a bit of a mystery to me. I know she moved to London when she was a teenager to become a singer and actor and it never really worked out for her. I only see her a couple of times a year but she never seems overly bothered about me and my sister, which feels strange considering how much our aunties and uncles on my mum's side of the family are obsessed with us.

The one thing the family loves to say about Val, though, is how she never talks about her real age. It always confuses me because she's really pretty and whenever my mum tells me how old she is I know I'm only a kid and don't really know these things, but she seems to look really good for her age to me. Mum always tells me not to talk about that though, so I don't mention it. Auntie Val's real age is apparently something none of us should ever mention out loud.

Anyway, I'm sitting watching everyone being bored by whatever Auntie Val is saying when Auntie Flo catches my eye, smiles and winks at me. Her entire demeanour says *"watch this, you'll like it"*, at which point she interrupts Val mid-sentence and says in a loud voice so the entire room can hear, *"forget all that anyway, Val, you must have been through the menopause by now at your age, haven't you?"*.

The room descends into silence for a split second before Auntie Val explodes into a rage: *"How dare you say that, I'm not old enough to go through the menopause, that's offensive and I can't believe you've just said it in front..."*

Whatever she goes on to say I can't hear anymore. The room has burst into life with some people talking in shocked tones, others desperately trying to calm Auntie Val down and the remainder telling Auntie Flo off for being rude.

Auntie Flo looks back at me with another wink and a shrug of the shoulders as if to say, *"what can I do? I'm just telling the truth"* with a wry grin on her face as my grandma berates her for being uncouth. She's just tossed a metaphorical hand grenade in the middle of the room and is now sitting back to soak up and appreciate her work.

I think it's absolutely hilarious and chuckle away to myself behind my hand in the corner, careful not to be seen by any of the adults.

On the long drive home in the car hours later, my parents are talking about how funny it was while, at the same time, telling me and my sister that type of behaviour isn't acceptable and Auntie Flo was very rude to do what she did. Message received, loud and clear.

* * *

Fast forward 30 years and one of the things I disliked in other people was when they were direct to the point of being rude. The people who tell the world they *'say what they mean'* as a cover for being offensive.

It wasn't until I did this work I realised I only disliked that behaviour because it's a part of me I've repressed since I was that little boy being taught Auntie Flo was rude and being like that isn't acceptable, so every time I wanted to tell someone how I really felt or just let loose with my feelings I'd repress it, leading to me disliking it in others.

What Do We Need To Do?

As with previous parts of the lessons I'm sharing, this doesn't mean it's okay to be rude to people or that everything we've been taught to repress since we were kids now needs to be blurted out to the world. I absolutely love thinking about my Auntie Flo and, at the same time, don't want to become like her in every way.

To unlock this stage we need to first recognise the darkest parts of ourselves we've been burying for decades, then accept they're a part of us just as much as all the parts we've been taught to value over the years.

We are all just flawed human beings with thoughts, emotions and character traits that aren't perfect and never will be, and that's okay.

When we can look at the things we don't like in others because we don't like them in ourselves; look at the things other people say about us that really hurt our feelings, and realise they are a part of us and that's okay, we can finally begin to feel good enough for being the human we are, rather than constantly feeling as though we're not good enough because there are huge parts of us we're repressing after being taught they're not acceptable.

This is where the idea of *"sometimes…and that's okay"* comes back into play. For me, that became *"sometimes I'm narcissistic and that's okay"* and *"sometimes I'm a failure and that's okay"*.

It's also important here to return to the Karate Kid training and think about labels and the stories we tell. When someone calls us narcissistic what do they really mean? The world of narcissism is complex in itself, but something I realised over time is most people have started using that word as a replacement for *'arrogant'* or *'egotistical'*, rather than its deeper true meaning, which can actually be an extremely strong thing to accuse someone of.

A quick internet search says narcissism is *"excessive interest in or admiration of oneself and one's physical appearance… selfishness, involving a sense of entitlement, a lack of empathy, and a need for admiration"*. If I'm completely and brutally honest with myself, is it fair that sometimes I display those characteristics? It's absolutely fair. I'd actually say in the modern, social media driven world those character traits appear in many millions if not billions of people these days. There's a big difference between *'being a narcissist'* and *'showing narcissistic characteristics at times'*.

And what about being a failure? If I look at everything I've done throughout my life, is it reasonable for some people to label those things as being failures? Yes, it is. We can all have different views on how we interpret many things, including success, and one of the real benefits of embracing this work is it enables us to stop looking at things in black and white terms and begin to see the world through the nuanced lens it needs to be viewed.

Something can simultaneously be a failure in some ways and a success in others. In fact, I'd say most things I've ever done can be described that way. Even things that appear to be complete failures give opportunities to learn, which turns them into something of a success, in my eyes at least. Again, there's a difference between *'being a failure'* and *'sometimes having failed at things'*.

The counterintuitive part of this is we've been taught to repress these things because the world teaches us they're bad – hoping that by repressing them they'll somehow go away and we can all get on with our lives with no issues. Unfortunately, that's just not how it works.

As we've seen, the things we repress just get pushed into our shadow and, rather than disappear, they follow us around every day, meddling in our lives without us knowing and causing us all sorts of pain and problems.

The solution, then, isn't to continue ignoring them, it's to really sit with them and understand them so we can bring them into our consciousness, stop being ashamed of a part of us and begin to make more conscious decisions about who we want to be and how we want to behave.

It's likely that up to this point your subconscious has been driving the vast majority of your life in the same way mine was in control of my life. It's only by having the courage to bring these things into the light and facing our demons we're able consciously to make changes we want to make.

Accepting How We Really Feel

A huge part of this work ties back into what we discussed in Chapter 11 about accepting, allowing and processing our real emotions, rather than repressing and denying the ones we've been taught not to like.

Having now discussed the parts of us we've been repressing in our shadow, it's time to look back again at identifying and processing emotions so you can be sure you're not burying anything.

A great story I love to tell to sum this up perfectly involves someone else I was working with who I love to bits. They were telling me about a childhood memory of an old friend who they'd known since they were very young. Their mum had often compared them to their friend when growing up, saying the usual things like, *"why can't you be more like X?"* and regularly comparing their school performances.

This went on for years until both of them wanted to go to the same highly-acclaimed university and applied at the same time. The person's friend was accepted but they didn't get in. When I asked how they felt about it, our conversation went like this:

Me: "So how did you feel when that happened?"

Them: "I was really happy for them. They're one of my best friends so I was happy they got in even though I didn't."

Me: "And what else did you feel?"

Them: "Nothing. That was it."

Me (with a smile): "Really? You didn't feel anything else that you just don't really want to say out loud?"

Them (smiling back): "No, like what?"

Me: "Like, 'how did that stupid bastard get a place when I didn't, I'm just as clever as they are, if not even cleverer, and I deserved that place more than they did, the stupid prick'."

Them (laughing out loud): "Haha, yep, that's exactly how I felt!"

Which sums up the challenge we face nicely. We all feel jealous sometimes. We all feel angry, resentful, judgmental, afraid, anxious, full of self-pity and a whole host of other things we've been taught aren't acceptable, but they are. They are acceptable. Every one of them. They're just normal human emotions and thoughts.

The way for us to move further forward through this adventure is to start recognising and allowing ourselves to feel all our emotions without judgment. Remember, they're just feelings that can't hurt us or hurt anyone else if we process them in healthy ways. In fact, the main way they can hurt us and others is when we repress them and they manifest in subconscious and unhealthy ways.

Think about our earlier discussion about repressed anger manifesting as rage. That is harmful to us and to the people around us and the solution is to allow and process our healthy anger in the first place, rather than repressing it as we've been programmed to do.

✎ Exercise

Here's an exercise I want to become as commonplace in the personal development and self-help worlds as daily gratitude journals.

Have you heard of them? If not, they're a really good idea and help us to be more grateful for the lives we already have. There are lots of different ways of keeping a gratitude journal but, in simple terms, it's just about writing down every day (or as often as you can) a few things you're grateful for in your life, big or small. It helps to remind us of the good things we have that we might otherwise take for granted.

This exercise is the other side of that coin, and one I haven't heard anyone else talk about.

I'd like you to write down all of the ways you really feel, or have felt, about events that have taken place over the past month – especially the emotions you might previously have been too ashamed to admit to yourself or to anyone else. It's important to be completely honest with yourself, again remembering this is for your eyes only.

I'd recommend doing this on loose paper rather than in a notebook or journal so you can destroy it afterwards if you want to avoid any risk of hurting someone's feelings by them finding and reading it, although it might prompt something you'd like to discuss calmly with someone else after you've processed it fully on paper anyway.

Your sentences might start with things like:

- "I am angry that..."
- "I am worried/anxious about..."
- "I feel insecure about..."
- "I was feeling sorry for myself when..."
- "I am grieving about..."
- "I was jealous of..."

Something else to look out for is when you might have repressed your *'understood'* emotions about things you've been taught are inappropriate. For example, did you find out someone you don't like had lost their job and (if you're completely honest with yourself) you were happy about it? You might even have felt joy at the news someone died, which none of us want to admit out loud.

Remember, we're all just flawed humans. Sometimes we have thoughts or emotions we'd rather not have, and the worst thing we can do is deny and repress them. Instead, notice them, accept them with a smile while being kind to yourself and allow it to pass, knowing it's just a thought or an emotion.

If you need to, go back over the other life events you've already written about earlier in the adventure and write about any emotions you haven't been truly honest about. This can often be the most difficult to do and therefore the most impactful, especially when we're writing about experiences with people we love.

Life is not black and white, so it's not only possible but highly likely that you will love your children, your partner or various other family members at the same time as you being angry with them, resenting them or being jealous of them for many reasons, big and small.

Feeling those emotions does not make you a bad person, it makes you human. Now is the time to start allowing yourself to be the full human you're meant to be, experiencing all your emotions.

After you've had some practice doing this for past events, I'd suggest getting into the habit, like the gratitude journal, of regularly writing about the emotions you've experienced throughout your day. Getting home from work and writing about how pissed off you are with your boss, and why, can help to accept, allow and process your emotions in a conscious and healthy way, without hurting yourself or anyone else. The same applies to any other emotions you've experienced throughout the day in any other circumstance, in particular in relation to any close family members or friends who might be pissing you off.

To help with this, I've found it's useful at the end of each day to quickly write out all of the things I have done during that day, before asking myself what emotions I felt around each experience. Without taking that step, it's amazing how often I will completely forget something that's had an impact on me without realising.

For example, becoming aware that I spent an hour flicking through Twitter, then reflecting that I actually felt angry, irritated or anxious when doing so helps not only to ensure I am processing emotions properly, but also helps me to reflect on what aspects of my life could be changed to improve my wellbeing.

Notes

The Most Addictive Drug on the Planet

It's finally time to get into the detail of something I've alluded to a couple of times already. I'm conscious this might cause some controversy, which is part and parcel of writing a book like this.

Now we've gone deep into the darkness inside us as well as exploring the multiple characters meeting our needs on a daily basis, I feel it's the right time to talk about the substance I think is the most addictive drug on the planet – one that secretly keeps us all locked in damaging cycles without being able to see things for what they are. Here, I hope we can break free from its power.

Have you guessed what it is? It's not heroin or alcohol. It's not social media or TV.

It's what I call *Victim Juice*: the addiction to being a victim.

I've never heard anyone else talk about this. Maybe because it's too uncomfortable to think about. Maybe because no-one really thinks about it. Whatever the reason, during my adventure I've realised it's a key part of life causing huge problems.

A Crucial Note

Before we get into detail, it's incredibly important to note the intention of this part. What I am about to discuss relates to situations in our lives when we consciously or subconsciously adopt the position of a victim in order to meet our needs.

That does not take away from the fact that there are often times when people *are* victims at a very serious level, mainly as a result of the behaviour of one or more other people. This part of the book is not intended in any way to diminish how damaging it is to be a victim of someone else's behaviour, wherever it lies on the scale.

It is especially not intended to diminish the impact of being a victim at a high level on the scale, whether that be in your private life or as a result of a large event that has caused serious harm or damage to you or the lives of your loved ones. It is extremely important to me that the intention of this part is not construed or used in a way that seeks to diminish or downplay the trauma experienced by millions of people around the world who suffer in such ways.

I have witnessed at close quarters the damage that can be done to large numbers of people through traumatic events that force them into being a victim in some way. This part is not intended to detract from the experiences of those people in any way.

The point is for us to become conscious of all the times we are voluntarily and subconsciously putting ourselves in the role of a victim on a daily basis in order to avoid taking responsibility for our lives and making the changes we say we want to make.

"We are very good lawyers
for our own mistakes.
And very good judges for
the mistakes of others"

(Paulo Coelho / HIPPIE)

Why We All Benefit from Being Victims

We all benefit in some way from being victims. All of us. Every human I've ever met and every one I've encountered through any form of media.

In some way, big or small, every one of us meets some of our needs through being a victim.

Let me explain.

At the time of writing, there are roughly seven-and-a-half billion people living on Planet Earth. I want you to think for a moment about yourself and every human you've ever encountered out of that huge number.

How many can you think of who routinely (or even intermittently) tell you the ways they have abused another human? Do you ever think about or acknowledge the way you abuse other humans?

To be clear, I don't mean by every now and then making flippant comments like, *"oh, sometimes I'm a right bitch"* or *"I know I'm a complete bastard at times"*.

I mean really sitting down and contemplating all of the ways you've really hurt someone. Really damaged them.

My bet would be you've hardly, if ever, done that yourself or heard anyone else do it. Yet we can all rattle off the ways our husband or wife are horrible to us. How selfish they are. How manipulative. How controlling.

We can all talk about ungrateful children who don't know they're born, or parents who just don't understand us; friends who don't communicate properly and piss us off; brothers and sisters who only ever think of themselves and not how their actions impact on everyone else; bosses who are demanding and mean or employees who are lazy and don't do what they're told.

We have all heard of liars and thieves, cheats and people who are or have been physically violent. Most prevalent in modern society, we all see other people on social media who are idiots, rude and offensive.

A planet of 7.5 billion people, every one of them a victim. But, logically, that can't make any sense, can it? If we're all victims, who are all of these nasty people who are abusing us? How is it always someone else?

Despite us all being able to easily identify all of these traits in other people, and how each of them is damaging to us, hardly anyone ever takes a moment to reflect on how we are guilty of the same things.

I should take a moment here to say that this, like the vast majority of other things, is not black and white. We are not either an abuser or a victim. Being a victim and being an abuser exists on a scale, like most other things in life.

If zero on the scale of victimhood is never acting as a victim, and 100 is always acting as a victim, we all exist on that scale somewhere, often at different levels at different stages of our life and in different situations.

But we are all on it. Likewise, in our roles as the abuser.

The problem with our current approach to this topic and the way our society approaches it, though, is once we paint ourselves in any way as the victim, we lose any comprehension or appreciation of the fact we are also, usually simultaneously, an abuser.

We focus on the way our husband or wife makes us feel in a certain situation and we completely overlook what we are doing in return or, often, in advance.

We complain about our children's attitude but don't stop to think about how we created it.

We bitch and moan about our destructive boss, and never take the time to think about what we're really like as an employee.

The list goes on.

It's not our fault. As with the rest of our programming it was installed in us at a young age and reaffirmed by the world in which we developed.

We were taught to be victims, in big and small ways. We listened to our mum complain about our dad and our dad moan about our mum. We heard our uncle call his boss a dickhead and our brother say his teacher always picked on him.

So, we copied what they did. Like we do with everything. Then, after a while, it just became second nature and we never stopped to consider what role we were playing in the things we spend so often complaining about in our lives.

We were sucked into the trap of enjoying the silent benefits of being a victim, so stopped being able to see that if everyone on the planet is a victim surely it makes sense that a good proportion of those people are also abusers.

As I walked down the path I'm on I realised it's not just a good proportion of people, it's everyone. I've never met a single person who isn't or hasn't in some way abused another human, usually in ways they will never see or acknowledge. Often because it would be too painful to do so.

I am and have been as guilty of it as everyone else. Some of the most difficult parts of transforming my life came with having to sit and look back with fresh eyes over all the ways in which I had abused the people in my life. Often the people closest to me.

The vast majority of it was unintentional. We usually don't mean to abuse someone else. The reasons we do will become apparent the further through these pages you go and may be apparent from what we've already discussed.

Sometimes, though, if we're really honest with ourselves, we do mean to. We are purposefully abusive, we just don't call it that.

We tell ourselves when we behave in ways we wouldn't accept in others that our behaviour is somehow different. That it doesn't really count because, well, it's us – which is enough for us to let ourselves off the hook.

More than that, we focus on why we're actually the victim in whatever scenario we happen to be in, and victims can't also be abusers, can they?

So, we happily skip past our own behaviour without so much as a second look, while pointing the finger at someone else.

If you're struggling with this concept, I'll give some specific examples after addressing another important language point.

A Change of Language

While you've been reading the previous sections you might have found your system recoiling at the very suggestion you might be an abuser. I've noticed that even though I have done enough work to be comfortable with the truth of my own role as an abuser in my past life (albeit not liking the thought), it's extremely difficult for people who love me to hear me talk in those terms. It's a reflection, I think, of most people's discomfort with the notion.

To try to make it a little easier for you to consider in what ways you have played that role in your life, I think it might be more beneficial to start talking about this in terms of victims and villains rather than victims and abusers. Instinctively, it feels as though most people would find it easier to identify occasionally as a villain than as an abuser, so we'll stick with that terminology going forward. Feel free, though, to use whatever language you need to be able to process what we're talking about.

The Romantic Partners

Maybe the most complex of victim-villain relationships, romantic partners[11] are the easiest to consider in these terms. Think about your own life for a second. If you're currently in a relationship, quickly think of the ways your partner pisses you off and causes you harm and pain on a regular basis.

Are they untidy? Do they appreciate you enough? Do they listen to what you say? Are they the life and soul of the party around their mates but around you they're like a bag of sweaty rags?

Add your own to that list. I'd guess it'll be pretty easy to do.

Now think of all the ways you cause damage to your partner. I'll wait.

The thing is, it's easy for us to see all the ways our partner is causing us harm and damage because we experience every little thing they do on a daily basis. And it's equally easy for us to dismiss the very same things we do to them.

---

[11] A term I'm using loosely to describe any form of relationship such as husband/wife, boyfriend/girlfriend, boyfriend/boyfriend, girlfriend/girlfriend or any other combination that might exist when you read this book – I appreciate there might be little actual romance in the relationship when these points are relevant...

Do you really listen to your partner when they speak to you? Do you think you appreciate them for what they contribute to your relationship? Do you try to control or manipulate them to get your own way? Do you make tiny comments every day that slowly chip away at their soul?

When they tell you about the things you do that really upset them, often seemingly small and insignificant things, do you ask them to tell you more about the ways your actions are hurting them or do you dismiss them with a laugh?

One of the biggest challenges that appears in this context links back to what we discussed around repressed anger manifesting as overt or covert rage, which will often come out in a romantic relationship. The problem is it's very easy for us to identify overt rage in ourselves or someone else and to recognise it as harmful, however, one of the most damaging behaviours I see when it comes to people being harmed by their partner is covert rage.

It's the little things every day that slowly torture someone but no-one can really see. I compare it to the difference between having your head chopped off with an axe, which is the equivalent to overt rage, and having your head chopped off by someone making one thousand tiny cuts, which is equivalent to covert rage.

In both scenarios you lose your head, but more people are likely to recognise someone chopping your head off with an axe as abuse than they are someone making a thousand tiny cuts because, in the latter situation, every time you suffer a little cut most people's natural reaction is to say, *'I can't see what you're complaining about, it's just a little cut'*.

If you stop to think about it properly, being brutally honest with yourself, can you see the ways in which you are the villain in any of your relationships in ways you might not previously have realised?

A story from a few years ago springs to mind when I think of this particular part of the problem and how we are mainly blind to our own behaviour while focusing on the harm we suffer from a partner.

I was still working as a corporate lawyer when an accountant contact of mine called to ask for help with a case. He had two clients, husband and wife, who were going through the bitterest of divorces. They'd been fighting for five years and were known in the local court system because of how toxic their case had become. Other lawyers had resigned from their positions because they were unwilling to remain involved in the dispute.

The couple had a business together and needed to agree a division of that business in order to finalise the divorce, which is why he called me.

Despite the less than appealing pitch, I agreed to speak to the husband and wife separately to see if there was a way I could help.

I had initial calls with each of them, after which I realised there was a way forward but not if we approached the challenge in a traditional way. One of the problems that had been repeating itself was whenever each side hired someone to help them, that person would quite quickly become emotionally attached to their client's side of the argument, resulting in ongoing battles between lawyers and advisors that mirrored the dispute between the couple.

I suggested a different approach – rather than act for either of them I would instead act as an independent deal-broker without providing advice to either party. That way we could be more confident we wouldn't just end up back in the same situation of two corporate lawyers fighting each other over their egos.

The couple agreed to the approach and things became really interesting.

Given I wasn't acting for either side and was taking a neutral position, I ended up in a unique place in their dispute. I listened carefully to both sides of the story around the divorce, which led to a realisation that has stayed with me to this day.

Whenever I spoke to either side I was convinced they were in the right. They told the story of how the other side was a monster and they were the victim of the other party's behaviour in such a compelling way it was impossible to see how they could be wrong. I could see how when they told that story to their friends, family and advisors, those people would of course agree with them that they were in the right, creating an echo chamber where everyone and everything around them confirmed their belief that they were the victim and the other party was the villain.

The difference for me, though, was I heard both sides of the compelling arguments, which could only lead to one conclusion. Both of them couldn't be right and, without knowing where the truth lay, I could be sure that it was somewhere in between the stories they were each telling.

Of most importance for the purposes of reaching a settlement, they were both absolutely convinced the other side didn't really want to conclude the divorce and that the other party was repeatedly putting obstacles in the way to prevent a conclusion being reached. They both told themselves compelling stories about why the other side was doing that.

By sitting in the middle and listening to both sides, I could assure each of them not only that the other person wasn't trying to sabotage the deal, but that they were both desperate to bring it to an end so they could get on with their lives.

We reached an agreed settlement within weeks, which my accountant contact who had referred the case to me thought was a miracle on the same level as Jesus walking on water.

The striking lesson I took from the whole thing, which is relevant to what we're discussing here, is neither side was able to see past their own story about how they were the victim long enough to consider in what ways they were also the villain. It was actually quite sad to think that if someone had been able to encourage them both to look at it from the other person's perspective from the beginning, they might have avoided years of trauma and pain.

The Employee and the Boss

Which side of this equation are you on?

Let's start with the employee. Think of all of the ways your boss pisses you off, or a boss has annoyed you in the past. Think of all of the ways they caused you damage every day, chipped away at your confidence or somehow undermined you.

How did that feel?

Now try to put yourself in their shoes. What do you think it's really like to manage you? If you had to put to one side for a second the idea that you're an ideal employee, in what ways might the way you act in work cause problems for another human who has to get you to do your job?

I once had an employee who rated himself as 10 out of 10 on a review. Perfect score. My rating of him as his boss was a six, and that was being generous.

While a slightly different example, I'm reminded of when I used to own houses and rent them to young professional tenants. One tenant in particular a few years into what became a very stressful venture declared with absolutely certainty one day that she was the *"perfect tenant"*.

She clearly believed that with all her soul when she said it to me. The problem was she had never been a landlord, so had no comprehension of how a perfect tenant behaved. Through my eyes she was the most difficult tenant I ever had, out of approximately 50.

If you're an employer or business owner, do the same thought exercise the other way around.

Can you suspend your victim status for a few minutes and think of all of the ways you might be causing your employees harm?

* * *

I appreciate this is not an easy or pleasant thing to think about, but it will become easier as we keep walking down the path and the reasons for changing our mindset around our status as victims will become clearer.

If you've already identified your own victim character, or a character who has victim-like character traits, you might have already begun to figure out why we embrace this role subconsciously so easily. It's because of the juice we get from playing the victim role.

From a human or emotional needs perspective, being the victim usually gives us certainty about our lives. If we know that we're hard done to by our husband or wife, we don't have to think about anything else. We can be certain everything is their fault.

We also gain significance from the same position, because being a victim makes us feel special. And, last but not least, we usually get love and connection because being the victim often ensures we receive bucket loads of sympathy from our friends and family.

No wonder victim juice is so addictive – it meets at least three of our basic emotional needs.

From a practical perspective, it can often help us to avoid taking responsibility and might help us to shy away from any number of things, from having to look after kids to doing something in work we don't want to do.

As with everything else in this chapter, the purpose is to reflect on all the ways we do this without deflecting to others. A common issue I see is whenever a really uncomfortable topic like this arises our incredibly clever team in the control deck of our mind tells us all the ways someone we know is like this. It's a great distraction tool that can be extremely difficult to overcome.

In fact, I first came up with this theory when I realised I'd been focusing daily on how someone in my old life used to play the victim role constantly. I noticed how much it irritated me and, going back to the shadow work we were doing earlier, had a sudden breakthrough that the only reason it could annoy me so much is if it was something I was repressing in myself.

As I paused for a few minutes, it became clear to me that by thinking about all the ways another person playing the victim was damaging my life, I was making myself a victim –meaning I was just as addicted to Victim Juice as the other person. It was an uncomfortable discovery to put it mildly.

The key, then, if you haven't already, is to reflect on and identify all the ways you are – or might be – putting yourself in the role of victim in your life. Again, it's only by identifying it and bringing it into your consciousness that you will be able to do anything about it.

Selfish Silences and Silent Contracts

A very subtle but common way in which we put ourselves into the role of victims in our day-to-day lives is by using silence as a tool while telling ourselves stories about what that silence means.

We use it in many different ways which I want to bring to your consciousness as part of this work so you can become aware of it. As with everything else, until we become aware of these things there's nothing we can do about them.

Taking the two points in reverse order, silent contracts ties in to what we've discussed around the stories we tell ourselves and the things we see in others that we dislike in ourselves. A silent contract is when you do something for someone else with the expectation they will do something in return, the kicker being you don't disclose any of this to them in advance.

Think of when you hold a door open for someone and become angry when they fail to thank you. If you stop to reflect on what that means, the first thing to notice is you're telling yourself a story that the only reason you hold the door open is to be selfless towards the other person, often a complete stranger. But that's a load of bollocks.

The only way it can be true that you're holding a door open solely for someone else is if you have no expectation whatsoever that they will do anything in return. It's the same as giving anyone else a gift or a compliment. When you hold a door open for someone and get angry when they didn't thank you, what really happened was you entered them into a silent contract without them knowing. You effectively said *"I will hold this door open for you if you say thank you to me afterwards"*. Crucially, you didn't ask them if they wanted to accept the offer.

If someone got angry with me now if I didn't thank them for holding a door open, depending on what mood I'm in I might say with a smile, *"I didn't ask you to open it for me"*. When you stop to think about it, it becomes quite ridiculous that we get annoyed with total strangers for doing things we expected of them without ever communicating it.

In our personal lives that might manifest itself as us taking the bins out in the expectation our partner would wash the dishes, without expressly saying that was our intention. Or giving someone a present expecting them to say thank you or to buy us a present of equal value in return. These silent contracts inevitably end up with us painting ourselves silently as victims whenever anyone doesn't fulfil their side of a deal they didn't even know existed.

The role of silence in our victimhood goes further when it comes to selfish silences. A selfish silence is when we bite our lip during a conversation and don't say what we really want to say, while telling ourselves the story we're doing it for the good of the other party. We tell ourselves we don't want to hurt their feelings or some other tale to justify us being in the right.

The problem, though, is it's often not solely for the other person's benefit. Lots of the time it's our ego avoiding giving another person the opportunity to prove us wrong about something by giving their point of view. Our silence is a way of arrogantly telling ourselves we know we're right, which elevates us in our mind above the person we're dealing with while simultaneously allowing our ego to paint us as the victim of the other person's behaviour.

Both selfish silences and silent contracts are forms of manipulation. They are ways we try to control the behaviour of others or the outcome of a situation without expressing what we really want to say or do. It's a way in which we meet our need for certainty, because we can tell ourselves inside our heads we know what would happen if we said or did X, Y or Z.

It's important to slowly begin to notice whenever we're staying silent in a conversation and asking ourselves what our real motive is, while also observing whenever we're entering people around us into silent contracts without their permission. When we notice both, the key is to break the silence in order to avoid our manipulative characters taking the mic and, instead, expressing ourselves openly and honestly, letting go of whatever the outcome might be.

After all, we actually very rarely know for sure what will happen in the future, it's only our ego telling us a story.

Beginning to See Ourselves

One of the most uncomfortable aspects of this work and beginning to see yourself for who you really are rather than the story you've been telling yourself is you might realise people have been telling you some of these truths for a while, often in heated arguments or when someone you don't like has told you something about yourself you've been quick to dismiss.

The only consolation is when anyone says something about us we don't like in the future, rather than dismiss it we can take it as an opportunity to learn something about ourselves that someone else sees. If it is something we have already identified about ourselves, we can follow the lead of Roman philosopher Marcus Aurelius who said:

> *"If you learn that someone is speaking ill of you,*
> *don't try to defend yourself against the rumours;*

*respond instead with, 'Yes, and he doesn't know the
half of it, because he could have said more'."*

I used to argue against people criticising me and all it achieved was making me unhappy, angry and anxious. I now find myself shrugging at insults and criticism and instead saying if they knew me as well as I now know myself they'd have far worse things to say.

This might be one of the most counterintuitive parts of this work. By seeing ourselves for who we really are, it releases us from the cage we'd built from the need to be more than we are and less than a whole human, and leads to inner peace.

The Gates of Hell

Last year I had my first experiences of the planet's natural psychedelic plants, which were incredible and would take far too much time to explain in too much detail here. One of the most profound messages I received while on my first mind-blowing trip that I'll share with you, though, involved Hell.

I realise how dramatic it sounds.

I was shown a vivid image of journeying to the Gates of Hell and, when I arrived, the only thing there was a full length mirror hanging on the gates. The only way to leave Hell was to go through the gates, and the only way through was to stand in front of the full-length mirror and look at yourself until you could truly see your own darkness.

As I confirmed to the planet, I had spent a long time exploring that darkness and could see it all. The gates opened and allowed me to enter. Inside Hell, my only task was to sit with my demons and learn to accept them as a part of me. To become comfortable sitting in my own darkness. Only then was it possible to leave Hell and return to the light.

The twist, though, was that by being able to enter Hell, see my demons and learn to accept them, the light I returned to was nothing like the light I'd left behind. It was the brightest and most blissful light I'd ever known. I spent the next two hours laughing my tits off while telling myself jokes inside my own head.

This is the most difficult and challenging part of the adventure. To be able to look at ourselves and truly see for the first time the pain we have caused to the people around us, often to the people we love the most. To be able to see all the ways we have manipulated and controlled, harmed, abused and undermined. Usually without intending to, but doing so nonetheless.

Are you able to do that now? Do you want to? If this part of the adventure is a step too far it's understandable. It's incredibly hard to really look at the ways we've been responsible for hurting those around us when we've only previously considered ourselves to be victims. If you're not ready to do that yet it's okay. We must all take whatever path is right for us at any given time.

If you are ready, though, the rewards on the other side of the darkness are worth it.

"We never lose our demons… We only learn to live above them."

(The Ancient One / Doctor Strange)

Sorry Seems to be the Hardest Word

Another huge counterintuitive sign-post on the other side of the darkness and on the way to inner peace came for me in the form of apologies. But not the apologies I thought would lead me there.

If you're anything like me you might have a few key incidents or relationships in your history that cause you mental anguish whenever you think about them. Often, the reason those things play on our mind is we've been telling ourselves the story for a while, potentially years, that we were in the right and the other person should apologise to us in order to give us what is often referred to as *'closure'*.

The problem is that those apologies very rarely come, usually because the other person is doing exactly the same as us by putting themselves in the role of victim.

A life-changing moment for me during the early part of my adventure was when I sat down and reflected on the few people and incidents in my life that regularly played on my mind, usually causing me to become angry about the past. Rather than do what I'd always done in the past and allow my ego to wind me up by telling me all the ways I'd been hard done to and was a victim, I reflected on all the ways the things I was complaining about were actually my responsibility.

Going back to what we discussed in Chapter 9, I took radical responsibility for everything that had happened and I considered for the first time all the things I needed to apologise for in relation to each situation.

I then took a pen and paper and wrote hand-written letters to each person, setting out my regrets about what had happened between us and all the things I was sorry for.

As if by magic, each of those incidents that had previously haunted me for years just dropped out of my head. When I looked inward instead of blaming the outside world for my problems, I found a peace I'd never experienced before.

How to Apologise

This might sound like a strange section to put in a book for adults. We all know how to apologise after all, don't we?

Something else I learnt along this adventure was the vast majority of us don't really know how to apologise properly. I've been both the giver and receiver of flawed apologies in the past and, if you've been on the receiving end of one, this might resonate with you.

Many of the apologies we give and receive are not really full apologies. They're pale imitations of what a true apology should be which, as with most other things we've discussed, come as a result of the way we've seen others apologise throughout our lives and have simply copied.

It's another area in which I'm sure there will be conflicting ideas, so here I'll set out a summary of my current views on the topic as well as some thoughts of an expert in the field, and leave you to consider how they sit with you.

In very simple terms, the key to a real apology is to make sure you're making it about you and your behaviour, and not about anything else. That might sound obvious but, if you think what apologies tend to sound like, they often follow one of the following forms:

- "If I did X then I'm sorry"
- "I'm sorry if you feel upset"

- "I'm sorry for doing X but it's because you did Y"

Do they sound like apologies you've made and heard in the past? Can you spot the problem with each of them?

In the first, the entire apology is couched in terms of the person giving it not really believing they did whatever it is they're apologising for. The word *"if"* at the start undermines the entire apology. You're either sorry for your behaviour or you're not, there can be no *"if"* involved.

The second is a classic form of apology that only seeks to apologise for the feelings of the other person and, again, avoids the provider of the apology actually taking responsibility for their actions. If I hear an apology of this nature these days, I will calmly and assertively tell the person speaking that they don't need to apologise for my emotions. My emotions are mine alone, and seeing as I won't apologise for them anymore there's no need for anyone else to.

The third and final example is another classic, which gives with one hand and takes away with the other. It says sorry while at the same time putting the blame at the other person's feet. It's saying the person really blames the other party for what happened, not that they take responsibility for their actions.

The key, then, is very simple. To apologise for something you must apologise for your behaviour, nothing else. There should be no reference to the other person, their behaviour or their involvement in what happened.

If you are apologising just to extract an apology from the other party, it is not a real apology. If you are apologising just to make a passive aggressive dig at the other party for their behaviour, it's not a real apology. If you do anything other than take full responsibility for your behaviour, it's not a real apology.

That means a real apology simply says, *"I'm sorry I was deceitful. I told lies and I'm really sorry I did"* or *"I'm sorry I was cruel. The things I said were unnecessary and I'm truly sorry"*.

Crucially, a true apology should also ask if there's any way we can make amends for how we behaved, which goes as simply as, *"Is there anything I can do to make up for my behaviour?"*.

To go a little further, the author Dr. Harrier Lerner says there are nine essential elements of a true apology, which are:

1   Does not include the word "but".
2   Keeps the focus on your actions and not the other person's response.
3   Includes an offer of reparation or restitution that fits the situation.
4   Does not over do.
5   Doesn't get caught up in who's more to blame or who started it.
6   Requires that you do your best to avoid a repeat performance.
7   Should not serve to silence.
8   Shouldn't be offered to make you feel better if it makes the other party feel worse.
9   Does not ask the hurt party to do anything, not even forgive.

While we've already covered most of the list and the rest is fairly self-explanatory, I want to highlight points six and eight before we move on.

If we apologise for something then repeat the same behaviour, the apology is completely undermined. That is especially the case if we repeat the behaviour again and again. I use the example that it's like punching someone in the face, saying, *"sorry for punching you"* then punching them again, repeating the same thing on a loop. Each time we do it, the apology becomes less of an apology and more of a manipulation technique.

Point eight can be trickier to deal with in practice because it is possible for apologies to make other people feel worse, especially if we're apologising for something they don't know about before we apologise. It's an area where I don't think there are any right or wrong answers, so if you're faced with a situation in which you're not certain whether your apology will make things worse or not I'd recommend talking it through with a therapist, coach or at least with someone you can trust to give you an honest and objective point of view.

It ties in with one of the steps in the Alcoholics Anonymous 12-step programme, which says we shouldn't cause harm to others when seeking to make amends, whether that's the person we're apologising to or a third party who might be caught up in our story.

Crucially, though, we also shouldn't use this as a get-out-of-jail-free card to avoid the responsibility of making an apology, which can be a knife-edge to walk on, hence outside advice and guidance being so helpful.

Last of all, I'd add something very basic to go above everything we've discussed. It might sound simple and obvious, but it's important to say.

You should only apologise if you're actually sorry for what you've done.

Too often I've witnessed and experienced people apologising because they don't want people to think badly of them. It's their people pleaser character taking the mic when they're not actually sorry at all for what they've done. I'd go as far as saying this is the main cause of the hollow apology examples I listed earlier.

When I wrote my apology letters a few years ago, someone I knew heard about them and decided they wanted to do a similar thing, so wrote an apology email to someone from their past and asked me to look at it to give my opinion.

The email had many of the words you'd expect to see in a typical apology, but my overriding impression and feeling was the person wasn't sorry at all and they were only sending the email because they thought they should.

When I gave that feedback, the person admitted that's exactly what was happening. I advised it was better not to send it at all in that case.

If you find yourself thinking you want to apologise to someone for something you're not actually sorry for, take some time to reflect on what your true intentions are in wanting to make an apology. You might find you're actually just trying to meet your own needs rather than doing it for the benefit of the other person.

In my experience, a hollow apology is worse than no apology at all. I would much rather someone told me they weren't sorry for their actions and explained why, than hear an empty apology designed only to manipulate me or others.

✎ Exercise

Think back to any events or incidents in your life that play on your mind, or anything else you consider you're owed an apology for, big or small.

Rather than sticking with the same story you've been telling yourself about those events, possibly for years, see if you can take everything we've been talking about and look at them from another perspective.

If you were looking at each of them from the other side and taking full responsibility for your behaviour and role in everything, what would you say was your responsibility?

If you can find how each incident was your responsibility, take a pen and paper and free write letters of apology to each person involved, using the rules for a real apology we've discussed.

There's no need to actually send the letters to anyone, the purpose of the exercise is for you to begin to practice how to gently bring any problems you face in life back to your behaviour and the things you're responsible for.

Obviously, if having completed the exercise you feel as though it might help to go through with the apologies, you can either send the letters or speak to each person direct, ensuring you follow the guidance we've discussed as far as possible and remembering this is another new skill we're learning so mistakes are likely to happen. If they do, be kind to yourself, give yourself credit for having the courage to make changes to your life and commit to learning from any mistakes.

Ideally, run any proposed apologies past a therapist or coach to get an independent view on how you're wording things before going ahead with them.

Notes

The Golden Parent Conundrum

Having been through the difficult work in this chapter, there's one more important point to note that links back to the very start of everything we've been talking about.

Something I used to take great pleasure in, mainly because I haven't got kids of my own, was asking close friends and family which of their kids was their favourite. The vast majority of people squirm in their seat before exclaiming loudly it's impossible to have a favourite and I wouldn't understand until I had my own.

My favourite people, though, would just reply with something like: *"Sally's my favourite. She tells jokes about poo while Max just cries all the time."*

I share that with you because the same dilemma applies to our parents. If you still have two parents and I asked you which is your favourite, what would you say? If you're like me your answer would be, *"it depends which of them has been winding me up most recently"*, which I guess is the honest answer if you've got kids as well.

When it comes to this work, though, I've found from people all around the world that as soon as we find out about programming from childhood playing such a big role in our lives, we tend to focus on one parent as being the main source of our problems.

Many people have what I'd describe as a golden parent, much like they have golden children, and find it almost impossible to see any of the problems they face in life as having originated from that person.

It's crucial we get beyond the stories we're telling ourselves in relation to this so we don't miss any important part of the work.

Maybe you had a parent who was always laughing and joking, never angry and always making things better for everyone around them, whereas your other parent tended to be moody, aggressive or negative a lot of the time.

The problem is the *'always positive'* parent is likely to have subconsciously taught us lots of fairly damaging traits without us realising, and obviously without meaning to. When you pause to reflect on the work we've done, a parent who is always positive, just like a child who is always positive, is almost certainly repressing emotions they don't want to face. If their role in their relationship with your other parent was always trying to make things better, it's likely they were people pleasers and have passed that trait on to you.

Go all the way back to the Audrey exercise in Chapter 4 and review the list of character traits of your parents or original caregivers. Having been through the work since then, can you see anything else in the make-up of either parent or caregiver that you've adopted and has caused you issues in life? If so, factor those things into the other exercises we've done to help understand where you originally learnt to behave the way you have until now.

If we have a golden parent, it's key we don't fall into the trap of blaming our non-golden parent for everything and overlooking what we learnt from the other partner that's caused us problems.

Notes

A Trick of the Mind

As we're moving through the toughest parts of this adventure together, it's worth always linking back to everything we've talked about already to remember the point of it all as well as making it easier to be aware of potential traps along the way.

First, remember at this point in your life it's likely the team in your control deck in your head and your cast of characters (your ego) has been running the show for decades, meaning they're unlikely to want to hand over control without a fight.

Our ego uses a whole host of tricks to attempt to keep us trapped in the life it has built for us including, for the purposes of this part, something I experienced regularly while trying to focus on my own darkness.

Whenever I found myself learning about shadows, victimhood and anything else, my ego would instantly point out all the ways those things applied to other people in my life. I'd find myself sitting focusing on others instead, as I intended, of focusing on my own behaviour. The ego is as brilliant as it is crafty.

The trick is to become aware of when your ego is trying to distract you from the real work and, when you notice, to bring yourself gently back to what you were meant to be doing, while being kind to yourself for having been distracted.

Of course, the things we're discussing will apply to everyone else in your life, but the whole point of this work is to focus on your own behaviour, not theirs, as yours is the only behaviour you can control, regardless of how much you might want to control others.

After that, it's key to remember the whole point of what we're talking about is to build our self-worth by understanding who we really are, learning to accept every part of us and, slowly but surely, taking conscious control over who we want to be in the future, rather than leaving it to our subconscious to decide on our behalf.

By understanding and accepting the darkest parts of ourselves, we can begin to understand and accept the darkest parts of every other flawed human on the planet. Then, rather than the world irritating us by reflecting back the parts of us we've repressed, we can move through life in peace, using a shrug of the shoulders and *"we're just all flawed humans"* as our new tag-line.

Every step forward we can take, no matter how big or small, adds to the self-worth power bar and moves us towards who and where we want to be.

Reminder:

1   Your world consists of a series of stories you tell yourself. Learn to understand what's real and what isn't.

2   Most things in life are not black and white. Don't let anyone convince you otherwise.

16

REUNITE

"I would rather be whole than good"

(Carl Jung)

It's incredibly fitting to begin this chapter with one of my favourite quotes that ties all the Karate Kid training we've been doing back to the very start of our adventure together.

Remember in Chapter 4 we discovered we were taught as children it was not okay to be a whole human, because in order to be acceptable to our caregivers we needed to be good, which meant repressing the parts of us the world considers to be bad and becoming less than whole as a result.

This part of the adventure is all about bringing everything together, so we can learn to be whole again.

The Purpose of Multiple Personality Work

It's time to dig out your list of characters. By this stage, you should hopefully have a good sized cast-list and be able to identify the needs they're meeting as well as whether or not you like each one.

As we're beginning to tie everything back to the start of the adventure, it's time to discuss the purpose of the multiple personality exercise we've been doing before going to its final stages.

As I said at the start of the book, the purpose of this work is to firstly see ourselves for who we truly are before being able to strip back the human built by other humans and rebuild in its place the human we want to be.

Alongside all the other exercises and work we've been doing, the multiple personality work is the single biggest part of being able to see for the first time who we really are, broken down into each little part of us.

Linking it all back to the original theory of the book, that all problems in life have at their root the issue that we have low self-worth and we don't think we're good enough, the key then is being able to see for the first time which parts of us we really don't like. The last column you should have completed for each of your characters should tell you in very simple terms whether you like or dislike each part of you.

If you are anything like me and everyone else I've ever taken through this work, it's highly likely you have a number of parts of yourself you simply don't like. As far as self-worth goes, at the moment it is highly unlikely you love the parts of yourself you don't like.

And, guess what? The parts of us we don't like and don't love are the parts of us we don't think are good enough, dragging our self-worth down.

Remembering The Bits We Like

Until a few months ago at this stage of the adventure my sole focus was on what I'll describe in the next section. I realised one day, though, that it's really important to remember this bit.

While there are likely to be large parts of yourself you don't like, there are also likely to be parts you really do like. Those parts are the bits we already love that help our self-worth.

It is crucial, therefore, that we don't overlook those parts when exploring our darkness and the parts we don't like. Remember there are already parts of you you're really happy with and have served you well throughout your life.

Don't lose sight of those parts as we go through the next sections.

Learning To Love The Parts We Dislike

After acknowledging and remembering the parts we do like about ourselves, the most important part of this entire exercise is to look at the parts we don't like and find a way to accept them, be grateful for them and love them.

I appreciate that might seem a stretch at the moment depending on the characters you have on your 'dislike' list, but stick with me and we'll get there together. This is another part of the adventure where I can guarantee the treasure is there, so if you can't find it we just need to keep digging.

The first step is to look at the emotional and practical needs each of those characters has been meeting for you until now. Ask yourself whether you can be grateful for them fulfilling those needs for you when you weren't able to meet them by using any of the characters you like or your true, original self. It's crucial here to remember you created every character on your list to serve a purpose in your life so, when you stop to think about it, it becomes a little strange that we don't like people we built to help us.

I like to picture this as a team in an office you manage. You recruited every one of the team and they've each been doing the role you hired them for all year. Now imagine all your characters lined up at the end of December, waiting to see if they're getting a Christmas bonus.

You've got all the team members you like standing together, laughing and smiling, excitedly waiting for the good news so they can go and celebrate at the Christmas party. Next to that group are all the people you don't like. The trouble-causers. There seems to be a grey cloud hanging over wherever they stand.

You bounce into the room, congratulating all the characters you like on a job well done. You give them their Christmas bonus in cash so they can go straight to the bar and you can all get blind drunk together and sing Mariah Carey songs on karaoke.

Then you turn to the workers in the other group. You tell them they're not getting a bonus this year and, to top it off, they can't come to the Christmas party because, quite frankly, you can't stand them. They've caused nothing but trouble in your life all year and you're sick of them.

Whoever the lead character is on your dislike list steps forward to confront you.

"Are you joking?! So, we spend all year sorting out all the shit jobs in this place, doing all the things none of that bunch of jokers wants to do, and not only do we not get thanked for it but you tell us you don't even like us? We've spent all year emptying the bins, cleaning up the communal kitchen and dealing with all the problem customers, while your happy-go-lucky characters have just been joking around doing fuck all! Can you tell me one serious problem any of them has sorted out for you all year? Go on, just one thing? I bet you can't, because whenever anything difficult comes up, that lot runs and hides. They pass the microphone to us to sort out your mess because you've never had the courage to sort it yourself. The way you treat us is an absolute disgrace."

If you're anything like me, until that rant you might not have thought of it like that. Every character on our list we dislike only exists because neither the real us nor any of the characters we like dealt with the thing that needed to be dealt with. No-one else met those needs for us, so our team in our control deck created someone who could deal with it for us. Then, after they've handled the problem, granted in a way we might not like but at least it was sorted, we come back and tell them we don't like them for what they did.

Seems a bit strange of us when you look at it like that, doesn't it?

Let me give you a couple of examples of a character I disliked and one someone I worked with disliked from his cast, to highlight the ways in which we might find we can be grateful for what they've done for us.

Learning to Love Bane

If you remember my character Bane from Chapter 12, he represented my rage. When I first did a version of this exercise I really did not like him one bit. He'd been so destructive in my life and caused so much damage, literally and metaphorically, I just wanted him to disappear and couldn't imagine ever being grateful for what he'd done for me.

One of the reasons I love doing this work in this way, though, is because by picturing each of the parts of me as different characters I can talk to each one like I would an old friend, which is really what they all are. I appreciate that might sound crazy, but I guess if you've stuck with me this far you're at least partly on board with the level of craziness I'm bringing to the party so we might as well carry on.

When I stopped one day to have a chat with Bane about what he'd done to my life, he made a life-changing point. Here's how the conversation went:

Me: "I just can't understand why you did the things you did. All those times you smashed something against a wall, or exploded at someone I love. You frightened me and you petrified them. Why did you do it?"

Bane: "I did it because you never said what you wanted to say. You spent your life biting your lip and tolerating your own life. Every hour of every day you refused to say the things that were important to you. Whenever you were angry and needed someone to just deal with that anger, the mic would just get passed from one of your nice characters to the next, every one of them refusing to deal with things."

Me: "I get that, but why did you deal with the problem in such a destructive way, why not do it in a way that didn't hurt me or other people?"

Bane: "Because I was built to stand at the end of the line. By the time the mic reached me it was too late and only something dramatic would work. I had to do something that resolved it once and for all, so I did. My explosions gave you something no-one else in your team did. It allowed you to express everything that had built up inside you that no-one else was willing to face. I know it wasn't the best way to handle it, but it's the only way I knew. I was just going off the programming we had in the system when the team in the control deck built me."

Me: "I suppose I can understand that."

Bane: "There's something else really important you're overlooking as well."

Me: "What's that?"

Bane: "You're assuming if I didn't exist your life would have been better without me."

Me: "Of course I am, you caused so much pain."

Bane: "But that's not true. If I hadn't been created to deal with this problem for you, there was another character waiting in the wings who had a different solution to the one I had."

Me: "I don't understand, who do you mean?"

Bane: "Without me being there to release some of the shit you were constantly building up, the next character waiting for the mic was the one who wanted to end it all. His solution was suicide."

Me: ...

Bane: "Lost for words?"

Me: "I'd just never thought of it like that. I always thought if you weren't there things would be better, but I can see now how much worse it could have been."

Bane: "I'm not saying what I did was a good solution, I'm just saying at least it kept you in the game long enough to get here."

*   *   *

From that moment I switched from not liking my rage character to being as grateful as I could be for him. He'd looked after me in ways I wasn't capable of doing, and no other character I'd built had been able to do. While Copey was busy having fun and being the centre of attention, he never, ever helped me to deal with my anger. He never helped me to process such an important emotion or find a way to make sure I was heard.

I realised it wasn't an exaggeration to say Bane saved my life. If it wasn't for him I can only imagine what might have happened. If I'd never been able to release those emotions, even in unhealthy ways, it frightens me to think of what I would have done as an alternative.

"You Live in his House"

Another story I really enjoy that illustrates how we can learn to love the characters we don't like comes from someone I've worked with for several months. He's an amazing man who I've really enjoyed guiding through this adventure and watching him change his life in spite of huge challenges he's had to overcome from his past.

One of his biggest challenges was a character I see fairly often who he'd learnt to use as his main go-to in difficult times. His dominant personality was a self-defeatist version of himself, who always looked for the negatives and talked him out of doing anything risky, always playing the safe option for fear of what might go wrong if he took a chance and what people might think or say if he failed.

When he identified him he really, really didn't like him. This is how our conversation went:

Me: "So tell me about what you don't like."

Him: "Well, the biggest thing is he stopped me from living my dream."

Me: "In what way? Tell me more."

Him: "About 12 years ago I wanted to pursue my dream of being an actor and entertainer. It's what I'd always wanted to do since I was a little boy and I had a chance to go for something that he stopped me going for because he was scared I'd fail and would make a fool of myself."

Me: "And what happened?"

Him: "I didn't go for the role and instead took a safe corporate job that I didn't want. If it wasn't for him I could be a rich, famous star now, and I really resent him for it."

Me: "That's true, you might have been really successful, but tell me how likely is it that people who want to become actors end up being rich and famous?"

Him: "Not very likely, it's really tough to make it in that world."

Me: "So, you're assuming if he didn't exist your life would be better. What if we pretend for a second the world without him might not be better. What might that world look like? What if he didn't stop you from becoming an actor?"

Him: "Well, I could have flopped and been an unemployed bum now."

Me: "And what happened with the life he encouraged you to choose?"

Him: "I did really well, got loads of promotions and paid a good salary."

Me: "So it sounds like you've got at least one thing you can be grateful to him for then."

Him: "What's that?"

Me: "You live in his house."

*   *   *

The point of the above examples is to illustrate how if we look at what the characters we dislike have brought to our lives from a different perspective, telling ourselves a different story about their role, we can find ways not only to be grateful for them but to love them for what they've done for us through the years when we weren't able to meet our needs in a healthy way.

When it comes to thinking our lives would have been better without them, as Winston Churchill said when I took him through this work:

"One must never forget when misfortunes come that it is quite possible they are saving one from something much worse."

We Don't Have to Like What We Accept

A stage of this exercise where people often get stuck is realising that finding ways to be grateful for what our characters have done for us does not mean we have to like what they did. Both Bane and I agree his solutions to our problems weren't ideal, they were just all he had at the time and the best he could come up with in the circumstances when backed into a corner.

The whole point of this is to enable us to see the darkest parts of ourselves that have previously been a plague on our lives. They have been operating from deep within our subconscious. Now we can bring them into our consciousness and find healthier ways of meeting the same needs.

✎ Exercise

Go back to your multiple personality list and for each character you've said you don't like, consider what they have done for you throughout your life that you can be grateful and love them for.

Remember it's not necessary for you to like what they did or how they handled the challenge of meeting your needs. The idea is to find ways to be grateful for how they looked after you until now to enable you to accept the parts of yourself you didn't previously like.

Notes

Reuniting the Team

The final stage of this work is to bring our team together in a way we've never done before.

Following the last exercise and speaking to each character to understand fully how we can be grateful for and love each one, I like to think of this phase as having a different type of talk with the parts of us who have collectively made up our ego for all these years.

This is the retirement chat.

Having accepted every part of us is valid, that we created each character for a reason and learning to love each one, the crucial final stage is to let each destructive part of our personality know we no longer need them.

From now on, their job will be to stay in the team as consultants and to teach the original version of us, Little You and Little Me, how to meet our needs in conscious and healthy ways. We can use the skills each character has developed over time and integrate them into our skill base to do the things we've never done for ourselves before. Like taking all our characters to one Rocky style training camp in the snowy mountains and asking them all to train Little Us to do everything we need.

Remember most of our characters were developed in our childhood when we didn't know any better ways of meeting our needs. Now we're grown-ups we can see ourselves for who we really are and know all about the needs we need to meet. We can make the conscious choice to meet those needs in healthy ways, meaning our destructive characters can move into a well-deserved retirement following their years of doing all the dirty work.

The question is how do we meet our needs in healthy ways so our more destructive characters can stay in retirement?

The first step is to review which emotional and practical needs each character has been meeting for us, and to think of all the practical ways we can meet those needs for ourselves long before the mic is passed all the way down the chain to the characters we didn't like.

Time for some more examples.

Retiring Bane

Bane existed for me to meet my emotional need for certainty and control, and to give me significance. From a practical perspective he was created to make me feel heard when neither the real me nor any of my other characters were saying what I wanted to say.

The practical step I needed to take to make sure Bane was happy to hang up his boots was, therefore, pretty simple. I needed to make sure I started to say the things I wanted to say rather than biting my lip and repressing my anger.

This is another part where the Karate Kid training we've been walking through on this adventure comes in.

Going back to Chapter 11, I needed to learn how to accept, allow and process my anger properly after learning it's a perfectly healthy emotion and not to be repressed anymore. After that, from Chapter 12 I needed to learn how to communicate my needs, wants and, most importantly, my boundaries, remembering as well that after setting and communicating my boundaries I had to learn how to defend them properly.

By consciously doing all this, I meet my needs for certainty, control and significance in a healthier way, as well as making sure I feel heard, so Bane naturally became redundant because I never reach a point in life where I've repressed my anger long enough that the mic reaches him.

Does that make sense?

I'll give some more general examples to help illustrate the point further.

Retiring Paul the Victim

As we discussed in the last chapter, I believe we all have a strong victim character in our cast-list, so it's important we discuss how that character can be encouraged to retire.

My victim character helped to meet my needs for love and connection, certainty and control and significance. From a practical perspective it helped me to avoid doing things I didn't want to do, to make people feel sorry for me when I was blaming the outside world for my problems and, maybe most importantly, allowed me to feel sorry for myself and avoid taking responsibility for my life.

As with Bane, then, the solution was simple, but not easy. To retire Paul the Victim I had to take radical responsibility for my life, in particular in relation to all the negative things I was blaming on other people or things.

By going through the exercises in the previous chapter and incorporating the other lessons we've discussed throughout this adventure, including being kind to myself, I learnt how to keep bringing my experiences of the world back to myself and asking in what ways the challenges I was facing were inside me being projected onto the world.

From there, I could begin to notice each individual circumstance in which Paul the Victim wanted to take the mic, and deal with whatever issue existed in a healthier way so he didn't need to.

Retiring Copey and Cope

Copey and Cope often both took the mic for me when I was feeling insecure or anxious. In general terms, the way for me to overcome them wanting to take control is to remind myself that feeling anxious is a completely normal way to feel, especially in uncomfortable or unusual situations. By doing so, I can retain the mic and stay present in situations where I would usually have allowed one of my characters to take over.

In practical terms, with Copey I learnt how to sing karaoke and dance in public without being drunk, and how to sit in large groups without feeling the need to numb any emotions with copious amounts of alcohol.

With Cope, I learnt how to identify when I might be tempted to use manipulation to get my own way in a situation and, instead, turn to vulnerability and honesty.

Given how prominent these characters were in my life, retiring them permanently is a work in progress and they do still pop up from time to time. When they do, though, it just serves as another gentle reminder that this work is ongoing, I am still a student and a flawed human being and I just need to learn for next time.

✎ Exercise

Go through each of the characters you didn't like on your list who you've hopefully learnt how to be grateful for and love, and figure out how for each one you can meet the needs they've been meeting for you in more conscious and healthy ways.

Come up with as many possible solutions as you can. There are no right or wrong answers, it's all about finding things that work for you in practice. This might be the smallest of things such as preventing your anxious character from distracting you from your feelings by free writing about your emotions whenever you spot them trying to distract you, or stopping your rage character getting on the mic by making sure you are accepting, allowing and processing your anger in a healthy way.

Notes

Simple Not Easy

We've already discussed this topic and it's worth reiterating here given how important it is.

Remember your characters were developed by your team in your control deck to serve a specific purpose and depending on your age as you read this they're likely to have been doing that successfully for decades. Given that, it's unlikely you'll be able to change your behaviours overnight, making this process relatively simple but not easy.

You might often see, as I do, people in the traditional personal development world telling you it's possible to completely transform your behaviour and, therefore, your life, overnight. While I agree we are able to change our beliefs overnight (you will hopefully have changed at least some of yours by the time you finish this book), my current view is most of our behaviours take time to change because we need to practice a new behaviour to replace an old one.

The only exceptions to that rule come when an old behaviour causes us so much pain that we have enough incentive to change overnight. If you can reach that stage with anything you've identified about yourself, that's fantastic. But don't expect it to happen with most of the behaviours you'll be seeking to change, which are likely to take time.

The Only Important Questions

It's time to share some wisdom from one of my favourite teachers from school, Mr Manning.

Mr Manning taught further maths to a very small group of us during our A-Levels, which are the qualifications we took between age 16 and 18 in England back when I was a lad.

At the end of our first few lessons Mr Manning would set us homework questions to do in the usual way and, at the beginning of the next lesson, would ask whether we'd done the work and whether we'd got any of the questions wrong. The answers were in the back of the textbook so we could check for ourselves, as we were trusted to do.

Despite our intelligence, or maybe because of it, we quickly realised we could get away with doing our homework just by telling Mr Manning at the start of each lesson we'd done it and had got all the questions right. It seemed like a simple solution that had no prospect of failure.

After a week or two, Mr Manning realised from our body language and the fact we weren't able to show an understanding in class of the questions he'd set for homework, that we weren't actually doing the work at home. He then told us something I'll never forget, and spoke to us in a way no teacher had ever spoken to us before. He spoke to us as adults.

Mr Manning told us in his direct and humorous way, that he already knew how to do maths and didn't need to pass his A-Levels at the end of the year because he already had the job he wanted. He said whether or not we wanted to pass our A-Levels and get the grades we needed to go to university was entirely up to us and, frankly, it didn't overly affect his life one way or another.

After that, he told us the point of this section. The only important questions he set us for homework were the ones we couldn't answer. If we could answer the questions properly that was great, because we understood how to do them and we'd be fine if similar questions came up on an exam. But if we couldn't figure out how to do one it was absolutely crucial he knew, because that was the only way he could help us to work it out.

That lesson applies just as much to this work. If you can't figure out how to be grateful for or love a character you dislike, or you can't work out in what ways you can meet the same needs in a conscious and healthy way, it's absolutely crucial you keep working at it until you find an answer rather than just skipping past it.

This is a key part of transforming your life to becoming the human you really want to be instead of the one created by other people, and it's another area where I can guarantee the treasure is there. If you can't find it now, keep digging and try approaching it from different angles until you can find the answers. If you can't figure it out the first time you look at it, allow it to roll around in your subconscious while you're going through your week, and ask your brain to figure it out for you. You'll be surprised how many problems can be solved that way.

If after all that you can't find the answer you're looking for, send an email to me at **questions@paul7cope.com** and I'll respond to as many questions as I can on my YouTube channel and podcast.

Who We Really Are

One of the most important parts of this section of the adventure links back to what we discussed in Chapter 13 about the stories we tell ourselves about who we are.

Look back to your list of *"I am"* statements from part 2 of the Fred exercise in Chapter 13. As we've discussed, the danger with those statements is they form a solid story about who we are that we then build an entire identity around when, as you've hopefully seen from the Bernard exercise from Chapter 14, the stories aren't usually totally true.

The key going forward from here is to become aware of each time you say something like *"I am..."* and ask yourself which *"I"* do you mean. Now you've seen all different sides of yourself, you might find it easier to accept that sometimes we're one thing and sometimes we're another, and that's okay.

Linking back to the shadow work in Chapter 15, it allows us to gently accept the darker sides of ourselves and, if we're not already, to also accept the lighter sides. If you constantly tell yourself you're a waste of space, it's time to begin to recognise that while you might sometimes be a waste of space, as we all can be (I love being a waste of space when I'm sitting in my underwear watching cartoons on TV), you're often not a waste of space at all, and it's okay to have both sides of your personality.

Likewise, it's okay that sometimes you're selfless and sometimes you're selfish, or sometimes you're happy and sometimes you're sad.

This all ties back to the dangers of black and white thinking. If we tell ourselves repeatedly a fixed story about who we are, it's no wonder we can't change. It's one of the reasons I'm not a big fan of the approach of Alcoholics Anonymous when everyone repeatedly tells themselves they're an alcoholic. That story then becomes so fixed it's impossible to move away from. Don't get me wrong, I'm a huge advocate of using whatever you can to live the life you want to live, so if being part of AA and abstaining entirely from alcohol works for you, that's great, I just don't currently believe it's always necessary.

Let me share a final story with you to tie that all together to end this chapter.

Falling Off the Wagon

One of my favourite people I've worked with came to me several months ago with severe concerns about his alcohol consumption and drug taking. He was worried that if he didn't get it under control it was going to derail his entire life and he'd lose everything, including his family.

We discussed my approach to solving these types of problems from their root, basically going through the work you've been doing in this book, and he decided he wanted to start.

Within about four sessions over around eight weeks, he started a call by laughing and saying to me that before the call he'd forgotten why he'd reached out to me in the first place, because his drinking and drug taking had completely disappeared.

This was weird, he said, because we hadn't spoken about drink or drugs once in our sessions. It's just another example of how focusing on the root of the problem (his low self-worth and not feeling good enough as a human) rather than the symptom (which manifested in this case through alcohol and drug addiction) is the best way to deal with problems we face.

The purpose of this story, though, is what happened a few weeks later.

Out of the blue I received an email midweek between our usual Zoom sessions. He told me he'd fucked up and fallen off the wagon. He'd been out on a binge, got pissed, taken a load of drugs and stayed out later than he told his partner he would. He was in trouble and beating himself up at being such a failure. I told him to just try to be kind to himself before we could speak about it properly in our next call.

This is how that conversation went:

Me: "So tell me what happened."

Him: "I just went out for a couple of drinks with a friend and got carried away. I ended up getting smashed, then the drugs came out and I stayed out much later than I was meant to, which got me in trouble. I feel like shit about it."

Me: "How many pints did you have?"

Him: "About 10."

Me: "And how many lines?"

Him: "Two or three."

Me: "And what time did you get home?"

Him: "About 2am."

Me: "Okay. So, before we started working together a few months ago, what would a typical night look like?"

Him: "Well, I'd usually drink about 20 pints, have a whole bag of coke and stay out until 7am."

Me: "Great. So, this is a win then."

Him: "What?"

Me: "This is a win. You've spent nearly 40 years being programmed in a way that led to you having chronically low self-worth and thinking you weren't good enough, which came out in an addiction to alcohol and drugs to help you numb the pain of life and repress your emotions. We've been working on a different way of thinking and feeling for a couple of months which led to you not drinking or taking any drugs in that whole time then, when you've gone back to them, you've taken far less than you would before and gone home five hours earlier than usual. That's a win. It's a step in the right direction. Rather than beat yourself up about it, we should be celebrating your progress."

Him: "Oh, shit. I hadn't thought of it like that."

Me: "Think about what we've been working on. Part of the problem is at a deep level you feel ashamed of yourself, going right back to when you were a little boy. When you try to stop drinking and taking drugs fully and you have a slip, you use language like 'I've fallen off the wagon' that just makes you feel even more ashamed of yourself and lowers your self-worth even more. It creates a vicious downward cycle that's even harder to break. The key is to be kind to yourself for the work you've done and give yourself credit for the progress you've made, which increases your self-worth, helps you to believe you are good enough and to break the cycle."

*   *   *

By embracing that approach rather than sticking to his old story about who he was, he was able to carry on the path we'd started and has now completely changed his life and his relationship to drink and drugs. He's able to have a few quiet drinks with friends when he wants to, but can stop when he chooses and hasn't touched drugs for months.

All of which has had a huge knock-on effect and created a virtuous cycle of him increasing his self-worth, which has rippled through the rest of his life.

He achieved all that by going through the exercises we've been doing, facing his own darkness, understanding who he really was and why each of his characters existed, then slowly taking conscious control of who was on the mic so he could meet all his emotional and practical needs in healthy ways, rather than leaving it to his subconscious and ego to meet them for him.

It's like magic.

Reminder:

1 Become the writer, producer and director of your life, not just the lead actor.

2 Self-sabotage does not exist.

17

MAKE PEACE

"There's a difference between knowing the path and walking the path."

(Morpheus / The Matrix)

We've reached the final part of the Karate Kid training where we tie everything together to find inner peace. You've hopefully already found yourself knowing how to do a few karate chops and self-defence moves as we've gone through the previous pages, so the purpose of this chapter is to make sure you're able to do the flying kick super-move as the climax to your movie, as well as understanding how everything else fits together to make you a black belt karate genius.

Ultimately, there's no point understanding all the things we've discussed unless we walk the walk as well as talking the talk.

Back to the Start

To go right back to the start of our adventure together, remember this all traces back to childhood, low self-worth and feelings that we're simply not good enough. The counterintuitive work we've been doing throughout the chapters of this book has been to understand fully at a deep level who we really are and who the human is that was created by other people, to enable us to deconstruct that human and build another in its place that we really want to be. To star in whatever musical we want instead of the one we were born into.

In mainstream terms, it's about getting beyond our ego to make sure the real us is on the mic and making the decisions in our lives, rather than characters we created in our childhood driving things.

We can't become the person we want to be and were always meant to be without first seeing the human that's been running us from our shadows. Once we shine a light on the part of us we've been repressing for decades we can bring it to our conscious mind and do something about it. We can consciously choose to act in a different way, whereas when we repress those parts of us they appear in our lives subconsciously without us realising.

This is the counterintuitive path to inner peace because when we see the darkest parts of ourselves reflected back at us by the world through the behaviour of others, rather than allowing that behaviour to anger and irritate us as it used to do, we can recognise it for what it is. We can see it as reflecting a part of us we've been taught not to like. We can say *"I do that as well"* or *"there's a part of me that wishes I could be like that"*.

From there, we can be kind to ourselves and show compassion to the person we would previously have judged, remembering we are all just flawed humans. Going back to what we talked about in Chapter 9, the key is to always bring everything back to us by taking radical responsibility and asking in what way are we responsible for the things we say we don't like.

After we've observed and shone a light on those parts of us, we can go back to the multiple personality work and ask ourselves in what way we would like to behave either to be more or less like the behaviour we've observed. Do we want to be more assertive and say what we mean more often? Or do we want to express our joy and let our hair down more? Would we like to be more relaxed and less uptight about everything, or allow ourselves to express our anger?

We can consciously choose to stop certain parts of us from taking the mic, without beating those parts of us up for not being good enough and we can train the real us, Little You and Little Me, to do all the things we weren't able to do when we were kids. We can do that by practising small things over and over again until they become our new automatic behaviours, remembering we're up against decades of being trained to behave in other ways, so it might take time to establish the new behaviours as permanent traits.

Becoming Who We Want to Be

The knock-on effect of this is we slowly become the human we want to be, letting go of the human we were built to be which, in turn, increases our score on the self-worth power bar and helps us to feel good enough.

On the other end of the spectrum if, for example, we were raised as people pleasers, it allows us to understand we don't always have to be liked and can be comfortable saying things to people that might lead to them not liking us as much as they did before. Or it might mean we're more comfortable saying stupid things or getting the answers to questions wrong when we were raised to believe that meant we weren't good enough.

Whatever your particular issues with your old self have been, you can slowly transform by building the human you were always meant to be instead of the one you were taught to be to please everyone else.

Going back to my example of my Auntie Flo, in my old black and white world I was taught subconsciously that I was good enough if I stayed quiet and didn't argue back against people or say things that upset others. As I did this work I realised that was causing me to repress my anger and hide who I really am. But I also didn't want to go to the other extreme of being someone constantly upsetting other people by saying whatever passes through my head at any given moment.

As part of the Karate Kid training, I now know I don't have to pick between a black or white extreme solution – I can pick a middle ground and adapt my approach to suit whatever situation I'm in. I can also accept I'm always going to be a student, there isn't a right or wrong answer and I'm not always going to do things the way I might ideally want to.

For example, I can calmly and assertively say what I want to say in any given situation, while being as kind and compassionate to the people around me as possible. If other people become upset with me as a result, as long as I've been kind and compassionate I am comfortable that I'm not responsible for their emotions in the same way they're not responsible for mine.

On the other hand, sometimes I can choose not to say anything because it's not appropriate in the circumstances. The important thing, though, is I am making that choice consciously rather than allowing my subconscious to decide which of my characters is taking the mic for me.

To give another example, someone I was working with was annoyed by people copying them into emails without saying whether they were meant to do anything about the content.

When we dug into why it annoyed him using Chapter 15's exercises, he realised he considered their behaviour lazy and there's a part of himself that's lazy, which he's been taught is not acceptable so he represses.

Now he can see that part of his shadow by shining a light on it, rather than just get irritated by it and say nothing, he can ask himself in what ways can he consciously deal with that scenario in the future to ensure things change. A simple solution is just to begin replying to people who copy him into those emails saying something like:

> *"Hi, it's not clear to me when you copy me into these emails whether I'm meant to do anything with them so, from now on, I just want to let you know that if you copy me in without any instructions I'm just going to delete the email without reading it. If that causes any problems please let me know."*

If we go back to the selfish silences part of Chapter 15, we can see that staying silent in this situation wasn't for the other person's benefit. Instead, it was to put the recipient of the emails in the role of victim because they could complain about the sender's behaviour. Staying silent allowed them to tell themselves they were in the right and avoid the risk of the other person not liking them for setting boundaries in an assertive and calm way.

By sending the email clearly stating boundaries we run the risk of people not liking us. However, the counterintuitive kicker in my experience is the opposite happens. In the vast majority of situations I've seen since beginning to practice this work, being able to calmly and assertively communicate needs, wants and boundaries to other people has a hugely positive impact on our lives, often leading to other people changing their behaviour in response.

Of course, things sometimes go wrong as they would when practising anything new but, in those circumstances, we can continue to communicate with people around us properly to repair any damage done while being kind to ourselves for any mistakes and remembering we're just students learning new things.

A Summary of the Path

In summary, the path we've followed is spotting the behaviour we don't like in others, recognising it in ourselves and becoming aware of which of our characters takes the mic when we behave the way that annoys us deep inside. We know now that is someone we were created to be, not who we want to be.

By understanding it all, it annoys us less and we can decide who we want to be, taking steps over time to practice a new behaviour.

Meanwhile, we are always remembering we're up against decades of training to be another way. So, the team in our head and our characters (our ego) are probably going to take some time to gently ease off the mic while we create new behaviour patterns. These changes *can* happen overnight, but often only really stick if we practice them over time.

It's simple and not easy. Little Us has to demand the mic from the characters who have been built to meet our needs and have been doing it subconsciously for years. Those characters might not want to give up their roles easily, hence it not being self-sabotage and more like self-protection.

We have to be assertive with the other parts of us, let them know we've been in training and we're ready to take control of situations we couldn't deal with when we were kids. We're adults now and don't have to follow the patterns we learnt as coping mechanisms when we were children.

Bruce Banner -v- The Incredible Hulk

A key part of this to note here is something I've heard referenced in other parts of the personal development and self-help worlds that I don't think helps. You might hear or think of this as an inner battle. A fight against your own ego as to who has control.

In my view it's a fight you can't win, which is why I don't encourage you to treat it as an inner battle.

Going back to my favourite comic-book analogy, think of Bruce Banner as Little You. He's the original version of the human. The Incredible Hulk represents the characters we built to survive when we couldn't meet our needs in healthy ways. He represents our ego. In our story, that's Little Me or Little You up against all the characters you've identified working as a team.

If that imbalance in numbers isn't enough to make you realise why we can't win an inner battle between our real self and our ego, think about it as the question being whether Bruce Banner can beat The Hulk in a fight. If Doctor Banner decided to have a fight against his inner monster, who do you think would win every single time?

I doubt it would be the tiny science man.

Which takes us back to what we've talked about throughout this work about being kind to ourselves and, specifically in relation to dealing with the characters we don't like, learning how to be grateful and love them for what they've done for us in our lives.

Doing that allows us to gently encourage them to retire rather than fighting parts of us. Remember that, from a self-worth perspective, fighting parts of ourselves only sends the subconscious a message that those parts of us are still not acceptable, keeping us locked in the *"I'm not good enough"* loop.

We break that cycle by accepting all parts of us and avoiding the inner battle. The best way to get our other characters to hand over the mic is to befriend them and gently explain to them why it's in everyone's interests for the real you to deal with things from now on, so they can enjoy their retirement as part of the team in the background.

The Power of Vulnerability

This is a huge part of the adventure I've purposefully left until the end of the training section of the book.

Before talking about it I'd again recommend you look up the work of Brene Brown in this area and consume all her books, Ted Talks and Netflix special.

I've already mentioned Brene when we were talking about shame, and her work around vulnerability goes hand in hand with that. It's incredibly impactful stuff in helping you transform your life.

The way I sum up this area is to think about how we've been taught to act in the world until now. In short, what we've learnt subconsciously has been to build our cast of characters, our ego, as a coat of armour and weapons against other people in the world, then approaching everything as a battle for us to win at all costs. In that way everything becomes a conflict.

A different way forward is embracing vulnerability and having the courage to take off our armour and put down our sword and shield before we expect anyone else to. Instead of treating everything as a battle between our egos, we lead with the real, vulnerable version of ourselves.

In practical terms, this looks like opening conversations by letting people know if I'm feeling afraid, anxious, annoyed or any other emotions I would never usually have talked about. I will let people know if I feel uncomfortable and that I'm still learning how to do all this properly, and ask out loud that people bear with me if I get upset or struggle to communicate properly.

While every sinew of my body would have been dead against this approach in the past, believing my ego was the most powerful part of me and the part best placed to achieve everything I wanted in life, since adopting this new way of living I have been blown away by its power.

When approaching other humans with our egos it only leads them to do the same, which inevitably can often result in conflict and pain for all sides. When leading with vulnerability, though, the impact can be incredible.

As Dave, my therapist, explained to me a while ago, egos cannot survive without another ego to fight against. If you drop your ego and lead with vulnerability, others are not usually able to sustain an egotistical attack on you without the energy of your ego to bounce off. I have witnessed time and time again the most powerful egos crumble when faced with vulnerability instead of fight.

Having been doing this work for a few years and doing everything I can to lead with vulnerability, I have never felt as strong and secure as I do now. The irony and counterintuitive part of this is that by being able to see all of myself, including all the darkness, and leading with vulnerability when dealing with others, including talking openly about my darkness and faults, it means there's little anyone can say that can deeply affect me.

It goes back to the Marcus Aurelius quote I mentioned in Chapter 15, that if anyone criticises me now I can accept it and know there's probably plenty of other stuff they could say about me if they knew me as well as I know myself. It makes me realise my approach to life before, with a coat of armour, sword and shield in most interactions was completely brittle and anyone could pierce it if they pointed at anything in my shadow I wasn't aware of and didn't like about myself.

Being vulnerable and understanding we are all just flawed human beings allows us to ask ourselves about ways we might be wrong and ways other people might be right, rather than stubbornly staying committed through our ego to opinions that we've developed emotional attachments to.

If you feel you have too many conflicts in your life, or you're the opposite and avoid conflicts because of how you feel around them or, like me, it's a bit of both, approaching situations in the future with vulnerability allows us to create a new story around dealing with important issues. Instead of calling them conflicts we can refer to them simply as conversations, which is what they ultimately are.

It's Okay to Come Back Later

As part of the resolving conflicts conversation another priceless lesson I learnt is that we don't have to resolve every issue as it arises. More often than not, the best thing we can do in the heat of the moment is allow ourselves to take in whatever has happened and process everything before coming back at some later date to discuss it.

By doing that we can avoid one of our more destructive characters hijacking the conversation by taking the mic when our emotions are heightened, and go through the things we've learnt to understand why something might be angering or irritating us before we try to go through it with another person.

Until we've mastered new ways of dealing with the world, using that time to pause and reflect is one of the most valuable things we can do to find more peace.

This also applies to things that might have happened in your life weeks, months or even years ago. There's nothing stopping you from going back to resolve an old issue if you feel you need to, hence some of the exercises we've already done around processing the past.

Maybe You're Right

This takes us to another powerful tool I learnt a few years ago, which I think originated with the spiritual author and speaker Wayne Dyer.

The story goes that whenever anyone said anything to Wayne about him or his work, for example one of his books, he would respond simply with, *"maybe you're right"*. Whether someone was telling him a book he'd written was the best they'd ever read, or it was the biggest pile of rubbish they'd ever seen, his response was the same.

It ties back to the idea that most things are only stories and aren't black and white, so when you stop to think about it it's possible for one person to think a book is awful and another to think the same book is brilliant.

Adopting the *"maybe you're right"* approach with a gentle shrug of our shoulders is a perfect addition to the work we've been doing, and can be used in practically every area of life.

Making Peace with the World

While we've talked a lot about doing this work to find inner peace, a huge part of finding that is making peace with the rest of the world.

By working hard to shine light on our own shadow we can slowly begin to realise everything we've discussed applies equally to every other human on the planet. So next time you're wondering why one day your partner is loving and the next day they're horrible, you can consider which of their characters have been taking the mic and why. You can ask in what ways you're contributing to their pain and what parts of their own shadow are being reflected back at them that they don't like, or which of yours is reflected back at you.

With complete strangers we can ask ourselves whether the stories we've been telling ourselves about them are true or whether there's any other way we could look at them that might lead us to have more compassion and empathy. We can ask where the information we're using to judge other people is coming from and how true it is on the scale. And, maybe most importantly, when we're tempted to paint ourselves as the goodies and other people as the baddies, we can ask ourselves in what ways those roles might be reversed.

We can learn to hold our views loosely and be prepared to change our minds by really listening to what others have to say rather than just waiting for our turn to speak.

More than anything, we can keep reminding ourselves we're all just flawed human beings and being compassionate towards ourselves and everyone else is a much more peaceful way forward than the alternative of judging ourselves and judging the entire world. Remember whenever we judge the outside world the root cause is we're secretly judging ourselves deep in our subconscious, so letting go of that judgment helps us to stop judging everyone else.

By really seeing our own darkness and understanding we're often just as much the baddies as we are the goodies, our compassion towards everyone else increases exponentially. This can help us to avoid arguments in our daily lives by realising once we find ourselves in an argument with anyone else we've both already lost. Instead of doubling down and leading with our ego in those situations, we can practice asking ourselves in what way we could be wrong while asking the other person more about why they think they're right.

Learning to Surf

Another analogy I often talk about with people I've coached involves surfing. When embarking on adventures like this many people think the aim is to iron out all the ups and downs in their lives, but that couldn't be further from the truth.

Think about what a healthy heartbeat looks like when someone is hooked up to a heart rate monitor in a hospital. Can you picture it? It goes up and down like waves. To take the analogy further, if we iron out those waves and we're left with a flat line, what does that mean on the heart rate monitor?

You've got it, it means we're dead. And being dead is not the aim of this work.

The key is to acknowledge that life is filled with waves. We have to have downs so we can appreciate and enjoy the ups, so rather than learning how to get rid of them this work is about learning how to be an amazing surfer and ride the waves. Our lives can transform completely once we embrace the downs as much as we savour the ups.

If you fully embrace this work, you're likely to find that your adventure is filled with huge ups and downs as you move into the next phase of your life. I often found it difficult, both in my emotional and physical healing adventures, when big steps forward were followed by crashes, which was when the wave analogy was most poignant. Even the best surfers in the world have to come off their board at the end of a big wave before regrouping and heading out in search of the next one. This work is no different.

Distractions from the Work

We've touched on this before and, as with all important points in life, it's worth repeating to make sure it goes in properly.

One of the crucial things to do when you decide to implement this work in your life is to notice when your ego is trying desperately to distract you from doing it. The main way I've noticed it does this, both with me and everyone I've ever guided through the adventure, is by encouraging us to focus our attention on something else. And when I say *'something'*, I mean absolutely anything.

The ego is brilliant at making us look at *The Prestige* and focus all our attention on there. So, for example, if you spend a fair proportion of your time worried about the sports team you support, focusing on your friend's dysfunctional relationships, obsessing over problems at work or what other people, the baddies, are doing on social media, you're falling for the oldest trick in the ego's repertoire. One thing for sure is the ego has lots of tricks.

The key whenever we notice this happening is to remind ourselves of the problem with magic tricks and bring everything back to us.

It's a reminder that whatever we see in the outside world is just a reflection of what's happening deep inside ourselves, and the most important thing to do is focus on that rather than whatever the world is showing us as a manifestation of our shadow.

Slowing Down is the Key

As you will have gathered as we've walked through these pages together, I'm not a big fan these days of most of the traditional personal development and self-help worlds. I've gone from loving what many teachers in that space preach to thinking not only is it not helpful but much of it is actually quite dangerous when you put it in the context of the work we've done together.

One of the things I dislike most about those worlds is the idea that to solve our problems in life we need to move faster. To work harder. To grind more. For generations now the entire Western world has been obsessed with getting faster, as though it's going to solve all our problems somehow if we can download a movie in two seconds instead of five.

What I realised a while ago is the main problem with going faster or working harder being the main aim is there's no upper limit. There's no point in time where we can look at each other and say, *"is this it, have we made it?"* so we just end up going faster and faster until we die, never feeling as though we ever went fast enough.

The secret the world really wants us to know is all around us in nature. The secret is that going slower is the solution, mainly because when we go slower there is a limit we can reach.

We can stop.

If I've learned anything during the past few years, it's that I am at my most peaceful when I reach a point where everything just seems to suspend in time and the world seemingly passes around me. To use another sporting analogy, it's like when a star player in a team game just seems to be able to drift through a game with everything moving around them rather than them desperately chasing everything else.

On the flip side, whenever I feel myself being pulled towards my old life of moving faster and being more productive in order to get things done, I feel myself becoming imbalanced again. When that happens I return to how the natural world tends to work and just move at my own speed. I slow down, breathe and reflect. I ask myself what part of my old patterns are kicking in to make me want to go faster, and usually discover it's something linked to self-worth, then I remind myself how that world and those patterns never made me content, which makes it fairly simple to return to my new ways.

I've gone from believing saving five minutes on every car journey is the target to thinking it isn't worth the extra anxiety that behaviour brings, and writing a book in six months rather than two weeks makes very little difference to the world.

Slowing down is the key.

What Balance Really Is

Seeing as we've just touched on this, I want to talk briefly about where most people go wrong when talking about finding balance.

I think when most of the Western world talks about balance that's not what they actually mean. They mean being right in the middle of everything in the sweet spot of whatever it is. So, for example, the perfect blend between working hard and having a happy home life.

But if you stop to think about it, that's not what balance looks like at all. If you don't believe me, put this book down for a second and stand on one leg for five minutes. Notice how many of those minutes you were right in the perfect sweet spot in the middle and how many of them you spent somewhere off the middle, gently correcting yourself one way or another.

If you don't want to do that, picture someone in a circus doing a high-wire balancing act. Can you see them? How much of their time are they just walking calmly down the centre of the wire with nothing happening, compared to how often they're moving from one side to the other, desperately correcting each time they move past centre, going too far the other way then over-correcting again.

That's what balance really is, and that's what happens to us in our lives. Which means expecting to find a place where we spend a considerable amount of time slap bang in the sweet spot of where we want to be is an unrealistic expectation we are unlikely to ever meet.

Instead, it's healthier to accept we will always be gently moving from one side to the other trying to figure things out and find that sweet spot and, in those beautiful moments when we do find it, we should savour them as much as we can in the knowledge they can't last forever. Which means when they stop we can be grateful for having experienced them rather than beating ourselves up for not having sustained that moment for all time.

The Power of Forgiveness

Another crucial part of making peace with ourselves and the outside world is to understand the power of forgiveness.

Many people when talking about this topic will focus on forgiving other people first, but to me that's no different to the main problem we face in life of focusing our attention on things outside of ourselves.

As with the rest of this work, the first step is to find a way to truly forgive ourselves for all the ways we've identified our shadow has been hurting others up to this point. If you haven't found anything you think you need to forgive yourself for yet, I'd suggest it's probably worth going back over the shadow exercises and thinking more deeply about the ways you've caused harm to the lives of other people.

Once you have found those things and done the work to ensure – as far as possible – your darkness is less likely to hurt anyone in the same way in the future, it's crucial you learn how to forgive yourself fully. As we'll see when it comes to love in a couple of chapters, unless and until you do that you will never be able to truly forgive someone else.

After you've accepted, allowed and processed any guilt or shame you have about your own past behaviour, the next step is to learn how to forgive the people in your life who have hurt you, even if they've never apologised properly for the way they behaved.

This is another area I struggled with for a while because the world tends to teach us we find 'closure' in these places through the actions of others, but I learnt that isn't usually true. If you are waiting for the outside world to do something before you can forgive and move on with your life you're likely to be waiting a long time, which will only cause you more harm.

Instead, understanding the reasons someone has acted the way they have based on everything you've learnt on this adventure and showing compassion towards the little person inside them who is just another flawed human being should hopefully be enough to enable you to forgive them for whatever they've done.

If you struggle with this, use a free writing exercise similar to the ones we've done on a few occasions to process all your emotions and understand fully what you're struggling to let go of. It may just be you've never really allowed yourself to process things properly. If that's the case, now's the time to do it so you can move on with your life.

Overcoming Addictions

As we've touched on previously, addictions of any sort are simply a symptom of deeper issues tracing back to childhood. Rather than focus on whatever addiction you or anyone else has, it is more important to remember the purpose of the addiction is simply to distract from emotions we've been taught are not safe to feel and to numb the pain of general life.

I appreciate it might sound insane, but whether someone is addicted to heroin or shopping the same root causes apply. It's why whenever I work with anyone who comes to me with an addiction problem, usually drugs (including alcohol), we spend very little, if any, time talking about the addiction itself. Our focus remains firmly on the Programming Experiences from childhood that have led to the person needing the addiction as a coping mechanism.

If you are experiencing any addictions the key is to focus on the work you've been doing during this adventure and understand what needs are being met through the addiction to something in the external world. Once you are able to identify the root causes and deal with them in the ways we've discussed, you're likely to find the addiction simply drifts away.

At the time of writing there has been plenty of discussion around large-scale addiction to social media. However, most of that debate focuses only on the symptom itself (the use of social media and how huge media companies are using psychological techniques to keep people trapped in addictive loops) rather than the root causes leading people to be susceptible to that type of manipulation.

Once you have dealt with the root causes, it doesn't matter what tricks any media company uses, you can simply choose not to use their platforms because you don't need them to fulfil your needs anymore. The same applies to any other addiction you can name, including addictions to emotions such as depression or self-pity.

Be Kind to Ourselves to Be Kind to Others

While we're talking about social media, it entertained me recently to see a campaign for people to be kind to others on the internet.

Rather than lots of people actually being kind to each other, though, I saw what I expected to see – most people shouting at other people telling them they need to be kind.

This is a perfect example of us not being able to see our own darkness while painting ourselves as the goodies and everyone else as the baddies.

Hopefully, I don't have to say this so deep into this adventure but, in case it's needed, shouting at other people to be kind is not being kind. In the same way that judging other people for being judgmental is also being judgmental.

It perfectly illustrates what we saw in the shadow work, with people seeing others being unkind and it annoying them because there's a repressed part of them that is also unkind, or wishes it could be more unkind in certain situations.

The secret to being able to be kind to others is, first and foremost, to learn how to be kind to ourselves. Unless we can face our own shadow and be kind to ourselves for being a flawed human being, we will never be able to be genuinely kind to any other flawed human.

Allowing Every Character to Process Emotions

Now you're aware there's not just one of you knocking around the planet, another key to finding peace is to be aware that sometimes more than one of your characters might need to process emotions in relation to any particular situation.

I had a very poignant moment in my adventure on this point when a while after leaving my marriage I realised I needed to delve into the emotions I was experiencing in order to accept, allow and process them. As we discussed in Chapter 11, I began free writing about everything I was feeling and that free writing turned into a letter to my ex-wife.

When I'd finished writing it I read it again and thought it summed up everything I felt and needed to say. The next day, however, I felt as though there was more that needed to come out. So, I did the same exercise again. This went on for five days, each day writing everything I felt in depth, accepting, allowing and processing it all. Each day I felt as though I was just saying similar things to the day before, just peeling the layers of the onion.

At the end of the week when I read through all five letters together, though, I realised something amazing. It was as though each letter had been written by a different person which, when we think about our multiple characters, made absolute sense.

One of the letters was full of sadness. Another full of apologies, regret and remorse. A third filled with anger and resentment. A fourth packed with grief and a fifth with, well, what the animal side of me missed from our relationship.

Even the hand writing changed slightly reflecting my state as I wrote each one. It was really powerful to see the whole range of emotions being processed, and showed the importance of allowing each character who needs to process something to do it fully.

In particular, it's crucial to allow each character to deal with its grief in whatever way it needs to. Remember grief is such a key emotion in our lives and any changes will impact on different parts of us in different ways.

Be sure to allow each part of you to process whatever it needs to.

Exercise

Go back to the Dorothy exercises (Parts 1 and 2) from Chapter 11 as well as any apology letters you've written from Chapter 15.

If you feel you need to, write letters to any people from your past expressing how any of your characters feel about your experiences with them. This might seem similar to the exercises from Chapter 11, but the subtle difference is saying the things you want to say to someone from your past can help process trapped emotions in a way the free writing exercises and letters of apology might not.

It's also worth noting you can come back to these exercises and do them as many times as you need as the onion keeps coming back for layers to be removed. Every time you write a letter you'll help to shift more repressed emotions from the past, which can help you find peace without ever having to send any of the letters to anyone.

If you do feel the urge to send anything you've written, I'd recommend leaving it for a few days to reflect and make sure it is something you really want to do. Ideally, talk it through with a therapist, coach or an objective, reliable friend or family member before going through with it. While these exercises can bring us a lot of relief and peace, sending the letters could do more harm to yourself and others.

How to Talk to Yourself

When we've spent so much of our lives being mean to ourselves inside our heads, it can actually be quite tricky to learn how to talk to yourself in a kind way.

The first thing to note is it takes practice, so doing it as often as you can on a daily basis is ideal. Also, to begin with, I'd recommend doing it out loud. I appreciate that might make you sound like a lunatic so it's worth limiting it mainly to when you're alone. Nevertheless, talking to yourself as though you're talking to someone else at the start of this usually helps to teach your subconscious what it's going to be doing from now on.

In this way, as with many other parts of this work, your best friend is often humour. If you can laugh while you're practising, it helps the team inside your control deck to realise life doesn't have to be quite so serious. The only thing to be careful of is that you don't default to using humour as a distraction from feeling emotions that make you uncomfortable.

If you still struggle with this, instead of thinking of it as talking to your current self, think of it as speaking to Little You and being kind to that little person who just wants to be loved unconditionally.

If you'd visited my apartment a year into doing this work you'd have definitely thought I had a screw loose. To add to the subliminal retraining of my brain, I'd bought a load of brightly-coloured sticky notes and written short messages on them before sticking them all around my apartment. They were on the fridge, above the cooker, on every door, on the bathroom mirror, on my laptop and all over the walls. They said things like:

- "Be kind to yourself"
- "You're only a student"

- "So, what?"
- "And then what happened?"
- "Sometimes…and that's okay"
- "Is there room for both?".

"So, what?" and *"And then what happened?"* are two of my favourite lines to say to myself and others during this work, because it's amazing how often we build something up to be a really big deal. Just by asking ourselves those two questions very gently and without judgment, we can often realise nothing actually happened, we'd just been winding ourselves up over nothing.

When you get further down the path doing this work, *"And then what happened?"* can reach extreme proportions because there's very little in life that actually has any dramatic impact if we accept it for what it is.

"They called me a liar!!"

"And then what happened?"

"Well, nothing, it just hurt my feelings."

"Oh, okay."

Abandoning black and white thinking and finding room for two or more things to exist at the same time has also been a game changer in my life. I find it hard to get into an argument about anything these days because it's very rare that a situation is black or white, so I usually just end up shrugging my shoulders and combining it with *"maybe you're right"*.

To add to this, as we discussed in Chapter 13, the vast majority of the pain and suffering in our lives comes from stories we invent about the world, which means one of the most impactful ways we can talk to ourselves in a way that brings us peace is to stop telling ourselves stories about the past or the future that aren't true.

This is most powerful when we are tempted to speculate about what another human thinks or feels about any given situation. Unless we are prepared to ask that person what they actually think or feel, the best thing we can do is learn how to become comfortable not knowing.

All of which leads me to that lovely, warm peaceful place right in the centre of the balancing high wire. I recommend you take whatever messages you feel are most impactful from this book and implement them wherever you can. The more often you can gently suggest to your subconscious the new behaviours you want to adopt, the better it will be.

A Rigid Dance

An incredible lesson I learned when interviewing Dr. Ed Tronick was something he said about the world and the way we see it.

He said we often look at things happening on a global scale and things happening in our daily lives and think they're chaotic when, in fact, the opposite is true.

He gave the example of a dysfunctional relationship in which each party causes the other harm. While to the people involved and to the outside world it might look as though the dysfunction is built on chaos, in reality each party is playing a very specific role in the show.

When one party does one thing, the other party reacts in the same way, just like in a well-rehearsed dance. As I stopped to reflect on that and thought of my past relationships and those of the people around me, I could see it with absolute clarity for the first time. My sister and I often joke that our parents have had the same argument before Sunday dinner every week for our entire lives. We are all guilty of doing the same things over and over again in the same rigid dance, filtering up to a global scale, which we'll talk more about in Chapter 21.

The Three Stages

In very basic terms, when it comes to our emotions what we're looking to do comes in three parts:

1   Identify our emotions
2   Accept, allow and process them all
3   Move on

My issue with much of the traditional personal development and self-help world is there's too much of a push to reach stage three, which is what causes additional damage to people who have already been taught to repress their emotions.

Being told to reframe feeling nervous as being excited does nothing other than remind our system of a story we learnt when we were a little kid that there's something wrong with being nervous. If you'd asked me before I began this work whether I ever felt nervous, I would have told you very enthusiastically that I never felt nerves, it was just excitement.

Now I'll tell you I'm nervous because I know there's nothing wrong with it. There will often be excitement mixed in with my nerves, but there's no point denying the nervousness or, to give it a different name, anxiety, because that's what was causing me so much of a problem for decades.

The key is to make sure even after doing this work we don't skip past stage two too quickly. Whenever I find myself moving away from the centre and not feeling great, it tends to be because

I've identified the emotions I'm feeling then told myself I've processed them to move on faster without properly doing it. Remember moving on too quickly is just another form of repression, which we want to avoid.

Getting to stage three is, though, important, and should happen naturally if we complete stages one and two fully. As we've discussed, moving towards our misunderstood emotions rather than away from them usually leads to them disappearing naturally in a fairly short space of time.

If we find ourselves wallowing without moving to stage three, it's important to gently ask why that might be the case. What are we gaining from wallowing in an emotion or making ourselves a victim?

Be The Parent You Wanted

An issue I've witnessed in a few people I've coached links back to a lesson I learnt from a friend I met in Bali a couple of years ago.

We were chatting one day and he was telling me about a conversation he'd had with his therapist about his dysfunctional relationship with his dad that continued to cause him pain despite putting a lot of work into therapy and trying to process his childhood and their ongoing problems.

His therapist said to him:

> *"You keep going back to this human, this man, asking him to be something he isn't. You keep expecting him to be the parent you wanted instead of the parent he is, and he's simply not capable of it. That's not his fault, it's just the way he is from the way he was raised as a child. When you were a child that was a perfectly normal behaviour pattern but, now you're an adult yourself, it's time to stop going back to*

that man and asking him to be something he isn't. It's time
to start being the parent to yourself that you want to be."

That lesson has always stuck with me and it's worth remembering if you find yourself having any ongoing challenges with your parents or original caregivers after doing this work. Remember they're just flawed humans as well.

It's time to be the parent to yourself you wanted them to be.

A Society of Children in Adult Bodies

I once heard the author and philosopher Alain de Botton sum up one of the world's main challenges very succinctly.

Given most people have never done any work of this nature and are, therefore, still carrying around with them thousands of scars from their childhood that have never been processed and dealt with, what we've actually ended up with is a society of children in adult bodies, rather than a society of grown-ups.

The world would make far more sense if we looked at most people as four-year-old children and assessed their behaviour on that basis. It's something I started doing a couple of years ago and it has had a profound impact on my life. It doesn't take much to look at a world leader, online influencer, celebrity or colleague in work and, if you picture them as a four year old, see all the issues they're still struggling to deal with. The 40-year-old body they're walking around in just causes confusion. I was exactly the same before doing this work and at times can still see the little boy inside me reacting to a world he wasn't built for.

The purpose of this work is to make sure as often as possible we're no longer part of the children in the adult bodies brigade.

✎ Exercise

To wrap up this chapter and the last stage of the Karate Kid training, I want to give you some exercises to practice that might seem simple but can have a huge effect on your development and transformation.

Part 1

The first is to do small things every day that you might never have dreamed of doing before because you'd be too worried about what other people might think or say, or because you told yourself a story that's just the way you are. You'll have to be honest with yourself and identify what those things are, and it doesn't matter how small or silly they seem. The whole point is to start with something small and build up.

So, for example, in my old life I would never have left the house wearing a shirt with any form of mark on it. If I'd spent half an hour ironing a shirt to perfection, then spotted just as I was leaving the house there was a tiny ink mark on the collar I would turn around and change the shirt. A small step for me, then, was to ignore any little marks I noticed on my shirts before leaving the house while observing how no-one cared and nothing happened.

After a while I slowly cared less about what people thought, reaching a point last year where I realised after recording a YouTube video that my jumper had crumbs all over it from a biscuit I'd eaten before shooting. The old me would have immediately deleted the video and re-recorded it to make sure it was perfect. As the new me I just shrugged my shoulders and said to myself, *"it doesn't need to be perfect, I'm just a flawed human"*.

If anyone does make any comment about whatever it is you've done, it's crucial to note their issue is not with you but with themselves, just as it was when we were judging other people for similar things. Once your own self-worth is repaired and we stop judging ourselves harshly internally, judging the outside world magically stops as well.

If things like that don't bother you, maybe it's something like every tin in your kitchen cupboard has to be turned with the label facing out or you can't sleep. If that's the case, practice leaving them facing the other way and accepting whatever emotions come up.

Something likely to apply to you that could bring a huge amount of value is changing the way you behave around social media. Simply spending less time on any of the platforms you use frequently can help and, specifically, posting less frequently looking for external validation, sympathy or attention – or stopping entirely using the platforms to judge other people and paint yourself as an angel – can all slowly help to build self-worth.

Find your own examples and start to gently change your behaviour towards something that gives you more peace.

Part 2

This might be the simplest and most powerful exercise I've ever done, and works particularly well for those of us who were raised to need credit for the things we do (most of us).

From now on, every week I want you to do a good deed for someone without telling anyone about it. If you tell anyone at all in order to get credit, whether that's a friend, relative, therapist or coach, it doesn't count.

As you read that it might sound like the easiest exercise in the world, but when I first did it I was shocked by how desperate I was to tell someone, anyone, about the good deed I'd done so they could tell me how good a person I was.

The point of this is to begin to practice the idea that our self-worth is in our control. If we can do good deeds and give ourselves credit for what we've done, we don't need any external validation to help us feel good about ourselves.

By doing these exercises combined with everything else you've already done, you will slowly but surely build your score on your self-worth power bar.

Remember, the small things are the big things.

Notes

"Be yourself, no matter what they say"

(Englishman in New York / Sting)

18

SOLVING LIFE'S PROBLEMS

Now we've finished the training part of the adventure, seeing as I called this book *"How To Solve Any Problem In Life"* I thought I should give you the biggest examples I can think of to illustrate the point, or you might just think I'm full of shit.

So, this part basically covers a few big topics I wanted to talk about that might play big roles in your life and should demonstrate where this work applies at the highest level.

If you've already peeked ahead at the titles to the next three chapters, I hope you'll at the very least acknowledge you're getting value for money for whatever you paid for this. There can't be many books in the world that tell you how to sort out all the shit in your life including your love life, changing the world and healing illnesses.

Hopefully you'll see how everything we've been talking about comes together to address some of the biggest challenges we face as humans.

19

THE PROBLEM WITH LOVE

"Fever isn't such
a new thing,
Fever started long ago"

(Fever / Little Willie John)

We might as well get stuck straight into one of the big topics.

Did you know that Eskimos have between 40 and 50 words for snow, and around another 70 for sea ice?

It makes sense when you pause for a second to think about it. Most of us live in places where snow and ice appear infrequently throughout the year. I met someone last year who had never seen snow at all in her 30 years on the planet.

So, we don't really need more than a couple of basic words for those things.

But imagine if where you lived was dominated by snow. It might make more sense, then, to have different words for the different types. You know, the soft fluffy stuff, the dirty, gritty stuff, the icy, slippy stuff, the deep stuff, the shallow stuff. You get the picture.

Having more words to easily describe what type of snow is outside would come in handy.

That might sound like a strange way to begin a chapter about love, until you ask yourself whether you have ever stopped to think how we use the word *"love"* in English. I hadn't until a few months ago and I don't think many people ever do.

We use the same word for the way we feel about our favourite food, our mum, our favourite sports team, the romantic partner we have a secure relationship with, the romantic partner we have a dysfunctional relationship with, our children, our dog, our dad, our nieces and nephews and our favourite hobby, to name just a few.

Isn't that a bit mad?

When I say, *"oh, I really love ice cream"* I don't mean I love it in the same way I love my niece and nephew. I'm not committed to helping ice cream live its best life and I won't always be there for it if it needs me (although I do expect it to be there whenever I need it).

Yet, despite developing this language for thousands of years, we've never thought it might be a good idea to come up with a few more options for us to describe accurately what we mean at any given moment when talking about this highly complex topic, even though other languages have done just that.

It's one of a number of problems we face.

New Definitions of Love

Before we go further, I think it's worth considering an important part of the earlier training and reflecting on the labels we use when talking about love. Ideally, I think we should be more specific about the types of love.

This is another topic I'm sure there are entire books about and one which we could talk about for hours. I've limited myself to four general categories I think cover most of what we need for the purposes of this chapter.

Endless Love

The version of love referenced most often when we talk about the people we love most is, I think, *"unconditional love"*. Sadly, in my experience and having thought about this for a while now, I don't think unconditional love exists very often, at least not in the way we generally mean.

If you think back to the very start of our time together on these pages and the things we discussed around our childhoods, you might have already realised we don't even usually show the truest form of unconditional love to our children and close family members.

Many of our problems in life actually trace back to us feeling the love we received was conditional upon many things, including not showing various emotions that our caregivers were not comfortable with, or behaving in certain ways.

For the most part, I think when we refer to unconditional love as the love we have towards our children and close family, what we really mean is a love that will never end. No matter what these people do to us we will always feel love for them.

I'll refer to that as *Endless Love*.

Hollywood Love

This is the area that really started me thinking about the topic of love. It's the type of love we've been taught by society, largely through Hollywood movies, songs and popular culture, that we should feel for each other in our romantic relationships.

It's the love we see as someone knocking down a door to save the person they were meant to be with. The one that says someone else is the missing half of us. That someone else completes us. That we all need to be rescued or should be rescuing someone else.

This type of love is, to me, the most dysfunctional form we have. The biggest problem, though, is it has been normalised by society to lead us all to believe it's what we should be searching for when, in fact, it's built on all the same problems we've been discussing throughout this adventure.

Committed Love

What starts as Hollywood Love often turns dysfunctional and burns out leading to painful separations or divorces. However, if a relationship built on any form of Hollywood Love lasts any reasonable period of time it mutates into what I'll describe as *Committed Love*.

What I mean by Committed Love is best explained through a short story. A woman in her fifties I was talking to a few years ago was explaining to me how she'd separated from her husband of 30 years after a very painful conversation. She confronted him after years of arguments and asked whether he ever really wanted to marry her. He said it was never his intention to get married or have kids, but he loved her so did both of those things for her. If he was living his life again, though, he might not have done either.

The lady was distraught because she said it was proof he never loved her. My view from the outside was different, though. I observed that despite her husband saying he might not have married her or had kids in another version of his life, he did both of those things for her and for the past 30 years had worked hard every day to provide for his family. They always had money for rent and food, and she could focus on raising the kids she always wanted.

I said that, to me, might be one of the purest forms of love there can be, albeit still dysfunctional. In some ways it's sacrificial and, at the very least, shows dedication and commitment to another human. If that doesn't represent a kind of love I'm not sure what does.

True Unconditional Love

Despite what I've said above, I do believe true unconditional love exists, I just don't believe it's really possible unless a human has done the work necessary to be able to love themselves for who they are, their darkness and their light before trying to love someone else.

It's only by being able to do that work are we then able to truly love someone else unconditionally. To tell them without any doubt we love them regardless of what they do or how they feel or behave. To let them know we want them to be themselves, no matter what that means for us. To tell them we love them even if it means they won't be a part of our play or see us ever again.

True unconditional love is truly selfless in every way, which is why we see so little of it.

I also believe we can move from the other forms of love to this purest form by working on ourselves, being vulnerable and communicating openly and honestly with each other. It takes time and work, but is possible.

Introducing Attachment Theory

Now we've explored some new ideas for definitions of different types of love, let me introduce you to one of my favourite topics. As with everything else you've read here, I'll give you my interpretation of attachment theory and leave it to the purists to point out where they think I'm wrong. If what follows interests you, I'd highly recommend reading more on the subject if you want to understand more about why your romantic relationships are the way they are.

In basic terms, attachment theory is all about how we learn to attach to other humans from a very young age. Which means, as with so many of the things we've talked about, the problems you face in your romantic relationships have less to do with what's going on now and more to do with when the magic trick started all those decades ago.

You form attachment styles based largely on the way you formed attachments with your original caregivers, and you're likely to have carried those styles right through your life into every romantic relationship you've ever had. You know those clichés that you end up marrying your mum or dad? Well, it's not all hocus pocus nonsense.

Different people describe attachment styles in different ways, but my favourite descriptions split them into four simple categories:

1 Secure Attachment

2 Anxious Attachment

3 Avoidant Attachment

4 Anxious/Avoidant Attachment

Secure Attachment

Secure is where we want to be. The Holy Grail of attachment. People with a secure attachment style are independent enough to look after themselves while being comfortable forming close relationships in a non-needy way. They'll give you space when you want it and communicate their wants and needs coolly and calmly like a Jedi.

When I first started learning about attachment styles I read that 50 percent of the population display a secure style, which to be frank shocked me. The only people I've ever met who I'd say display a truly secure attachment style are people who have done this type of work for years and figured out all their own shit, which is probably about two per cent of the people I've had contact with over the years.

To check my observation against the statistics I'd read, I asked my therapist what his experience was in his years on the planet and he said similar to me.

So, if 50 percent of the people out there do really have a secure attachment style they seem to be hiding it pretty well from me and Dave at least.

Anxious Attachment

Stereotypically associated more with women than men (but see later on this), people with an anxious attachment style tend to be quite needy in relationships. They're the people who constantly want to be with the other person, phone repeatedly to see where you are and basically won't leave you alone, needing all kinds of reassurance about themselves and the relationship.

Avoidant Attachment

Stereotypically associated more with men than women (although also see later), people with an avoidant attachment style tend to want more space and feel smothered quite easily. They like to keep people at a distance and not get too close.

This was my predominant attachment style before I did any of this work.

Anxious/Avoidant Attachment

This is the place nobody wants to be. As the name suggests it's a combination of the other two troublesome styles and leads to a fucked up place where a person is partly really needy while simultaneously not wanting to get too close.

As you can imagine, that's a tricky combination. It's also where I ended up by the time I left my marriage a few years ago.

It's Not Black and White

To continue a big theme from the earlier training, as you might have already realised we tend not to just have one style. Instead, we usually display a combination of the different areas, landing in different places on the scale for each one.

For example, you might display a strong anxious attachment style with a touch of avoidant and a sprinkling of secure. If you want to find out what your attachment style is, which I'd recommend doing, visit **paul7cope.com/attachment** and follow the links to a free online test.

It's also possible over time to change your attachment style, both in a positive and negative direction. As I've mentioned, during my last relationship I became less and less secure over the years, falling from predominantly avoidant with a touch of secure and anxious to full blown anxious/avoidant.

The good news, though, is it's also possible to move in the other direction, which I believe is another natural consequence of doing the work in this book. When I last took the online test I mentioned above, I had thankfully moved firmly into the secure attachment space.

"This love has taken its toll on me"

(This Love / Maroon Five)

Why Every Relationship You Have is at Least a Little Bit Fucked

As with many other things we experience, when it comes to our romantic attachment the universe has a twisted way of trying to help us work out our shit from when we were kids.

In basic terms, this means we tend to be drawn to people based on our respective attachment styles. Secure people tend to be drawn to other secure people, with anxious and avoidant people drawn to each other. This is also where Hollywood Love comes back into the picture to help illustrate why so many of our relationships are doomed before they even start.

Unless you've been raised under a rock or in a commune with no access to Hollywood movies, you're likely to have watched hundreds if not thousands of movies over the years that normalise the dysfunctional connection between anxious and avoidant attachment styles. There are also very famous scenes in movies that sum up the problem completely.

As a young boy, I must have watched the movie *Pretty Woman* a thousand times, because it was one of the movies my big sister was obsessed with. *Pretty Woman* was watched by millions of people worldwide and seen as a beautiful story of love overcoming all odds.

In reality, it was a story about a millionaire with serious psychological and emotional problems from his childhood forming a dysfunctional attachment to a sex-worker, who had a similar upbringing. The closing scene portrays the myth that has been so damaging to people of all genders for generations – the concept that we exist in relationships to save each other.

The other famous movie scene that springs to mind that melted a generation of women's hearts was in *Jerry Maguire* when

Tom Cruise's character turned to Renée Zellweger's and said the immortal line: *"you complete me."* I still remember now the impact that scene had yet, when we look at it from the perspective of this work and attachment theory, it's just another example of an avoidant personality type forming a dysfunctional attachment to an anxious personality type and both sides thinking the other person is the missing half of their coin.

The problem is we humans are not able to fill the missing parts of us externally, whether that's through working harder, taking drugs, gambling, buying lots of things or, in this case, through attaching to another human and expecting them to *"complete us"*.

Sadly, as most of us have learnt consciously and subconsciously from all kinds of inputs over the years, including movies and most relationships we've seen as examples to replicate, our subconscious believes that is the way forward, hence most of our relationships being at least a little bit fucked until we learn how to un-fuck them.

"I've Got Some Bad News For You"

When I first started to learn about this topic, one of the earliest articles I read was a blog post written by the author Mark Manson. It contained a line that has always stuck with me.

It said something along the lines of, *"if you find you're always attracting psychopaths into your life, I've got some bad news for you…"* and linked to another article exploring the things we've discussed about how we end up being attracted to other humans.

The way I like to think about this in simple terms in an attempt to help you move past the idea that most of the problems in your relationships are the other person's fault (if you are still thinking that after everything we've discussed) goes back to the concept of scaled thinking we discussed earlier.

In basic terms, think of what we've been discussing as a straight line scale from zero to 100 with zero being completely fucked and 100 being the most secure person you can imagine.

When you look at your current partner or, if you're single, your previous partners, what score would you give them? As we talked about right at the start of the book, go with whatever number first pops into your head rather than thinking about it for very long.

My theory is wherever you think your partner is on the scale, you're probably within about five points of them either side. So, if you think your partner is a completely imbalanced, insecure lunatic with an anxious/avoidant attachment style, and you scored them a lowly eight out of 100 on the scale, your score is likely to be between three and 13.

Why, you might ask, would I come to this conclusion? Well, if you were more emotionally and psychologically secure yourself, you wouldn't be in a relationship with someone who is so fucked up.

The way out, then, is to do the work in this book or other work like it, to move further up the scale into a secure place so you can either create or attract a more stable, secure relationship.

A Rigid Dance

If you recognise any of yourself or your relationships in what I've described, it's likely another point we discussed earlier plays a large role in your life.

Remember I mentioned Dr. Ed Tronick describing how we view much of the world as chaotic when it's actually a rigid dance? That might be most apparent in romantic relationships.

I mentioned earlier my parents and the same little arguments they've been having for decades. Can you think of any similar examples in your life? Does your partner, or a previous partner, always do one thing and you always tend to respond in the same way, usually just focusing on their behaviour and complaining about them rather than thinking of how you're contributing to the very thing you say you hate?

If you've been in a relationship for a while, it's highly likely you and your partner have been doing a well-rehearsed dance for years, back and forth, step for step, without ever realising.

Living in a Co-Dependent World

This is another area where countless books have been written exploring and debating the detail, so I mention it here only to introduce you to the topic in case you want to delve further into it.

There are many definitions of co-dependency so let's stick for now with the general reference point of Wikipedia, which defines a co-dependent person as:

> "...someone who cannot function on their own and whose thinking and behaviour is instead organised around another person, process, or substance. Many co-dependents place a lower priority on their own needs, while being excessively preoccupied with the needs of others."

As with many other things on this adventure, I first started looking at co-dependency because I could see that my romantic partners over the years, who typically displayed strong anxious attachment styles, were clearly also co-dependent.

I vividly remember at times completing application forms for various things and when it asked *"do you have any dependents?"* I would think *"yes, my partner"*.

Interestingly, though, the further down this path I travelled and the more I began to focus on myself rather than the external world, including other people, I had another breakthrough I wasn't expecting.

I was co-dependent as well.

In all the literature I've read about co-dependency, as with most other topics, people generally seem to want to put everyone in a nice, neat, black and white box. You're either co-dependent or you're not and, if you're in a relationship with a co-dependent person, they're the co-dependent one and you're the poor victim. I see this sort of message repeated over and over in different areas of psychology and human behaviour.

As I often see, though, and as we've already seen in the work we've been doing together, it's rarely the case that we can see something in others that isn't somehow in us as well.

To give you a basic summary of my current beliefs in this area, if the definition of a co-dependent person as set out earlier ties in well with humans who display an anxious attachment style, that would suggest if we follow the usual attachment patterns that people with an avoidant attachment style end up in relationships with co-dependent (anxious) people.

For a while when I first looked into this, that's exactly what I could see. Then my confirmation bias helped me to only see the ways in which that was the correct assessment of my relationships.

Luckily, though, another part of our Karate Kid training kicked in and I started to question the stories I was telling myself because every now and then I'd read something about co-dependency and couldn't help but see a part of me in it as well.

If you stop to think about it, if one person in a relationship is co-dependent and organises their thinking and behaviour around the other person (in my case, my partners being dependent on me) that leads directly to the other person doing the exact same thing back in the other direction without being aware of it.

I would respond to my ex-partner's dependency needs by allowing them and enabling them to be dependent on me, while of course complaining about it the whole time and saying how much I hated it. In doing so, though, I was organising my thinking and behaviours around them in a co-dependency loop.

This is best summed up by a line I read in a book many years ago. When talking about this topic it was saying how people who live with someone who is clearly co-dependent will say *"they need me"*. The question in the book that stopped me in my tracks and I've repeated ever since simply said, *"do they need you, or do you need them to need you?"*.

If we tie all this back into the emotional needs work we did as part of the multiple personality exercise, we can start to see that no matter what we're doing in life, especially in our relationships, we are meeting our own needs first and foremost. We might be telling ourselves a story that everything we do is for someone else, for someone who depends on us, but the reality is we are meeting our own needs through however we behave.

This results in us living in a world full of co-dependent people, with that co-dependency built on the same root cause as everything else in life; our low self-worth and feelings that we're not good enough.

Might As Well Face it, You're Addicted to Love

As the famous philosopher Robert Palmer said in 1985, you might as well face it, you're addicted to love.

We've touched on the topic of addiction throughout the book and it's a huge part of our lives I believe is rooted in our low self-worth. Sadly, many of our experiences of love or, as we can now call it, Hollywood Love, actually bear all the hallmarks of addiction.

Think about it. The intermittent rewards of moments when everything is just right give us hope things can be perfect. They are interspersed with misery and a longing to have those moments back. And it's intertwined with the dysfunction explained by attachment theory and how we usually meet our needs subconsciously in unhealthy ways.

It all means if our self-worth is low and we don't feel good enough, we're likely to be in a relationship we're addicted to on some level – which partly explains why difficult relationships can be so difficult to leave.

We might say we're unhappy, but our addiction is serving multiple purposes in our life that we haven't previously understood.

How To Fix It

Given I'm talking about this in the context of everything else we've discussed, you might not be at all surprised to hear my proposed solution to this problem is the same as the solution to every other challenge in life.

Being co-dependent, displaying anything other than a secure attachment style and being addicted to love are all rooted in us having low self-worth and not feeling good enough. The simple solution, then, is to repair our self-worth and make sure we feel good enough.

Doing the work we've already been through helps us to become more secure and enables us to form healthy relationships with others rather than the dysfunctional ones we've been taught to form since we were children.

Rather than following the Hollywood story that we're all half of a complete picture and need someone else to complete the other half, the key is understanding healthy relationships are formed between two humans who are already 100 percent whole themselves, not needing anyone else to complete them.

When two complete humans come together they can then create an even more powerful team built on True Unconditional Love. If we don't make the changes necessary to break free from Hollywood Love to move into True Unconditional Love, though, I believe it's inevitable we will end up in a form of Committed Love relationship.

The trick to break from the pattern we're in is to learn how to truly love ourselves first before we can love anyone else unconditionally.

"Those three words, They're said too much, They're not enough"

(Chasing Cars / Snow Patrol)

Redefining Self-Love

This leads me to share with you a huge breakthrough I had on my adventure when working with one of my coaches. I briefly mentioned this story in Chapter 1 and wanted to share the details with you.

I had already done lots of work over 18 months and had reached a point where I felt pretty good, secure and at peace. One day after speaking publicly to a group of students about the first book I wrote and enjoying the experience, Jim asked me a very simple question:

"When you were up there speaking, did you love yourself?"

The pause before I answered said everything. If he'd asked me if I love my mum or dad I would have said *"yes"* without hesitation, yet when it came to whether I loved myself, I paused, which meant the answer couldn't have been an unconditional *"yes"*.

It led to me reflecting on that point and asking myself why I still couldn't say I loved myself fully. Rather than explain my conclusion to you, I'm going to share an extract of the email I sent to Jim telling him about my breakthrough:

"When I stopped to think about it, when I think of the word 'love' I always have problems, and have for years. I was reading something on Friday that summed it up nicely, which said we use the same word when describing how we feel about pizza, our favourite city, our sports team, our parents, our kids, our mates, our romantic partners, etc, but they're all different types of love, so when I ask if I love myself it raises questions straight away. I've also always resented people using the phrase "I love you" as a catch all to try to cover up less than loving behaviour...

More importantly, I realised that I've always associated the word 'love" with "good', because when I was little I felt as though I received more love by being good and wasn't loved when I was bad. So, when you ask do I love myself, I internalise that as 'am I good?', and my answer to that question after all the work I've done is no, I'm good and bad, so if I use the same meaning as I had growing up I can't possibly love myself because 'love' is only for good people.

On top of that is the 'they love themselves' line that we use in society to describe egotistical people and how they walk around 'loving themselves', which people say in a very negative way. So, 'loving yourself' in my head is actually loving your own ego, not loving the true you.

That led me to coming up with my own definition of what I think love is and what I want it to be, and that is unconditional love. The love that I would want to give to any kid I had and the type that everyone talks about but very few people actually give.

By reframing it that way, I found myself straight away being able to answer the question differently. If I ask, do I unconditionally love myself, the good and the bad, including the ego and every other part of my personality, the light and the dark, I can happily say yes. There are parts of myself that I don't like sometimes, but I understand why they exist and I love them even though I might not like them.

Then, after all of that, I was doing more free writing last night about what I actually care about and what I want to do, and it led me to a pretty overwhelming breakthrough.

For a long time I've acknowledged that the world we live in is all make believe, but as I wrote last night I came to an even deeper realisation, that even I only exist as a series of stories, as do we all.

Who I think I am is just a story, and who everyone else thinks I am is the same. I know from the past two years how even my own story about myself is probably wrong at any given time, which means there's no way of knowing who I actually am and, if we take everything all the way back to the beginning, we are actually just a part of the universe in the same way a tree is, we just add loads of stories on top to try to give everything some meaning.

The planet doesn't differentiate between us as humans and any other thing, so everything about us is just a creation, including our names, our identities and, most importantly for where I am right now, our physical pain and our imaginary limitations.

So, the upshot of all of that craziness is that for the first time in my life, I can say from my soul rather than my intellect, that I do unconditionally love all of me, because there's nothing not to love. I love myself in the same way I love my dog, the sea and the trees. When I don't like parts of me, I can and do still love those parts of me.

It's helped me to let go of loads of shit that I was still holding on to and for the first time, to really believe deep inside that I will heal and I can do whatever I want because nothing really matters, including what anyone else thinks. I've realised I knew that intellectually before, but I feel it in a different way now."

Skipping past the references to the universe and us being just like trees for now, you can hopefully see how the breakthroughs I described in that email tie in to the work we've been going through in which we've explored the darkest parts of ourselves that we might not like but can learn to love.

By referring to that as True Unconditional Love, I found it much easier to find a place where I can say I love myself. As far as relationships are concerned, that means I can now approach them from a position of having a secure attachment style, not being codependent and not needing an addiction to another person to fill any of my needs.

Multiple Personalities in Relationships

It's also worth touching back again on our multiple personalities when it comes to relationships. A big part of this work I've loved as I've developed over time is once I understood my own multiple personalities I could begin to see them in everyone else. This helps to understand why one moment your partner can be the most loving person in the world and the next they're a complete bastard. It's different characters taking their mic to meet different needs of theirs at different times.

If you've ever had a connection with someone inside a relationship that for some reason just doesn't work, chances are it's because the connection was between a part of each of you that only ever came out intermittently at the same time, your inner children. The parts of you free from the darkness of the world.

But the chances are your inner child and their inner child were or are usually buried beneath multiple other characters, all created to protect Little You and Little Them from the pain of being a human.

So, the deep connection you felt was or is real, but only between parts of you and them that you've probably both neglected for so long they very rarely take the microphone. At all other times it's your other personalities trying desperately to match with each other and, if your relationships have been anything like mine, often failing miserably.

If you take a step back and think about it, it makes perfect sense.

If my self-pity character is trying to exist at the same time as my partner's hyper productive character, they're not going to have much in common, especially when neither acknowledges their own existence and needs.

The key is to understand and accept who all of these personalities are, so that we can begin making conscious decisions over who takes the mic at any given time and understanding not only when one of our characters have taken the mic, but when one of our partner's has taken theirs, too.

Changing the Dance

All of this leads us to a place where we can change a dysfunctional relationship by making a conscious choice not to carry on in the same rigid dance we've probably been doing for years.

Next time your partner says the thing that usually makes you scream or cry or go silent or storm from the room, you can assess which of your characters usually takes the mic in that moment and why, and choose consciously to keep Little You on the mic, leading with vulnerability and getting to the root of the problem rather than focusing on *The Prestige*.

If you stop dancing the other person can't carry on without you, which forces change.

"You're nobody till somebody
loves you, you're nobody
till somebody cares
You may be king,
you may possess the
world and his gold,
but gold won't bring
you happiness
when you're growing old"

(You're Nobody Till Somebody Loves You /
Russ Morgan, Larry Stock, James Cavanaugh)

The Love You Truly Need

While I love that song, sadly it ties into what we've discussed about movies and popular culture teaching us for generations that we need external things to make us happy.

I believe the sentiment of the song is true, but the kicker is the real love you need is your own. Without it you can't ever truly be peaceful, you can never truly receive anyone else's love and you can never truly give it to someone else.

To live the best life we can live I believe the ideal scenario is for our lives to be filled with True Unconditional Love and for us to build real connections with as many other humans as possible. We can't have that, though, without first doing the work to make sure we truly love ourselves.

20

HEALING ILLNESSES

"All the lies they have told me, they make me wanna shiver."

(AKA…Broken Arrow / Noel Gallagher's High Flying Birds)

I've purposefully left this chapter until late in the book.

Most of what I've already shared with you is enough to lead many people in my life to think I'm nuts, so I don't tend to share it unless people really want to hear about it. But what I'm about to share with you takes things to another level altogether.

If you've enjoyed at least some of what you've read so far, maybe even completed some of the exercises and had some realisations about your life you weren't expecting, then I hope you will at the very least continue to read what's coming with an open mind.

I appreciate before I start that at first glance this can be mind blowing. I often think back to what the old version of me would make of what I now believe about the world, and it makes me laugh thinking about his cynical response. He would think I'd lost my marbles.

My aim, as it has been throughout the book, is to take something that might at first seem crazy and slowly walk you to a place where it makes absolutely perfect sense.

Let's see how we get on.

An Unusual Disclaimer

At this point before talking about health-related matters, most authors will insert a disclaimer telling you to speak to your doctor before making any decisions about your health.

While I think that is still a wise thing to do in most circumstances, what I really want you to take from this chapter is to start treating your health as I've encouraged you to treat the rest of your life since Chapter 9 – by taking full responsibility for yourself and stop deferring responsibility to others.

Please do not read anything on these pages and follow them blindly. It is absolutely crucial you take responsibility for your health, taking on board as much information from as many sources as possible before making your own decision about what's right for you. You might read what follows and think it's all nonsense, you might be completely convinced by it or anything in between those two extremes – all of which are perfectly acceptable responses.

The old lawyer in me is obliged to say I am not a health professional in any shape or form, and I only share what is to come for informational purposes. I therefore accept no responsibility if you decide to adopt in your life anything I discuss and end up turning into a pigeon.

A Little Bit of History

It's important to begin with a little bit of medical history.

Up until the 1600s, what I will loosely describe as the Western medical world believed that our human system was one whole thing. The world predominantly believed human beings were spiritual beings; the body and soul were one.

There was another line of thought, however, which was that the spiritual approach was preventing advances in medical science, leading in the 17th century to Rene Descartes introducing the idea of the mind and body being separate, which paved the way for what we now widely accept as the modern Western medical approach.

Our medical professional largely, therefore, treats our body as a machine that is in no way related to our mind.

Which is the first place I want to ask you to be open to another idea.

The Car Mechanic

We talked earlier about my idea that the creation of humans is like a big car production line.

I want to take that analogy to the next level and, to do so, would like you to picture a fancy modern car. It can be anything you like, you just need to know its make and choose a colour. It's best to pick something you'd really love to have yourself.

You might pick a red Ferrari, a gunmetal grey Aston Martin, a yellow Ford or a black Renault. Whatever you choose, I want you to imagine it having all the features a modern car would have.

Electronic remote control locks, voice activation and, above all, a really complex onboard computer system running everything.

Have you got something? Can you picture the sophisticated machine?

Great. Now, imagine one day you're driving down the road in your highly complex vehicle and it starts playing up. Nothing major at first, just a bit of noise that sounds like it's coming from the engine.

You take the car to a mechanic you trust with your life. He dresses just like a mechanic and has all the bits in his garage you'd expect a mechanic to have. You've been going to the same mechanic for years, as have your parents before you, and you trust everything the mechanic says.

He takes the car and looks over it for half an hour before coming back and telling you there's nothing physically wrong with it. None of the physical bits of the car are faulty.

You ask whether it could have anything to do with the onboard computer system that runs everything, and the mechanic says it can't be that because the onboard computer system has nothing to do with the physical operation of the car. He says to just keep driving the vehicle and it'll probably sort itself out.

He says if the noise is bothering you he can give you some ear-plugs to use while you're driving so you can't hear it.

You take his word for there being nothing wrong, accept his offer of earplugs and drive off.

A week later the noise is getting so loud you can't hear your music regardless of how high you turn the volume and speaking to passengers is impossible, so you take the car back to the garage and have the following conversation.

Mick the Mechanic: "*I've checked everything in the body of the car and there's no real cause of the problem.*"

You: "*Are you sure it's nothing to do with the onboard computer system, Mick? Doesn't that run everything else in the car so it is at least worth thinking about?*"

Mick: "*No, the whole industry agrees it's got nothing to do with the computer system so we only look at the physical stuff. We've seen this problem loads of times before and we call it Loud Car-itis. There's no cause of it and no cure for it.*"

You: "*Oh, Loud Car-itis sounds really serious, is it?*"

Mick: "*Yeah, it's pretty serious and, like I say, can't be fixed, but we can give you some stuff to cover up the noise and there's a product one of the big car repair manufacturers makes that you can use.*"

You: "*Oh, right. What are they then?*"

Mick: "*Well, we've got a bigger pair of earplugs for you to wear so you can't hear the noise as much, and we've got this wax you rub on the outside of the car every day for the rest of your life.*"

You: "*That doesn't seem like a solution, it's just sort of papering over the cracks.*"

Mick: "*I know, yeah, but that's what we all do, there's no other way.*"

You: "*Are you sure it's not even worth looking at the onboard computer system? Surely that's got something to do with it?*"

Mick: "*No, it's definitely got nothing to do with that.*"

*   *   *

If that was a real conversation, would you just accept the mechanic's position that it's got nothing to do with the onboard computer system, or would you try to find a mechanic who's at least willing to consider the computer system might have something to do with it?

What if you found out there were other mechanics who believed the onboard computer system is the cause of the problem and they use methods not accepted by the rest of the car repair business that completely fix the problem?

Would you want to speak to those mechanics to find the real cause of the Loud Car-itis so you could fix your car instead of spending the rest of your life putting up with the noise, wearing earplugs and rubbing a weird wax on the outside that seems to have no real effect?

Who Repaired that Cut?

Do you remember the last time you cut yourself? It doesn't matter how big it was, it might have been a little paper cut or you nearly chopping your arm off with a chainsaw, as long as the result was it fully healed.

If you can easily look at the part of your body you cut now just take a little look. Maybe you can see a scar or maybe there's no evidence of it whatsoever. Now ask yourself who repaired it. What happened that took your body from bleeding through your skin to being whole again?

It's not a trick question. The answer is what a kid would give, your body fixed itself. Even in the extreme example of nearly losing your arm in a chainsaw accident, the doctor's job is to perform emergency surgery to stitch things back together and stop you bleeding to death and, after that, it's your body that fixes itself. It slowly joins everything back together and seals up the hole from which the blood was escaping.

"That's Just the Placebo Effect"

Do you know what a placebo is? I'd guess you've heard of it, but I'll give a quick summary just in case you're not sure.

A placebo is commonly used in trials of a new drug, when pharmaceutical companies and the health profession are trying to measure the effectiveness of the new medicine. In simple terms a test group will be divided into two, say 100 people in each group, with one group given the trial drug and the other group given a sugar pill, a placebo, and told they are being given the drug. Nobody knows which group they're in.

Each group will be measured after the trial to see whether the experimental drug was successful or not. In a successful drug trial, 70 of the 100 people in the group that received the drug might have recovered from whatever the drug was intended to help them recover from, and 30 people recovered in the group that received the placebo.

The pharmaceutical and health industries use that data to show the new drug is effective and should be rolled out.

That's all pretty straightforward, right?

So, here's a conversation I had with a doctor about the results of a drug trial like the imaginary one I used above.

Me: "Can you just sum up the results of that trial for me please, doc?"

Doctor: "Of course, it was a really successful trial. Seventy percent of the group who received the new drug recovered fully, whereas only 30 percent of the group that received the placebo recovered, proving the drug is effective."

Me: "Sounds good. What about the 30 people who got better just by taking a sugar pill though?"

Doctor: "Oh, that's just the placebo effect."

[30 seconds later]

Me: "Hang on. So, you're saying 30 people in the group that didn't get the drug got better anyway, just because they believed they were being given a drug that would make them better?"

Doctor: "Yes, like I said, it's just the placebo effect."

Doctors are Great

Before we go any further into this discussion, I want to make clear I don't have anything against doctors or the Western medical profession in general. Developments in Western medicine have saved hundreds of millions of lives over the past few hundred years and should quite rightly be celebrated.

Discoveries like penicillin and antibiotics have revolutionised medicine and have led to us leading healthier and longer lives than the generations of humans that went before us, and the surgical world performs modern miracles every day, putting humans back together who would have no chance of survival years ago. In that regard, doctors are fantastic.

My problem, as it often is with the world, is that our tendency to view everything as black or white usually leads to us missing nuances that could be really valuable to us all.

"These are mediocre times…
People are starting to lose hope.
It's hard for many to believe
there are extraordinary
things inside themselves
as well as others"

(Elijah Price / Unbreakable)

Healing Ourselves

Where this has all been leading is a door on the hotel corridor I walked through a few years ago that completely changed my view of the world. Before I pushed that door open I had no idea this part existed, despite it already being full of millions of people.

The world I found was one where people believe we are able to heal ourselves from all kinds of illnesses in the same way our bodies repair cuts or join broken bones back together.

While at the moment the people in this world represent a minority of humans, especially in the West, I truly believe that within 50 years what I'm about to talk to you about will be common practice, and we'll look back at the past few hundred years as the dark ages.

The Mind-Body Connection

Going back to my story about the car mechanic earlier, you might have already spotted the analogy between the car, our bodies and our minds.

Sadly, that story pretty much reflects my experiences inside the Western medical world over the past 40 years while I've been treated for all kinds of issues including "growing pains", psoriasis (a skin condition), Crohn's disease (a bowel condition) and ankylosing spondylitis (a bone and joint condition).

The Western medical profession doesn't have an explanation for any of those conditions, but the pharmaceutical industry has products designed to take our minds off them all, ranging from creams and lotions to rub on the outside of our bodies, to heavy duty drugs to be pumped into our bodies through an infusion.

None of those things, however, cure anything. They simply treat the symptoms.

Do you have any health conditions doctors are unable to explain? Bear in mind even things like asthma and eczema fall into that category, as well as most bowel conditions, stomach problems such as acid indigestion, arthritis and other bone conditions, fibromyalgia and, at the most serious end of the scale, cancer.

Maybe you, like me, have been told the common story that your health condition is caused by your body attacking itself. I used to hear that line and nod along, thinking isn't it strange that my body attacks itself without questioning it further.

That all changed a few years ago, though, when I walked through the door on the hotel corridor of the mind-body connection and started to open my mind to a very simple idea – that the mind and the body are inextricably linked.

If you stop to think about that statement it doesn't exactly seem controversial given that our heads are physically attached to our bodies and our brains basically run everything. Yet the Western medical world is largely not interested in that idea at all. It does not believe our onboard computer systems have anything to do with the overall health of our physical bodies.

Does that sound rational to you? If we wouldn't accept that explanation about our cars and their onboard computer systems, why should we accept it about our bodies without any challenge?

Dissociative Identity Disorder and Health

In the most extreme cases, the multiple personalities we've talked so much about become so extreme they manifest as dissociative identity disorder (formerly known as multiple personality disorder), although I'm acutely aware that statement would be laughed at by mental-health professionals, who would say what I've described in this book in relation to multiple personalities has no association with dissociative identity disorder.

The main reason I mention the disorder, though, is there are numerous reported cases of people with multiple personalities displaying a health condition in one of their personality states that doesn't appear in another. For example, they might be diabetic when one of their personalities is manifesting but not when another is on the mic.

How that doesn't lead every medical professional in the world to want to delve into the mind-body connection would completely baffle me if I didn't understand human behaviour the way I do, but it still amazes me how it can be overlooked so easily.

Just stop to think about that. Forgetting anything else we've discussed or will go on to discuss, there are cases of humans who have a serious physical condition when their mind thinks they're one person that disappears entirely when their mind thinks it's another person.

How can that possibly be the case if the condition is solely physical? Note that if a person with dissociative identity disorder breaks their arm, they have a broken arm regardless of which personality is in charge because the broken arm is a physical problem.

Could there be a clearer example of the mind body connection in action, when we have literal examples of different minds appearing in the same body and controlling what are otherwise considered to be physical health problems?

Our Multiple Personalities and Health

To explore this topic further, we need to go back to the start of our adventure together and walk through it one step at a time.

Let's start with our learning to repress emotions when we're children and remembering emotions are just chemical reactions inside our bodies. Again, in very crude terms, if we don't let those chemical reactions process in the way they were meant to, what do we think happens to them?

Remember as well what we discussed briefly about how other animals release trauma from their bodies by physically shaking. Rather than shake out and release our trauma we keep it locked inside our bodies, allowing it to accumulate day after day, month after month, year after year.

While doing that, our control deck team is busy developing different characters to help us meet our needs in subconscious and unhealthy ways, often because we aren't processing our emotions properly.

When these two things combine, they can lead to us developing health problems to meet our needs.

Does that sound hard to believe?

Observe the Ways you Benefit

Much of what you've read in this book I either learnt from or was inspired by the coach I discovered in New York after going through the door on the hotel corridor into this new world where I found people healing themselves from unexplained illnesses using the power of their minds.

I remember vividly a conversation I had with Ralph in the early weeks of us working together. He said to me:

> *"I want you to observe and write down this week all the ways you benefit from your illnesses."*

Before I tell you my reaction to that instruction, it's important to point out the reason I'd gone to Ralph in the first place was because I hated my illnesses. I had been plagued by Crohn's disease and ankylosing spondylitis for years and was desperate for them to disappear. So, for the person to whom I'd turned for help to suggest I benefitted from them in any way led to a response along the lines of: *"Are you fucking kidding me?"*

After he stopped laughing at my predictable reaction, he told me to just do it with an open mind and we could discuss it the week after.

By the following week I had a list of benefits as long as my arm. Here are a few of them:

- My pain helps me to avoid doing things I don't want to do because I use it as an excuse
- I get more attention from my family because of my stiff back and pain
- My illnesses allow me to feel special and different to other people
- When I achieve something, like running a marathon or starting a business, I get extra significance because I achieved it even though I've got illnesses.

If we look at this through the prism of the multiple personality work we've done, the list above is of the practical needs I was meeting through my illnesses.

When looking at the emotional needs, I was gaining certainty because my story around my health conditions was so fixed. I gained significance by being different to other people and by knowing I was still achieving things in spite of being in so much pain, which I usually kept secret (making me feel even more significant). I also got greater love and connection with my family from the attention they gave me over the conditions.

From first thinking health problems caused me nothing but pain, I could suddenly see ways I was actually benefitting from having them.

The Poor Health Character

Even after I discovered all the ways I benefitted from having health problems, it wasn't until my first experiences with the planet's natural psychedelic plants that I had even more breakthroughs about even deeper benefits the poor health character developed by my control deck had been giving me.

Lying on the floor of a jungle in Mexico, I suddenly realised two huge benefits that character provides.

He allows me to feel sorry for myself and for my serious side to come out, which are both sides of me I repress because I was ashamed of them. I have openly said to myself for years I can't stand the idea of being boring, and I realised I was deeply insecure about not being interesting.

I always wanted to be charismatic, entertaining and fun, which led to me repressing the side of me that is boring or serious. Without me realising, my unexplained health conditions forced me to display those sides of my true self.

Summarising My Poor Health Character

Name

Poor Health Paul

Character Traits

Lethargic, grumpy, self-pitying, quiet, boring, intense, serious.

Triggers

In the past I would have said the trigger for Poor Health Paul to come out was whenever I felt in pain, but I know now that's not the case. The pain and other symptoms came out because I was repressing my emotions.

Human Needs Being Met

Certainty and control, significance and ego, love and connection.

Practical Needs Being Met

I use him as an excuse not to do things I don't want to do. I get more sympathy because of him, I feel more connected to my family because of him, he helps me to feel special, he allows me to feel sorry for myself and to be more serious and boring.

✎ Exercise – Part 1

Now it's your turn. If you have any illnesses or health issues of any type that doctors tell you can't be cured, physical or mental, whether it's asthma, eczema, allergies, a painful hip you can't overcome, depression, back pain, bowel problems, ADHD, migraines, stomach issues or anything else, I want you to observe all the ways you benefit from them.

If you can't think of them straight away, observe as you go through your week whether anything comes up. Do you complain about the health condition to someone and it gets you attention and love? Do you post about it on social media for the same thing? Do you ever use it as an excuse to get out of doing something you don't want to do? Does it allow you to feel sorry for yourself?

Notes

✎ Exercise - Part 2

After you've done the initial part of the exercise focusing just on the benefits you get from any form of illness, I want you to go through the multiple personality process for that side of yourself like my summary above so you can see the traits and triggers as well. Go as far as the emotional and practical needs in your character table and we'll come back to the rest later.

Notes

"It's despite the evidence, not for the lack of it, that we practice the way we do."

(Dr. Gabor Maté / All The Rage (Saved by Sarno))

Mainstream Support

I appreciate this might all sound like woo-woo nonsense, even if you are open-minded enough to consider it as a possibility.

The real kicker, though, is summed up by Gabor Maté's quote above. There is mainstream evidence supporting everything I've been talking about, including the ACE Study we discussed in Chapter 4. Medical research published in respected medical journals that simply disappears without a trace and is hardly acknowledged by the establishment in Western medicine.

If that's the case, you might ask why we're not spending more time, money and energy working on healing humans through the power of our minds rather than pumping us full of drugs that serve only to treat symptoms.

Why Are We Stuck?

Here's another key part of life that ties neatly into many of the things we've already talked about.

When I have spoken over the years to a range of senior doctors and consultants about my various conditions and asked whether there are any other approaches we could take or if there's any other research outside of the standard Western approach of treating the symptoms of illnesses with drugs, I've mainly been met with smiles, laughter and dismissive attitudes.

The only time in the decades I've been in the medical system asking these questions that anyone entered into a real conversation with me was when I mentioned it to a doctor who was born in Malaysia and had lived in England for many years. He actually showed interest in the discussion and told me many of the illnesses common to the Western world simply weren't seen in Malaysia until very recently, as a Western lifestyle had been creeping into their culture.

While that's just one anecdote and we should be careful to come to any conclusions based on anecdotes (despite what we tend to do in life), it's interesting that he was at least willing to entertain the conversation.

The other senior doctors and consultants I've dealt with over the years have been brought up in, trained and paid by the Western medical world. Think back to our discussions around confirmation bias, the stories we tell ourselves and, in particular, the sunk cost reality, and you might start to see why there's so much reluctance to even consider a different approach.

Consider one of the consultants I have been dealing with for the past few years. She is a really lovely, caring woman in her forties or early fifties, who I believe wants the best for me and her other patients. When I last saw her and asked if there was any new research into these illnesses, she immediately began talking about new drug trials that were showing promise. I smiled politely and left the hospital having informed her I wouldn't be taking any more drugs for my conditions, which was met by a tilt of her head and a pitying response pleading with me to go back onto the drugs because it was in my best interests to do so.

Now think about that consultant's life. She has most likely been trained in the Western medical system her entire career, dating back decades. As we've discussed, that system is built on the idea that our mind has little to do with our physical illnesses. When it cannot find a physical cause of a problem it assumes there is no cause or cure, and focuses on the use of pharmaceutical drugs to treat symptoms.

Now consider how much of that world is funded. The global pharmaceutical industry was valued at over 300 billion US dollars in 2020 and, sadly, has a huge influence on how we approach treating illnesses. Regardless of anything else, common sense tells us that if you are part of a system reliant on people taking drugs to treat the symptoms of their illnesses, there is a huge financial disincentive to ever look into potential cures that don't require drugs and would cost little to nothing to roll out.

I'll say that again in a different way in case it's not clear. If most of the unexplained illnesses we experience can be cured through the power of our minds and eating more healthy food, one of the biggest and most influential industries on the planet would radically reduce in size, losing billions of dollars of revenue.

Now consider how it works on an individual level for most doctors. If you have spent your entire professional life telling yourself the story that you're helping people by prescribing medicines that carry with them risk and side effects, letting go of that story becomes so difficult it's practically impossible for most.

Confirmation bias will lead you to ignore any studies suggesting the way you and your industry has operated for generations might be flawed, and the sunk cost reality will mean you have so much invested in what you've already done it's just too difficult to leave behind.

Factor into everything that doctors are just as likely as the rest of us to suffer from low self-worth, and the chances of individuals living within a professional echo chamber telling each other they're all definitely right are extremely high.

For a doctor to admit what they might have been doing for decades could be wrong and, potentially, harmful to the people they've been dedicating their lives to helping takes huge levels of self-worth. Remember at an individual level a doctor has an incentive to carry on believing in the thing that pays their rent or mortgage and feeds their family.

At an industry level, it's obvious why the placebo effect is dismissed so readily. Why would any pharmaceutical company want to explore the idea that patients can heal themselves without the need for the drugs it manufactures?

It's worth pausing to reflect on the example I gave before of a conversation with a doctor around a drug trial. If we lived in a world that wasn't driven by financial profits, as soon as we did the first trial showing anyone healing just by believing they were being given a drug, all of our time, money and energy would surely be put into exploring why that happens.

Instead, we can see it all going into the development of drugs that only treat symptoms, cost our societies billions of pounds, dollars or euros every year and usually have hundreds of potentially damaging side effects.

If we zoom out and look at the Western medical industry in those terms, it becomes much easier to understand why there's no interest in what I've shared with you in this chapter being explored properly.

I can tell you from personal experience that no doctor or consultant has ever explored with me what the true cause of my conditions might be. We have never discussed my psychology or capacity to process my emotions, and have never discussed my childhood despite the ACE Study having been published in the late 1990s.

What Should We Do?

If anything you've read has struck a chord or caught your attention in any way, I'll reiterate what I said at the start of the chapter. The only way any of us can escape the loop we're stuck in is to take full responsibility for our health at a personal level.

While I wouldn't encourage you to do this before exploring fully any health conditions you're experiencing, I took the decision a few years ago to stop taking the biological drugs I had been receiving as an infusion every eight to 10 weeks at hospital for the previous 15 years.

It would be unfair of me to omit from this chapter the fact that when I was first given newly-developed drugs to treat the symptoms of Crohn's disease and ankylosing spondylitis I was the happiest man alive. At the time I referred to those drugs as a miracle given the way in which they eased the symptoms that had been hampering my life so badly in the years leading up to receiving them for the first time.

When I look back now, though, I wonder what would have happened if, when I first showed any symptoms of unexplained illness, I'd been introduced to the world in which I now believe.

I'm certain there would have been no need for experimental drugs to be used because I wouldn't have endured years of suffering. I have spoken first hand to enough people who discovered the world of the mind-body connection soon after being diagnosed with an apparently incurable illness and completely healed to believe the same could have happened to me over 20 years ago.

If you are willing to take full responsibility for your own health, regardless of how big or small any health problems you're experiencing are, the key is to completely change the way you think about what those health conditions represent.

> "For years I've been treating The Hulk like some kind of disease, something to get rid of. But then I started looking at him like the cure."

(Bruce Banner/The Hulk / Avengers: End Game)

Illness is Our Friend

Which takes us back to my favourite companion through the adventure we've been on together, The Incredible Hulk.

At the moment, we look at whatever health problems we face as just that – a problem, a disease or an illness. While this might sound like a crazy thing to say out loud, the secret is to stop looking at them in that way and, instead, to start thinking about them as our friends.

In the Avengers movies, Bruce Banner ultimately resolved his issues with The Hulk by considering him in a completely different way. Rather than try desperately to get rid of him as he'd always done before, he joined forces with him and started to see him as the cure, not the illness.

What is it Trying to Tell Us?

If we approach any illness from the perspective of the team in our control deck trying to solve problems, what we can see happening is when the team was struggling to get our needs met using the characters it had already created, it reached a point where it had to hit the big red emergency button and bring health issues into the game.

The way I like to think about why some of us get some illnesses or health conditions and some get others, is when our team meets to discuss how it can solve the challenge of meeting our needs, it looks at what's available to it in our genetic operating system. So, if, for example, your body has a switch allowing your team to turn on Crohn's disease, it will use that option. If, though, your genetic make-up doesn't have that option but it does have chronic back pain available, the team will use that instead. The same goes for depression or things like ADHD.

In my example, as is the case for many people who suffer from illnesses or other health conditions, when I look back I can see now my team was gradually escalating the severity of the options it was turning to as the years passed. When I was a little boy I experienced chronic pain in my legs that would make me scream at night, forcing my parents to run into my room and flood me with love and attention. Doctors dismissed those as "growing pains" even though I think it's fairly widely accepted it's not meant to cause us intense levels of pain to grow.

After growing pains I developed whooping cough, then the skin condition psoriasis as a teenager, followed by a stiff neck and back when I was 17 (later diagnosed as ankylosing spondylitis), then acid indigestion and Crohn's disease when I was in my mid-twenties.

All the way through, my mind and body were simply trying to tell me something wasn't right inside me. That's all illness and pain are. It's our system putting up a huge red flag telling us something needs to change, the only problem is – because we haven't been taught to look at it like that – instead of figuring out what's wrong and changing it we carry on and pump ourselves full of drugs to treat the symptoms.

It's also important to note this isn't restricted to serious or chronic health conditions. It can be as simple as a sudden outbreak of spots, a rash on your legs or serious toothache no-one can explain. If there's no other explanation for it, such as an allergic reaction or response to an environmental factor, treat it as your body acting as a barometer for what's happening inside your mind and system and ask yourself what's happening.

Are you repressing anger? Are you feeling anxious but not processing it properly? Are there any other emotions you're refusing to deal with because of issues tracing all the way back to your childhood?

Remember the reason we develop the characters in our life we don't like is because we are not comfortable dealing with our emotions healthily and consciously, so the team in our control deck comes up with a different solution for us.

It's no different with health issues. When we are exposed to an emotion we simply don't want to feel, our friendly team develops a way to distract us from that emotion. It's ingenious when you think about it. Rather than have to face the fact we're angry, anxious or hurt, all our focus goes to the pain in the middle of our back or the red, painful rash on our skin instead of where it really needs to go.

I now see any pain or illness I experience as my inner friend doing whatever it can to force me to be who I'm really meant to be and experience my emotions for what they are.

Put simply, illness and pain are usually either something our system is using to distract us from feeling an emotion we don't want to feel or they are a warning of something not being right inside our body, or both.

Experiencing Trauma

We've already discussed the impact trauma has on our lives from a very young age and have now tied that into how the repression of emotions can lead to health problems. It's also worth noting, though, the impact traumatic events later in life can have that lead to the sudden onset of illnesses or health issues.

A few years ago, my sister, her husband and their two young children were woken in the early hours of the morning by a complete stranger banging on the front door and screaming at them to get out. When they first woke, in shock, they thought someone was breaking in to steal from them, which would have been traumatic enough. After a few seconds to wake and gather their thoughts, though, they realised the kind-hearted passer-by was alerting them to the fact the house adjoining theirs was on fire.

The family was forced into the road at 2am and had to stand and watch while the fire brigade desperately tried to stop their house from joining the house next door in burning down. As you can imagine, it was a severely traumatic experience for all of them.

I share this with you because of what happened next. Up until that moment in her life, my then 36-year-old sister had never had any problem with her body processing vitamin B12. In the months that followed, however, she found herself regularly feeling lethargic so visited her doctor for a check-up to be informed following tests that she now had a vitamin B12 deficiency and would need to attend hospital every few weeks to have a vitamin supplement injected into her system.

At no point did anyone in the medical world ask why after 36 years on the planet with no issues in this area, the body of this otherwise healthy woman suddenly stopped processing vitamin B12. Instead, they did what they usually do with things they don't understand – say there's no cause, no cure and the only way forward is to be injected with something that someone makes money from producing.

I hear and read about stories similar to this often. If you pause and reflect on any health issues you've developed in later years, can you now link them to any life events when you might have repressed emotions because they were painful to process? Maybe they followed the birth of your children, the loss of a job, the death of someone close to you or any number of other events that, when you look back with fresh eyes you can see you struggled with emotionally.

Doing the Work

Once we've changed our perception of health conditions from being our enemy to being our friend, as with our other destructive characters we can figure out how we are benefitting from the condition we say we don't want.

We can then deal with the repressed emotions that led to the illness and find ways to meet our needs consciously and healthily instead of leaving it to our subconscious to deal with.

When we fully engage with this, it's just a matter of time before our body catches up with our mind and illnesses we were previously told were incurable just disappear.

It has been incredible to watch how many people I've worked with to resolve other issues such as drug addiction or depression have reported during our work together that some health condition I wasn't aware of just disappeared as we'd been doing the work.

Chronic acid indigestion that used to keep them awake at night regardless of how many ant-acid drugs they took had vanished. Back pain disappeared. Reliance on medication drifted away.

If you are still sceptical, look up a few of the people I've listed in the resources chapter at the end of the book or do a simple online search for people who have cured themselves of supposedly incurable illnesses doing work just like this. You can see for yourself. I will also be publishing on my YouTube channel and podcast interviews I carried out with one of my coaches and his clients who have all fully healed from unexplained conditions.

In the context of all the other work we've done, if we go back to the multiple personality work and the destructive characters we developed over time to meet the needs we weren't able to meet ourselves, the poor health parts of us are just another element we need to follow through the same process.

What we need to do next, then, is complete the multiple personality work for our health conditions.

✎ Exercise

Thinking back to the table you created for the multiple personality work, it's time to figure out how you can be grateful for any health condition or illness rather than treating it as something you want to get rid of. Then consider how you can meet the needs it's meeting for you in a conscious and healthy way.

Notes

Making Peace with Poor Health Paul

As I reflected on everything my health conditions had given to me over the years, as with my other destructive characters I began finding it quite easy to be grateful for – and love – my poor health character.

Since I was a little boy he's been finding ways to get me more attention, love and connection when I didn't know how to ask for it consciously. As I've grown up, he's helped me to feel special when I might not otherwise have done, helped to meet my need for significance and given me easy ways out of situations I wasn't able to handle in healthier ways.

I get upset now when I think of everything he's done for me throughout my entire life. When I stopped thinking of him as an enemy, I realised he's my oldest friend. He's always been there for me when I needed him, and always found ways to help me meet needs I couldn't meet myself.

When I look at my life now from a zoomed out perspective, I also realise I wouldn't have met my coach Ralph or learnt about half of the things I now love so much if I'd never had poor health. This book probably wouldn't exist and I might not be living the life I am.

When I look at Poor Health Paul like that, it's impossible not to be grateful for him and love him.

Retiring Poor Health Paul

One of the challenges I've faced in retiring my poor health character comes from what I've just shared. While many people I've seen miraculously heal from various health conditions have done so relatively quickly, I've been on my adventure for three years without all my symptoms totally disappearing.

I realised just through the course of writing this book that a reason for that could be my complete switch from hating my health conditions and wanting them to disappear, to realising they've always been there to help me and I actually don't know what the world looks like without them.

It's time for me to let go of my oldest friend and there's a part of me that just doesn't want to say goodbye because I'm afraid to.

What I have been able to do is slowly make sure the real me is meeting as many of the emotional and practical needs Poor Health Paul would have previously met, and doing it in conscious and healthy ways.

For example, whenever I feel the urge to use my pain as an excuse not to do something, I ask myself why I really don't want to do it and, if there's another reason, I refuse to use my pain as the excuse. By continuing to use the pain or any health condition as an excuse, all we are doing is confirming to our team in the control deck we still need it to meet our needs, which will result in it staying on the mic.

As I'm observing my emotions, if I notice I'm feeling sorry for myself for something, I allow myself to feel that emotion without the need for the pain and without feeling ashamed of feeling that way. We all have many things in life to feel sorry for ourselves about, so we don't need health problems to allow us to feel that emotion.

I remember on my fortieth birthday walking into my parents' house and seeing my niece sitting on the couch clearly feeling sorry for herself. *"Are you feeling sorry for yourself today?"* I asked, in as gentle a way as I could, to which she responded by giving me a suspicious look. My teenage niece isn't used to people asking if she's feeling sorry for herself without it usually being followed by the statement, *"I don't know what you've got to feel sorry for yourself about, you've got a wonderful life"*.

To settle her concerns, I followed my question up with, *"I've been feeling sorry for myself all morning"*. *"Why?"* she asked. *"Well, I went to look at a new apartment that I was excited about and thought I'd want to live in but, when I got there, I realised the photos must have been taken ages ago because the place was really scruffy, and the area it was in was horrible. I found myself walking away from it and just started crying thinking about where my life is and how it wasn't meant to be this way. By the time I was 40 I was meant to have a family of my own, a big house, a successful career and all the other things we're told will make us happy when we're growing up, but I don't have any of those things."*

"But I thought you loved your life?" my niece replied. *"I do. I've created the life I want to live rather than the one I thought I had to live, but that doesn't stop me also feeling sadness and grief about the other life I had that I've lost. It's not black and white, both things can exist at the same time. So sometimes I just need to feel sorry for myself for a while and it's okay to feel that way even if your life is generally great. Shall we just sit here for a while and feel sorry for ourselves together?"*

My niece accepted my offer and we both allowed our emotions to process fully before spending the rest of the day laughing and joking together, after our self-pity had passed naturally without being suppressed.

I approach feeling serious or being boring in the same way now. If I find myself being insecure about potentially boring someone, I do my best to accept that side of me so I don't need the poor health side to take the mic.

Don't get me wrong, as with all the characters we've had in our lives for decades, it's not always an easy process to keep them off the mic and it takes daily practice and being kind to ourselves when we make mistakes, but it's a work in progress that's worthwhile.

As the weeks and months pass, I can feel my poor health character slowly moving into full retirement.

Links to Karate Kid Training

I think it's important to note how our health conditions also link to a few of the other parts of the Karate Kid training we've been doing together, so you can see how it all ties together in another aspect of life.

One thing I see often is the relief and satisfaction we humans get when a person in a white jacket at a hospital or doctor's surgery gives us a name for what's wrong with us.

If we're feeling lethargic, in pain, stiff or any one or more other symptoms, we've been conditioned to not want to see it just as a bit of pain or a bit of stiffness. Instead, we like someone we see as qualified to put a label on it for us. The problem with labels though, as in the rest of life, is once we have a tag for something we attach meaning to that label and become fixated with it.

So, as soon as my pain and stiffness became the very serious sounding *"ankylosing spondylitis"* I was able to attach meaning to that label, enabling me to find more and more ways to meet my needs through it.

Those labels are also usually rooted in black and white thinking, because generally the Western medical world will say we either have a certain condition or we don't, whereas I see it as being much healthier to view health conditions on a scale as we've discussed doing with many other parts of life.

When someone I worked with described to me his ADHD symptoms, he described exactly how my brain operates – it just sounded like his brain was a little more distracted than mine at times. It had led to the black and white diagnosis of the ADHD label and, the next phase of our training that goes hand in hand with all this, him starting to tell himself stories about what having ADHD means.

He would tell me a story that because he's got ADHD he struggles to write things out clearly because his condition stops him processing things from his brain onto a page properly. I pointed out gently over time that he would often explain things like that to me in a beautifully crafted email, which proved the story he was telling himself and telling me wasn't true.

Once we started to break down those stories and the black and white thinking, he could slowly let go of the idea that he has a debilitating illness called ADHD and, instead, just talk about his brain sometimes getting over excited or struggling to concentrate. Both of which are totally normal human experiences.

Importantly, we could then also begin to focus on the benefits of his brain being the way it is. Much like a characteristic I recognised in my brain, it meant weird and wonderful ideas that at the very least are entertaining to think about and, every now and then, have greater value to the outside world.

On my own adventure, despite using phrases like ankylosing spondylitis, Crohn's disease and psoriasis to describe issues to you throughout this book, once I learnt all about this world I stopped referring to myself as having any of those conditions and stopped using the labels entirely.

When I have back or neck pain now I just refer to it as back or neck pain, which immediately stops it becoming bigger than what it needs to be. Psoriasis just becomes a bit of a rash and Crohn's disease is my bowels being a bit off. All of which just points me back to the root of the problems, rather than getting distracted by the end of the magic trick.

Getting Worse Before Getting Better

If you decide to go down this path to resolve any health issues you have, it's important to note things can get worse before they get better. They certainly did for me although they don't for everyone.

First, my body had to detoxify from serious medication it had been pumped full of for over 15 years. And from a psychological and emotional perspective my ego wasn't ready to give up without a fight the solution it had found as the greatest distraction from the emotions I didn't want to feel and the system it had created to meet so many of my needs.

As you read in my origins story, weeks after taking the decision to stop my anti-inflammatory infusions I found myself lying on my bedroom floor after deciding it would help with the pain in my back, before realising I couldn't get up because the pain was so intense.

I was living on my own with my dog then and my phone was in another room so, as Tilly came up to start licking my face thinking I was playing a game, I just burst out laughing at the realisation I was basically going to end my days lying on that floor.

After waking from a sleep it took me about an hour to slowly make my way in agony from that position, up onto the bed and finally into a standing position.

From that day, though, I slowly recovered and, around two years later, show practically no signs of Crohn's disease, have minimal psoriasis on my skin and, despite still having some pain and tension in my back, live a full and normal life without any medication.

I have fully healed in my mind, I'm just waiting for my body to catch up fully having been experiencing these problems for over two decades. There's no way to know how long the healing process will take once you embark on this part of the adventure, but the total belief healing is possible is a key part to it all.

Observing how pain and other symptoms can increase as the mind's way of desperately trying to keep us distracted from the root cause of the problem, repressed emotions, means we can remember the pain is not actually real. Instead, it's created by the mind as a distraction technique, so focusing on the emotions we would otherwise be repressing is the solution.

As you do this, you might notice pain you previously thought was physical and fixed begins to move around your body, skin conditions fade in one part of your body or flare up in another or something you hadn't previously experienced suddenly appears. If this happens it's an incredible sign you're on your way to healing because it's your body admitting to you the issues aren't real.

Stop to think about that. If you break your arm it's a physical issue so the pain is in your arm. You don't wake up one day and it's moved from your arm to your leg. But chronic pain doesn't work in the same way. I have often watched with fascination since beginning this work at how one day the pain that used to be firmly in the middle of my back will have shifted to my bum or my knees. When that first started happening I knew I was into the final stages of healing.

Likewise, with other physical symptoms like skin conditions, as they ease on one part of our body and flare up on another it's a sign you've got it on the run.

Some people, however, don't go through any of that. For many, just learning about this concept and learning to deal with their emotions properly leads to rapid, often instant, healing. I have witnessed that first hand in friends and clients who have healed within a few days, and have heard many stories of healing overnight.

Maybe that will be you.

Releasing Trapped Emotions

If you decide to explore the path of healing illnesses through the mind-body connection, it's worth noting one of the basic explanations for our repressed emotions manifesting as illnesses in our physical body. Put simply, when the chemical reactions of emotions aren't released from our bodies they lodge somewhere in our cells and stay trapped.

When we go through the process of releasing often decades old trapped emotions, then, we often find we need to release them physically – much like animals shaking off trauma.

I have cried more in the past couple of years than I had in the 38 preceding years combined, often physically shaking as I sobbed, with tears and snot running down my face like a baby. The release I felt after every cry was palpable, and you might experience something similar as you begin to release years of repressed emotions.

You may also find your body needs more sleep to process

everything. Things can shift in other ways, too – notably people reporting (as I experienced) needing to go to the toilet more often while your system releases trapped anger, anxiety and fear in particular.

Last, but not least, spending as much time as possible belly laughing is also an incredibly powerful and fun way to release trapped emotions. When you stop to think about it, the way our bodies move when crying and laughing uncontrollably are the same, hence both methods being great ways to release.

This is where the worlds of somatic healing and similar processes are worth looking into.

Other Considerations

It's worth noting there are many possible causes of health problems in our complex systems, ranging from our diets to genetics to serious physical issues. It is important then to make sure we don't have any other causes of health challenges we're facing by being checked out by a doctor before embarking on anything I've discussed.

The key though, I think, is to look out for the language doctors often use to disguise when they're really saying, *"I don't know what's wrong so we just give this thing a scary-sounding name to make it sound real"*.

One of my favourite recent discoveries in the course of writing this book has been to hear for the first time a phrase doctors use when trying to sound clever; saying an illness is *"idiopathic"*.

That sounds fancy and important doesn't it? Until you discover the meaning of idiopathic is:

"Relating to or denoting any disease or condition which arises spontaneously or for which the cause is unknown."

Which means the medical profession has even gone as far as making up a fancy word to distract us from the fact they're really saying, *"we don't know what it is"*.

All of which means if I do ever need to see a doctor again about something I can't resolve myself, a direct question I will ask in as nice a way as possible is: *"Are you please able to tell me with certainty what the cause of this condition is and what the cure is?"*

If they aren't able to answer that question with anything approaching absolute certainty, I go back to the likelihood that the cause is in the onboard computer system or something else within my control.

Whenever we're dealing with the traditional medical world it's also worthwhile remembering that medical studies, research and surveys can be useful and interesting, but they are often flawed by their very nature because they report averages. Even if something can cure 70 percent of people, that means 30 out of every 100 people won't be healed by it – and you could very easily be one of those 30.

You are unique and should approach your health that way, which is why taking responsibility for yourself is so important. What works for me might not work for you and vice versa, which is why I'm sharing in the resources chapter a list of other people who are established in this world, each of whom has a slightly different approach to healing illnesses.

If you like the idea of what we've been talking about, I'd encourage you to check out each of the people listed and decide for yourself what approach fits best for you. My intention is to introduce you to this world to enable you to transform your life in ways you might not previously have thought possible. I don't need you to believe the same things I do or approach everything in the same way I do, it's much more important to me that you find a way that works for you.

While I am a huge believer and advocate of the mind-body connection and its ability to heal illnesses, I also believe what we put into our bodies has a huge bearing on our health. Going back to the car analogy, if our minds are the equivalent of the onboard computer system, what we put as fuel into our engine has a big impact on how well our vehicle runs. We might be able to cure many illnesses through the work in this book, but we can never reach the full potential our bodies have without the correct fuel.

On that side of things, I'd recommend looking into developments around gut health and its impact on the rest of our systems, as well as looking at whether any particular foods don't agree with your unique system. I can tell you from experience that I feel so much better when I eat more fresh fruits and vegetables and less processed or junk food. The same applies to the regular Western past-time of drinking alcohol. If you regularly drink alcohol you are filling your body with a depressant drug that prevents it functioning properly.

The obvious diet points aside, I should point out that if you believe repressed emotions can be the root cause of health conditions it's worth being wary of anything that tells you a specific diet or routine can be the sole solution to a health problem. Before discovering the things I have about the mind-body connection, I tried everything from diets limited only to salad to acupuncture in my ears and daily routines of exercise and meditation.

The issue with anything of that nature is the root cause of the problem is our low self-worth and feelings that we're not good enough. By adopting a new diet or routine we can be setting ourselves up to make things worse because, if we slip up on that new diet or new routine, which we often do, we can end up feeling worse about ourselves, lowering our self-worth and, therefore, not recovering.

As I did when focusing on a juice fast as a way of healing, I ended up worsening my self-hate spiral which could never have led to a good place. My view, although clearly biased because of how much I believe in the world I am now in, is the main focus should first be on making sure you are kind to yourself and repairing your self-worth, before testing anything else.

I have a theory that might never be able to be accurately tested that often people who embark on a new diet, routine or juice fast to heal illnesses end up healing partly because they are treating their bodies with more care from a biological perspective, but mainly because it's often the first time in their lives they've shown themselves total love and put themselves first.

It's also worth noting the people I've met first hand who have healed fully by doing the work we've discussed in this book have not changed their routines or diet significantly in any other way, save that they usually end up taking better care of themselves generally once they repair their self-worth and feel good enough. Those people had often previously tried a whole range of crazy or popular diets or routines such as cutting gluten from their food or not eating anything containing starch, but found once they healed through the mind-body connection they were free to eat whatever they wanted.

Think of the car analogy. If there's a problem with the onboard computer system, you have to repair the computer for the problem to be fixed properly. Once that's done you can make sure the car is running at peak capacity by ensuring you're using the best fuel, but you can't fix the original problem just by using better fuel.

I have also had incredible experiences with intense breathwork such as a method known as "rebirthing" and with plant-based psychedelic medicines, both of which played key roles in my healing process. I would strongly recommend you looking into both if you are interested in this area.

The Celebrity Story Arc

To round off this chapter, I wanted to highlight how many famous stories there are that seem to tie in perfectly to the work we've been discussing throughout this book, including how repressed emotions can lead to serious health problems.

While I don't want to discuss any individual in detail, in the resources chapter at the end of the book I've listed some stories that are worth looking up and documentaries worth watching. You can see for yourself the pattern in the story arc of many people who achieved great things in the world we've created while seemingly suffering from all the issues we've discussed, culminating at some point in serious physical pain that doctors are not able to find a cause or cure for.

Notice when following any of those stories how often an operation is performed to solve what is considered to be a physical problem, only for the pain or apparent physical problem to simply move to another part of the body.

If you watch those stories and tie them into your own life, the lives of people you know and the things we've discussed in this book, I'll leave you to reach your own conclusions about how real any of this is.

21

CHANGING THE WORLD

"Reality is merely an illusion, albeit a very persistent one"

(Albert Einstein)

To borrow and tweak a famous line from Bill Shankly, a legendary adopted son of my home city of Liverpool – life is a simple game, complicated by idiots.

Unfortunately, in this scenario we're the idiots. It's not entirely our fault we ended up here, though – we have been led astray for generations by a series of idiots driven by their low self-worth to create a world where most humans are largely miserable.

We are, however, now responsible for continuing the idiocy.

Fortunately, as we've discovered, taking responsibility for where we've ended up means we have the possibility to change it which, ultimately, is what this book is all about.

As we've seen already, a mistake I see most people making in life is trying to solve a problem by starting in the middle rather than going back to the root, which applies to trying to change the world as much as anything else.

So, before we get into how we can change the world, I think it's worth going back to the beginning and summarising how we ended up where we are. I've taken the liberty, therefore, of summarising the entirety of the development of humans from when we first started talking to now. Bear in mind when reading that it's a summary, but is all based on absolute fact so you're safe to believe every word of it.

The History of Humanity

A very long time ago, humans were walking around the planet naked, just like every other animal. They barked at each other, ate the food growing from the ground and from the trees, and shit all over the floor.

One day, one of the humans opened his mouth to bark at another human and, instead of his usual growl coming out, he said: *"Eh, you, my name's Billy, what's yours?"* Another naked man looked back at him, confused, and replied: *"How did you learn to do that? Hang on, I'm doing it now. That's mad! I think my name's Paddy."* *"That's great,"* said Billy. *"Do you fancy a pint?"*

After discovering they could talk, Billy and Paddy went to the local jungle pub and had a chat over a pint of beer.

"It's mad this, isn't it? How long do you reckon we've been able to do this for?"

"No idea, mate, but I've got a funny feeling it's going to change things for us."

At that moment, another human appeared over the horizon and started walking towards Billy and Paddy. As the human moved closer, though, the men could see something was different about this human. It had more flesh on its chest, which the men found strangely attractive, and appeared to have a cave between its legs where their dangly bits were.

"Hello, what's your name?" said Billy. *"I'm Sally. I've been living over the hill but heard you two chatting so thought I'd come across to see what was going on".*

As Sally was talking, Paddy started gesticulating towards Billy trying to get his attention. *"What is it?"* said Billy, annoyed at being interrupted. *"I'm not sure I should have said anything,"* said Paddy. *"But since Sally came over your dangly bit looks like it's not dangling anymore. Is it pointing at me for a reason?"*

"Oh, shit," said Billy *"Why the fuck has it done that?"*

"Let me have a look," Sally said and reached over to inspect what was happening. As Sally and her pointy chest things got closer, Billy realised they might have something to do with the development. *"Erm, I know this sounds a bit mad, but my pointy thing that used to be a dangly thing is getting very excited and keeps telling me it wants to go in your cave."*

"That is an interesting development," said Sally.

The humans decided while they were figuring out what was going on the men would wrap some cloth around their waists to cover their dangly bits, and Sally agreed she'd cover up her cave and pointy chest things to avoid any mishaps.

After a few more pints and a discussion around what they should do next, Billy, Paddy and Sally decided they'd have a look for any other humans who had learnt to say things with their mouths, and went off over the hill to the next field.

After a few days they'd found quite a lot of people who realised they could also say things with their mouths once Billy, Paddy or Sally had said something to them.

To cut a long story a little bit shorter, the humans all lived happily together for a while just getting on with life the way they had before, laughing and joking around and shitting on the floor.

Then, one day, one of the pointy chest humans, Barbara, said to the others: *"I'm bored, should we do something new?"*

Little did they know at that time, Barbara's expression of boredom would change the world forever. To try to impress Barbara in the hope she'd let him put his pointy thing in her cave, Paddy started coming up with new ideas for things to do.

He suggested they put some bits of old trees together to make things to sleep under so they didn't get wet when it rained. He rolled a load of leaves together and started kicking them around, encouraging others to chase him while he tried to kick what he called a "ball" into a big hole in the mountain side.

After watching Paddy doing all that, a few of the other humans started coming up with ideas, with Delila making things for them to sleep on that could go into the things that Paddy was making with bits of trees, and Colin stretching some strings over some wood and starting to make sounds none of the humans had heard before.

It turned out years later that in the same week the first talking humans had invented property development, football, IKEA and guitar music.

From there things snowballed and within months they'd created an entire village built around the jungle pub, with houses, live music on a Saturday night and monthly visits to walk around a one-way system in a big shed to source pre-built furniture.

Other humans had realised they could catch, cook and eat some of the other animals, and everyone had started to trade things with each other, with the guitar players agreeing to play only in return for a cooked pig and Paddy refusing to build anymore houses unless he received four cows, a chest of drawers and two tickets to the big football game in return for each one.

After a while that all just became too much like hard work, so Sally came up with a golden solution. One day she came into the village with a pile of tokens she'd made with pictures of her face on them and told everyone from then on instead of trading things they'd just trade tokens, and they'd agree in advance how many tokens each thing was worth.

Everyone agreed it was the best idea they'd heard since Larry had found a way to stop them shitting all over their own floors.

For a while everything went smoothly until, one day, Billy got bored and suggested to Paddy they should start a new game consisting solely of who could collect the most tokens with Sally's face on. Paddy asked what the point was, and Billy said if they could get as many tokens as possible, it would mean they could be the most powerful humans in the village and make everyone else do stuff for them. Paddy liked the idea of that and, seeing as he was the only human who could build houses, decided to join in.

Over the next few years, Paddy and Billy collected loads and loads of tokens, piling them up in a big building Paddy had built specially for this purpose. Once the other humans could see how many tokens Paddy and Billy had, they started asking if they could do things for them in return for some tokens.

Paddy said he'd lend them a few tokens but they'd have to give him back more than he lent to them, and Billy said they could do some jobs for his mates in return for a very small number of tokens, while he collected five times as many from the people he outsourced the villagers to.

A few of the humans thought that sounded like an awful idea and carried on doing what they were doing before, making their own tokens by doing stuff directly for other humans, but loads of the villagers thought Paddy and Billy were great, so started borrowing tokens and doing jobs in return for a small handful of tokens each week.

While this was all going on, one day, out of the blue a human calling himself Arthur came riding into the village on the back of a horse, which the other humans had never seen before, holding a big sharp, pointy thing above his head.

"I am your king!" declared Arthur. *"What the fuck are you talking about?"* replied Billy, before all the other villagers came out to see what all the fuss was about.

"I am your king!" repeated Arthur. *"I didn't know we had a king,"* shouted Sally. *"I thought we were part of an autonomous collective. Who made you king?"*

"The Lady of the Lake, her arm clad in the purest shimmering samite, held aloft Excalibur from the bosom of the water, signifying by divine providence that I, Arthur, was to carry Excalibur. THAT is why I am your king!" Arthur said, forcefully.

Billy piped up again: *"Strange women lying in ponds distributing swords is no basis for a system of government. Supreme executive power derives from a mandate from the masses, not from some... farcical aquatic ceremony. You can't expect to wield supreme executive power just because some watery tart threw a sword at you."*[12]

---

[12] I'll give you bonus points on the adventure if you know where I borrowed this scene from.

At that point Arthur trotted over to Billy and said: *"Can I have a word in private?"* Billy agreed but only if Paddy, Delila and Sally could come with him. Arthur agreed.

Arthur: "Look, I've got this scam going that I've been running all over the country. It's working well so if I let you in on it will you promise not to cause any trouble?"

Billy: "I'm listening."

Arthur: "Well, most of these humans haven't got a clue what's going on, so what I've been doing everywhere else is telling everyone I'm the big boss because I was given this sharp pointy thing by a woman in a lake."

Billy: "Is that true?"

Arthur: "Is what true?"

Billy: "The story about the woman in the lake?"

Arthur: "Don't be ridiculous, I just made it up so the people in my village would do what I said and I wouldn't have to do any work."

Billy: "Oh, right."

Arthur: "Anyway, what I've been doing everywhere else is making an agreement with the humans who have been making stuff and collecting loads of tokens"

Billy: "Hang on, there are other humans doing that already?"

Arthur: "Yes, did you think you were the only ones who'd got bored and started coming up with mad ideas?"

Billy: "I suppose so, yeah, but anyway get on with this agreement you were talking about."

Arthur: "Right, well the agreement is I get to carry on being king with my family and mates, we keep everyone in check with the story about the woman in the lake, and we keep you protected so you can keep collecting loads of tokens and doing whatever you want."

Billy: "Sounds like a decent plan, but what if we don't agree?"

Arthur: "Well, this might not have come from a woman in a lake but no-one else has figured out how to make one yet, so I'll chop your heads off if you don't go along with the plan."

Billy: "Okay, sounds like a compelling argument, we're in. What next?"

Arthur: "Well, we just convince everyone else using a propaganda campaign through the local pub and my mate Rupert's news spreading service that we're all more important than them and they need to work harder to make sure we can sit around doing nothing while they build big houses for us to live in, paid for by them."

Billy: "You think they'll buy it?"

Arthur: "Maybe not at first, but we'll chop a few heads off then once everyone gets used to the idea they'll forget it all started from us just making shit up and will go along with it forever."

Billy: "I mean, that sounds highly unlikely but we might as well give it a go. How do we start?"

Arthur: "Well, the first thing we need to do is divide the villagers so they start seeing each other as different to themselves. Once we've done that, we can give some free houses to the ones who can't work because they're too ill and some free tokens to buy enough bread to stay alive, then tell all the ones who are working for you to look down their noses at the ones living in free houses who aren't working and getting free tokens."

Billy: "But, hang on, aren't you living in free houses and not working while you get free tokens from us?"

Arthur: "Yes, but that's different."

Billy: "Why?"

Arthur: "Well, because I've got the big sharp pointy thing, we're living in really big, fancy free houses that make us look special, you're giving us loads of free tokens so we look even more important and, aside from anything else, it's my plan."

Billy: "And you don't think anyone will get onto this and cause trouble?"

Arthur: "Look, a few of them might, but we'll just make out they're all insane using Rupert's news service. I promise it will work, it's working everywhere else."

Billy: "Okay, let's do it."

* * *

And that is how the world we live in today first started. Over the years Billy, Sally, Paddy, Delila and Arthur passed on their plan to their kids after they'd established it in the early years. It turned out Arthur was right and very few people ever questioned what they'd been told so, through the centuries, what the early humans had started just grew and grew.

What started with us humans just wandering around the place being pretty happy had ended up with most of us spending our days in big, concrete blocks with glass walls working to make Billy and Paddy's descendants lots of money, with many of us trained to look down our noses at poor people living in houses provided by the state living off tiny amounts of money provided by the state, while simultaneously worshipping Arthur's descendants who are still living in massive houses provided by the state while living off loads of money provided by the state.

The kicker to it all is that it's all make believe, created by other humans years ago. None of it is real.

Remember, three quarters of **life** is a lie.

Flawed Attempts to Change the World

I used to want to change the world and I've met, seen and heard many others who want to do the same thing.

The problem is when we say that phrase it's usually our ego talking, we really mean we want to change the entire world by ourselves and, most importantly, we want the world to see us doing it and to give us credit for it.

What I've realised since embarking on this adventure, transforming my life, repairing my self-worth and taking my ego in hand, is that none of us can change the world. Not by ourselves.

No-one ever has and no-one ever will.

If you don't believe me, think of any of the most famous individuals who have gone before us seeking to change the world and ask yourself whether they truly succeeded.

I remember Ralph on this topic asking me once if I'd heard of a bloke called Jesus. I said the name rang a bell. Ralph pointed out, very wisely, that Jesus might be the most famous of all the people who have attempted to change the world. He was apparently the son of the fella who created the entire universe, so I'd say he had a bit of an advantage over you and me when it comes to having a chance of changing the whole thing. He also didn't have social media to contend with.

He ended up being nailed to a cross in public before he'd turned 40 and, despite his apparent work and sacrifice, the world in which we live could still do with a fair bit of changing.

If Jesus couldn't do it, maybe we should give up on the idea of one person ever being able to change the entire world for us.

Another Way

If we can agree it's not a wise idea to keep trying the same thing over and over again and expecting different results which, as Albert Einstein famously said, is the definition of insanity, maybe we can look at how people have tried to change things in the past and, based on the things we've been learning on our adventure together, try a different approach.

One of the main problems I see is the same one we experience in our individual lives being replicated on a global scale. When wanting anything to change, most people spend most of their time pointing their finger at others expecting them to change rather than looking at themselves.

We spend our time discussing how a different government would change things or a different system altogether. We blame the structures in place and think if we change the structures we'll change the world. But if we look around the world at different structures and different systems, and we look through the generations at different governments we can see that basically nothing has ever changed. You can look at stories from the Roman Empire or political satire from the 1970s and you'll basically see the same issues on repeat.

The reason for that is clear if we zoom out to look at the bigger picture. The problem with every flawed organisation, system, government or country is they're made up of flawed humans. Yet instead of focusing on the flawed humans making up the flawed collective, we focus on the collective and expect that to somehow miraculously change without the humans inside it changing as well.

This takes us back on a wider scale to the victim mentality we discussed in Chapter 15. It's easier for us to all blame the systems in which we operate than to take responsibility for our lives. This does not mean many of the systems in which we operate aren't flawed and shouldn't be changed, remember it's not black and white. It does mean, in my view, we should be looking at both at the same time, because changing any systems without changing ourselves will only lead to the same outcomes we've always had.

"Am I a part of the cure, Or am I part of the disease"

(Clocks / Coldplay)

Angels and Demons

This takes us back to another point we've discussed previously, that we all tend to see ourselves as the goodies and the other side, whoever they may be, as the baddies. We see ourselves as angels and others as demons.

Aside from a handful of people, I firmly believe the vast majority of people do what they do because they have good intentions. Even the baddies in the movies we watch don't think they're baddies, they just have a different idea to the other side of what's best for the world at large.

The key is for us all to take a step back and look at things with fresh eyes from a place of no ego in order to assess whether the position we're taking can be challenged in any way, but that's not possible until we do the work to set our own ego aside.

Without doing that, we repeatedly end up in a situation akin to George Orwell's *Animal Farm*, where people with good intentions take over a flawed system only to see their own flaws leading them to operate a similarly flawed structure.

By doing the work in this book, or work like it, to see our own darkness and enable us to admit in what ways we might be the baddies, we are more able to listen to what our so-called enemies or rivals say or think and process it without bias. It's by coming together and listening to opposing views reasonably and rationally without attacking each other or allowing our egos to take over that we'll make real progress. Without that, we are doomed to simply repeat the mistakes of the past on loop.

I believe that in the vast majority of situations if you are not willing or able to calmly and rationally listen to the other side of whatever conversation you are in, you are part of the disease not part of the cure, regardless of the story you are telling yourself.

Polarised Tribes

As far as I can see, what prevents us more than anything else from coming together and listening to each other reasonably and rationally to solve the world's problems is our subconscious enrolment in polarised tribes. We join groups that seem so far removed from the group with an alternative view to us that we can no longer see any way we can even discuss topics calmly, let alone resolve them.

To solve this part of the problem we need to trace back how we end up in polarised tribes to begin with. Let's again walk step by step through the work we've been doing.

We start out as individuals with low self-worth, often without realising it. From there we hear a story about any particular topic that we believe and decide to adopt it as our position. The first issue here, though, is the world immediately pushes us towards taking a black or white stance in relation to whatever the topic happens to be which, as we've seen, is damaging in itself.

From there, given in the modern world we can always find people who agree with whatever our position is, we subconsciously fall into a bubble where everyone reflects back to us what we already think. That convinces us we're the goodies and people on the other side of the argument are the baddies.

By this point we have long since formed an emotional attachment to our view by referring to it as *"my opinion"*, which means it is now attached to our self-worth.

All of those factors together mean it becomes incredibly difficult for us to engage in a rational conversation about any complex topic because we inevitably end up with our ego battling egos on the other side of the debate, getting us nowhere other than more divided than when we started.

The big question is how do we overcome these hurdles to enable us to even begin to talk to each other healthily again?

How to Break from Polarised Tribes

This is where doing the work solves the root causes of the problems again.

By doing everything we've been talking about we can begin by ensuring our own self-worth is high and we feel we're good enough regardless of our opinion on any given topic. From there we can gently challenge the stories we've been told or have been telling ourselves and make sure we adopt scaled thinking in relation to whatever we're discussing rather than falling into the trap of black and white thinking. We can ask ourselves whether there's room for two things to exist at once.

We can then hold whatever opinion we form loosely, referring to it as *"an opinion"* or *"my current opinion"* rather than *"my opinion"*, enabling us to open ourselves to opinions that might lead to us changing our minds, while actively avoiding falling into echo chamber bubbles with people who just say the same things back to us on repeat.

When we are able to do all this, suddenly we can see the potential for ourselves to be the baddies alongside anyone who disagrees with us or, better still, to see us all as flawed human beings with good intentions, which opens us to the possibility of discussing challenging topics calmly, rationally and reasonably.

All of which exponentially increases our chances of changing things for the better.

Viral Growth

So, rather than focusing on changing the world by changing all 7.5 billion people on the planet at once, changing systems, organisations or governments, we first have to change ourselves.

The key is shifting what's inside us to repair the damage we've carried for decades, holding us back from realising who we're truly meant to be.

Once we've successfully done that, we can see if we're able to help just one other person to do the same because that's how we really change the world. One person at a time, starting with you and me.

If each person who changes themselves to repair their self-worth and take their ego in hand then helps one person do the same thing, then that person helps one person and on, and on, we end up with viral growth of inner peace and contentment, which ultimately results in a changed world.

Without uncontrolled egos, unrepaired childhood trauma and billions of humans walking around not thinking they're good enough, there would be no wars. Nobody would go hungry. We could create systems that actually do what they're intended to do, without greed, self-interest or corruption destroying them.

If we can be generous and kind to ourselves in our most difficult times, maybe we can do the same to everyone else when they struggle, rather than the point-scoring negativity we have now that serves only to make us feel worse about ourselves and each other.

Seeing Beyond the Stories

Before wrapping up this chapter, I wanted to share with you one of the best books I've read over the past few years and strongly recommend that you read.

Factfulness: Ten Reasons We're Wrong About The World - And Why Things Are Better Than You Think, by Hans Rosling, Ola Rosling and Anna Rosling Rönnlund, is an unexpectedly uplifting read about what the world really looks like if we are able to break away from the stories we're told and zoom out to the bigger picture.

This might sound like a strange thing to include in a chapter about changing the world, especially in the context that I'd guess you, like I used to, might think the world is in desperate need of change.

In many ways, however, as the authors point out through detailed examples in the book, the world is generally in a much better state than you might think. The problem, as it tends to be in a 24 hour, seven days a week news media world, is our focus is always directed at where there are problems. When we can zoom in on any part of the globe there are always problems somewhere for us to look at, which can give us the false impression things are worse than they are.

A line I recall being repeated throughout the book is things can be bad and getting better, which applies to so many of the topics we're led to believe are worse than they've ever been. It's crucial to understand the psychology of attention driving our media, which is basically that we're more likely to click on dramatic, fearful news than we are to click on positive, uplifting news.

The root of that, to me, is also based on our low self-worth. I have noticed since doing this work I have less interest in any dark, dramatic or fearful news, and even less interest in dark, murder filled entertainment programmes I used to love in my old life. When I see a media outlet now reporting things in black and white terms in order to create and trade off the division it causes, I have no interest in giving it any attention.

The simple reality is we're able to change the world simply by changing our perception of it, by seeing it for what it really is rather than what we're being misled into thinking it is by media companies incentivised to keep us in fear.

As we've already discussed, regardless of whether we're ever able to go on to solve problems that do remain on a global scale, we can control our experience of the world by changing our inner state rather than focusing on everything outside us that's beyond our control.

Running in the Wrong Direction

Last but not least, I want to share with you a message I received during both of my first psychedelic experiences at the end of last year.

I could write an entire book about those adventures and I'm conscious you might have wildly different views from me on whether there's any merit in messages we might be given while experiencing psychedelic plants provided by the planet. However, it's important to me to share this last thing when it comes to the changes we might want to make to our civilisation in the future.

One of the messages I received was very simple: we're running in the wrong direction.

Humans come from the planet in the same way all other animals do. We might have a small number of us who know how to make electricity, WiFi and iPhones but, fundamentally, what gives us peace and fulfilment tends to be quite simple. A small number of our species has us running head first as fast as we can into integration with machines, when the reality is our origins and our true destiny lies in integration with the planet.

It's no coincidence that the more we move into a digital world the lower our self-worth becomes and the more issues we see such as depression, suicide and all kinds of health problems, both physical and mental.

Regardless of anything else, if we want to find more peace and fulfilment in our lives it's crucial we move back towards our natural place on the planet.

"And when the broken
hearted people living
in the world agree
There will be an answer,
let it be.
For though they may
be parted, there is still a
chance that they will see
There will be an answer,
let it be."

(Let It Be / The Beatles)

22

WHAT NEXT?

"I've been fighting with
one arm tied behind my back.
But what happens when
I'm finally set free?"

(Carol Danvers / Captain Marvel)

As you know, one of the main purposes of the adventure we've been on has been for you to deconstruct the human constructed by others to enable you to become the human you were always meant to be.

By understanding the root of all problems lies in childhood, repairing your self-worth and accepting you are good enough, the world in which you live will transform forever. But that is just the start. Just the foundation on which you can build whatever life you want to live.

From here, the things you used to see as holding you back can melt away, but only if you continue to do the work needed to make that happen. Remember we cannot undo decades of programming overnight without practising on a daily basis and re-training our system to begin operating in the way we want it to work.

This chapter, then, is all about how to figure out what to do next.

Caterpillar to Butterfly

The first thing to bear in mind is that if you truly want to transform your life, doing so can be a challenging process both for you and for those around you, who are more than happy with the role you've been playing in Mamma Mia for the past few decades.

Remember those people might not totally understand or be fully supportive of any changes you want to make, which is where understanding your wants and needs and creating boundaries becomes so crucial to building the life you really want to live.

It's worth considering it's often much more difficult for us to really transform if we stay in the same environments we were always in. Through the process of becoming the person I want to be I have changed my career, left an unhappy marriage and fundamentally changed where and how I live on a day-to-day basis. Many people I have guided along this path have done one or more of the same things.

That's not to say you can't change your life without making fundamental changes to your environment, although you might find it more difficult to change completely without some environmental tweaks.

In particular, you might need some time to go into a cocoon to look after yourself first and foremost while you're doing the hardest parts of this work. Think of it like a caterpillar when it's going through the process of becoming the butterfly it was always meant to be. To complete that transformation it protects itself in its own little world for a period of time before coming out to the wider world in its new form.

I'd recommend at least considering doing something similar.

There Are No Shortcuts

I said this at the start of this part of the book and want to repeat it at the end.

A question I often see people asking anyone who tries to encourage others to transform their lives is, *"what's the shortcut?"*.

Most people don't want to change what they eat or work harder in the gym to get a six-pack, they want to be able to carry on eating cakes on their couch while someone gives them a pill.

The problem is shortcuts almost never exist and, especially in this area, trying to take them actually does nothing other than keep you from ever reaching the place you want to reach.

Another counterintuitive aspect of this whole adventure is part of the way we build our self-worth is by doing the hard work ourselves. By achieving things we didn't think we could do, often very small things one step at a time, we slowly teach our system we are good enough which, in turn, increases our score on the self-worth power bar gradually over time, which is the most sustainable way to grow.

The Chinese Bamboo Tree

One of my favourite analogies to talk about in relation to this work is the Chinese bamboo tree.

After planting a bamboo tree you're unlikely to see any growth for around five years. You water and fertilise it, year after year, with no apparent changes. Then, in the fifth year, the tree suddenly grows around 90 feet in six weeks.

I want you to start thinking about transforming your life like a Chinese bamboo tree.

Whenever we want to make sustainable changes, we expect results overnight. I remember someone once asking my old personal trainer in May whether he could get him in shape for the summer. *"Of course,"* my trainer said. *"Assuming you mean next summer, not this one"*.

Many personal trainers or weight-loss regimes might tell you they can get you ripped in the space of a couple of months, but what they won't tell you is whatever method they use is unlikely to work over the long term. If you want a great body, the best thing you can do is put the work in consistently over a period of time that transforms the way you think about health and fitness. This work is no different.

While it might look to the outside world the Chinese bamboo tree isn't doing anything for the first five years of its life, it's spending its time growing its roots and laying a solid foundation for the rapid growth it can see ahead.

That's exactly what this work is. While you will no doubt start to see changes and results fairly quickly, real-life transformations are achieved through a change of behaviour over the long term. So, as you do this work I'd urge you to start thinking of what your life can be in a year or five years from now, rather than expecting it to miraculously transform in a month.

Where most people go wrong when attempting any change is expecting miracles overnight. They overestimate what can be done in a month and completely underestimate what can be achieved in a year or a decade.

It was four years ago my law firm came to an end. Since that time I've been working towards where I am now, one step at a time. Which leads us to another powerful analogy.

The Steam Train and The Scooter

Without knowing it when we start our lives we are usually put on a steam train. It has a fixed track, very few stops and, once it gets going, it's almost impossible to change direction.

The steam train takes us through school, maybe university or some other form of training, the search for a life partner, the attachment to a career, hopefully at least one child, then a pretty steady existence until we retire and, ultimately, die.

It's the same journey most other people we know go on, which is why it feels so comfortable and safe even if we don't like it. When we hit a point in our life where we think we might want to change direction, though, we suddenly realise even attempting to change tracks with the train would be a nightmare. On top of that, the idea of changing from this train to another one fills us with dread because the pressure on that other train and track being better than the one we're on is huge. What if we get it wrong? What will everyone think? What if we fail? We'll then just be stuck on a different train on a different track forever.

Doing this work, though, enables you to jump off the train in full motion, like Wonder Woman or Jason Bourne, onto the back of a scooter. And switching the train for a scooter changes everything.

Now, rather than being stuck on one track forever or, sometimes worse, deciding whether to switch to another track and sticking to that for the rest of your life, you can now figure out the general direction in which you want to head and work out the best way to get there along the way.

Sometimes you'll find yourself going down dead ends or realise you're going in the wrong direction but, unlike when you were on the train, if that happens you can quickly change direction again and make sure you're back heading towards where you wanted to go. Then, if along the way you realise the place you were heading for isn't where you want to go anymore, you can change that as well.

Doing this work and repairing your self-worth gives you total freedom to do whatever you want to do with your life without fear of what other people might think or what might happen if it doesn't work out. If you're not sure what you want to do or where you want to go, you can just keep trying new things until you find something you like.

Being Better Than Yesterday Is Bollocks

Something I hear a lot in the traditional personal development world is the idea that to create a great life you don't need to be better than anyone else, you just need to be better than you were yesterday.

While I agree we shouldn't be comparing ourselves to others if we want a peaceful life, I think the idea of always being better than we were yesterday is a load of bollocks.

If we're always better than we were yesterday our progress in life would be a straight line, always going up and always getting better. To expect that to happen is unrealistic at best and damaging at worst. No-one's life gets better in a straight line. Some days we'll do better than others and some days we'll do worse. The secret is to aim for an upward trajectory of progress, so when you zoom out on the picture of your life you can see you're generally heading in the direction you want to go.

Think of it like the stock market graph. If you zoom in at any moment things might look like they're getting worse, but when you zoom out and observe the same chart over a number of years it's generally going in the right direction.

Better to reflect on progress you've made since the same time a year or five years ago than to always aim to be doing better than you were yesterday.

Changing Your Career

If part of transforming your life involves changing your career or your business I'd recommend reading my first book, *The 7 Secrets to Change Your Career*, which will guide you step by step through the process I developed when changing my own career years ago.

We have covered and will cover a few of the things discussed in that book, so if you decide to buy it expect some repetition, however, I don't want to spend too much time here focusing solely on your work when for the purposes of this book I'm more interested in your life as a whole.

You can read or listen to the first chapters of that book for free before deciding if it's for you by visiting changeyourcareer.org

"But I Don't Know What I Want To Do"

If after doing this work you do realise you want to change any part of your life, you might find you're telling yourself the story you don't know what you want to do. The first thing to note here, especially when it comes to big questions like, *"do I want to be in this relationship?"* or *"do I want to stay in this job?"*, is that it's almost certain you do know what you want to do.

Someone said to me many years ago before I'd ever started on this path that people generally do know what they want, they just don't want to admit it to themselves, usually because of fear, insecurity and anxiety about what admitting the truth might mean. I can empathise with that because when I look back at my old life I can say with hindsight I always knew deep down what I really wanted to do, I was just too afraid to do it.

The job of a coach or therapist, then, is simply to help you admit to yourself what you really want to do.

✎ Exercise

To do this exercise effectively I need you to suspend any connection with what you believe reality to look like right now.

I want you to imagine you don't have anything holding you back. You have as much money as you want and nothing can go wrong. In that situation, what would you do with your life? Try not to go straight to the lottery-winner dream of *"I'd lie on a beach drinking cocktails all day"* because, generally speaking, that dream soon loses its appeal when lottery winners realise they have no meaning to their lives.

Instead, think of it like how do you want to spend your days and who with? Where do you want to live? Do you want a romantic partner and, if you already have one, do you want it to be that person? Do you want to sing or play guitar in front of crowds of people, do stand-up comedy, act, dance or join the circus? What did you dream of when you were a little kid that you still want to do today? Do you fantasise about quitting your corporate job to open a restaurant or start a gardening business? Or do you dream of quitting your gardening business to start a corporate job?

Whatever it is, write it down. If you need to, free write about this on loose paper to avoid anyone you might not want to from reading it. The purpose is to write out the dream without any restrictions. Don't let your brain pre-empt what you really want to write down by telling you it's not possible. If it does that, remind it you're just playing a game.

Notes

The Search Engine in Your Head

When it comes to changing our lives, a basic difference I see between people who do and people who don't is how the search engine in their heads responds to search queries.

Even before doing this work my search engine operated in a way that allowed me to do things other people wouldn't do. It struck me I could be in the same situation as most people and where I would find solutions to problems, they would just find more problems.

If this isn't making any sense, think back to the exercise you've just done and ask yourself whether as you were doing it your brain was looking for all the ways you could achieve your dreams, or whether it was telling you all the things stopping you achieving them.

For most people, their search engine does the latter. It frames searches as, *"Brain, please tell me all the ways I can't do this thing"*. My search engine and the search engine of people who consistently make changes in their lives frames the searches as, *"Brain, please tell me all the ways I can do this thing and all the ways I can solve any hurdles in my way"*.

If your search engine has always looked for the ways you can't do things, after doing this work it's time to start gently encouraging it to switch to the other setting. You might find the negative search setting was installed as part of your childhood Programming Experiences and is linked to low self-worth resulting in fear of what might happen if you even attempt to do something new. As you now know, though, you have the power to change that subconscious programming if you so choose.

Making a Conscious Choice

It's crucial to note here that before doing this work your life was mainly being operated by your subconscious so, to a certain extent, you had an excuse for not living the life you really wanted to live.

After doing this work, though, you are now aware of how your system operates and all the ways you're meeting your needs using the characters you've been developing since childhood.

The key, then, is to remember you are now in charge of the decisions you make, whether you decide to make changes or not. It might sound like another counterintuitive thing for me to say, but doing this work doesn't necessarily mean you have to transform your life drastically.

You can change things just by fully understanding why you do the things you do and accepting them for what they are. So, for example, if you realise you only live in the place you do because you're actually frightened of what life might be like if you took the chance to move, rather than blame it on other people like you might have done before you can just take ownership of your decision and acknowledge you would move to a different place but you're too afraid to do it.

Doing that can, in itself, help to give you inner peace and contentment. The simple reality is often our lack of inner peace comes from the fact we're constantly bullshitting ourselves and other people about who we really are and what we really want. Learning about those things and cutting out the bullshit can work wonders by itself.

There's No Perfect Life

When I was growing up without realising it I always thought there was a perfect life I could build. A perfect job with a perfect home, a perfect wife with a perfect family in a perfect place.

When I spent three months in Bali towards the start of my adventure, though, which was the closest thing I've experienced to what most people would describe as paradise, I had a life-changing breakthrough. I realised there's no such thing as a perfect life.

Bali might be my favourite place on the planet. The people are wonderful; kind, happy and friendly. The island has everything you might want, from beaches and forests to little villages and built-up towns. I spent three months with some of the most amazing people I could ever wish to meet, enjoying deep and meaningful conversations about the universe interspersed with dancing, singing and loads of laughter.

And as well as all that, it wasn't home. When I travel I have to speak more slowly because my accent is difficult for people to understand. I missed my family and my city, and didn't have anyone to watch football with or talk about Jordan Henderson to. The WiFi was dodgy at times and the roads didn't work properly.

I realised there's no such thing as perfection because there will always be a trade-off or compromise. To live in a place with happy, smiley, kind people who are so laid back they're practically horizontal, you have to accept their biggest skill isn't going to be building a place with great infrastructure. And if you want great infrastructure you're going to have to accept the people who create great systems also need to implement stricter rules to make sure everything works properly, meaning it's not as laid back.

If your wider family doesn't live near a beach in a sunny country, you're usually going to have to choose between two things you love. If you work for yourself you're unlikely to get the same stability you might get from working for a big corporation, and if you want to eat cakes and ice cream every day you're less likely to be able to have that dream body.

There can be no perfect romantic partner, parent, child or friend for us because none of us are perfect, which means we're not the perfect romantic partner, parent, child or friend to anyone else. We are all flawed just as life is flawed.

As strange as it might sound, accepting that helps us to take another step to inner peace and contentment. It is all built on the foundations of understanding our own darkness and accepting our imperfections as we accept the imperfections in everyone and everything else.

Finding Joy

Something else I learnt from my time in Bali, and since then along my adventure, is that one of the secrets to living our best life is to get back to something we used to do naturally as children but have generally been taught to repress as the years have progressed. We need to discover more ways of finding joy in our lives.

We can find joy in the smallest of moments. In singing and dancing in the shower, playing a silly game with our friends or listening to a kid laugh. Finding ways of filling our lives with as many of those moments as possible is transformational in itself.

✎ Exercise

This is a simple and enjoyable exercise once you get into it, although it can be challenging for us adults who have been living a fairly mundane life for a while.

I just want you to write down everything in life that brings you joy, from the smallest to the biggest. It could be anything from putting your head on a fresh pillow, to celebrating a goal scored by your favourite football team to rubbing snake oil on your genitals on a lazy Sunday afternoon.

List as many as you can, whatever they are.

Notes

Becoming Who You Want to Be

When we begin to get a clearer picture of who we really want to be after stripping back the layers of characters we've been using as a smokescreen for years, it's time to learn how to slowly change our lives to embrace that new version of us.

The first thing that springs to mind is one of my favourite quotes from the past few years, taken from Glennon Doyle's book, Untamed:

"Stop asking people for directions to places they've never been"

I've repeated that quote so often to people I've coached over the past year that I've now added my own piece to it. Not only should we stop asking people for directions to places they've never been, but we should also stop listening to people who volunteer directions without us asking.

This might make sense to you without any further explanation but, just in case it doesn't, what I'm referring to here is how often in life we listen to advice of other flawed humans who've never done the thing we're trying to do.

If you decide you want to transform your life to start being the person you always wanted to be, you might find sharing your new, enthusiastic plan with people who've never done that themselves might only lead to you receiving advice and directions you don't want and aren't helpful.

You might even find it's worse than that.

Crabs in Buckets

There's an old story I've heard a number of times over the years about a man walking past a guy on a beach who was catching crabs.

The passer-by noticed the fisherman had been throwing the crabs in a bucket with no lid and one of the crabs was climbing up the side trying to escape, so mentioned it to the fisherman.

"Oh, don't worry," the fisherman replied. *"Whenever one of them tries to climb out the others pull it back in."*

I've got no idea whether that's a true reflection of the behaviour of crabs in buckets, but it makes for a good story to highlight this point so it's worth sharing.

Sadly, you might discover when you decide you want to escape the bucket you're in, the people you know who have no interest in leaving the bucket will, consciously or subconsciously, try to convince you to stay. If you find the people closest to you doing this, either in subtle or obvious ways, it's worth spending some time considering why that might be and seeking to figure out whether you can either encourage them to come with you or, at the very least, stop dragging your leg in an attempt to stop you escaping.

In my experience, the main driving force behind others wanting to keep you in the same world as them is fear, which is possible to overcome. The question is whether you need to help them to overcome their fear or whether you can simply ignore their concerns and carry on regardless. The option you take is likely to depend on which person is trying to keep you in the bucket and what role they play in your life.

If it's one of your friends you might simply be able to ignore anything they have to say about your new plans but if, for example, it's your partner, it might take a bit more consideration as to what you want to do next given it's difficult to continue a romantic relationship with someone who lives in a different bucket to you.

As we discussed about taking responsibility, this is another area in which the more people you can surround yourself with who are on a similar path to you, the easier it will be to do the work you want to do. It's no different to any other part of life. If you want to stop drinking alcohol and spend all your time with heavy drinkers, it's going to be more difficult to give up. If you want to eat more healthily but everyone you hang around with only wants to eat burgers and pizzas, you're creating additional hurdles for you to overcome.

This doesn't mean we can't spend time with people who aren't on the same path as us, it might just mean we have to be more selective about the time we spend with those people and, most importantly, that we have to set healthy boundaries around what we need and want in our new lives.

One True Fan

An infamous article in the personal development world you might have come across is called *"1,000 True Fans"* by Kevin Kelly.

The concept of the article is we don't actually need thousands or millions of customers to make a project commercially viable, we just need 1,000 true fans who will buy anything we produce, whether that's a song, a guitar or a designer wheelbarrow.

It's a concept I like when it comes to helping people find a way of making money from the things they love, so I'd recommend you search for it and have a read if that's something you might be interested in.

For the purposes of our adventure together, it's another concept I've adapted to apply to building a life that brings you inner peace, contentment and joy.

My version of Kevin Kelly's idea is called *"One True Fan"* and is built on the idea that the things we do in life to bring us joy and fulfilment don't need to be commercially viable or make us any money at all.

I've recently been taking singing lessons because I've loved singing karaoke for years and, in my new life, thought it might be good to learn how to be the best singer I can be, seeing as I get so much joy from it.

My teacher told me the sad thing for him when watching most people when it comes to singing in the modern world, is many of us have given up singing entirely because we've been told on too many occasions we can't sing. We've started to judge each other so much about something we used to do in society as a common way of bonding with other humans, that lots of people have lost the joy of the experience from their lives altogether.

It reminded me of a conversation I had with one of my uncles when he told me he used to love to dance until he married my auntie. It didn't take too many occasions on which she told him he was embarrassing her with his freestyling dance moves before he gave up completely.

Which is where my *"One True Fan"* concept comes in.

After doing this work and beginning to build your self-worth it's time to start doing the things in life again you love to do, even if it makes you no money and even if no-one else thinks it's any good.

Do you love to dance but have two left feet? Fantastic, start dancing again at every given opportunity and ignore what anyone else says. Do you love to sing but people tell you you're tone deaf? Great, time to dust off those vocal chords and make a comeback.

Whatever it is you enjoy in life, the only person you need the support of is yourself. We don't need to make everything into a commercially viable enterprise, there are plenty of other things we can do to make money. This is all about starting to do the things in life again you love, whether that's trainspotting, painting, playing guitar, reading comic books, knitting or any other weird or wonderful endeavour.

Core Values

There are lots of exercises you can do to figure out what you want to do in your life as a new job or career, which you can see in my first book, but the one overarching exercise I want you to do for the purposes of this book is based around your core values as a human.

I've learnt over time that one of the biggest keys to living the lives we want to live is staying true to our values. If we don't do that, it's practically impossible to live a peaceful and fulfilling life. The problem is usually that we have no idea what our core values are, hence this exercise.

✎ Exercise

For this you'll need a timer of some sort. If you've got a smartphone you can just use the stopwatch or countdown timer on there.

Using the timer, do the following in three separate stages:

1. In no more than two minutes, write down your top 10 values from the list below.

2. In no more than 45 seconds, from the list of 10 write down your top five values.

3. In no more than 15 seconds, write down your top two values from the list of five.

The point of the timer is to force you to go with your instincts rather than think about it too much, so make sure you do it with the timer.

Acceptance	Charity	Fun	Learning	Sincerity
Accomplishment	Cleanliness	Generosity	Liberty	Spirituality
Accountability	Clear	Gratitude	Love	Spontaneous
Accuracy	Clever	Growth	Loyalty	Stability
Achievement	Comfort	Happiness	Passion	Strength
Balance	Commitment	Hard work	Patience	Success
Beauty	Confidence	Harmony	Peace	Support
Boldness	Connection	Health	Prosperity	Trust
Bravery	Contribution	Honesty	Recognition	Truth
Brilliance	Dedication	Honour	Respect	Understanding
Calm	Dependability	Hope	Responsibility	Uniqueness
Candour	Determination	Independence	Security	Vision
Capable	Enthusiasm	Individuality	Service	Wealth
Careful	Family	Joy	Sharing	Winning
Certainty	Freedom	Kindness	Significance	Wisdom
Challenge	Friendship	Leadership	Simplicity	

Once you've identified your top two values, begin thinking about whether decisions you're making in life are in line with your values or not. If they're not, ask yourself why you're making them and whether you really want to do something else if you're being completely honest with yourself.

Notes

A Jar of Self-Love

This is another concept I've borrowed and adapted from the mainstream personal development world that I first heard of on a Tim Ferriss podcast years ago. I think in his example this idea was called 'The Jar of Awesome' or something along those lines, but the purpose is very similar.

One of the things I see people struggle with most when doing this work is breaking free from the self-hate inner voice that has plagued them their whole lives and to give themselves credit for the work they're doing. It's not always easy to turn off that monologue, so it takes time, patience and being kind to ourselves to gently move away from it to a healthier internal dialogue.

The purpose of the Jar of Self-Love is to help you to make sure you're giving yourself credit for the progress you make as you move through your adventure, so that your ego cannot deny the progress exists.

Without little tricks like this, I find our ego is extremely good at convincing us we're not actually making any progress and we should just abandon the whole thing to go back to the way we used to be. Remember us talking about there being no such thing as self-sabotage? This is one of the areas we see it most prominently. Our existing identity will do everything it can to protect itself, so we need to do whatever we can to gently educate it into realising the way we want to go forward is better for everyone.

The basic idea is to buy a glass jar to be kept in a prominent place in your home. Next, write down on a small piece of paper – brightly coloured notes are perfect for this – every time you achieve something, no matter how big or small, that you're happy with on your new adventure. So, for example, it might be that you spoke up in a meeting at work and expressed how something is pissing you off, and you would never have done that before because you were too worried about what people might think. Write it down and put it in the jar.

Next you might find yourself calmly explaining to your partner why something that happens regularly in your lives together isn't acceptable to you, which you would never have done before. Write it down and put it in the jar.

The whole point is you start to build a physical representation of the progress you're making, that your ego cannot ignore. The key is to be kind enough to yourself to make sure you're noticing and writing down every little thing you do to move forward, because the small things are the big things in this work.

Over time, you will see the jar slowly filling up and you can every now and then, whenever you need a little boost, empty the jar and read about all the progress you've been making, giving yourself credit for that progress without needing it from anyone else.

"Slow is smooth and smooth is fast"

(Bob Lee Swagger / Shooter)

It Takes Time

It's worth stressing again this work takes time and is not a quick fix. The more you can see it as being the same as looking after your physical health the easier it will be to accept this is not something to be done for a few months then discarded. Just like working out and eating healthily, if you stop doing the work it's practically impossible to maintain the same results.

I always remind myself and the people I work with that I lived the first 38 years of my life based on the operating system I had installed in my childhood and have only been practising using the new operating system for three years. It's not until I'm 76 years old that I'll be able to say I've lived as many years with the new system as I did with the old system. So I'm bound to make mistakes and it's bound to take time to undo the old programming while I replace it with the new stuff.

While writing this chapter I took a sip of my drink and for some inexplicable reason my body said to itself, *"I think we breathe this stuff you know, let's try that"*, which led to me temporarily choking on a sip of water. As a 40-year-old man I must have swallowed drinks millions of times in my life, yet my insane system sometimes still thinks it's worth seeing whether we should breathe liquid rather than swallow it. I've got no idea why it still does that, but it serves as a great example of how we can still make mistakes doing things we've been practising for years, so we can go easy on ourselves when learning an entirely new way of living our lives.

Everything we've talked about is part of working on the self-worth muscle, which we need to continue to do in order to build it and maintain its strength over time. Just like any other muscle in your body, it's not something you can do once or twice then forget about. This is all about consistent work to create a new life, not a quick fix.

Make it Your Own

I feel very like Simon Cowell on *The X Factor* writing this bit.

I've seen many coaches, therapists and teachers of all kinds over the years, and something stands out to me as a key difference between those who are really effective and those who aren't.

Those who aren't tend to teach from a position of insecurity or ego. They tell you the only way to do things is the way they do them and force you to replicate them precisely.

I'm not a fan of that approach.

The people I've seen who I have really loved over the years are people who encourage us to listen to what they've shared, take in the bits that make sense to us, discard the rest and open ourselves to learning as much as we can from as many different sources as we can to ensure we're interpreting whatever we're learning in whatever way fits our lives best.

While you and I share all the same traits of flawed humans, we are also both unique. Which means it's imperative for you to truly internalise this work that you adapt it and make it your own so it works properly in your life.

Much of what you've read in this book has been a mash-up of things I've learnt from all different sources. I'd hear one thing from one coach, join it with something my therapist said and wrap it in a word of wisdom from another coach, then realise I could spin it all into a story about my dog or The Incredible Hulk and it'd make more sense to me. Each of the people who taught me along the way might read my interpretation and think it's a load of nonsense, but it works for me and allows me to adapt as I move through my own adventure if ever anything isn't working.

I encourage you to treat this work, as with the rest of your life from now, as an experiment for you to figure out as you go along. There are usually no right or wrong answers and no black and white solutions. What works for you might not work for me and vice versa, so it's about testing little things every day and figuring out what works best for you.

The Universe

You can change the heading of this section to whatever you believe was in charge of putting this mad place together in the first place. If you're religious you might call that God, or whatever you call God and, if you're not, you might call it energy or something else. I refer to it generally as the universe.

After stripping back the stories we've been brought up with and beginning to see, hear and feel the world for what it truly is, a common shared experience for most who embark upon this adventure is beginning to receive messages from the universe.

This is another part of my life where the old version of me would think the new version had lost his marbles, but it is what it is.

Basically, you might start seeing things that happen to you as either a challenge sent by the universe to test your newly-developed skills or as a reward for the work you've been putting in.

You can expect to see both as time passes, so I encourage you to embrace whatever comes your way and use it to help your work. Whether the universe sends me tests or rewards I make sure I show my appreciation by saying a little thank you. We are, after all, just tiny parts of a huge show, the vast majority of which we have absolutely no control over, so I think it's worth getting along nicely with whoever or whatever is in charge.

As with everything else, though, you're free to form your own view and act accordingly.

Getting Back to Basics

Another story I love originates from a former president of the United States. Before any major meeting this president used to make sure the people he would be speaking to had enjoyed plenty of sleep, food and drink, and had been to the bathroom.

I think it's a great philosophy to incorporate into our daily lives.

While you can obviously see how much I love the work we've been talking about, given I've written an entire book on the subject, I've realised over the years we can sometimes get too caught up in the seriousness of what's happening in our world. Are we depressed? Are we repressing our emotions? Do we really love our partner? Is it really okay to keep talking about playing with your genitals to complete strangers?

But, often, we don't need to go that far or deep to solve our problems. Think about when a baby cries. We don't start wondering immediately whether they've been traumatised by their appearance in the world (although from now on maybe it will cross our minds more), we just start checking things like does their nappy need changing, do they need to be fed or watered, or do they need a sleep.

I've trained myself in my new life to ask those questions whenever I'm not feeling at my best. It's incredible how often what starts as a thought that I might be feeling sad is really just that I haven't eaten anything since waking up and I need some food for energy.

One of the biggest game changers in my life that I recommend to everyone I work with, is the crazy idea that we should all be getting much more sleep than we currently are, and we should take a nap at least once a day.

I look back now at the old personal development world I used to love and how many tricks, tools and techniques it gives for hacking the world by making sure you smash the day from the moment you wake up at 6am. Everything from special coffees to make you forget you're so tired to keeping your running gear on the floor next to your bed to give yourself a better chance of going for that run you promised yourself you'd do.

Here's a different idea for you to play around with and see how well it fits. Instead of setting your alarm for some ungodly hour and from the moment you open your eyes finding "hacks" to get you through the day before you can come back to bed, just sleep more so when you wake up you don't need any hacks, tricks or tools to get through your life.

I know, I know, it sounds like a wild idea, doesn't it? Add into that the further idea that you should take at least one nap every day and people might just start saying you're lazy. The old me would definitely say the new me is a lazy little piece of shit, but then the old me wanted to kill himself and the new me strolls around through life without a care in the world, so I know who I'm listening to from now on.

It's another area that when you stop to think about for a while is insane. Half the world doesn't get enough sleep and thinks that's a sign of success, while the other half of the world sleeps when it wants and has an afternoon nap as part of its culture. The sleepy part of the world tends to live longer and report greater levels of peace and happiness, yet the *"sleep is for babies"* part of the world still looks down its nose at those lazy countries. No wonder their gross domestic product isn't as high as ours, eh? And, as we all know, GDP is the only measure of happiness worth anything to us humans. I mean, it's not that it's just a figment of someone's imagination and means absolutely nothing to any of us, is it?

If you're shouting at the page that it's okay for me to say we should get more sleep because I'm lucky I've got a life where I can sleep whenever I want, you might have been missing the point of the book and might need to go back over it again.

Remember, I used to be just like everyone else in the Western world who believed all the bullshit we've all been told. In fact, I wasn't just like them, I was one of the biggest advocates of that way of life. Work hard, sleep less, find life hacks to succeed. And once I realised it was all a load of bollocks I ripped it down and built a life that began with one thing at the top of my list to design around: *"I don't want to have to set an alarm to get up every day."*

That's it. That was the number one thing on my list when it came to re-designing my life. There were plenty of other things as well, but I can say with absolute certainty now that designing a life around getting as much rest as I need has been a complete game changer.

These days, if I find myself feeling tired at 9pm, instead of telling myself I need to stay up longer to do more work or watch something on TV to make my life worthwhile, I just go to bed and sleep.

I couldn't recommend it highly enough.

Ultimately, a lot of what we've talked about is about cultivating more awareness around our lives, which also factors into this section's focus. Becoming more aware of whether we're just tired, hungry or thirsty rather than depressed is priceless. On another level, being aware of what fuel we're putting into our systems as we discussed briefly in Chapter 20 is also key.

Since starting to take better care of myself both psychologically, emotionally and through what I eat and drink, I am now much more aware of how I feel the day after eating a takeaway or drinking alcohol. There are times I will wake up feeling depressed or lethargic and realise it's because the day before I'd made the conscious decision to have a drink with friends or be a slob in front of the TV with a KFC.

I don't beat myself up about those decisions, I just make sure I'm aware of the choices I'm making and how they will inevitably factor into how I feel, rather than doing what I used to do, which was drinking alcohol five nights a week and wondering why I felt so awful.

A Thought for Parents

As we've touched on the topic of things you might be saying are okay for me and different for you, lots of this book talks about our own childhoods and how we raise children in this world, and I'm extremely conscious I don't have any kids of my own. It's something I'm always quick to stress when I'm talking to people with children because I hate it when anyone tries to make out they know what it feels like to be part of another section of society they have no idea about.

It's the same when it comes to conversations about race and gender. I am a white man so I have no idea what it's like to be any other race or any other gender. I also have no idea what it's like to be a parent, although I imagine it's simultaneously capable of being the most demanding and most rewarding role on the planet.

If you have read any of this book and worry about what you might have programmed or are programming into your kids, I'd recommend reading *The Book You Wish Your Parents Had Read* by Philippa Perry. It was recommended to me by a mate who had been implementing its ideas to good effect with his little girl and said it sounded very similar to the work I talk about in this book.

The benefit of Philippa's book is it gives you direct advice about how to speak to and deal with your children in ways that will encourage them to accept and process their emotions in healthy ways rather than repress them.

It's worth highlighting, though, my current view is that the greatest gift you can give to your children is to do this work properly yourself. While teaching them how to handle their emotions properly is great, remember kids mainly learn by copying what you do, not doing what you say. So, if you tell them to process their anger properly but they watch you repressing it on a daily basis and making passive aggressive comments towards your partner as a result, they'll more than likely just copy what you're doing.

The people I've guided along this path who have kids have all reported significantly improved relationships with them regardless of how old their children are. Being able to be vulnerable and show up as their true selves, talking openly and honestly about their emotions and their mistakes in life has led to a very welcome but usually unintended consequence of the work.

Mismatch and Repair

The really good news when it comes to any mistakes you might have made unintentionally with your children and, indeed, with any other relationships in your life, is that the mistake isn't the key part.

In their book, *The Power of Discord*, Ed Tronick and Claudia Gold talk about the idea of mismatch and repair, which I think gives everyone hope for the future.

The key is life is not about avoiding any form of trauma, mistakes or mismatches with other people. We are all flawed humans and we are bound to make mistakes along the way, falling out of step with people we love and accidentally traumatising our children. The most important part of any human relationship is the way in which we repair any mismatch.

When I heard this for the first time it made absolute sense to me. I think back to all my closest relationships and they're not close because we've never experienced problems, they're close *because* we've had challenges we've overcome together.

Whether it's family, friends or business relationships, the strongest bonds have formed through repairing mismatches after they've taken place.

The good news, then, is by doing the work we've discussed, taking responsibility for your actions and approaching your relationships with a new sense of vulnerability and openness, you are much more likely to be able to repair any mismatches and mistakes from the past, regardless of how far back they go.

Traditional Financial Freedom Does Not Exist

When using this work as a foundation from which to build a new life, I want you to be aware of something I noticed many years ago before starting down this path and before realising it applied to me as well.

You might have seen in the traditional personal development world a lot of talk about the idea of financial freedom. It's basically the idea you can make enough money to give yourself total freedom in life and, ironically, the amount of money you need to give yourself financial freedom is not usually that high.

The problem with that idea is it's another load of bollocks. I realised over the years that I knew and encountered lots of people who had more money than they knew what to do with. They were sitting on pots of cash that someone else would look at and view as financial freedom, but they weren't free at all. In fact, the more money they had the more trapped they felt.

I knew one couple who complained about the life they had. It was too busy and hectic and they wished they could change it. They envied me at the time because I'd started to change my life and they wanted to do the same but couldn't afford to, they said. They went on to reveal they had half a million pounds worth of equity in their house. At the same time, I was a quarter of a million pounds in debt. We were three quarters of a million pounds in wealth apart from each other, yet it was me making changes to my life while they stayed stuck.

It was during that period I realised we can make as much money as we want, but without emotional freedom we can never be free. It makes perfect sense when you think about it. Most of us, including me in my old life, are trying to earn more money partly because we're trying to fill a hole inside us we think can be filled from the outside. We don't feel good enough about ourselves and we think having more money will fix it. But it never does because it never can. You'll just keep earning more money until one day you'll die with loads of money and that big, fat hole still sitting inside you.

The irony is true financial freedom doesn't come from having more money, it comes from having inner peace. Since transforming my life I no longer need to earn as much money as I possibly can, to become a millionaire or drive sports cars to try to make me happy. I'm happy and content anyway. Don't get me wrong, if my life leads me to a place in which I can comfortably buy my dream car and fly around in a private jet I will more than happily do so. I have no problem with materialistic possessions that might make our lives a little nicer, but the beauty of this work is I don't need any of that anymore. I'm good enough just as I am, whether that means I'm driving around in a beat up second-hand car or a shiny red Ferrari.

Focus on repairing your self-worth and feeling good enough, and you'll be more financially free than you ever dreamed possible.

Don't Underestimate Yourself

As we near the end of this chapter, it's important to point out a common area where we all tend to go wrong until we truly learn to feel good enough about ourselves and fill our self-worth power bar.

Most humans totally underestimate what they can do and massively overestimate what everyone else can do. It's one of the reasons it's really important to me to share with you all the ways I fuck up and make mistakes. Without doing that, it's too easy to look at someone who looks like they've achieved something you'd like to achieve and think it's not possible for you because you don't have whatever it is they have.

The reality goes back to us all being flawed human beings. If you've stuck with me this long into this adventure it's because we're more alike than we are not alike. We are both totally flawed and have been working on dysfunctional operating systems for decades. The only difference between you and me right now is likely to be I started this work a few years ago and you've either recently started or are just about to. Or maybe you've been doing it for longer than me and have just read this out of curiosity. Wherever you are on your own adventure you are more than capable of transforming your life if you choose to.

Don't allow the stories you tell yourself about other people to hold you back.

The Benefit of Working with Someone

To loop back to something we discussed right at the start of our time together, if you're not already doing so I'd strongly recommend you find a therapist and/or a coach (both if possible) to work with to help you along this path.

I've done as much as I can to portray the work I'd do with you in one-on-one sessions, but there's no substitute for working with someone directly and being able to dive into their specific life challenges.

Having a therapist or coach will help you in ways you might not consider possible provided, of course, you choose someone who's a good fit for you. Go back to the tips in Chapter 2 for how I'd recommend finding the right person to work with if you can't remember them.

The beauty of working with someone directly is they can help you get past the parts of the exercises you get stuck on, just like Mr Manning.

Try Not to Become (More of) a Bellend

This is a very important point to make as we draw all these shenanigans to an end.

Often when people begin working on themselves in order to change their lives there is a tendency for them to either become a bellend or, if they were already one, to enhance their bellend status further. If you're not British and don't know what a bellend is, I'll leave it for you to do some homework as a side exercise rather than describe it to you.

I actually think the traditional personal development and self-help worlds that teach toxic positivity are more likely to create bellends than the work in this book. They tend to be the people on social media constantly telling you to love everything and smile. You might have guessed by now I'm not a big fan of all that.

While the work we've talked about does its best to stay well clear of all that nonsense, there's still a risk of our ego finding new ways to take control of our lives without us realising by showing up as an uber-enlightened person who portrays themselves as being better than everyone else as a result of doing this work. I fell into that trap for a period during my own adventure, which is why I can warn you about it now.

In fairness to those of us who temporarily go down that path, it tends to be motivated by the enthusiasm for how powerful this work can be and wanting everyone we know to do the same work and change their lives. After a while, though, comes the realisation that people will only do this work when the time is right for them, that time will often never come and our banging on about how enlightened and knowledgeable we are about all this is very rarely welcomed.

A good rule of thumb to follow is to only offer to share any of this with anyone who asks for help. Think of it as being Batman and you are only allowed to help people who send out the bat signal. If they don't send out the signal, it's not for you to get involved. Wanting to get involved with things that have nothing to do with you is more likely to be your ego trying to meet your own needs than anything else.

Finding balance and practising keeping your ego to one side is the best defence against falling into this trap.

Bring Everything Back to You

Ultimately, where I found complete peace and contentment was through the ability over time to always bring my experience of the world back to me. Whenever something or someone annoys, irritates or angers me, I quickly and gently bring it back to what inside me has been touched by whatever has happened.

I think about my personalities and needs, as well as the shadow work we covered in Chapter 15. I take radical responsibility for everything rather than pointing my finger at the outside world and blaming it for however I think or feel.

I see many people who are able to do this 95 per cent of the time, but still come across things they aren't willing or able to take responsibility for. When I see that happening, I see there's still an element of fear that is preventing the person from wanting to look at themselves and face their own darkness in whatever the situation is. Maybe it's with a close family member or a romantic partner and the idea of looking at themselves is just too painful.

If that happens to you, think of the deep sea diving analogy we discussed earlier. Maybe it's just something you need to come back to at a later stage once you've acclimatised to the depth you've reached. Whatever happens, I encourage you to do your best to bring everything back to you and take responsibility 100 per cent of the time. That, to me, is where complete peace and contentment lies.

A Cheat Sheet

To wrap things up, I thought it might be helpful to have a handy little cheat sheet containing just a few of the principles and ideas we've discussed as an easy reference point.

These are the types of things I'd put on sticky notes around my house to remind my subconscious of the new programming we're installing. It might be worth doing something similar.

1   Take radical responsibility for everything.
2   Be kind to myself.
3   What's the real problem?
4   Life is simple, not easy.
5   It's an opinion, not my opinion.
6   I'm always a student.
7   Is there room for both?
8   The small things are the big things.
9   The problem isn't my thoughts or emotions.
10 "Sometimes…and that's okay."
11 There's more than one of me. Who's on the mic?
12 It's better to be whole than good.
13 Write it down or say it out loud.
14 Stop bullshitting myself.

15 How do I know it's true?

16 Meeting my needs subconsciously means meeting them in unhealthy ways.

17 I am not responsible for the emotions of others.

18 Adopt scaled thinking to avoid black and white thinking.

19 Look out for confirmation bias.

20 What I dislike in others I dislike in me.

21 Life is about learning to surf the waves, not flattening them.

22 The treasure is always there.

23 Maybe they're right.

"I'm gonna clear out my head
I'm gonna get myself straight
I know it's never too late
To make a brand new start"

(Brand New Start / Paul Weller)

23

THE END OF THE
BEGINNING

"Every man dies,
but not every man really lives."

(William Wallace / Braveheart)

We've finally reached the end of this part of the adventure together, although it's not the end of the end, it's more like the end of the beginning.

There are just a few more things I want to share before we part ways.

The Certainty of Misery

If you've been doing the multiple personality work as we've moved through the book, you might have noticed a common need your characters are trying to meet for you is the need for certainty and control.

When I did this work for the first time I was shocked by how big a need for certainty I had. I always thought my main driver was uncertainty and variety, but I realised even in my search for change and diversity in life I need certainty.

The reality is humans crave certainty and security in different ways. The main problem with that, though, is generally we're more likely to choose certain misery than risk the uncertainty associated with changing things. It's one of the reasons most of us stay in less than fulfilling relationships and jobs. Better the Devil you know.

Sadly, we tend not to change until the pain of staying the way we are is greater than the pain we associate with the risk of change.

If you decide to do the work we've discussed hopefully the fear of change will lessen, allowing you to make the changes you really want to make.

There But For The Grace of God Go I

That's a line I often find myself saying inside my head or out-wardly to others.

Once we have truly done the work to see our shadow for the first time, we can begin to really have compassion for others. I have upset family members in recent times by saying that line when talking about people with serious drug addictions whose lives have gone off the rails in ways most of humanity isn't prepared to accept.

When I say in a sliding doors world that could have been me, most people won't accept it. But when you stop to reflect on everything we've discussed it makes sense. We are effectively all addicts living in an addicted world. Those who became addicted to hardcore drugs, often at a young age, simply fell into a path any one of us could have done in different circumstances. If you think your addiction to your phone is any different to an addiction to heroin you're sadly kidding yourself.

I consider myself lucky that the circumstances of my life never exposed me to things I might have found more difficult to break free from. That makes it really easy to show compassion for people with serious drug addictions or challenges in their lives I haven't specifically faced.

We are basically the same people and I hope doing the work in this book and facing your own darkness will help you find more compassion towards those less fortunate than us.

What Are We Doing?

I've been playing around with different titles for this section but I think the one I've settled on is perfect.

When I look at the world with fresh eyes since doing this work and removing the stories I used to convince myself were true, I often just sit back and ask myself what the fuck we're all doing.

We're basically a simple species with simple needs. And yet we've allowed our civilisation to be led to a fairly unhappy and unfulfilling place by some of its most dysfunctional members. They aren't happy with themselves and encourage us to follow their path, which we do blindly even though it makes us miserable.

I look around me at people who spend every day racing around doing things they don't want to do, in jobs they never would have picked as kids, stressed out, miserable, longing for a few hours or a couple of days here and there when they can take a break.

The world we have built fills me with sadness. I often struggle to witness it. To be a part of it. I was once part of the problem, blinded by the promise that vast financial wealth and untold material riches would satisfy me. Yet now I see how what we have built leaves so many behind.

We think of ourselves as the most advanced species on this planet, yet we have built and maintained systems for generations that create misery and pain for billions of humans. For mums and dads, brothers and sisters, husbands, wives, sons and daughters. We think we're advanced because a handful of us know how to make iPhones, but the truth is most of us wouldn't survive a month if someone turned off the electricity. Our pets would last longer than we would.

The twist in this story, though, is even those who do their best to maintain the systems our ancestors built are no better off than most. They might have bigger numbers showing on their imaginary bank balance, they might live in grander houses and wear more expensive clothes, but when they look in the mirror at night they see the same flaws you and I see. They feel the same hole deep inside their soul.

We are all flawed human beings. All struggling. Most never feeling good enough. The irony is those holding on to what we've built would be best served by letting it go.

The reality is material things don't make people happy. The world in which we live has taught us that chasing possessions and money will make us happy, but it never will. If you completed the exercise in the last chapter to figure out what brings you joy in your life you might have realised, like I and everyone else I've taken through it, that most things that bring you real joy aren't materialistic at all. They don't cost money.

The things we love most in life tend to be spending time with the people we love. With our friends and family. Making each other laugh and playing games, yet we've built a world in which connection and love has been replaced by a never ending search for more money and possessions, none of which ever makes us fulfilled.

It saddens me when I look at many of the world leaders and billionaires who have shaped the world in which we live and I see an emptiness behind their eyes. Most of them are just being led subconsciously by their childhood Programming Experiences just as you and I were. The only difference is they've absolutely aced the game and combined their low self-worth with special talents that have catapulted them to the top of the dysfunctional, make-believe society we created.

Once they're up there we all then follow their lead as though what they say is in our best interests, but I simply can't see how that's the case anymore.

I see a greater drive to move deeper into a technological world and I despair. Part of creating a content, peaceful and fulfilling life for me has been spending less time staring at my phone and more time doing things that bring me joy. I hear the same story again and again from people who live a similar life to me.

On the other side of the coin, as we move further into a tech world and further away from the world we were created to live in, depression, suicide, drug addiction and unexplained health problems are sky rocketing. Children are committing suicide in record numbers before they've had a chance to experience life for what it can be.

It's absolutely heartbreaking, yet we continue to follow that path blindly thinking there's no other way. Maybe, though, it's time to revert to a place closer to where we started.

We have an opportunity, maybe the last opportunity before this is all over for another civilisation of humans. A chance to make things right. To turn away from the dysfunctional world we have built and move back towards where we are meant to be. To use the technology we've created to add to our lives rather than becoming slaves to it.

The Greatest Invention

The truth we all seem to completely forget is we live on a magical, living organism floating through space, not on a dead rock.

A story I love to tell when talking about the deepest and most philosophical part of all this involves picturing yourself appearing on one of those TV shows in which people try to get wealthy people to invest in their business ideas. In the UK it's called *Dragon's Den* and in the US it's *Shark Tank*.

We live in a world where we think the greatest thing anyone has ever done is to make a smartphone, a computer or any one of a number of other technological inventions. There are people driving us towards a place where our fridge will be able to speak to our microwave, as though that's something humanity desperately needs. It will make some people a lot of money though so, you know, that's the main thing.

Imagine if you were appearing on one of those TV shows and your invention was a seed. Just a tiny, little seed from, let's say, an apple.

This is how I picture the conversation going:

Rich person: "So, what have you brought us today?"

You: "It's this." [You hold a tiny brown seed between your thumb and first finger, and the rich people squint to try to see it from a few metres away]

Rich person: "And what the fuck is that?"

You: "It's a seed."

Rich person: "A seed?"

You: "Yes, a seed."

Rich person: "And what does it do?"

You: "Well, if I put it in the soil outside and leave it for a few years, it will turn into an apple tree."

Rich person: "Oh fuck off, that's ridiculous. [looking over at the producers off camera] Is this a wind up?"

You: "No, honestly, it's real. If I put this little thing in the ground outside it will turn into an apple tree."

Rich person: "So, what, we don't need to do anything like investing more money in it to make it grow, pumping it full of artificial chemicals or outsourcing something to India?"

You: "Nope."

Rich person: "Well, you're going to have to explain how it works."

You: "It's pretty complicated and I'm not entirely sure, but basically this little seed has everything it needs to turn into an apple tree, and the soil outside is full of nutrients that will feed it while the rain from the sky will provide water to help it grow."

Rich person: "You just put it in the ground and the soil feeds it?"

You: "Yes"

Rich person: "That sounds fanciful at best, isn't soil just dirt?"

You: "No, it's actually more like magic sand full of invisible goodness."

Rich person: "So no investment other than putting it in the ground and leaving it for a few years?"

You: "That's right."

Rich person: "And where do we plug it in?"

You: "It doesn't need to be plugged in."

Rich person: "What, you mean it charges wirelessly?"

You: "No, it doesn't need any power."

Rich person: "Well how does it grow?"

You: "It gets energy from the sun?"

Rich person: "I mean this is getting ridiculous now. So, you're telling me this tiny little thing just goes in the ground and is fed by the mud and rain, and energised by the sun?"

You: "Exactly."

Rich person: "Sounds like you've gone insane, sunshine. But seeing as we're on TV let's go with it and assume everything you've said is real, how do we monetise it?"

You: "What do you mean?"

Rich person: "Well, can we, like, put adverts on it or use it to mine people's personal data, anything useful like that?"

You: "Well, I suppose you could nail some posters to it once the tree has grown, but I'm not sure why you'd want to."

Rich person: "Well what does it do if we can't monetise it for advertising revenue or trick people into giving us their personal data?"

You: "Erm, it makes apples."

Rich person: "And?"

You: "Well, it literally makes something we can eat and keep us alive that's really healthy, full of vitamins and tastes delicious."

Rich person: "And can we sell the apples?"

You: "Yes."

Rich person: "I just don't see where the market is to be honest. Come back when you've got an app we can use to get more personal data from people."

* * *

I tell that story mainly just because it entertains me but its basic point is to highlight how we've lost sight of the magic of our planet while becoming mesmerised by technology that in some ways makes our lives better and in many ways makes them much, much worse.

Nothing we invent can ever or will ever come close to the magic of Earth, but we never stop to think about how incredible it is because we're too busy arguing with strangers on Twitter or sad-posting on Facebook.

This isn't me becoming an old man having turned 40 and saying we need to go back to the good old days, but it is me asking a question. Namely: Isn't it time for us to start questioning the path we're on and looking to find a better, healthier balance between the world we came from and the one our dysfunctional leaders have been building for years, just so they could make more money and have more control?

Remember most of what has been created wasn't for the good of humanity – it began because clever people started to understand the flaws in our operating systems and realised those flaws could be exploited to make money. Since then, and since a world was established where making more money was the ultimate goal, we've just been on one long road to destruction, with very few of us ever pausing to ask why we're doing it even though we're fundamentally unhappy.

Remember as well that everything man-made that we see in the world is make believe. It was all created by other humans and the passage of time has convinced us it's all real, but it's not really. We can change anything we choose to change. We can move the walls. We can bend the spoons.

"If we can forgive
what's been done to us,
If we can forgive what
we've done to others,
If we can leave our stories behind,
Our being victims and villains,
Only then can we maybe
rescue the world"

(Chuck Palahniuk)

Only Those Who Know They're Demons Can Save the World

If we do want to change things, I think where the world has always gone wrong, where people have always gone wrong, is in thinking that it will be the angels who save humanity.

That could never have been the case, because the problem with people who tell themselves they're angels is they haven't accepted their darkness. They do not yet understand they are the monsters they most fear. They are part of the problem.

The issue is even if those people take control all that results is a different type of darkness because unless you already know you're a monster you can't put in place anything to protect yourself, the world and the people around you from your shadow.

If we want to save the world we don't need angels, we need demons. Those who have faced their darkness and accepted it. Those who understand humans are deeply-flawed creatures. Imperfect. Dark. And those that know our beauty lies in our darkness as much as it lies in our light.

Only those who understand their own shadow can have a chance of making changes that truly impact the world. Of transforming humanity.

That's what I dream of. A day when billions of people can look in the mirror, see their own darkness and accept it as a true part of themselves. Maybe then we will have peace. Maybe then we will stop judging ourselves and each other. Maybe then our compassion and our love will overcome our fear and our hate.

At the end of it all, though, there's only one person whose love you need in order to build a peaceful and fulfilling life. Your own. Once you have your own love, you can then begin to think about the love of others, both giving and receiving, and how that can add untold value to your life.

But without securing your own love first, the love of no other person on the planet, given or received, can give you what you need. And you can't truly have your own love without loving every part of you, including the darkness. Remember you are the only person who will be there from the moment you were born to the moment you die, so being your own best friend and loving yourself is the biggest gift you can ever give to yourself.

None of us can change the world alone, but we can change ourselves. We can change humanity one person at a time. It's time to stop pointing the finger at everyone else. To look at ourselves, to search deep inside and accept everyone around us for who they are, by acknowledging that the worst in them is the worst in us.

None of us can ever be perfect. We will always be flawed. But we can be imperfect and flawed together.

Time to Say Goodbye

As I said earlier, it's time for us to say goodbye now but this is only the end of the beginning. How many parts there are in your adventure, though, is entirely up to you.

For me, the path continues and I can't be sure where it will lead. I hope you enjoyed the part of the road we shared and I hope you managed to find some peace and light after facing your darkness. If you didn't, I hope you will consider going back to the beginning and going through the exercises again, or pursuing the next part of your adventure in some other way.

If you didn't find your treasure, I can still guarantee it's there. Perhaps I wasn't a good enough guide. If so, that's on me and I hope you'll keep looking for what I know is there. Remember, you are unique but not different. We are all flawed humans and we all share the same histories, needs and desires.

For my part, I dare to dream of a brighter future for us all. Maybe it's too late, or maybe this is the first time in human civilisation we will collectively come together and build a world where we can all be peaceful and content. None of us can know for sure. What I do know is for whatever time I have left on this incredible planet I will help as many people as I can to find the world I have found. Maybe if enough of us find it, together we can build a place for those who believe in the same things. Imagine all the people, living life in peace.

I'd love to end this like a superhero movie. I'd love to tell you I'm your saviour or someone else is coming to rescue you. But I can't do that. I'm not a hero. I'm not special. I used to think I was and even wish I was, and now I know that was just my ego giving me something I couldn't give to myself at the time. Now I've given myself that gift I know I'm not here to save the world.

Instead, there's good news and bad news. The bad news is there isn't a hero. No-one's coming to rescue you. No knight in shining armour or beautiful princess. No government or billionaire in an expensive flying suit.

The good news, though, is you don't need any of them to change your life. You can be the superhero in your own adventure. Your own Wonder Woman. Your own Iron Man. Your own non-binary flying warrior (insert the name of that superhero yourself when Disney or DC Comics create it in the years after I wrote this).

The only question is do you want to be your own hero? It's the bit they don't stress enough in the stories. To be the hero takes sacrifice. It takes the strength to be different to those around you in order to be who you really are. To accept your darkness. To dare to venture to the Gates of Hell and stare into the full-length mirror long enough to truly see yourself.

To pass through the gates and learn to be comfortable in the fire, before being able to rise into the light as your true self. To embrace the world and float through its chaos, holding everything you once believed to be certain with a loose grip. To shrug at the people you once considered enemies and say, *"maybe you're right"*. To know you aren't special and you're not here to save the world by yourself. To be part of the cure instead of being part of the disease.

The path is simple to follow, it's just not easy. The treasure is there if you want it, but only if you're prepared to walk through that dark cave you never wanted to enter.

I can't tell you what to do, only you can decide. And you must do what's right for you. I can't change the world, I can only change myself and ask you whether you're willing to do what it takes to join me.

I can ask if you're willing to be brave enough to change, because that's what this really is. I know I told you it's an adventure, it's your adventure, and that's true. What I might not have said enough is how much courage it takes to begin your quest and how much more courage it takes to see it through, even when the days are dark and it feels as though things are getting worse before they get better.

Things often get worse before they get better, that's just the way hero stories go. I'd like you to decide to start your hero journey and only you can choose whether it's time for you or not.

If you do decide to follow this path, though, you won't be alone. You'll be surrounded by thousands of other flawed humans all embarking on their own adventures, all doing whatever they can to change the world. Together. As one. Hand in hand, helping each other from the floor whenever we fall.

After writing this I'm going to retreat into the world I've been building for a while. A world of peace and contentment. A world filled with love, hope and laughter. I'd love you to join me there. It's fairly quiet with so many people still too distracted by the world where I used to live. There aren't many of us here but I'm hopeful it will get busier before I leave this planet, whenever that may be. Maybe I'll see you here one day.

Until then, that's all the snake oil I've got for you for now. Remember if you rub it on your genitals it might make them lovely and soft, but it's unlikely to transform your life.

I'll leave it to you to decide what you want to do next but, whatever you do, be kind to yourself.

Take care,

Paul
Liverpool, May 2021

"And in the end,
the love we take
is equal to the
love we make"

(The End / The Beatles)

THANK YOU

I want to thank you for dedicating your money and, more importantly, your precious time to reading this book. It means more than I can articulate that anyone would want to read what I have to say and I feel incredibly humble that of all the books you could read you chose this one.

I hope it has added something to your life, even if that has just been something new to think about.

If you liked the book and think it could help someone else you know, please share it with them. I find myself and the people I've coached often saying we wish this stuff could be taught to children in schools, because if we'd learnt it as children there would be much less suffering in the world. So, feel free to share it far and wide and to pass around the same copy to as many people as you want.

Whatever you thought of what you've read, if you have a spare two minutes I'd also be extremely grateful if you can leave a review on any online platform you like, especially anywhere you bought the book from.

Whether you leave a good review, a bad one or somewhere in between, it's important to me for people to be able to see an honest assessment of these pages before deciding whether they want to dedicate some of their life to reading them.

At the end of the day, whether you thought this was the best book you've ever read or an absolute pile of rubbish, maybe you're right.

Thanks again

RESOURCES

Key Books

Becoming Supernatural (Dr. Joe Dispenza)

Codependent No More (Melody Beattie)

DARE (Barry McDonough)

Daring Greatly (Brene Brown)

Factfulness (Hans Rosling, Ola Rosling and Anna Rosling Rönnlund)

Healing Back Pain (Dr. John Sarno)

How to Overcome Your Childhood (Alain de Botton)

Letting Go (David Hawkins)

Man's Search for Meaning (Viktor Frankl)

Recovery (Russell Brand)

The Body Keeps The Score (Bessel Van Der Kolk)

The Book You Wish Your Parents Had Read (Philippa Perry)

The Gifts of Imperfection (Brene Brown)

The Monk Who Sold His Ferrari (Robin Sharma)

The Power of Discord (Dr. Ed Tronick and Dr. Claudia Gold)

The Power of Now (Eckhart Tolle)

The Power of Vulnerability (Brene Brown)

The Silenced Child (Dr. Claudia Gold)

The Six Pillars of Self Esteem (Dr. Nathaniel Branden)

The State of Affairs (Esther Perel)

The Surrender Experiment (Michael A. Singer)

The Truth (Neil Strauss)

Untamed (Glennon Doyle)

Waking the Tiger (Peter Levine)

When Anger Scares You (John Francis Lynch)

When the Body Says No (Dr. Gabor Mate)

You Are The Placebo (Dr. Joe Dispenza)

Documentaries and Movies

The Matrix (1999)

Fight Club (1999)

Big Fish (2003)

Avatar (2009)

About Time (2013)

Unbreakable (2000)

Split (2016)

Glass (2019)

Rocketman (2019)

All the Rage (Saved by Sarno) (2016)

Andy Murray: Resurfacing (2019)

Brene Brown: The Call To Courage (2019)

Avicii: True Stories (2017)

Chasing the Present (2019)

Tiger (2021)

Super Juice Me (2015)

Fat, Sick and Nearly Dead (2010)

Follow The Incredible Hulk's story arc as described in the book through the following movies:

The Incredible Hulk (2008)

The Avengers (2012)

Avengers: End Game (2019)

Blogs, Podcasts and YouTube Channels

Mark Manson (Blog)

Teal Swan (YouTube)

The Joe Rogan Experience (Spotify/Podcast)

The School of Life (YouTube)

The Tim Ferriss Show (Podcast)

Other People to Check Out

Alain de Botton

Byron Katie

Esther Perel

Dr. Gabor Mate

Dr. Joe Dispenza

Dr. John Sarno

Marissa Peer

Wim Hof

My Therapist and Coaches

David Kirk (www.dkpsychotherapy.co.uk)

Ralph Ruiz (https://ralphitness.com)

Jim Hughes (www.becomeuntamed.com)

Nicole Parsons (www.nicoleparsons.co.uk)

Printed in Great Britain
by Amazon

73331382R00368